Errata

- On page 183, lines 22 and 23 should read:

    Stress-final implied-offbeat pattern at the opening of a line
    (midline stress-final patterns are much less frequent)

- On page 184, line 1 should read:

    Stress-final implied-offbeat pattern other than at the opening of a line

- On page 184, line 6 should read:

    Stress-initial implied-offbeat pattern at the fifth position

- On page 233, the first scanned passage should appear as follows:

    Theme this but little heard of among Men —
      ò   B o B o   B   ŏ   B ô B

- On page 233, the second scanned passage should appear as follows:

                                the soul
    Remembering how she felt, but what she felt
                        -s -s +s   +s
    Remembering not, retains an obscure sense
                            ŏ   B ô B
    Of possible sublimity

- On page 272, the scanned passage in note 19 should appear as follows:

    And Tiresias and Phineus, prophets old
    B̄   o B ŏ   B o   B o B

The Passion of Meter

The Passion of Meter

A Study of Wordsworth's

Metrical Art

Brennan O'Donnell

The Kent State University Press

Kent, Ohio, and London, England

© 1995 by The Kent State University Press, Kent, Ohio 44242
ALL RIGHTS RESERVED
Library of Congress Catalog Card Number 94-30735
ISBN 0-87338-510-1

Manufactured in the United States of America

Library of Congress Cataloging-in-Publication Data

O'Donnell, Brennan, 1958–
The passion of meter : a study of Wordsworth's metrical art / Brennan O'Donnell.
p. cm.
Includes bibliographical references and index.
ISBN 0-87338-510-1
1. Wordsworth, William, 1770–1850 – Versification. 2. English language – 19th century – Versification. 3. English language – 19th century – Rhythm. 4. Metrical phonology. I. Title.
PR5897.O36   1995
821'.7 – dc20   94-30735

British Library Cataloging-in-Publication data are available.

For Angela

Contents

Acknowledgments ix

Abbreviations xi

Introduction: An Ear for Poetry 1

PART ONE: *The Passion of Meter*

1. Similitude in Dissimilitude 21
2. Metrical Tension and Varieties of Voice 48

PART TWO: *The Versification of Poems*

3. "Words in Tuneful Order": Wordsworth's Early Versification, *An Evening Walk* and *Descriptive Sketches* 71
4. Varieties of Rhyme: The Stanzaic Verse of the *Lyrical Ballads* 115
5. "Infinitely the Most Difficult Metre to Manage": Characteristics of Wordsworth's Blank Verse 179

Conclusion: On the Power of Sound 238

Notes 249

Bibliography 276

Index 285

Acknowledgments

Completion of this book was assisted by a Junior Faculty Sabbatical grant from the Loyola College Center for the Humanities. Research at the Wordsworth Library, Grasmere, was made possible by a grant from the Loyola College Faculty Development Committee. I am grateful to members of the Steering Committee of the Center for the Humanities, to my colleagues on the Faculty Development Committee, and to David F. Roswell, dean of the College of Arts and Sciences, for their generous support and encouragement.

Material from the Dove Cottage manuscripts is quoted by kind permission of The Wordsworth Trust. I am grateful to Robert Woof for granting access to the Dove Cottage collection and to Jeffrey Cowton for his kind assistance during the time of my work at the Wordsworth Library.

I have been most fortunate in having had the benefit of Mark L. Reed's eye, ear, and critical judgment at several important stages in the development of this study. Anyone familiar with his work will know why I say that I cannot exaggerate the value of his teaching and advice. My debt to T. V. F. Brogan is one I share with all students of English versification. I cannot imagine sorting through the vast and diversified literature on prosody without the sure guidance of his research. In addition, I am grateful for his careful reading of my manuscript and for his advice and encouragement in the final stages of the work.

To the late Harold I. Shapiro I owe a large part of whatever ability I have to (in his words) "get it right." Reading a poem with tact and with sensitivity to rhythmic and sonic structures and patterns was always a joyful activity for him, and he had a rare ability to communicate that joy to his students.

My wife, Angela, a student of Hal Shapiro's, has been my best reader and best help. This book is dedicated to her.

Abbreviations

BL	Samuel Taylor Coleridge, *Biographia Literaria; or, Biographical Sketches of My Literary Life and Opinions*, ed. James Engell and W. Jackson Bate (Princeton, N.J., 1983). 2 vols.
Brogan	T. V. F. Brogan, *English Versification, 1570–1980. A Reference Guide with a Global Appendix* (Baltimore, 1981).
DC MS	Dove Cottage Manuscript.
DS	William Wordsworth, *Descriptive Sketches* (London, 1793).
EW	William Wordsworth, *An Evening Walk* (London, 1793).
EY	*The Letters of William and Dorothy Wordsworth, The Early Years, 1787–1805*, ed. Ernest de Selincourt; revised, Chester L. Shaver (Oxford, 1967).
LB	*Lyrical Ballads*. The several editions cited are distinguished in the text and notes by dates of publication.
LY 1	*The Letters of William and Dorothy Wordsworth, The Later Years, Part I, 1821–1828*, ed. Ernest de Selincourt; revised, Alan G. Hill (Oxford, 1978).
LY 2	*The Letters of William and Dorothy Wordsworth, The Later Years, Part II, 1829–1834*, ed. Ernest de Selincourt; revised, Alan G. Hill (Oxford, 1979).
LY 3	*The Letters of William and Dorothy Wordsworth, The Later Years, Part III, 1835–1839*, ed. Ernest de Selincourt; revised, Alan G. Hill (Oxford, 1982).
LY 4	*The Letters of William and Dorothy Wordsworth, The Later Years, Part IV, 1840–1853*, ed. Ernest de Selincourt; revised, Alan G. Hill (Oxford, 1988).
MY 1	*The Letters of William and Dorothy Wordsworth, The Middle Years, Part I, 1806–1811*, ed. Ernest de Selincourt; revised, Mary Moorman (Oxford, 1969).
MY 2	*The Letters of William and Dorothy Wordsworth, The Middle Years, Part II, 1812–1820*, ed. Ernest de Selincourt; revised, Mary Moorman and Alan G. Hill (Oxford, 1970).
Prose	*The Prose Works of William Wordsworth*, ed. W. J. B. Owen and J. W. Smyser (Oxford, 1974). 3 vols.

PW	*Poetical Works.* Used alone, refers to *The Poetical Works of William Wordsworth,* ed. Ernest de Selincourt and Helen Darbishire (Oxford, 1940–49). 5 vols. Where accompanied by date, refers to the edition of Wordsworth's *Poetical Works* so dated (between 1827 and 1849–50).
13-Bk Prelude	*The Prelude,* MSS A–B text (1805–6), in the version edited by Mark L. Reed, *The Thirteen-Book Prelude* (Ithaca, N.Y., 1991). 2 vols.
14-Bk Prelude	*The Prelude,* MSS D–E text (1831–33), in the version edited by W. J. B. Owen, *The Fourteen-Book Prelude* (Ithaca, N.Y., 1985).
Reed *CEY*	Mark L. Reed, *Wordsworth: The Chronology of the Early Years, 1770–1799* (Cambridge, Mass., 1967).
Reed *CMY*	Mark L. Reed, *Wordsworth: The Chronology of the Middle Years, 1800–1815* (Cambridge, Mass., 1975).
STCL	*Collected Letters of Samuel Taylor Coleridge,* ed. E. L. Griggs (Oxford, 1956–71). 6 vols.
STCPW	*The Complete Poetical Works of Samuel Taylor Coleridge,* ed. E. H. Coleridge (London, 1912). 2 vols.

Introduction
An Ear for Poetry

> In recent years we have come to read the inner complexity of Romantic poetry with increasing delicacy and sophistication. . . . But we know surprisingly little—or, perhaps, have forgotten too much—about the actual literary conditions of the time. Hence we tend to read the poetry as a centering of psychological stresses or of historical and philosophical forces, ignoring much that is crucial to any poet as practitioner of a craft.
> —Stuart Curran, *Poetic Form and British Romanticism*

In 1836, Barron Field predicted in a letter to Wordsworth that future readers of the poet's work would come to appreciate how "deeply" he had "studied the sound as well as the sense of poetry."[1] Field was a very close reader of Wordsworth. He was "fascinated," in Stephen Gill's words, "with the poet as technician," and had as detailed a knowledge of the minutiae of Wordsworth's verse as anyone outside the Wordsworth household.[2] Field also had a good ear for poetry. He was right to insist upon a deep, fundamental relationship between the sound of Wordsworth's verse—its rhythm and rhyme, its patterns of consonant and vowel sounds, its employment of conventional verse and stanza structures—and the matter of his poetry.

The very fact that Field saw a need to assure the sixty-six-year-old poet that "one day" these structures of his verse would be appreciated, however, indicates a curious anomaly in Wordsworth's critical reception. Skill in versification, defined broadly as the ability to marshal the physical resources of language to good effect, is, as John Hollander says, a "necessary condition" (though of course not a sufficient one) of poetry.[3] In Wordsworth's own terms, "Sensibility to harmony of numbers, and the power of producing it," is "invariably" attendant upon the other "powers requisite for the production of poetry" listed in the 1815 Preface

to *Poems* (*Prose* 3:26–27). A poet, in other words, is by definition a writer who "studies the sound as well as the sense." Possessed to an unusual degree of powers that are liberally dispensed to all of humanity—observation and description, sensibility, reflection, imagination and fancy, invention, and judgment—the poet is also distinguished by the "accomplishment of verse" from the many poets "sown / By nature" whose words do not endure, or endure only in the poet's "sensuous incarnation" of them in rhythmic and sonorous forms.[4] By the time Field made his comment on the sound of Wordsworth's verse, Wordsworth was already generally acknowledged to be a powerful and important poet. Nevertheless, in Field's remark we hear an intelligent and sensitive correspondent, a man whose critical opinion Wordsworth valued, saying in effect that one day Wordsworth would be acknowledged to have been a capable writer of verse, as well as a great poet.

As peculiar as Field's assessment of Wordsworth's reputation may sound when stated baldly, it in fact accurately summarizes a view that pervades critical commentaries from as early as the 1790s to the present. To survey Wordsworth's critical reputation is to see that he is commonly regarded as a major poet who is at best only minimally concerned with a fundamental and pervasive aspect of the poet's art. Wordsworthians and commentators on the romantic period and on the history of English poetry and prosody have tended, with some notable exceptions, to deprecate, dismiss as irrelevant, or simply ignore the particularities and peculiarities of Wordsworth's verse considered as verse.[5] Thus, while Wordsworth criticism in recent years has delved ever deeper, and with what Stuart Curran calls "increasing delicacy and sophistication," into the textual and linguistic detail of poems, it has left virtually untouched major issues related to the rules, conventions, effects, and peculiarities of Wordsworth's metrical art. Wordsworth's metrical theory and practice—his understanding of the part played by meter in general or by particular metrical forms in the writing and reading of poems and the rules and habits underlying his management of metrical scheme, rhythm, rhyme, assonance, alliteration, and other patternings of sound in relation to sense—remain largely unexamined.

Neglect of the metrical, rhythmic, and auditory in Wordsworth's verse is of course partly a symptom of a general neglect of such qualities in much literary criticism of the mid- to late-twentieth century. As several commentators recently have noted, the explicit attempts of many modernist and postmodernist poetic schools and movements to diminish the role of the poem as a temporal and oral art dependent for full realization upon metrical and auditory qualities has had important consequences

for reading earlier poetry. Concentration on the image, abandonment of rhyme, calculated unmetricality or arhythmicality, innovative breaking of traditional metrical forms, concrete poetry, the use of typographical means to call attention to the text of the poem as text—these and many other methods and tendencies in recent poetry have helped to create a critical climate inhospitable to metrical and sonic analysis of relatively more traditional verse.[6] Insofar as criticism of poetry in the past seventy years has, as David Perkins argues, "devoted itself largely to explaining and defending" contemporary tendencies, it has "taught us, in reading [all] poetry, to bring to bear categories of attention appropriate to modern poetry, and [to] activate these same categories in reading poetry of the past."[7] The elegance of Surrey falls on deaf ears, whereas Wyatt's more "modern" roughness draws praise; the rhythms of Donne and Browning make those of Herbert and Tennyson seem merely tame by comparison.[8] Deconstructive theories have made many academic critics suspicious of approaches to poetry that place value on the means through which the poet achieves a distinctive "voice." If the poem is a "text" among texts (and not, say, an imitation of a speech act or a set of directions for vocal performance), then extrasemantic elements (all of those things that make the text a made thing requiring for full understanding sensual apprehension of something other than black marks on white space) are of little intrinsic interest. Many approaches to poetry recently in favor—among them the various "cultural studies" methods—tend to discourage any critical approach that values literary language as a consciously and intentionally shaped medium significantly set apart from other kinds of "discourse."[9]

Other reasons for neglect of Wordsworth's metrical art are specific to Wordsworth and are directly traceable either to theoretical problems raised by his prose comments on the subject or to intrinsic difficulties created by his practice. This is, after all, the poet who seemed eager to deflect attention away from the craft of verse when he defined poetry as the "spontaneous overflow of powerful feelings" (*Prose* 1:149). The poet is not a maker of verses but "a man speaking to men" (*Prose* 1:138). This is the Wordsworth who chimed in with contemporary voices calling for a new kind of poetry, one based on the recognition that there is no "*essential* difference between the language of prose and metrical composition" (*Prose* 1:135). This is the reforming poet who said that meter was historically the "great temptation" to the manifold abuses that enervate contemporary poetry, as it encourages the substitution of inflated and specialized poetic diction and wrenched syntax for the common language of good sense (*Prose* 1:161). The Preface to *Lyrical Ballads* (with its appen-

dix) has become a lens through which Wordsworth's attitudes toward metrical art have been viewed, despite Wordsworth's explicit claims that its arguments are applicable primarily to the poems originally published as *Lyrical Ballads*. Complicating the issues raised in the Preface, too, is Coleridge's influential disparagement of its arguments. Beginning with *Biographia Literaria*, a tradition of interpretation develops according to which Wordsworth's confusion about issues of diction and metrical craft manifests itself in extreme "inconstancy," or "inequality" of style.[10]

The most important reasons for the traditional ambivalence toward Wordsworth's metrical art stem, of course, from his practice. Literary historians of whatever stamp or inclination tend, consciously or not, to favor a progressive model, emphasizing "development." According to such models, whatever presents itself as epoch-making or anticipatory of later developments is of more consequence than the actual practices of a poet engaged, as Wordsworth was engaged, in assimilation and subtle modification of a complex set of conventions and tools of the trade. For all of his suspicions about the power of metrical language to lead the poet astray, Wordsworth was in matters of versification a deeply traditional poet from the start. He knew in minute detail how Spenser, Daniel, Shakespeare, Ben Jonson, Anne Finch (Countess of Winchelsea), Milton, Dryden, Pope, Thomson, Burns, Cowper, Charlotte Smith, and Beattie (not to mention scores of others) composed verse because he was engaged from his youth onward in memorizing and imitating these poets. Throughout his career and his corpus, Wordsworth gives evidence to support his claim (and the testimony of those who knew him) that he held vast stores of the verse of his predecessors in his memory—that he was, in a physical sense, informed by the rhythms of the English poetic past.[11] His most characteristic lines are perfectly traditional accentual-syllabic decasyllabics or octosyllabics. Even the most cursory survey of his selection and use of verse forms shows that he regarded regular, traditional, and recognizable verse patterns and stanzas as important means for framing his own individual voices.[12] Wordsworth's five volumes of *Poetical Works* contain nearly ninety different stanza forms in addition to a large bulk of extraordinarily varied blank verse (both dramatic and nondramatic) and more than five hundred sonnets (mostly Italian and Miltonic, but a few Shakespearean). These ninety forms include Chaucerian rhyme royal, Spenserian stanzas, tail rhyme, a number of stanzas invented by and traditionally associated with Jacobean lyricists, heroic couplets, elegiac stanzas, the Burns stanza, and *ottava rima*.[13]

In a postromantic climate in which originality tends to be equated with breaking through or out of the old, such tendencies seem to be at

odds with the image of the revolutionary Wordsworth, who according to Hazlitt heralded an age in which "rhyme was looked upon as a relic of the feudal system, and regular meter was abolished along with regular government."[14] Verse composed on principles that challenge the mainstream English accentual-syllabic tradition dominating English poetry from Chaucer through the middle of the nineteenth century tends, insofar as it may be regarded as a step toward modern developments, to assert greater claims on the attention of the twentieth-century critic than does verse that is, like Wordsworth's, firmly entrenched in that tradition.[15] Blake's Preface to *Jerusalem,* with its call for the liberation of poetry from Miltonic "fetters" and from subjugation to the "daughters of memory" and their mnemonic forms, provides a convenient point of reference for definitions of a properly "romantic" and revolutionary position with regard to metrical forms. And Blake's long line in the "prophetic" books provides an example of romantic metrical form as originating with the individual poet. (One must make one's own meter or be enslaved to another's.) In comparison with such manifestos and such practice, Wordsworth's versification lends itself to censure as representing at least a partial failure to effect a genuinely "romantic" liberation of the spirit of poetry from its exile in the Egypt of its own remembered past.[16]

The most influential late-nineteenth- and early-twentieth-century compendium of prosodic opinion, George Saintsbury's monumental *History of English Prosody,* is also (unfortunately for Wordsworth's critical reception) an excellent example of this kind of thinking. For Saintsbury, Blake and, especially, Coleridge led the way in establishing a "romantic revival." They liberated English verse from a numerical conception of the line (a syllabic prosody in which the number of total syllables in the line is strictly governed) and instituted a foot-based prosody that, in allowing latitude in the total number of syllables so long as the number and placement of stressed syllables remains consistent, is more adaptable to the actual qualities of spoken English. The Coleridge of *Rime of the Ancient Mariner* and *Christabel* is figuratively the hero of Saintsbury's providential history: his verse is the "match" that "kindled the torch of revived true English prosody" (foot-based, accentual verse) after a dark time of Continental influence (manifested in a prevalent syllabism, a Frenchified corruption). Saintsbury's Coleridge anticipates and paves the way for a great efflorescence of prosodic innovation and variety in the later nineteenth century. As the "knife that set the prisoner free, the mallet that knocked the block from the dog-shores and sent the ship careering into a sea hitherto silent, soon to be full of magical voices," Coleridge's verse helps to make possible Shelley, Browning, and

Swinburne (3:60). Saintsbury's Wordsworth belongs to an age before the great liberation (or rekindling, or "revival") and is presumably still imprisoned on the silent "dog-shores." His contribution to the history of prosody is summed up by Saintsbury in what is probably the most succinct formulation in print of the critical bifurcation of Wordsworth the poet and Wordsworth the metrical writer: "In no great poet does prosody play so small a part" (3:74).

This study argues for Field's ear against Saintsbury's. It argues, that is, for the desirability of an ear open to the possibility of important and unexpected sources of interest and creative tension in the metrical forms and sensuous patterns of Wordsworth's verse (whether or not these are anticipatory of later developments) and against the tendency to ignore or deprecate whatever fails to conform to our postromantic conceptions of appropriate musicality. The book pursues the broad argument that a proper understanding both of Wordsworth's individual poems and of his overall achievement as a poet requires much more careful attention to subtleties of his versification than has been common in the critical tradition. Toward this end, it provides a critical and historical context within which Wordsworth may be read metrically, describes and illustrates some of the more important characteristics of his metrical practice in a wide range of verse forms, and traces significant relationships between his management of the minutiae of his versification and some of the larger tendencies and concerns of his poetry as a whole.

By the phrase "reading metrically," I mean nothing more nor less than reading with attention to the poet's own expressed sense of the significance of metrical choices and uses and with some understanding of the many and complex ways in which the selection and use of verse kinds and patterns informs the poet's composition and affects the reader's experience of the poem. Wordsworth offers a great deal of evidence in his critical prose, letters, and conversations of his concern with these elements of his art. And his poems everywhere demonstrate that he habitually regarded the complex patterning of rhythmic and sonic elements within the context of conventional use to be a deeply vital and constitutive element of meaning. This evidence suggests that for Wordsworth a genuinely original poetic voice was, like the natural objects that he described in attacking the authenticity (and naturalness) of MacPherson's "Ossian," always "distinct" but never "defined into absolute independent singleness" ("Essay Supplementary to the Preface" of 1815; *Prose* 3:77). In matters related to versification, as in so many other aspects of his thought and art, Wordsworth argues in theory and practice for continuity with difference (or similitude in dissimilitude), inviting his

readers to hear his voice both as distinct from any other and as a part of a chorus of English poets. The history of English poetry, like the structure of *The Prelude*, or the physical movement involved in writing and reading successive lines of verse, moves forward by and through periodic returns. Each line of Wordsworth's verse is an unpredictable sequence of sounds and stresses unique to the poet, the poem, and the speaker; each line is at the same time a repetition of a predictable abstract type. That type, moreover, is resonant with echoes of past use. To "hear" the poetry is to sense in the structure and movement of the verse itself what is characteristic of (or required by) the forms employed by Wordsworth, what is uniquely Wordsworth's own in the employment of these forms, and how he exploits the tensions between the two.

Part 1, "The Passion of Meter," presents a reading of Wordsworth's prose comments about metrical art in the prefaces, letters, notes, and conversations. These initial chapters (1 and 2) reassess what Wordsworth actually said about the significance of meter and other schematic elements of verse (in contrast to what he is commonly taken to have said) and set forth in some detail the simple but rather strict rules and conventions of the metrical system that Wordsworth had internalized by the time he was fourteen and continued to follow throughout his career. (This system was, even during Wordsworth's lifetime, recognized as slightly old-fashioned and today requires some historical reconstruction if we are to read Wordsworth's verse as he may have assumed it would be read.) Wordsworth's prose comments center primarily on tensions inherent in the expressive use of the language of intense passion for the purposes of providing a salutary kind of pleasure. The poet's duty to give pleasure restricts him in matters of versification to what has pleased many and pleased long—that is, to a severely limited range of fixed, familiar, and conventional patterns of arrangement of sound and rhythm. At the same time, Wordsworth's definition of a poem as a "spontaneous overflow of powerful feeling" commits him to a language organized according to the dictates of a genuinely motivating passion. This language is vitally rhythmic (as is all passionate expression) but innocent of the abstract metrical forms of literary convention. Wordsworth describes the poet as an artist who engages in a process of "fitting" the syntax and rhythms of impassioned speech to the conventional arrangements of metrical form for the purposes of exploring, in a manner that will be pleasurable for a reader, the "fluxes and refluxes" of the human mind under the influence of various motivating feelings.

This notion of tense opposition between what Wordsworth calls the "passion of the sense" (or "passion of the subject") and the "passion of

meter" marks a significant distinction between Wordsworth's theories and the better-known (and widely embraced and promulgated) theories of Coleridge. Coleridge describes successful metrical art as involving the reconciliation of tensions within an overarching unity of effect. In good poems, those purely metrical cues and restraints that Wordsworth calls the "passion of meter" are entirely subordinated to the "passion of the sense": they become expressive markers of an impulse toward restraint that naturally opposes the overflow of emotion. Wordsworth's delineation of two distinct, equal and opposite "passions" is grounded in his own central aesthetic principle of "similitude in dissimilitude" and "dissimilitude in similitude." For Wordsworth, the pleasure to be derived from metrical language does not necessarily depend on meter being subordinated to diction (nor on diction being subordinated to meter), but on the complex oppositional relationship between artfully structured language in metrical forms and the actual language of passion. According to this view, metrical form does not function solely (as it does for Coleridge) as one among many indications of a heightened state of passion; it is (or can be) a kind of counter-presence in the poem, which may, when appropriate, be subordinated for specific expressive or emblematic purposes to the passion of the sense. Thus, Wordsworth's theory properly understood encompasses the Coleridgean notion of successful metrical composition as productive of a unified whole in which tensions are fully reconciled (a unity in multeity) but does not limit its definition to this one possibility. Wordsworth leaves open the possibility, and desirability, of a very wide range of relationships between expressive motives of poetic speakers and the metrical frames in which these are presented by the poet. What for Coleridge is a distressing "inconstancy" in Wordsworth's fitting of diction to metrical scheme (the same poet who is capable of the first twenty-four lines of "Tintern Abbey" is also strangely capable of the final three stanzas of "The Sailor's Mother") may be seen, through close attention to the implications for metrical analysis of Wordsworth's discussion of similitude in dissimilitude, as constancy to another (and more properly Wordsworthian) aesthetic principle.[17]

Wordsworth's views, then, may be regarded as a challenge to the reader to pay extraordinarily close attention to the minutiae of metrical forms, to relationships between forms and subjects and among various forms, and to the poet's management of rhythm, rhyme, assonance, alliteration, and the like. In refusing to fix by theoretical fiat the precise role played by these elements, Wordsworth denies his reader the comfort of taking for granted the function of meter in any one poem or body of

poems. Wordsworth's prose comments hint at a broad range of possibilities in his fitting of diction to metrical arrangement and thereby challenge the reader to pay close attention both to the metrical peculiarities of each poem and to the varieties of metrical art on display throughout the corpus as a whole. The remainder of the book pursues, largely through examples, the argument that accepting Wordsworth's challenge does indeed open up hitherto unapprehended complexities and sources of interest in the poetry itself.

Part 2, "The Versification of Poems" (chapters 3 to 5), focuses on Wordsworth's practice in poems selected to suggest the range, variety, and complexity of his versification. Chapter 3 treats characteristics of his early verse, with particular attention paid to his first significant published poems, *An Evening Walk* and *Descriptive Sketches*. Chapter 4 focuses on stanzaic verse through an overview of and individual readings of stanzaic poems in Wordsworth's first deliberately structured collection of shorter poems, the 1800 *Lyrical Ballads*. Chapter 5 distinguishes varieties of Wordsworth's blank verse and surveys his accomplishment in what he thought to be the "most difficult metre to manage." The study concludes with an essay on Wordsworth's "On the Power of Sound" as a retrospective mythic defense of the pervasive importance of his metrical art. Throughout the study, the arguments and readings also are intended to demonstrate in practical terms the importance of attention to metrical complexity in reading individual poems.

In the course of those sections of the book that focus on readings, I am also engaged in elucidating the climate of opinion surrounding the practice of verse composition during Wordsworth's age. The romantic period is a time of rapid change in theory and practice both, and Wordsworth was well aware of this. He learned the basics of his craft during a period remarkable for its uniformity of practice and opinion and published his major work in a climate of intense debate about the nature and function—and even value—of verse. By the time he died, practice and theory in England were both characterized as pervasively by diversity and experimentation as they were by uniformity in his youth. In Wordsworth's youth, the heroic couplets of Dryden, Waller, and especially Pope had defined the technical limits of the heroic line. Edward Bysshe's *Art of English Poetry* ruled the day.[18] The heroic line contained ten syllables and ten syllables only; hypermetrical syllables were not allowed, were routinely lopped off by contraction or elision, and were, if not subject to one or another rule for syllabic reduction, mightily offensive to the ear of the cultivated reader. Even-numbered syllables were stressed; odd were not (with only a few variations allowed). Pauses

were to be employed midline, after the fourth, fifth, or sixth syllable. Run-on lines were discouraged. These practices were so firmly institutionalized by the 1770s that Samuel Johnson could proclaim, apparently without a tinge of irony, that to attempt improvements beyond what Pope had been able to accomplish would be "dangerous."[19]

During Wordsworth's lifetime, English literature saw many "dangerous" attempts at improvement. Critics argued against Pope's contractions and elisions as unnatural and called for looser restrictions on the number of syllables admitted per line, arguing all the while for the desirability of more "natural" pronunciation. Milton's blank verse—heavily indebted to Italian models, and to many eighteenth-century ears exceedingly wild and sublime—was increasingly cited as a musically various, liberating alternative to Dryden's urbanity and correctness. The greater availability of more accurate texts of the elder English poets—especially of Chaucer and Shakespeare—meant that more and more the model on which poets' formed their style was English rather than classical. A vogue for popular English and Scottish song and baladry brought verse from an oral and musical tradition into respectability—and the romantic poets drew freely on the language, and eventually on the rhythms, of Bishop Percy's *Reliques of Ancient English Poetry,* Robert Burns's Highland songs, Scott's *Minstrelsy of the Scottish Border,* and other collections of "extraliterary" verse. Following such models, Coleridge and others fashioned the verse that would eventually contribute to the breakup of what had been a fairly uniform tradition of accentual-syllabic verse from Chaucer to Wordsworth.

Such innovations make the romantic period a watershed in the history of versification. And it is important to know that Wordsworth persisted for the most part in writing relatively strict accentual-syllabic verse in the midst of this rapid change. By the 1840s, Wordsworth was admitting that he could not accustom his ear to the "freer movement" of the accentual verse of younger poets, in which "redundant syllables" caused more "deviation" from "the common Iambic movement" than he would allow in his own verse.[20] I would argue that by mid- to late century, those subtleties of his verse that stem from his strict adherence to tradition (elision of extrametrical syllables and a uniform placement of stress that makes small variation significant, for example) were already becoming lost on most readers (as they certainly are lost on Saintsbury). What is needed, then, is an approach something like that pursued by musicologists of the "period music" or "original instruments" school, who seek to restore in performance a feel for how a seventeenth- or eighteenth-century piece may have been performed during the lifetime

of the composer. Wordsworth, Hazlitt tells us, created a strange and unsettling effect by "chaunting" his verse.[21] He certainly wrote a kind of verse that his own contemporaries found challenging in the range and variety of its "fittings" of language to meter. I would not wish to argue that the only good reading of a Wordsworth poem is one that reenacts the rhythmic and auditory effects of a period-style performance. Even if such could confidently be defined and imitated, there is no need to teach students to chant Wordsworth.[22] Nevertheless, I do think that respecting the differences between our assumptions and Wordsworth's, insofar as these are recoverable in the texts themselves, may enable readers of Wordsworth and the romantics to hear expressive subtleties—and to grasp with the mind's ear emblematic possibilities—that otherwise would be lost.

NOTE ON SCANSIONS AND PROSODIC TERMINOLOGY

The primary focus of this study is Wordsworth's poetry, not prosodic theory. Accordingly, I have attempted to introduce in the discussions and readings that follow as little specialized prosodic language as is consonant with the ends of precision and sufficiency of description. At the same time, it would be foolish to ignore the opportunities for subtlety of analysis that linguistic study of prosodic elements has afforded literary criticism in the second half of the twentieth century. One of the chief reasons Saintsbury fails to value (or even understand) Wordsworth's metrical art is that Wordsworth's prosodic peculiarities are not well described by Saintsbury's foot-based system of "iambics" and "trochaics" and "trisyllabic substitution." So, although adopting the standard foot-based terminology developed most fully and influentially by Saintsbury would have had the advantage of familiarity, it also may have imported into the discussion assumptions according to which the real sources of tension in Wordsworth's verse would remain indescribable.

Fortunately for my purposes, a system of scansion has been developed that lends itself well to analysis of the kinds of subtleties that distinguish Wordsworth's verse. Derek Attridge's *The Rhythms of English Poetry* (1982) sets forth a set of rules that is both simple and remarkably powerful in its explanatory force. The usefulness of Attridge's system as an analytic tool stems in part from his grounding of the work firmly in linguistic prosody, which takes account of the actual phonetic content and physical structure of a poetic utterance, and in part from his literary tact, which makes him sensitive (as strictly linguistic prosodists sometimes are not)

to the force of those specifically literary conventions that impinge upon this actual phonetic content. Attridge's system, that is, allows its user to take account of the fact that in any adequate reading of a metrical line a reader feels the line to be a locus at which an abstract pattern and an actual, quantifiable sequence of physical impulses intersect in a single "complex experience" (172).[23]

Attridge defines the line as a meeting (or "marriage") of a conventional pattern of expectations—an arrangement of a certain number of "offbeats" and "beats," in which a natural tendency of English speakers to alternate strong and weak syllables is formalized—and a variable "realization" of this pattern in an actual sequence of relatively strong ("stressed") or relatively weak ("unstressed") syllables. An "iambic pentameter" line is *metrically* a "five-beat" line in the pattern "o B" (or offbeat-beat):

o B o B o B o B o B

The actual pattern of relatively strong and relatively weak stresses that realizes this pattern is the line's *rhythm* (marked above the line with the symbols [-s] and [+s]):[24]

-s +s -s +s -s +s -s +s -s +s
Our walk was far among the ancient trees
("To M.H.," l. 1)

Metrical interest springs from the variety of kinds and degrees of complexity and tension that are possible in this marriage of metrical form and realization. The example above is a relatively simple realization. Because it realizes the metrical scheme following only the "base rules"—a stressed syllable realizes a beat and an unstressed syllable realizes an offbeat—it may adequately be described using only the basic schema of "o"s and "B"s under the line:[25]

Our walk was far among the ancient trees
o B o B o B o B o B

Of course, even this highly regular actual line does not fully conform to or realize the metrical pattern, if only because the actual stress value and phonetic content of each stressed syllable is different from all other stressed syllables (and the same is true of the unstressed). The metrical form is merely binary, whereas the actual sounds of the syllables are

distinguished by pitch, duration, timbre, loudness, and the like. Each [+s] or [-s] is not equal to every other stress or nonstress (whereas a beat is a beat and an offbeat an offbeat), and this level of variation can be significant (both expressively and emblematically). For purposes of metrical scansion, however, this is a line with little or no tension between meter and rhythm.

The most common kinds of tension occur when an unstressed syllable falls in a beat position or when a stressed syllable falls in an offbeat position.[26] In the first case, and when the syllable in question occurs between two unstressed syllables, the influence of the meter may cause the unstressed syllable to be "promoted." The symbol [B̄] designates a beat realized by a syllable other than a [+s] (either a [-s] or [s]):

              -s   s   -s
Too weak to labour in the harvest field
o B o B o B̄ o B o B
("A Narrow Girdle of Rough Stones and Crags," l. 69)

Unstressed syllables also fall quite frequently in the first (beat) position in verse that normally begins with a stress (trochaic tetrameter, for example):

Feeling tunes your voice, fair Princess!
And your brow is free from scorn
B̄ o   B o B o B
("The Armenian Lady's Love," ll. 43–44)

They are also common in the last (beat) position of iambic lines:

And dances with the daffodils
o B o   B o B o B̄
("I wandered lonely as a cloud," l. 24)

                      such, perhaps,
As have no slight or trivial influence
o B   o B   o B o B o B̄
("Tintern Abbey," ll. 31–32)

Attridge accounts for these tendencies by expanding the promotion rule to include unstressed syllables occurring "with a line-boundary on one side and an unstressed syllable on the other" (167).

"Demotion" of a syllable occurs when a stressed syllable between two stressed syllables falls in an offbeat position. The symbol [ȯ] denotes a demotion:

    +s +s   +s
   As thou seem'st now to do; might one day trace
    o B ȯ B o B
   ("It is no Spirit who from heaven hath flown," l. 14)

Because stressed syllables are very common in the first (offbeat) position of lines, the demotion rule is expanded to include a stressed syllable after a line boundary and before a stressed syllable:

        He heard the South
  +s +s -s +s
  Make subterraneous music, like the noise
   ȯ B o B
            ("Michael," ll. 50–51)

Promotion and demotion are subtle means for achieving expressive effects and for lending variety and interest to metrical language. The presence of promoted syllables tends to increase the speed of the line, as the light syllables in beat positions are felt to move more quickly than do full stresses. Demotion, which tends to slow the line, is of the two effects the more disruptive, as it also tends to produce a sense of separation among the affected stressed syllables (or the line boundary and stressed syllable).

Promotion and demotion involve minute differences in the degrees of stress required by syllables to realize beat and offbeat positions. More potentially disruptive kinds of variation stem from changes in the expected order and sequence of stress and nonstress. "Implied offbeats" occur when two stressed syllables occur in sequence, without a line boundary or a contiguous third stress allowing demotion. They are designated by the symbol [ô]:

   For from the summit of BLACK COMB (dread name
          B ô B
   Derived from clouds and storms!)
      ("View from the Top of Black Comb," ll. 2–3)

Implied offbeats may be felt as a slight pause between stressed syllables, or as an "eddy in the smooth flow of the verse" (Attridge 173).

In accentual-syllabic verse such as Wordsworth's—in which not only the number of strong stresses, but the total number of stresses in a line is strictly controlled—implied offbeats usually occur in conjunction with certain other compensatory features, called "pairing conditions." These conditions are in some cases specific to a particular kind of verse and are subject to several variations, so I will limit myself here in this general description to those that come into play most frequently in Wordsworth's verse. The "implied offbeat condition" requires that an implied offbeat must either immediately follow or precede a nonfinal "double offbeat." The double offbeat, or an offbeat position realized by two unstressed syllables, is marked with the symbol [ŏ]:

                -s -s   +s   +s
For from the summit of BLACK COMB (dread name
                ŏ   B ô B
Derived from clouds and storms!)
                                ("View . . . Black Comb," ll. 2–3)

           +s   +s   -s -s
Even more than when I tripp'd lightly as they
           B   ô B   ŏ
                                ("Ode," l. 196)

The first of these examples employs a "stress final" pairing; the second, a "stress initial" pairing.

In Wordsworth's iambic verse, double offbeats also may occur, and frequently do, in observance of an "initial inversion condition." In the iambic pentameter line (five-beat accentual-syllabic verse in duple rising rhythm), realization of the first (offbeat) position with a [+s] is so common that it must be recognized as a part of the "metrical set." The "initial inversion condition" (or "substitution" of a trochaic opening for the usual iambic) states that the initial offbeat "may be omitted only if the first beat is immediately followed by a double offbeat":

O there is blessing in this gentle Breeze
B   ŏ B o B̄ o B o B
                              (*14-Bk Prelude* 1.1)²⁷

Occurrences of double offbeats, except in observance of the implied offbeat condition or the initial inversion condition, are rare in Wordsworth's verse in duple rhythms (iambic or trochaic).

The variant symbols [B̄, ó, ô, ŏ] provide a means for indicating graphically and precisely occurrences of various kinds of rhythmic play and tension within the metrical set. The several kinds of departures from the metrical rule may be ranked in the following order according to the amount of tension or disruption they tend to cause (from least to most disruptive): promotion, demotion, stress-initial pairing, stress-final pairing. Combinations within a line of more than one variant, of course, tend to increase the complexity of the line.

A final attraction of this system for the purposes of this study should be sufficiently obvious from this description of it: although it allows for more accurate and subtle treatment of metrical variety and complexity than do Saintsburian foot-based systems, it does not dogmatically exclude the familiar terminology of "iambic," "trochaic," and the like. (The use of "initial inversion condition," in which the notion of an inverted first foot is latent, is a good example.) So long as the concepts of feet and substitutions are not allowed to obscure the actual experience of the verse, in which effects often encompass structures greater than two- or three-syllable groups, there is no reason why the structure Attridge calls a "five-beat" line in duple rising rhythm ("o B") should not be described, in terms familiar to Wordsworth and his contemporaries, as "iambic pentameter." "Five-beat" and "pentameter," "four-beat" and "tetrameter," "rising rhythm" and "iambic," "falling rhythm" and "trochaic" may be used (and are used in this study) interchangeably.

DESCRIPTIONS OF STANZA FORMS

In descriptions of stanza forms, lowercase letters describe the rhyme scheme of the stanza: *a* endings rhyme with other *a* endings within the stanza, *b* lines with *b* lines, and so forth. The notation *aabb* represents a structure of repeating couplets; *abab* represents cross rhymes; *abba* represents envelope or embedded rhyme. Subscript numerals refer to the number of beats per line. The stanza $a_4b_3a_4b_3$, for example, is a cross-rhymed stanza with alternating four- and three-beat lines.

Terminology used to describe rhyme is adopted from William Harmon's "Rhyme in English Verse: History, Structures, Functions."[28] Harmon's category of "promoted" rhyme allows description of effects of rhyme akin to the metrical promotion and demotion discussed above.

Promoted rhyme may occur when rhyming syllables bear unequal degrees of stress:

+s
And I could with my days to be
o B

s
Bound each to each by natural piety.
o B̄

("My heart leaps up," ll. 8–9)

Promotion also occurs in pairs of rhyming syllables in which neither is felt to carry the full stress value required both by the meter and by the rhyme. Harmon provides the examples "light / infinite"; "liberty / merrily" (371).

Harmon's terms "consonance rhyme" and "assonance rhyme" make sense of the muddle created by terms such as "slant rhyme" and "half rhyme." A consonance rhyme is an imperfect rhyme in which concluding consonants are shared and vowel sounds differ (craze/froze); an assonance rhyme employs identical vowel sounds but differs in the final consonant sound (save/grey). "Augmented rhyme" replaces "feminine rhyme" or "double rhyme" for pairs such as lying/dying and is defined as a perfect rhyme (lie/die) augmented by *homoeoteleuton* (ing/ing). Augmented rhyme is designated in stanza descriptions using a subscript line following the letter: $a_4 b_{-3} a_4 b_{-3}$ describes a stanza in which the second and fourth lines regularly employ augmented rhyme.

PART ONE

The Passion of Meter

1
Similitude in Dissimilitude

> It would not be a useless employment to apply this principle [of the pleasure stemming from the perception of similitude in dissimilitude] to the consideration of metre, and to show that metre is hence enabled to afford much pleasure, and to point out in what manner that pleasure is produced.
> —Wordsworth, Preface to *Lyrical Ballads* (*Prose* 1:149)

"THE GREAT SPRING OF ACTIVITY"

One of the simplest and least-assuming statements about meter in the Preface to *Lyrical Ballads* is also one of the most important for understanding Wordsworth's metrical art.[1] Having listed in rapid succession a number of reasons why he has chosen to write in strict, traditional meters, even while admittedly striving to employ a language as free as possible from the usual distinctions between metrical language and the language of "all other men who feel vividly and see clearly" (*Prose* 1:142), Wordsworth calls upon the experience of his reader:

> All that it is *necessary* to say . . . upon this subject, may be effected by affirming, what few persons will deny, that, of two descriptions, either of passions, manners, or characters, each of them equally well executed, the one in prose and the other in verse, the verse will be read a hundred times where the prose is read once. (*Prose* 1:151)

Good metrical poetry needs no other justification beyond the fact that it invites and rewards rereading. It invites rereading, Wordsworth contends, because the act of reading verse is an inherently and complexly pleasurable activity. Wordsworth's attempt to identify the source of the pleasure arising from composition in meter leads him to the central statement of his metrical theory:

> Among the chief ... causes [upon which the pleasure received from metrical language depends] is to be reckoned a principle which must be well known to those who have made any of the Arts the object of accurate reflection; I mean the pleasure which the mind derives from the perception of similitude in dissimilitude. (*Prose* 1:149)

The "principle" discussed here Wordsworth calls "the great spring of the activity of our minds and their chief feeder." It is also the source of "sexual appetite, and all the passions connected with it." It is the very "life of our ordinary conversation; and upon the accuracy with which similitude in dissimilitude, and dissimilitude in similitude are perceived, depend our taste and our moral feelings" (*Prose* 1:149).[2] Wordsworth declines to enter into a "systematic" treatment of the topic as it relates specifically to metrical issues (saying instead that it would "not be a useless employment" to do so); nevertheless, the Preface does provide a number of strong indications of the direction such a treatment might take. This is especially true when the partial and relatively narrowly focused arguments advanced in the Preface are considered within the context of some of Wordsworth's many statements about meter, rhythm, rhyme, and other elements of versification in his essays, letters, notes, and conversations.

Underlying the entire discussion of meter and diction in the Preface to *Lyrical Ballads* is Wordsworth's assumption that the poet is by definition bound to provide a particular kind of salutary pleasure: the "end of Poetry is to produce excitement in coexistence with an overbalance of pleasure" (*Prose* 1:147). The "pleasure which a Poet may rationally endeavour to impart" (1:119) is itself complex. Because the passion involved in poetry frequently issues from "an unusual and irregular state of the mind," it "may be carried beyond its proper bounds" by powerful words "or images and feelings [that] have an undue proportion of pain connected with them" (1:147). In such cases, meter, operating as a familiar and constant presence in the midst of uncommon and unsettling passion, may act to oppose and to temper this excitement: "Now the co-presence of something regular, something to which the mind has been accustomed in various moods and in a less excited state, cannot but have great efficacy in tempering and restraining the passion by an intertexture of ordinary feeling, and of feeling not strictly and necessarily connected with the passion" (1:147).

The words "co-presence" and "intertexture" are of fundamental importance in Wordsworth's theories. They maintain a distinction, upon which Wordsworth frequently insists, between two potentially opposi-

tional activities: the selection of "real" language (a selection that theoretically follows no rules but those dictated by the passion itself) and the "fitting" of that language to metrical arrangement (which involves a complex process of framing passionate language in conventional form for aesthetic purposes). These two processes correspond roughly to the dynamics suggested in Wordsworth's familiar description of a poem as a "spontaneous overflow" of feeling, "recollected in tranquility": feeling overflows in expressive syntactic structures, figures, and imagery; metrical arrangement and all of the patterns of rhythm and sound that go along with it may be regarded as a sign of the presence of the tranquilly purposeful mind directing and shaping the passion toward the proper ends of poetry.

Because meter functions as a sign of purposefulness, and because it stimulates associations between the generating passions of a poem and moods and states of mind other than those that are the immediate occasion of the poem ("in a less excited state"), the effects of metrical organization are not, and cannot be, entirely subordinate to the impulses of that generating passion. Two systems of organization are at work, and in good verse they will be felt as interconnected and dynamic "co-presence[s]"—a passionate overflow of spontaneous emotion and an "intertexture" of "ordinary feeling . . . not strictly and necessarily connected with the passion."

The potential complexity of the "intertexture" of meter and diction (and its genuine contrariety) is developed further on in Wordsworth's argument when he makes the seemingly contradictory claim that meter frequently performs a function directly opposite to that mentioned in the preceding quotation. In cases in which the "Poet's words should be incommensurate with the passion" and "inadequate to raise the Reader to a height of desirable excitement," meter may "impart" the requisite passion "(unless the Poet's choice of his metre has been grossly injudicious)":

> In the feelings of pleasure which the Reader has been accustomed to connect with metre in general, and in the feeling . . . which he has been accustomed to connect with that particular movement of metre, there will be found something which will greatly contribute to impart passion to the words, and to effect the complex end which the Poet proposes to himself. (1:149)

Wordsworth recognizes here that it is probable, the complexities and insufficiencies of language being what they are, that many parts of his

own, or any poet's, work will be too personal or too idiosyncratic to convey successfully the full intensity of the passion. In such cases, the intrinsic pleasures issuing from the sonic patterns and rhythmic movement of verse itself, and from its powerful ability to call up associations between such movement and previous experiences of pleasure in measured language, will help supply the deficiency. The "complex end" of the poem, that is, may be effected by unusually passionate language couched in rhythmic structures that temper the impulses of the passion, or by language which in some cases fails to embody satisfactorily what Wordsworth calls elsewhere "the passion of the subject" but which nevertheless commands and repays attention because its physical properties are organized in an insistent and inherently pleasurable way.[3]

In both of these cases, the poet depends heavily on the relationship between meter and diction to create a sense of the difference between the language of "real life" and the language of poetry. Meter, says Wordsworth, contributes "imperceptibly" to "make up a complex feeling of delight" through "an indistinct perception perpetually renewed of language closely resembling that of real life, and yet, in the circumstance of metre, differing from it so widely" (*Prose* 1:151). The same idea is discernible in the following paragraph of the Preface, when Wordsworth says that in these poems he "endeavoured to bring [his] language *near to* the language of men" (1:151; emphasis added). He states clearly that he understands the extremely subtle—even "imperceptible"—intrinsic pleasures of meter and consciously seeks to use these in creating an idiom somewhere between the language of common life and something that feels more significant and perhaps more permanent and directly communicative than does that frequently unpredictable language, subject as it is to becoming incommunicative through its very familiarity. He strives for an idiom that may be perceived to be "near" to speech. At the same time, he consciously creates a context in which specifically idiomatic tendencies (in the sense of radically personal and individual) will be modified by virtue of his voluntary obedience to a system of organization that he shares with all poets in a four-hundred-year-old tradition of accentual-syllabic verse.

One of the chief effects of the poet's use of metrical language as Wordsworth defines it is that it creates a potentially pleasurable sense of aesthetic distance between the language of the poem and the "language really used by men." The operation of language itself, and especially the complex interplay of mind with and against language, becomes

objectified through the reader's consciousness of the movements and turnings of verse. Wordsworth suggests that no matter how successful a poem is in employing language that is informed by an occasion of real passion, and no matter how it resists the limiting influence of preconditioned notions derived from other poems, meter itself will tend to counter, for better or for worse, these distinguishing and individuating impulses through its "tendency... to divest language, in a certain degree, of its reality, and thus to throw a sort of half-consciousness of unsubstantial existence over the whole composition" (1:147). The presence of meter works continually and subtly to impress the reader with the obviously composed, overdetermined nature of the speech. Each phrase, each word, even each syllable is simultaneously able to be apprehended as an element of the syntax of expressive passion, as an element of an overarching, conventional pattern of repeated stress and sound, or (strangely and even mysteriously) both. Does the sequence "meadow, grove, and stream" take the form that it takes primarily as an index of a mind moving figuratively from fixity and containment to change and fluidity? Or is it also—or even more fundamentally—evidence of an ear attuned to the slowing effect of a late pause after an unstressed syllable (move "meadow" to the second position in the string of nouns and note how the line lurches forward at its close) and to the pleasures of assonance operating in contiguous syllables that are simultaneously distinguished by degree of stress (méad-ŏw, gróve)? Wordsworth's discussion suggests that he holds such intersections of distinct motives as a deep source of the enduring pleasures of verse.[4]

To take another example virtually at random, did the "well-dressed" woman walking by the side of Loch Ketterine in "Stepping Westward" actually say, as Wordsworth claims she said, the metrically tractable phrase "What you are stepping westward?" or has Wordsworth transformed it in his tranquil recollection? Is the fit between this supposedly actual salutation and the metrical scheme of the poem an instance of an actual and chance utterance approximating a metrical form (which instance thereby dictates the choice of the metrical frame that will control the rest of the poem), or has the actual speech been recomposed in conformity with Wordsworth's need for an eight-syllable line with end rhyme:

"What you are stepping westward?"—"Yea."

The point, of course, is that the demands of both systems—expressive syntax and metrical form—are fulfilled by the same speech instance. I

would argue that this issue of simultaneous fulfillment, raised by the very act of quoting speech metrically, goes a long way toward explaining why the salutation proves so powerful to the speaker of "Stepping Westward." As an instance of actual speech that catches the poet's ear—an ear attuned by training to distinctions between permanently pleasurable utterance and the ephemeral noise of much daily discourse—it is more than a merely courteous form of address or a gesture insignificant beyond its conventional form. Instead, the greeting (like a poem) seems to embody the very spirit of a particular kind of human communication, and that spirit is communicated in large part through the contours of its physical form—it had the "very sound of courtesy" (l. 20). Whether or not the line has been revised, the effect on the ear and in the mind is a conviction that there is, or can be, a kind of poetry in the sound of everyday speech.

THE PASSION OF METER

In a letter of 1804 to John Thelwall, Wordsworth puts some of these issues in more practical terms and within a context that may help to show more concretely what is peculiarly Wordsworthian about his ideas concerning the "intertexture" of metrical frame and expressive motives. Thelwall was at this time promulgating an innovative theory of meter as part of his campaign to reform English elocutionary principles. Following the work of Joshua Steele and others, Thelwall argued for a system of scansion based on analogies between musical quantities and the metrical treatment of syllables, through which he believed the music of English verse could be liberated from the narrow strictures of neoclassical conceptions of the line. Thelwall apparently had raised one of the central issues of his work—the correct, natural, and appropriately musical recitation of verse—and had asked for Wordsworth's opinion. Judging from Wordsworth's response, it seems that Thelwall had voiced some such opinion as is contained in the following quotation from his *Selections for the Illustration of a Course of Instructions on the Rhythmus and Utterance of the English Language* (London, 1812):[5]

> From my system of reading verse, I preclude all peculiarities of tone, all arbitrary accents, quantities and pauses; all helping out the verse, as it is called, by clenches and closes, independent of the *grammatical* construction of the sentence. All must depend upon

the sense, the sentiment, and the feeling. . . . I know of no such
distinction as a *verse mouth* and a *prose mouth:* I want only a distinct,
a sonorous, an articulative mouth. (xv–xvi)

In responding, Wordsworth says that he is in broad agreement with
Thelwall's "general rule" that "the art of verse should not compell you
to read in . . . emphasis etc that violates the nature of prose." But he also
wishes to impose certain important "limitations":

This rule should be taken with limitations for not to speak of other
reasons as long as verse shall have the marked termination that
rhyme gives it and as long as blank verse shall be printed in lines,
it will be Physically impossible to pronounce the last words or
syllables of the lines with the same indifference, as the others, i.e.
not to give them an intonation of one kind or an other, or to follow
them with a pause, not called out for by the passion of the subject,
but by the *passion of metre* merely. (*EY,* 434; emphasis added)

The connection that the letter makes between metrical form and inescapable physical restraint is clearly related to the statements in the Preface concerning meter as a co-presence and intertexture of powers not strictly or exclusively stemming from "the passion of the subject." It also represents a fundamental contradiction of the commonly held notion that Wordsworth regarded meter (or could have regarded it as a practical matter) as a mere ornament.[6] In stating that verse cannot share the rhythmic characteristics of prose "merely" ("not to speak of other reasons") because the metrical arrangement of language makes it "Physically impossible" for the eye, ear, and speech organs to ignore rhymes or line endings, Wordsworth suggests that metrical form acts, for poet and reader both, as a force almost as inevitable as gravity. It may (and must) be resisted, but its power cannot simply be willed away. Such a view suggests further that Wordsworth thought of formal rhythmic patterning as incorporating into the poem basic laws external to the individual instance of speech and that these laws can and do assert themselves in verse with the force of a "passion"—a powerful word in Wordsworth's criticism—whether or not that passion is perfectly consonant at any given point with the poet's or the speaker's passion. The metrical form of a line itself, its length and its internal structure, imports its own passion into the poem. It is, therefore, for better or for worse, never a neutral or invisible element. It functions as a counter-presence,

a fixed system of organization that either significantly cooperates with or significantly resists the organizing tendencies originating in the passion of the subject.

Wordsworth's comments also provide important and hitherto overlooked evidence about his understanding of the interplay of diction, syntax, and meter in the writing, reading, or recitation of verse.[7] Thelwall, in concert with a number of revisionary prosodists writing in the period 1770–1815, insists that the true genius of English verse music consists in its relative freedom from the restraints of an abstract metrical rule.[8] Thelwall therefore advocates the subordination of meter to the rhythms of speech. (Note in the quotation from Thelwall that "grammatical" constraints—or what twentieth-century prosodists would call "syntactic stress" requirements—alone are to establish the essential rhythmic character of the composition.) Wordsworth's response shows him arguing, characteristically, against the grain. Wordsworth will grant that close similarity in the grammatical organization of a poem and a passage of good, passionate prose is a desirable aim. As early as January 1798 he copied into the Alfoxden notebook a strong statement on the subject: "distortion" of the "natural order and connection of . . . words" solely for the sake of distancing metrical language from prose is the "worst fault that poetry can have."[9] Beginning in the late 1790s his own verse shows greater and greater subtlety in his use of naturalistic syntactic structures (compared, for example, with *Descriptive Sketches*). And the Preface to *Lyrical Ballads* is, of course, famous and infamous for its insistence on the shared idiom of speech, prose, and verse. In the letter to Thelwall, however, Wordsworth clearly refuses to blunt what he takes to be a clear distinction between the actual experience of reading metered and unmetered language. Wordsworth's language will approximate the speech and prose of passion and good sense, but that language will be shaped by and presented in a conventional pattern that will distinguish it sharply and definitively from these other forms of expression. Whereas the tendency in Thelwall and in many other romantic prosodists is to collapse this distinction in practice by making "grammar" (or "prose sense") the sole cue in determining rhythm in performance, Wordsworth insists that the predictable passion of the meter and the widely variable passions of the subject form two distinct systems of organization that the poet fits to one another.[10] The metrical poem, for Wordsworth, is characterized by tension between two "passions" that assert themselves in the tense interplay of phrase and measured line. The thoroughgoing dissimilarity, issuing from this tension, between

a reader's experience of verse and of other forms of verbal expression is as important as the fact that the metered poem uses elements common to all passionate uses of language."

The letter to Thelwall continues with even more practical matters, as Wordsworth gives a brief description of his "very simple" rules for his pentameters:

> 1st and 2nd syllables long or short indifferently except where the Passion of the sense cries out for one in preference 3d 5th 7th 9th short etc according to the regular laws of the Iambic. This the general rule. But I can scarcely say that I admit any limits to the dislocation of the verse, that is I know none that may not be justified by some passion or other. (*EY*, 434)

Wordsworth's rules are, as he says, simple. But they also reveal a great deal about the principles of his entire prosodic system, especially when read along with his comments on "similitude in dissimilitude" and the "passion of meter" and in the context of late-eighteenth-century attitudes about meter. I shall take up this latter topic in more detail below; but at present I wish only to observe that Wordsworth's definition of his line as a fixed number of syllables, his insistence upon observing the "regular laws of the iambic" in the alternation of "long" and "short" syllables,[12] and his sense that variation produces expressive "dislocation" in the line suggest that he was possessed of a more developed (if less polemically useful) sense of the complexities of the issues than were Thelwall and many others who were writing during this period of prosodic innovation (or, in Hazlitt's view, of revolution).

Thelwall's system, for example, which has been praised in the twentieth century as a *locus classicus* of romantic liberalizing tendencies, rejects both syllable counting and the concept of abstract metrical "feet," advocating instead the application of musical terms and concepts to the study and recitation of verse.[13] For Thelwall, describing a line in terms of numbered syllables occupying locations in the line makes no sense, because it is the number of equally timed "cadences" that determine the form of the line, and these cadences may contain variable numbers of syllables (just as musical measures contain variable numbers of notes performed in equal time). The heroic line, which Wordsworth describes as decasyllabic and five-footed, is for Thelwall "six *proportioned,* but varied cadences," now "theoretically degraded into five disproportioned and incongruous feet" (iii–iv). A "cadence" is "a portion of tuneable

sound, beginning heavy and ending light," but the "heavy" syllable or even the entire cadence may consist of a "hiatus or pause" that functions like a musical rest. Thelwall scans the heroic line thus (I have simplified his elaborate markings in the interest of clarity):

      (/)   - / - / - / - / - /
    (pause)Then / fables / yet have / feign'd, or / fear con / ceived
      (/)   / - - / - (/) - - / - /
     — / Gorgons and / Hydras / (pause) and Chi / meras / dire.
                                                       (Thelwall, xlvii)

For Thelwall, no merely theoretical or abstract conception of the line or foot may be allowed to impinge upon the natural "rhythmus" of English speech. His vehement refusal to allow for elision of syllables is a good case in point. Thelwall calls the common eighteenth-century practice of dropping syllables in typography and pronunciation in accordance with a numerical definition of the line a "barbarous expedient." The harmony of the verse of Shakespeare, Milton, and all the "best writers," in fact, depends on the frequent introduction of a "syllable more than is counted in the bar," an effect that Thelwall calls "appogiatura" (xlviii).[14] In Thelwall's system, even instances in Dryden or Pope of strictly decasyllabic lines achieved by typographical elision or contraction of extrametrical syllables are to be given full pronunciation (the symbol [ᵕ] marks the "appogiaturae"):

                Th'*offended,* suff'ring in th'*Offenders* name
                                ("Religio Laici," l. 108)

                  ᵕ   ᵕ   ᵕ
                The offended suffering in the Offenders name
                                    (Thelwall's scansion)

                A mightier Pow'r the strong direction sends
                And sev'ral men impels to sev'ral ends.
                          ("An Essay on Man," epistle 2, ll. 165–66)

                        ᵕ
                A mightier Power the strong direction sends
                  ᵕ   ᵕ
                And several men impels to several ends.
                                    (Thelwall's scansion)

For Thelwall (and increasingly for readers in the romantic period) a commitment to the rhythms of speech diminishes the role of meter conceived of as a fixed abstraction or idea of order to which linguistic material is fitted.[15] During a time of theoretical and practical loosening of constraints on the English line, then, Wordsworth's decidedly syllabic definition of his pentameters marks him as an exception.

Appreciating Wordsworth's resistance to contemporary developments in prosodic theory and practice is of primary importance in reading Wordsworth metrically. Indeed, I think that many twentieth-century commentators have failed to hear the music of Wordsworth's verse in part because the attitude toward verse pronunciation and performance that Thelwall espouses more closely approximates our own than does Wordsworth's.[16] If the eighteenth century insisted too heavily on metrical order at the expense of the rhythmic subtleties of natural speech pronunciation, the twentieth century has arguably lost a sense of the metrical as anything other than a recurrence of speech cadences.[17] In many twentieth-century linguistic accounts of prosody, tension between abstract metrical frame and actual speech rhythm is resolved, as it is for Thelwall, by subordination of the merely metrical to the phonetic. In Thelwall's terms, no influence on performance other than the "grammatical" may be admitted. For Wordsworth, however, meter (an abstract norm) and rhythm (the actual pattern of stress and unstress in a given performance) are distinct and may not be collapsed into a single entity. In his early work, Wordsworth did habitually elide extrametrical syllables; and throughout his corpus his continued adherence to a syllabic definition of the line makes the effect that Thelwall calls "appogiatura" considerably more complex than the mere grace note it has become for Thelwall. Moreover, when Wordsworth speaks of the "passion of meter" and of a felt "dislocation" of pattern in a particularly expressive line, he reveals that he does in fact, as a practical matter, conceive of the line as a locus or intersection of two different systems of organization. The passion of the sense produces dislocations that are felt in relation to—but that do not redefine the essential metrical pattern of—the line. Another way to put this is that the physical realization of speech in phonetic patterns of alternate stress, pitch, timbre, and duration is only part of what the line really is: in fact, the verse line is a complex combination of an unrealized and unrealizable repeating abstract pattern and a unique and widely variable phonetic instance.

For Wordsworth, then, each verse, even each syllable, represents at least potentially a marriage of widely variable phonetic occurrence and a fundamental and invariable pattern.[18] This tension is useful to

Wordsworth in two ways that may be singled out here as deserving of more attention than others: (1) for its potential expressive effects or uses, and (2) for its potential as an emblem or trope participating with other, more overtly significant, kinds of expressions of interest in the power of language and the power of sound.[19] Expressive effects—what Wordsworth calls tracing the "fluxes and refluxes" of the mind in the act of expressing itself—are registered as varying degrees of tension between phrase and line, between actual rhythm and abstract meter. Emblematic uses are made possible by the fact that Wordsworth's dual and dynamic conception of meter allows each line to be regarded potentially as a site either of cooperating or of competing power from within and without. Which words and which syllables manifest themselves in the poem at the beck and call of the passion of the sense? Which owe their incorporation to the passion of the meter? To what degree is the "selection" of language the poet's own selection and to what degree is it dictated to him through the ear? Is the language of any metered poem best regarded as an instance of an idealized reality (a fixed and immutable idea of order informing language selected from everyday speech) or of a realized ideal (enduring patterns and harmonies discovered in the very midst of the "language really used by men")?[20] Such questions are a part of the very texture of verse written according to the principles set forth in Wordsworth's discussions.

In the letter to Thelwall, Wordsworth quotes the following verse from "The Old Cumberland Beggar," calling it the "most dislocated line I know of in my writing" (*EY*, 434):

> Impressed on the white road;—in the same line.

To perceive this or any other verse as "dislocated," one must in some sense be able to perceive two entities simultaneously: a syllable cannot be dislocated unless the reader somehow is able to perceive the normal pattern of syllabic-stress "locations" despite the displacement. The issue of exactly how this perception occurs is complex and has been the source of a great deal of confusion in the history of prosody.[21] It may be worthwhile, then, to set forth here some basic points concerning my assumptions about these issues.

Derek Attridge's *Rhythms of English Poetry* provides a discussion of the sources of tension in traditional English verse in terms that are conveniently adaptable to Wordsworth's theory and practice. Attridge argues that good regular verse (traditional accentual-syllabic verse of the kind Wordsworth writes) is able to impress a reader as deeper, richer, and

more resonant than speech or prose because of its "deep roots in human physiology and psychology" (151). Verse arises from a "natural tension" between variety and regularity that is embodied in all language: "The voice, or rather the speech faculty of the human brain, enjoys its freedom to range over a finely graduated scale of intensities, timbres, pitches, and durations, but also feels the pull towards simple patterns and repetitions" (18). Meter formalizes this natural tension, taking advantage of and heightening its inherently pleasurable operation. At an even deeper level verse formalizes the basic physical rhythm of tension and release, exertion and relaxation, in the speech apparatus itself: "the action of the muscles controlling the lungs, and the relationship between this pulmonary activity and the movements of the speech organs higher up the vocal tract" all participate in sympathetic movement in accordance with the movements of verse (59). Regular verse, that is, brings into operation normal and habitual physical impulses common to all speech but also imposes upon those impulses a heightened sense of pattern. The sense of a regularized pattern is perceived by the reader as a "metrical set" (Attridge's term for what Wordsworth would call the "passion of meter" or the "regular laws of the iambic"), which may or may not be consonant with the actual speech impulses at any one point in a verse, but which coincides with those impulses frequently enough to be felt as a regulating presence. Verse is defined neither by its metrical scheme nor by its rhythmic impulses. It is a third thing: a pattern variously realized.

Attridge argues that the metrical set "confers on the language [of a metered poem] a degree of rhythmic (and semantic) complexity beyond the reach of the ordinary spoken language" (313). Pervasive tensions between speech act and metrical set in any given realization of the line create a sense of "optionality" or of the possibility of alternate realizations of that same line. "If you prefer to emphasize the regularity of the metre," says Attridge, "the resolute irregularity of the language will be felt pulling against you; if you let speech rhythms have their head, the periodicity of the beat will exercise a counter-claim: both readings, however, will register the inherent tension of the line" (313). "Inherent tension," skillfully controlled by the poet, can create a feeling that the line or passage cannot be fully realized in any one performance. The optionality of good regular verse is so deeply a part of verse rhythm itself that it "remains effective" whether an individual reading chooses to emphasize metrical regularity or irregular speech rhythms.

To return to Wordsworth's example of expressive dislocation, here is the verse from the "Old Cumberland Beggar," scanned as Attridge would scan it. Symbols above the line, [-s] and [+s], denote unstressed and

stressed syllables; symbols below the line denote the alternating pattern of five "offbeats" ([o] and variations) with five "beats" [B] that is the metrical set employed in Wordsworth's poem (see Note on Scansions and Prosodic Terminology):

    -s   +s   -s -s +s +s   -s -s +s +s
Impressed on the white road;—in the same line
  o   B   ŏ   B ô B   ŏ   B ô B

The scansion shows more graphically than would a foot-based description exactly why "dislocated" is an accurate description of what occurs in the relationship between the general rule and the realization. In a foot-based scansion, the line would be described as having two pyrrhics and two spondees "substituted" for iambs, as if each two-syllable unit were detachable and modifications within a "foot" did not affect the structure of other parts of the line. Attridge's system shows both the "general law of the Iambic" below the line (in the alternation of offbeats and beats) and the actual, variable realization of the pattern in strong and weak stresses. An "iambic pentameter" line with little tension or dislocation is one in which the offbeat-beat pattern is "realized" or fulfilled with regularly alternating [-s] and [+s] syllables. The coincidence of offbeat with [-s] and beat with [+s] in such a line is registered by the simplicity of the line beneath the example (which uses only the basic forms of the offbeat and beat symbols):

To Books, our daily fare prescrib'd, I turn'd
 o B   o   B o B   o   B   o B
                                              (*13-Bk Prelude* 3.524)

The variant forms of the offbeat symbols—[ŏ] and [ô]—needed to describe the example from "The Old Cumberland Beggar" indicate the exact points of tension between pattern and realization. The symbol [ŏ] indicates the realization of an offbeat (a position normally occupied by a single unstressed syllable) with two unstressed syllables; the symbol [ô] indicates an "implied offbeat," or a place in the verse where the expected alternation of beat and offbeat is disrupted, in compensation for the earlier double offbeat. The effect of dislocation in Wordsworth's line results from the perception that in two separate instances one of the pairs of stresses in the usual pattern -s +s -s +s has been forced out of its normal place, forming the pattern -s -s +s +s ("on the white road"; "in the same line"). Physically, the dislocation is registered by a more-

than-usual rapidity (as the two syllables realizing the offbeat are hurried through) followed by a compensatory slowing (naturally caused by two contiguous strong stresses). Wordsworth says that it is at these points of tension that the passion of the speaker will be felt: to one who is able to enter into the passion, the line will be metrically expressive; for a passive reader impervious to the passion, it will be merely awkward.

Such tensions, felt in minute physical impulses, between the expectation of regular alternation and the widely variable possibilities available for the realization of pattern, give metrical language what Attridge calls its "reputation for qualities of density, complexity, and subtlety." The presentation of the complex phonetic variety of speech in relation to a simple and fundamental pattern "enables us to hear not a speech, but speech": "Another way of putting this is that metre, by freeing the spoken language from its univocal straitjacket, invests it with the kind of openness and multiplicity that is normally the special prerogative of the written text" (314). In more Wordsworthian terms, strict metrical arrangement allows the poet to create physical embodiments of living thought and feeling that resist reduction to a fixed and univocal dead letter. The metrical law that is bent but not broken, the line that is adequately defined neither by its ideal form nor by its concrete realization, provide tensions through which the poet can seem to incorporate into the poem itself extralinguistic powers that run deeper than (or overflow) the fixed limits of the poem.

Metrical poetry in Wordsworth's view invites—even requires—rereading in part because it keeps the mind constantly and actively aware that any single reading is "a" reading. In its encouragement of dual perception of the same order of words, it encourages a kind of oscillation of mind which in turn helps create a feeling that the resources of the line or passage are never entirely exhausted by a single reading. By allowing the mind to hover between competing alternatives in the realization of a line or passage, regular meter allows the language of the poem to be perceived as alive with possibility and potentiality: the dead letter, well versified, is revived in each new performance of the verse. Emphasize the "prose pattern" (or what Thelwall calls the emphasis required by the "grammatical construction" alone) of any complex instance of the kind of verse that Wordsworth describes and the metrical set will intrude upon the reading; sing it in perfect accord with a fixed idea of order and its recalcitrancies as a language in everyday use will work against the regularizing impulses. Without a metrical context, one might read thus:

```
-s   +s    +s  +s    -s  -s  -s  +s
My heart leaps up when I behold
```

Once the line is recognized as conforming to a recognizable verse pattern, whether it is called a "four beat line in rising rhythm" or "iambic tetrameter," the possibility of the following singsong reading is registered at some level of the reader's consciousness:

```
-s  +s   -s  +s   -s +s -s +s
My heart leaps up when I behold
 o  B    o   B    o B  o  B
```

A good metrical reading will provide a "complex feeling of delight" through "an indistinct perception perpetually renewed of language closely resembling that of real life, and yet, in the circumstance of metre," and in this case end rhyme, "differing from it so widely" (*Prose* 1:151). One may read the line expressively thus:

```
-s  +s   +s  +s   -s  s -s +s
My heart leaps up when I behold
 o  B    ȯ   B    o B̄  o  B
```

But because of the metrical set, the excluded possibilities will still hover around the line. Placed significantly in an offbeat position, the syllable "leaps" dislocates the verse, and contributes obviously to its expressive force. In a poem about the speaker's paradoxical wish to have the continuity of his life founded on a sustained ability to make a break with the order of things, such invocation of a scheme through a "dislocation" of it may also be regarded as emblematic of the ways of "natural piety." In John Hollander's terms, what was merely a "scheme" or conventional pattern can become, at such points in the verse, a trope.

Wordsworth's verse, in these matters, as in so many others, is indebted primarily to the mainstream tradition of Chaucer, Spenser, Shakespeare, and Milton. That is, he describes and writes perfectly traditional accentual-syllabic English verse, not different in the essentials of its laws and practice from the verse of the poets in whose company he wished to be placed by posterity. Wordsworth's need to explain fine points of his understanding of the "passion of meter" to Thelwall suggests, however, that he was conscious that his refusal to subordinate metrical pattern entirely to natural rhythms (or vice versa) marked him as something of a traditionalist in the midst of prosodic upheaval. The evidence of Hazlitt's well-known description of Wordsworth's manner of "chaunt[ing]" his own poems suggests that he may even have cultivated in recitation a style that would mark his

versified speech as more rhythmically regular and more impressively sonorous than natural or dramatic speech. And we know that Hazlitt, for one, found the "equable, sustained, and internal chaunt" not at all to his taste.[22] Whatever Hazlitt's suspicions were about Wordsworth's chaunt—suspicions shared in a general way in Thelwall's dismissal of "verse mouth" and in much prosodic theory of the later eighteenth century and after—they do give evidence that Wordsworth in fact considered the "equable," "sustained," and obviously measured qualities of his verse to be as important to his overall purposes as was his idiosyncratic movement toward more natural diction and syntax. It would seem that Wordsworth's "chaunt" habitually functioned as a marker of the distinction between metrical language and speech by conveying through pronunciation and intonation a sense of the metrical equalities (or equivalencies, or measures) against which meaningful variation might be felt and gauged: patterned alternation of stresses; repetition of equivalent line lengths; or, where applicable, recurrence of rhyme, stanza length and structure, assonance, alliteration. To Hazlitt's ear, and perhaps also to Thelwall's, Wordsworth's stylized and enchanted speech seemed strange and incongruous. One contention of the arguments and readings that form subsequent chapters of this book is that appreciating the tensions arising from Wordsworth's metrical "chaunt" and how these tensions function both expressively and emblematically is an important part of the experience of reading Wordsworth's poems as poems.

"FITTING TO METRICAL ARRANGEMENT"

My discussion of metrical similitude in dissimilitude and of the statements in the letter to Thelwall may at first glance seem to contradict some of the better-known statements about the enervating influence of poetic artifice in Wordsworth's prose, letters, and conversations. In fact, it may be seen as entirely consonant with the whole body of Wordsworth's statements, which give evidence throughout of the poet's healthy refusal to be limited by the standard dichotomies that fracture much thinking and writing about meter: freedom *versus* restraint, expressive natural speech *versus* artificially patterned rhythms, subordination of meter to syntax *versus* subordination of syntax to meter. For Wordsworth, as for all poets who use the resources of the accentual-syllabic tradition to good effect, the whole point of verse composition is to bring opposing systems of organization into complex interplay with one another. And Wordsworth's statements about meter, considered as a whole, steadfastly insist on the potential for genuine

interplay, as they resist the temptation to regard one system as axiomatically subordinate to the other.

Take, for example, Wordsworth's discussion in the Preface to *Lyrical Ballads* of the experimental nature of the collection. The poems are presented in the hope that they may be "of some use" in discovering whether, and to what degree, the combination of common language with metrical form may produce pleasurable poems:

> It [the first volume of *Lyrical Ballads*] was published, as an experiment, which, I hoped, might be of some use to ascertain, how far, by fitting to metrical arrangement a selection of the real language of men in a state of vivid sensation, that sort of pleasure and that quantity of pleasure may be imparted, which a Poet may rationally endeavour to impart. (*Prose* 1:119)

Wordsworth's emphasis on the "real language of men" has received a great deal of critical attention. The rules of the "arrangement" to which this diction is fitted, the implications of the metaphor implied in the word "fitting," and its relationship to the "endeavour to impart" pleasure have been less frequently explored. Taken together, and in the context of late-eighteenth-century metrical theory and practice, these elements make the passage much more complex and consciously challenging than may appear at first sight.

Insofar as Wordsworth's statement calls for the use of the real language of men, it represents a break with the attitudes of a majority of eighteenth-century writers of, and about, metrical language. Writers of the generation to which Wordsworth responds in theory and practice tended to hold that metrical arrangement legitimately dictates the kind of language that may be used, as well as its syntactical structures. Much influential eighteenth-century metrical theory rested on the assumption that a chief and desirable function of meter was its tendency to improve and chasten the language itself through the example of an elevated, more highly wrought, idiom. The superimposition of rational patterns of arrangement on the unruly phonetic material of the language tended to be regarded as a means for distinguishing the language so produced from the "real language of men." Meter chastened language, excluding inharmonious words and phrases, encouraging "poetic" variants of commonly used words ("e'en," and "ere," for example), and enforcing an elaborate system of elision and contraction of supernumerary syllables (the system that Thelwall brands as "barbarous" in his *Selections*). Indeed, as Paul Fussell has argued, it appears that eighteenth-century readers

derived a good deal of pleasure simply from the fact that metered language was presented as something other than individuated and idiosyncratic "real language."[23]

Late-seventeenth- and eighteenth-century commentaries are full of dicta justifying on aesthetic principles the kind of artifice that Thelwall derides as "helping out the verse." Scores of writers make the analogy between verse and the dance, arguing that versified language ought to sound "as much different from the language of ordinary discourse . . . as the movements of dance are from common walking."[24] Although later writers, including Thelwall, deny that Milton used poetic contractions and elisions, Addison praises what he takes to be Milton's particularly elaborate use of these techniques as an effective "Method of raising his Language, as far as the nature of our Tongue will permit" above the level both of common speech and unmetered prose.[25] Other writers emphasize the power of strict rules of versification to place welcome shackles on poetic "enthusiasm." In Dryden's well-known words, the "rule and line" imposed by rhyme and meter on "lawless imagination" ensure that the language of poetry will be tempered by the "second thoughts" of judgment.[26] Edward Manwaring goes so far as to equate poetical numbers with geometric form: "The best interpreters of poetical Numbers are those who apply the rules of Music and Geometry to poetry."[27] Poetic diction is ideal speech, bearing approximately the same relationship to real language as a circle does to a naturally round shape. It is language purged of the merely individualized or accidental, right down to the minutiae of its rhythms.

In contrast to these views, Wordsworth's emphasis on real language generated spontaneously under the influence of strong emotion implies a tendency to liberate the selection of diction, the particularities of syntax, and perhaps even the minutiae of pronunciation from the demands and strictures of metrical arrangement. Indeed, part of the burden of the definition of the poet as "a man speaking to men" is that he is not, primarily, "man making verses." And Wordsworth's historical survey of the corruption of modern poetry included in the 1802 appendix to the Preface focuses on meter as a chief cause of or "passport" to the inanities and gaudiness of modern poetic diction. Insofar as meter tends to lead the poet to choose and arrange his words in accordance with conventionally pleasing patterns of sound, whether or not these patterns are appropriate expressions of the passions that the poem seeks to express, it can be a deleterious influence, as Wordsworth seeks to show through his analyses of syntactic distortion and mellifluous yet empty phrases and epithets in Cowper's "Verses Supposed to be Written by Alexander

Selkirk." The problem, in brief, is that meter can, and frequently does, draw the poet's and reader's attention away from the chief focus of the poem—the modifying effects of passion on perceptions—and toward the poet in his capacity as merely a manufacturer of verse.[28] Such verse will be displeasing to the well-disposed reader because it expresses something other than what it pretends on the surface to express; that is, instead of (or along with) the effects of joy or grief or longing, the poem expresses the poet's pride as a manipulator of language. Wordsworth describes the resultant pleasure of reading such verse as a kind of flattery: extravagant verse impresses "a notion of the peculiarity and exaltation of the Poet's character" and flatters the "Reader's self-love by bringing him nearer to a sympathy with that character" (*Prose* 1:162). The reader's pleasure is a debased pleasure stemming from a sense of participation in a game or exclusionary trick.[29] Such pleasure, needless to say, is the very antithesis of the kind of deep and permanent pleasure, open to human beings as human beings (and not as "poets" or "gentlemen" or the like), that Wordsworth aims to communicate.

These tendencies in Wordsworth's comments would seem to place them in the tradition of writing about meter that culminates in nineteenth- and twentieth-century organic theory and practice, which is characterized by the view that metrical form is properly considered as much an outgrowth of the passion as are the diction and syntax. Meter is subordinate to expression and functions only to misrepresent that expression when its power as a regularizing element or fixed precondition of composition is in evidence. Such well-known statements as Coleridge's "no work of art dare want its appropriate form" or Emerson's call for "Not meters, but a meter-making argument" suggest a way of looking at poetic form directly opposed to the more abstract, numerical, and rationalizing tendencies of earlier theorists.[30] Whereas eighteenth-century theorists tend to gravitate toward analogies between poetic organization and dancing, civilized restraint, and geometric form, romantic and postromantic writers on versification prefer images of growth and elaboration, in which outer shape expresses inner vitality.[31]

Many of Wordsworth's statements about poetic craft suggest that he did think of the relation between expression and metrical form in terms of an organic model. For example, in the Preface to *Poems* (1815), he argues that "the law of long syllable and short must not be so inflexible,—the letter of metre must not be so impassive to the spirit of versification,—as to deprive the Reader of all voluntary power to modulate, in subordination to the sense, the music of the poem" (*Prose* 3:29–30). In 1814, he reportedly took Dryden to task for having commented that the poet is

at times indebted to rhyme for his thoughts, and suggested that such opinions were directly at odds with Dryden's own achievement.[32] And, in a late sonnet that has been taken by commentators as a *locus classicus* of organic theory (*"A Poet!*—He hath put his heart to school"), he uses the figures of the "bloom of the Meadow-flower" and the grandeur of the "Forest-tree" as analogues for a kind of creativity that "comes not by casting in a formal mould, / But of its *own* divine vitality" (*PW* 3:52).[33]

As important as it is not to underestimate what might be called the organic, naturalistic, or expressive tendencies of Wordsworth's views concerning the relation between diction and meter, expression and form, however, it must also be acknowledged that the phrase "by fitting to metrical arrangement" implies at least as strong a tendency toward the older view of the processes by which verses are constructed, a process that involves—in Fussell's words describing standard eighteenth-century practice—"fitting existing materials into a preconceived plan" (48). If part of the notion of a "preconceived plan" is the metrical form of a poem, it must be admitted that Wordsworth's idea of fitting presumes a significant amount of preconception. Meter, in this view, cannot properly be spoken of as a wholly organic outgrowth of the process of creation, or as wholly an element of individual expression. It does not stem from the expressive use of diction alone and cannot be entirely subordinated to the demands of particular syntactical instances. Meter remains a constant, a set of flexible yet demanding rules, imposing uniform limitations on the particular poet's or speaker's individuated expression.[34]

This ambivalence about the power of meter appears throughout Wordsworth's comments on the subject. Even in the statement about the primacy of the "spirit of the versification" over the "letter of the meter," the subtle use of "so" in the phrase "the letter of the meter must not be so impassive to the spirit of versification" keeps the two elements in complex opposition. And for every statement stressing inner vitality over external form, one can find a corresponding recognition of the good poet's respect for and obligation to the recalcitrance of metrical, stanzaic, or repeating sonic structures. Dryden's reliance on rhyme for "second thoughts" draws Wordsworth's disapproval, yet elsewhere he makes a point very similar to Dryden's in comparing English and Italian as poetic languages. The relative difficulty of rhyming in English, says Wordsworth, imposes a salutary degree of difficulty on the English poet. Thomas Moore paraphrases Wordsworth's conversation thus: "In struggling with words one [is] led to give birth to and dwell upon thoughts, while, on the contrary, an easy and mellifluous language [is] apt to tempt, by its facility, into negligence, and to lead the poet to substitute music for

thought."³⁵ A similar attitude concerning the poet's reliance on the recalcitrance of language also informs the arguments in the Preface to *Lyrical Ballads,* as when Wordsworth argues that an important source of the pleasure arising from writing and reading metrical verse is the "sense of difficulty overcome" (*Prose* 1:151).

Such passages may be found throughout Wordsworth's prose and letters. In a letter to William Rowan Hamilton, Wordsworth counsels Hamilton not to be misled by Milton's claim to be "pouring easy his unpremeditated verse" but to keep clearly in mind that "the composition of verse is infinitely more of an art than Men are prepared to believe, and absolute success in it depends upon innumerable minutiae" (*LY* 2:454).³⁶ In the same passage he praises the versification of *Paradise Lost* as containing "more proofs of skill acquired by practice" than any other poem he can name. Even "A Poet—he hath put his heart to school," which expresses contempt for the poet who casts his expression in a "formal mould," confronts the reader with the obvious fact of its own formal mould. It is a perfectly regular Petrarchan sonnet, structurally as predictable as can be. Its octave indicts the poet who "feels by rule," and its sestet provides the speaker's alternative to such feeling. The conventional rhetorical turn occurs, as expected, at line 9. And the rhyme scheme is one of the strictest possible, as well as among the strictest of the various rhyme schemes that Wordsworth employs in all of his five-hundred-plus published sonnets: abbabaab cdcdcd. Either Wordsworth was deaf to such irony, or issues concerning the relationship between inner vitality and externally imposed form in Wordsworth's art are considerably more complex than they have commonly been taken to be.

Wordsworth's phrasings in the Thelwall letter, his use of the metaphor of "fitting" in the Preface to *Lyrical Ballads,* and his lifelong and corpus-wide employment of fixed, conventional metrical forms all suggest that his attitudes concerning the issue of metrical form and poetic expression are too complex to be described as they normally are in terms of a simple dichotomy between organic and mechanic, expressive and rhetorical, liberal and conservative, or neoclassical and romantic theories and practices. Wordsworth places maximum emphasis on the importance of both artful arrangement and spontaneous expression. These elements, it will be argued, represent for Wordsworth, and are meant to represent for his reader, complementary powers in dynamic and rhythmic relationship, contributing finally to what in the Preface he repeatedly calls the "complex end" of a poem. The poet fits language to meter—an idealized and abstracted conception of the line—but the

language he fits is a selection of the "real." Wordsworth recognizes and values the power of meter to regularize, elevate, or otherwise distance the language of a poem from the language of everyday life, while at the same time he refuses to adopt an already codified and distanced language, because such language would be insufficiently powerful to mingle with and move what he calls the "blood & vital juices of our minds" ("Essay on Morals," *Prose* 1:103).

Most important, the use in the Preface of the participle "fitting" and the strict limitation of the goals of the poetic experiment implied in the phrase "how far" also imply that Wordsworth saw a poem as a meeting ground for such opposition. The phrasing suggests that a chief interest of the poems so described ought to be the continuous process of fitting, not so much the accomplishment of a single and determining fit. Wordsworth does not say that the poet fits real language to metrical composition in order to produce a poem of seamless texture that contains no traces of the process through which it was made. He says that he is concerned with the question of "how far" a poem, which is an attempt or experiment in the process of fitting the genuine language of passion to the purposes and ends of art, may provide a lasting kind of pleasurable excitement.[37]

"Many are the poets that are sown / By Nature": the powers requisite to the production of poetry—observation and description, sensibility, reflection, imagination and fancy, invention, and judgment—are according to Wordsworth freely and abundantly given to mankind. But only those few with "sensibility to harmony of numbers, and the power of producing it," write powerful poems.[38] These few have the "accomplishment of verse."

"KNOWN HABITS OF ASSOCIATION"

Thus far, I have been intent on tracing Wordsworth's concern with the ways in which good poetry establishes an original and active relationship between the poet's diction and meter, between speech rhythms and metrical frames. Wordsworth's concern in this regard is implicit in many of the larger, not specifically metrical, issues taken up in the Preface and elsewhere—for example, in his frequent mention of his aims in drawing subjects from common experience, from "nothing more than what we are." The poet's use of subjects from shared experience invites the reader to experience a pleasing sense of the similarities and differences between the actual experience and its poetic representation. Under the influence

of this pleasure, the mind gains perspective on its own processes and may be led to a fuller understanding of its "primary laws" (*Prose* 1:123). Similarly, the language of common life, when fitted to metrical frames, produces a creative sense of strangeness. The perceived difference between that metered, numbered language and the actual material from which it is drawn, is for Wordsworth a supremely important source of the power of poetry. In good poems it may tease us out of ourselves, resituating the mind and giving a new insight into the manifold ways in which linguistic habits shape thought and perception.

Such salutary, active, and original interaction between diction and meter is, of course, not achieved without struggle. And although Wordsworth shows confidence in his own ability to use meter creatively, and in his reader's ability to respond properly to that use, he is also constantly aware, in theory and practice, of the potentially deleterious effects of what he calls the "blind association of pleasure which has been previously received from works of rhyme or metre of the same or similar construction." Wordsworth, it must be remembered, was writing for readers whose experience of contemporary metrical writing had, in his view, very likely constricted their ability to respond fully to new and original combinations of diction and meter. Thus, the conditioning, even enchanting power of meter to "pave the way" for all sorts of excrescences had to be explained fully.

The key passage in which Wordsworth discusses this "symbolic" or "exponential" function of meter shows clearly his concern with, and respect for, both the passion of meter and the burden of the poetic past:

> It is supposed, that by the act of writing in verse an Author makes a formal engagement that he will gratify certain known habits of association; that he not only thus apprises the Reader that certain classes of ideas and expressions will be found in his book, but that others will be carefully excluded. This exponent or symbol held forth by metrical language must in different eras of literature have excited very different expectations. (*Prose* 1:123)

Just as meter exerts a basic, physical influence based on the fundamental interplay of tension and release, variety and uniformity, freedom and restraint, so it exercises a power to associate one poem or type of poem with another. Wordsworth assumes that most readers of his poems come to them with experience of the rhythms, expressions, structures, and ideas of other poems in their minds, and that the metrical arrangement of language signals to them to expect combinations of metrical form and

"classes of ideas and expressions" consonant with those with which they are familiar and comfortable.

This aspect of the statement has been noted as demonstrating Wordsworth's "modern" conception of literary convention and as a significant refutation of "most linguistic models of the production or the reading of English verse" insofar as these models assume a "maker or reader" with "no memory and no range of reading," operating in "a world of poetic language sacred to motherless Muses."[39] Wordsworth here shows his awareness that poems are neither written nor read in a vacuum and that a chief source of the power of a poem comes through the tendency of meter to encourage comparison between a new composition and poems that already exist. Wordsworth is careful to distinguish, here and throughout the Preface, between those aspects of poetic art that are permanent and those that are not, between the fundamental laws that govern poetic pleasure and the arbitrary association of pleasure and its objects that is the product of fashion. That meter leads a reader to expect to have "known habits of association" gratified is a permanent part of the poet's art and of the reader's experience of the poem. It is as much a law as the physical law that prohibits meter to be read as prose or as a transcription of speech. If, however, this symbolic or exponential power "must in different eras of literature have excited very different expectations," then the particular "habits of association" that any given reader in any era of literary history desires to have "gratified" are to a large extent the arbitrary and transitory products of fashion, stemming from the mind's tendency to allow itself to be dictated to, to be lulled into rest by the comfortable and familiar.

When Wordsworth says that he knows that it "will undoubtedly appear to many persons that I have not fulfilled an engagement thus voluntarily contracted" (*Prose* 1:123), he is not claiming, as it has frequently been assumed, that the poet somehow may extricate himself from the expectations that meter encourages. Wordsworth never claims that his own poems will be—or ought to be—exceptions to the rule.[40] Nor does he suggest that his poetry will please his (small) audience despite his use of meter. On the contrary, he argues that all poetry that continues to please beyond the limits imposed by the fashions of its own era does so in part because the poet uses the power of meter to associate old with new, the familiar with the strange, thereby setting up creative tension between what is expected and what is provided. Poetic pleasure comes not through the poet's fulfillment of a preordained conception of any one kind of relationship between meter and language but through artful confrontation and reformation of deeply ingrained habits of association,

including those habits that inform the reader's experience at the most minute levels of the physical impulses of the verse.

Wordsworth's theory implies that good poetry will always exercise a power to reform taste through active engagement of habits of association. The aim of the music of his verse, then, no less than of his larger poetic program, is to "rectify . . . feelings," to give "new compositions of feeling" and to "render . . . feelings more sane, pure and permanent" (*EY*, 355). His belief in the necessity of confrontation between poet and reader is a chief reason why he anticipates a difficult relationship between his poems and his contemporary audience. Many of his readers, he knows, will "frequently have to struggle with feelings of strangeness and awkwardness [in the *Lyrical Ballads*]": "They will look round for poetry, and will be induced to inquire by what species of courtesy these attempts can be permitted to assume that title" (*Prose* 1:123). It is a fact of human nature that "we not only wish to be pleased, but to be pleased in that particular way in which we have been accustomed to be pleased" (1:157). Wordsworth consciously writes a type of poetry that furnishes the reader with challenges to this inclination: he offers "new friends," but "only on condition of his [reader's] abandoning old friends" (1:157).

Wordsworth nevertheless shows his respect for the tendency of his readers to cling to "old friends," calling the source of this tendency an "honourable bigotry." He sees no reason why poems, good or bad, from which a reader has received great pleasure ought not to be cherished. In fact, as *The Prelude* acknowledges, the tendency of immature readers to be carried away by the attractions of overwrought and "glittering verse" is to be recognized not as a fault but as a manifestation of noble aspiration, a "wish for something loftier, more adorned, / Than is the common aspect, daily garb / Of human life" (*14-Bk Prelude* 5.593, 577–79). Such "bigotry" is probably an important element in the tension requisite to the "complex feeling of delight" that is Wordsworth's aim. The important thing is that the reader resist the temptation to translate an "honourable" love of "old friends" into a set of rigid formulae that circumscribe his ability to respond to other, differently conceived, poems. To do so would reduce reading, which is properly regarded as an active undertaking involving "the exertion of a co-operating *power* in the mind of the Reader" ("Essay, Supplementary to the Preface" [1815]; *Prose* 3:81), to an entirely passive and mechanical undertaking through which no sympathy could be generated for anything or anyone outside of the reader's circle of "old friends."[41] In the Preface to *Poems* (1815), Wordsworth argues that some form of this bigotry exists in the readers of every age, and is a chief reason why original poets must create the taste by which they are

appreciated. Composition in meter will always imply, through association with other, more familiar poems, a relationship between a new poem and old poems; original creation will always fail in some degree to conform to the expectations produced through familiarity with old poems. The poet's road takes him not around but through the "honourable bigotry" bred by familiarity.

2
Metrical Tension and Varieties of Voice

WORDSWORTH'S METERS AND COLERIDGE ON METER

Wordsworth's emphasis on the "pleasure arising from the perception of similitude in dissimilitude, and dissimilitude in similitude," leaves ample room for—and even requires—a metrical practice exhibiting a wide variety of relationships among diction, syntax, and metrical form and verse pattern. Wordsworth was as much interested in the poem as a locus of active tensions between competing powers as he was in it as a *locus amoenus* characterized by achieved balance and harmonious unity of complementary elements. Wordsworth's poem is a Garden of Adonis, not a Bowre of Bliss.

The poet's meter and his selection of diction are distinct elements, yet are capable of being "exquisitely fitted" to one another. Meter functions as an external source both of fixed laws grounded in physicality and of passions produced by recollection of previously encountered works of art. It serves both as a force that, by resisting individual freedom and variation, makes such freedom and variation possible and as a standard against which the variation so produced may be recognized as significant. According to Wordsworth's theory, metrical form may be subordinated to the "passion of the sense," functioning primarily as an expressive reinforcement of the speaker's passions and habits of association. But it need not be. In fact, Wordsworth's discussion and practice suggest that he regarded such fitting as the exception to the rule—useful in the delineation of a particular frame of mind but not the exclusive aim of the poet's art at all times. More often than not meter participates in the creation of a complex sense of the poem as an "intertexture" of potentially opposing elements. The passion of meter can and does provide a type of "interference" that heightens and improves the "co-exist[ing]" pleasure produced by the passion (*Prose* 1:145). In Wordsworth's view, therefore, writing in meter does not require any one kind of diction, nor does it impose rigid requirements on syntactic elements. All that is

required is an original and dynamic relationship between the two patterns of organization sufficient to encourage and sustain active and pleasurable reading.

Given these attitudes, it is no wonder that Coleridge found the discussion of meter in the Preface unsatisfactory. Wordsworth's ideas concerning metricality and "similitude in dissimilitude," despite superficial similarities with Coleridge's ideas about the "reconciliation of discordant elements," are seriously at odds with Coleridge's own specifically organic theories, all of which flow from his view of the harmonious poem as a self-contained "unity" in which "*all* of the parts . . . must be assimilated to the more *important* and *essential* parts" (*BL* 2:72).[1] For Coleridge, the passion of the meter originates in "the balance in the mind effected by that spontaneous effort which strives to hold in check the workings of passion." It therefore follows that "the elements of metre owe their existence to a state of increased excitement," and that the language accompanying meter's signal of this "state" ought also to be the language of "excitement" (2:64). Whereas Wordsworth's theory emphasizes the "intertexture" of often-conflicting elements arising from different sources, Coleridge holds that there ought to be a complementary balance and correspondence between the excitement produced by the meter of a poem and that produced by the diction.[2]

Coleridge's conception of the poem as a unity and balance of formal elements stems from and is of a piece with his definition of the poet as one in whom excitement produces an extraordinary degree of imaginative, specifically synthetic, activity:

> The poet, described in *ideal* perfection, brings the whole soul of man into activity, with the subordination of its faculties to each other, according to their relative worth and dignity. He diffuses a tone, and a spirit of unity, that blends, and (as it were) *fuses,* each into each, by that synthetic and magical power, to which we have exclusively appropriated the name of imagination. This power . . . reveals itself in the balance or reconciliation of opposite or discordant qualities. (2:15–16)

It is precisely this extraordinary power to subordinate parts to wholes that is lacking in the speech of any speaker other than the "Poet" (and particularly so in the speech of the common man, who is the source of Wordsworth's "real language"): "There is a want of that prospectiveness of mind, that surview, which enables a man to foresee the whole of what he is to convey, appertaining to any one point; and by this means to

subordinate and arrange the different parts according to their relative importance, as to convey it at once, and as an organized whole" (2:58). It follows that a good poem, which Coleridge defines as "that species of composition, which . . . is discriminated by proposing to itself such delight from the *whole,* as is compatible with a distinct gratification from each component *part*" (2:13), cannot be the result of the kind of genuine and frequently unresolvable tension between diction and meter that Wordsworth conceives to be a chief effect of arranging "real" language in meter. Such a theory, argues Coleridge, could not have been behind the composition of those of Wordsworth's poems that are singled out for praise in *Biographia Literaria* as supreme examples of the operation of that "synthetic and magical power, . . . imagination"; rather, the theory has led Wordsworth into the composition of such "failures" as "Alice Fell," "Anecdote for Fathers," and "The Sailor's Mother," in which the presence of meter only heightens the unredeemably prosaic character of the poems.

As I sought to show in the preceding chapter, everything about Wordsworth's own theory and practice suggests that he never regarded this Coleridgean drive toward synthesis and unity of diction and meter as the exclusive aim of his verse. Indeed, Wordsworth does not merely acknowledge what Coleridge calls "inconstancy" of style; he embraces it as an integral part of what he takes to be the poet's chief task. That task is the imitation—for the purposes of providing a kind of pleasure that may induce sympathy and aid understanding—of the fullest possible range of the manifold operations of the mind under the influences of various passions. What Wordsworth calls tracing the "fluxes and refluxes" of the vastly complex human mind does not merely admit of a wide range of accommodations between diction and meter; it demands it.[3]

Wordsworth certainly regards the preeminently imaginative mind in its highest pitch of excitement (the Coleridgean ideal poet) as an important—perhaps even the most important—subject for his poetry. And in poems or parts of poems that aim at the "surview" of which such minds under such conditions are capable, the appropriate interrelation between diction and metrical form will be a blending or fusion of discordant elements. The harmonious unity of metrical form, elaborate syntax, and sonorous diction will suggest in such cases that there is indeed something natural and inevitable about the conformity of the language to the overarching structures of an organizing and unifying intelligence. At the same time, Wordsworth's theory—and Wordsworth's poetry—is everywhere attuned to the fact that most human minds at most times (and all minds at some times) lack for one reason or another this imaginative and

preeminently poetic surview. Wordsworth's verse contracts (or expands, depending upon one's perspective) to encompass the distempered mind of the Mad Mother as well as the "mind of Man" celebrated in the peroration of *The Prelude* as "a thousand times more beautiful than the earth / On which he dwells" (*14-Bk Prelude* 14.450–52). The bewildered cries of the speaker of "The Last of the Flock," the bemused and wandering narrator of "The Idiot Boy," the playful singer of "Written in March" ("The Cock is Crowing"), and the sententious rhetorician of "Humanity" are as "Wordsworthian" as the supremely synthesizing voice of "Tintern Abbey."[4] The "Poems of the Imagination," after all, form only one of eighteen categories into which Wordsworth would eventually divide his poetical works beginning in 1815. There is place in Wordsworth's corpus for Poems of the Fancy, Poems of the Affections, Poems Referring to the Period of Old Age, and so on. Wordsworth's discussion of meter, with its emphasis on meter as a "superadded" element or as a "co-presence," theoretically allows him an unlimited range of possibility in the fitting of diction to meter for the purpose of exploring a broad range of the infinitely complex processes through which mind and language "act and react" on each other.

Coleridge's analysis in *Biographia Literaria*, then, may be regarded as the fullest, most philosophical description of a typically Wordsworthian relationship between diction and meter, a relationship that is, however, only one of many that Wordsworth allows in theory and explores in practice. Whereas Coleridge characteristically works from a theory based on the unifying powers of metrical arrangement, Wordsworth's theory tends to emphasize difference and variety. It leaves open the possibility of an entire range of stylistic accommodations appropriate to the poetic delineation of "what we are." The difference of opinion on this matter may be seen as finally of a piece with so many of the crucial differences between the two men on aesthetic and philosophical issues. The distinction made long ago by John Jones is still useful: for all that the two poets shared, says Jones, "the theme of the one [Coleridge] was unity and of the other [Wordsworth] significant relation." Coleridge's poet fuses, blends, and reconciles; Wordsworth's engages in a dynamic process of fitting that only sometimes results in such significant reconciliation. Coleridge's poem or poetic corpus is or strives to be a unified organism in which each is subordinated to all; Wordsworth's is a "frame of things" in which what is individual, idiosyncratic, disorderly, or recalcitrant is placed in significant relation to the whole.[5] Just as Wordsworth's thematic emphasis on the processes of "fitting" mind to nature (and nature to mind) tends to emphasize the absolute importance both of the individual

mind and of what resists and remains unencompassed by the individual mind, so his "fitting" of language to meter brings to the foreground intricacies in the relationship between individual motives of speech and preordained structures of relationship that are not able to be subordinated entirely to merely personal expression. Finally, whereas Coleridge's specifically organic-aesthetic views tend to encourage a response to the poem as a self-contained object, expressive of a unity of complementary forces that inhere in the structures of the poem itself, Wordsworth's different views tend to stress the power of the poem as a vehicle for communication between poet and reader, the end of which is the creation of an open-ended and dynamic relationship.

METRICAL FORM AND RELATIONSHIP: THE EXAMPLE OF "THE SAILOR'S MOTHER"

It may be worthwhile at this point to discuss some of the chief points of difference between Wordsworth's and Coleridge's views on these matters with reference to a particular poem. Because Coleridge singles out "The Sailor's Mother" as an especially good example of the deleterious influence of Wordsworth's theories, that poem will serve as a convenient focus of attention.

For Coleridge, "The Sailor's Mother" is one of a number of works in Wordsworth's corpus that employ diction and syntax so prosaic that they "would have been more delightful . . . in prose" (*BL* 2:69). Indeed, the poem represents, according to Coleridge, "the only fair instance . . . in all Mr. Wordsworth's writings of an *actual* adoption, or true imitation of the *real* and *very* language of *low* and *rustic life*" (2:71). Coleridge hopes to show that the combination of such diction and metrical arrangement must result in failure and bases his explanation on his own view of what Wordsworth calls the "symbolic" or "exponential" power of meter. Coleridge's sense of this power is purposely more restricted than is Wordsworth's:

> Metre in itself is simply a stimulant of the attention, and therefore excites the question: Why is the attention thus stimulated? Now the question cannot be answered by the pleasure of the metre itself: for this we have shown to be *conditional* and dependent on the appropriateness of the thoughts and expressions, to which the metrical form is superadded. Neither can I conceive any other

answer that can be rationally given, short of this: I write in metre, because I am about to use a language different from that of prose. (*BL* 2:69)

As has been suggested, Wordsworth would agree entirely with Coleridge that meter acts as a "stimulant of the attention." He would not grant, however, that the poet must necessarily fulfill the promise to "use a language different from that of prose." For Wordsworth, whether or not and to what extent the language of a poem will differ from the language of prose will be dictated by passion or excitement itself, not by the use and habit that meter always to some degree stimulates. Coleridge's limitation of the proper relationship between meter and diction exclusively to a symbiotic union of complementary powers drawn from the same source (the state of excitement) implicitly dismisses as irrational Wordsworth's view of meter. For Wordsworth, the permanent possibility that meter will provide opposition to the passion of the sense is the crucial element of the contribution that meter makes to the "complex end" of a poem. That opposition may manifest itself through the simple recalcitrance of the "passion of meter," through the invitation that metrical forms extend to the reader to engage in comparison and contrast between the poem under consideration and other poems, or through the tendency of meter to "divest language, in a certain degree, of its reality." In fact, it is the ability of meter to provide contrast to diction, both when the diction abounds in passion and when it (significantly) lacks it, that makes it the only artificially contrived element necessary to produce poetic pleasure. In Wordsworth's theory, the power of meter alone frees the poet from the need to employ gaudy figures and language, gross and violent imagery or situations, or any other "colours of style" (*Prose* 1:145) in effecting poetic pleasure. It is only those readers who "greatly underrate the power of metre in itself" who require, in order to be pleased, that the poet employ "the other artificial distinctions of style with which meter is usually accompanied" (1:145).

"The Sailor's Mother" confronts the reader from the outset with a markedly incongruous relationship between humble subject and elaborate stanza form. The poem describes a speaker's account of his chance meeting with a woman who tells him a simple tale in simple words. Yet in its structure and movement and its literary associations, the stanza with which Wordsworth chose to frame this tale has nothing to do with that speech of "low and rustic life" that Coleridge says is truly imitated in the poem:

> And, thus continuing, she said,
> I had a Son, who many a day
> Sail'd on the seas; but he is dead;
> In Denmark he was cast away;
> And I have been as far as Hull, to see
> What clothes he might have left, or other property.[6]

The length of the stanza itself, and especially the concluding pentameter and hexameter couplet (which suggests Spenser's influence), provides it with a formal integrity unusual in the stanzas of short narrative poems on subjects from common life—particularly when the narrative is as stark as Wordsworth's is. The couplet functions as a rhythmic summation or turn, slowing the pace established by the tetrameter of lines 1 to 4 and providing in purely rhythmic terms an exaggerated sense of closure.

In fact, the structure employed in the concluding lines of these stanzas is more likely to have been associated with odes than with narrative verse in the later eighteenth century. Prior's ten-line adaptation of the Spenserian stanza in his influential "Ode, Humbly Inscribed to the Queen" (1706) helped to establish and perpetuate the use of a hexameter close in odic stanzas.[7] This use persisted at least as late as Coleridge's "Ode to the Departing Year" (1796) and "Dejection: An Ode" (1804) and Wordsworth's "Ode: Intimations of Immortality" (the first four stanzas of which were composed in March 1802, the same month and year in which "The Sailor's Mother" was composed). Gray used a hexameter close in a largely tetrameter stanza in his "Ode to Adversity" (1748), from which Wordsworth borrowed the stanza of his "Ode to Duty."[8] And a stanza identical to the one used in "The Sailor's Mother" is employed by Cowper in his translation of Antonio Francini's "Ode: Addressed to . . . John Milton" (c. 1792; published 1808). Coleridge uses the form twice in works which, though not strictly odic, are generically and stylistically more elevated than Wordsworth's homely tale: the juvenile poem "Nil Pejus est Caelibe Vita" (1787; published 1893) and the meditative "A Day Dream" ("My eyes make pictures" [1802?; published 1828]), the latter of which refers to itself as a "tender lay" (l. 33).[9]

Wordsworth's use of a much more rhythmically elaborate, insistently lyrical metrical frame than might be thought appropriate for a homely tale told in simple words would seem to be an extreme example of that "intertexture" of opposing feeling that he values as a source of poetic pleasure. The significance of this opposition becomes more apparent as one recognizes that the poem as a whole is structured according to an internal stylistic opposition: stanzas 1, 2, and most of 3 are devoted to a

narrator-speaker's account of the meeting; stanzas 4, 5, and 6 consist almost entirely of the quoted speech of the sailor's mother. Everything about the mere mechanism of the poem tends toward a presentation of obvious contrasts.[10]

The speaker whose voice begins "The Sailor's Mother" is represented by Wordsworth through a style in which speech motives and metrical imperatives are virtually free from tension:

> One morning (raw it was and wet,
> A foggy day in winter time)
> A Woman in the road I met,
> Not old, though something past her prime:
> Majestic in her person, tall and straight;
> And like a Roman matron's was her mien and gait.

The only rhythmic complexity is the very mild sense of promotion of the word "in" in line 3:

> A Woman in the road I met
> o B o B̄ o B o B

The end-stopped lines, punctuated by full-stressed and perfect rhymes, tend to correspond to self-contained syntactical structures. Each line thus maintains its integrity while contributing to the whole. The full stop at the end of the fourth line effectively divides the quatrain from the couplet, allowing the final lines to perform their expected function as a summation or turn to the stanza and producing a satisfying sense of closure. The repetition of *w* sounds throughout the first three lines, the *m* and *n* sounds in the concluding couplet, and the slow pace of the hexameter describing the woman's stately "mien and gait," all produce a conventionally harmonious sense of pattern. Together they form a fairly elaborate texture of rhythm and sound that acts to reinforce the elements of formal composition and patterning in the description of the woman. Such details as his immediate placing of the woman within the frame of her expected span of life ("something past her prime") or his likening of her posture and "gait" to a figure representative of a kind or class of woman known to him through art and literature ("like a Roman matron's") show the speaker to be predisposed toward the kind of "surview" that Coleridge identifies as the preeminently poetic movement of mind. And the particularities and structures of his language may be seen as an expression or objectification of his habitual tendency to place

particular phenomena (from syllables and phrases to events and strangers met on the road) in relation to structures and patterns within which they are accorded significance beyond the particular.

In stanza 2, Wordsworth provides a different kind of evidence that this speaker's perceptions are informed by more-than-usual powers of thought and feeling, as the plain "woman" becomes, through the effect on him of her "majestic" bearing, a proof of the survival of an "ancient Spirit":

> The ancient Spirit is not dead;
> Old times, thought I, are breathing there;
> Proud was I that my country bred
> Such strength, a dignity so fair
>
> (ll. 7–10)

The metrical style swells with the speaker's pride. Line 9 introduces the first real rhythmic complexity in the poem, in the ambiguous placement of "I" in the third position. The initial beat (or "first foot inversion") would tend to encourage the demotion of "I" in a double offbeat (because of a strong expectation encouraged by the metrical set that what Attridge calls the "initial inversion condition" will be fulfilled):[11]

```
    +s   -s  s   s
Proud was I that my country bred
  B    ŏ   B̄  o  B  o  B
```

One would feel more sure of this rhythmic realization, however, were it not for the relatively weak "that" in the fourth position.

One effect of this small ambiguity is to make the initial inversion insistent; that is, the pattern **B ŏ B** (usually realized +s -s -s +s) is emphasized by the slight tension involved in realizing it. The pattern is one of the most common features of the five-beat line. Here it appears in a four-beat, enjambed verse followed by a strong pause after the second syllable in the following line. Taken together, these elements tend to suggest rhythms more common in the heroic line than in four-beat "native" verse and help to give the phrase (from "Proud" to "strength") a rhythmic form and sense of weightiness appropriate to the elevation of the woman to a kind of heroic status:

```
Proud was I that my country bred / such strength
  B    ŏ  B  o  B  o  B   o    B
```

Wordsworth signals his speaker's turn of mind, then, through affective and emblematic uses of meter both: semantic elements conform easily to abstract, conventional literary structures (the line and the stanza). These elements create the music appropriate to what the speaker calls his initial "lofty thoughts" and indicate through their relationship the abstracting power of the speaker's mind. Parts and wholes are in easy relationship. Individual sounds drop easily into patterns, as the particularized "woman" on the road becomes a walking embodiment of "Spirit."

Neither the conventional harmonies nor the abstraction of the figure of the woman persist, however. The contrast is stark between the style of the stanzas devoted to the speaker's speech and the style of the quotations attributed to the sailor's mother. Her first line, in response to the speaker's question about what she carries beneath her cloak, contains the only conventionally harmonious, patterned speech attributed to her:

> A simple burthen, Sir, a little Singing-Bird.
>
> (l. 18)

The alliteration ("simple . . . Sir . . . Singing"; "burthen . . . Bird") and the restricted sonic range and repetition of the vowels give the verse a faint hint of a more songlike rhythm than has been established to this point. This effect probably results in large part from the assonance in "Sir" and "Bird," which tends to divide the hexameter aurally into two three-beat units (a tendency that it has even without this hint of internal rhyme):

> A simple burden, Sir
> o B o B o B
> A little singing bird.
> o B o B o B

The rhythmic shift is especially apparent given the earlier use of the hexameter (stanzas 1 and 2) as an unbroken unit carrying a summation in stately tones.

The contrasts continue in the first full stanza of quoted speech:

> The Bird and Cage they both were his:
> 'Twas my Son's Bird; and neat and trim
> He kept it: many voyages

>   This Singing-bird hath gone with him;
>   When last he sailed, he left the Bird behind;
>   As it might be, perhaps, from bodings of his mind.
>   (ll. 25–30)

The sources of formal tension are many. Neither the individual lines nor the four-beat quatrain has any real integrity. The rhymes in the run-on lines are, as Coleridge notes, barely noticeable (2:70). The rhyme of "his"/"voyages" is particularly troublesome, as it is both imperfect (really a consonance rhyme) and what William Harmon calls "promoted": that is, the final syllable of "voyages" requires, at least theoretically, an exaggerated degree of stress, or "promotion," to fulfill the phonetic conditions necessary to rhyme.[12] "They" in the first line is syntactically superfluous. It functions here, as so frequently in later eighteenth-century poetry, as a means for approximating colloquial speech. It may be worth noting that such devices are made effective in part through the strict syllabic constraints of the meter, since the redundant "natural" word choice also serves to fulfill a purely metrical requirement. Incongruously, the natural speech fits the metrical frame perfectly.

Other sources of tension include the rhythm of the second line, which introduces the first real rhythmic dislocation in the poem (a -s -s +s +s group, or what Attridge calls a "stress-final implied offbeat formation"):

>   'Twas my Son's Bird; and neat and trim
>   ŏ   B ô B
>   He kept it

This verse, leading as it does to an enjambment and a midline pause after an unstressed syllable in the next verse, asserts strongly an emerging natural speech rhythm that disrupts significantly the sense of the more formal organizational patterns of the stanza itself (and of the stanza as it had been employed in presenting the speaker's own words). The syntax of the hexameter, with its double pause, again (as in line 18) resists the tendency of the couplet to suggest closure.[13] Finally, the facile and pleasant alliteration of the initial stanza of the poem is replaced here by eight occurrences of an initial *b* sound, which serve to snag the rhythm ("he left the *b*ird *b*ehind / As it might *b*e, perhaps, from *b*odings").

If Wordsworth thought that the presence in a poem of such speech, which conforms so little to the expectations of the metrical pattern, was in and of itself sufficient cause for condemnation, he could hardly have done a worse job concealing his deficiencies in the stanzas devoted to

the speech of the Sailor's Mother. If he had simply wished to imitate, unobtrusively, simple speech, he could have followed the example of many contemporaries (Burns or Southey, for example) and used, as indeed he had used in several of the *Lyrical Ballads,* a simple common measure stanza or tetrameter couplets. Either of these forms would have decreased the number and kinds of formal expectations and structural divisions that mark the failure of the woman's voice to fall into line. (This is precisely what Coleridge registers about the verse when he suggests that the speech would have been better had it been in prose.) Conversely, if Wordsworth wished to soften what Coleridge calls the "abrupt downfall" (*BL* 2:71) that occurs in moving from the speaker's harmonious and elevated use of the stanza into the quoted speech of the woman, he could have done so. He chose, however, to make the stylistic contrast so clear and inescapable that he forces the reader to consider the possibility that the clash of dissimilar uses of the same metrical frame is itself an integral part of the poem's subject. What, then, might the comparative "failure" of the woman's voice to conform to expectations signify?

The formal context in which the Sailor's Mother speaks allows the reader the obvious opportunity to see in what ways her habits of mind differ from those of the speaker. Whereas the speaker's stanzas are full of abstract nouns ("ancient spirit," "Old times," "my country," "such strength," "a dignity") and adjectives describing the qualities of things ("raw," "wet," "foggy," "majestic"), the woman's diction is characterized by the use of concrete nouns ("seas," "bird," "cage") and simple verbs that relate the objects of her experience to one another and ultimately to a central signifier—"my son." Whereas the speaker's style stands as evidence of his ability and tendency to organize his world by assimilating discrete parts of his experience within larger structures and categories, the woman's style expresses a complete preoccupation with particularity, with hard fact couched in the simplest narrative form. Words matter to her only insofar as they point to particular facts and things; facts and things matter only as they are connected with her son.

The clash of styles in "The Sailor's Mother," then, may be regarded as having been calculated to bring into direct opposition the mind of the "wise man" with that of the "rustic" (the terms are Coleridge's): one speaker is habitually predisposed to seek and "discover and express those *connections* of things, or those relative *bearings* of fact to fact, from which some more or less general law is deducible"; the other is limited to "*insulated facts*" (*BL* 2:52–53).[14] Coleridge regards the concern of the "rustic" with "insulated facts" as evidence of "imperfect development" of faculties. Rustic speech is unpoetic because it issues from a mind

constrained to "scanty experience" or "traditional belief." The evidence of Wordsworth's poem (and the burden of his theory), however, suggests that he regarded the larger relationship between the speaker's imaginative poetic surview and the limited and concrete concerns of the woman as poetic in itself. For all of the stark differences between the two voices, they are inextricably bound to one another by the obvious fact of their dissimilar fitting to a common and aesthetically insistent stanza form. And the relationship brought out through such "fitting" works to illuminate tendencies in both of the speakers, as it invites the reader to an active engagement of the similitude lurking within the dissimilitude.

In more concrete terms, the juxtaposition of voices ensures that neither voice will quite "fit" its metrical frame seamlessly. If there is something strikingly prosaic, commonsensical, and matter-of-fact about the woman's speech, there is also something a bit too "lofty" in the speaker's stylized abstraction of the woman. (This point is made explicit in the speaker's initial difficulty in reconciling his "pride" at seeing this embodiment of "ancient spirit" with the fact that she addresses him as a beggar—"I looked at her again, nor did my pride abate. / When from these lofty thoughts I woke.") The incongruity is produced in part by the poet's use of a metrical frame that carries associations with more elevated kinds of poetry than this. For the speaker, the spectacle of the woman carrying the caged bird has a much more universal figurative significance than that which the woman herself is capable of seeing. (In this connection, it may be appropriate to emphasize once again the Spenserian associations of the hexameter final line of these stanzas.) But the suggestion remains, too, that with gains come losses, or that his discovery of the general law of which the particular woman is an instance may not, in fact, give sufficient weight to the irreducible particularity of the woman as a "mere" sailor's mother begging "in the road."

Last words are important words:

> "And now, God help me for my little wit!
> I trail it with me, Sir! he took so much delight in it."
>
> (ll. 34–35)

The poem ends with quoted speech, with no rounding off or summation by the original speaker. The unimpressive rhyme of "wit / it" and the ending of the poem so baldly with a pronoun further frustrate any residual sense one might have of the couplet as the appropriate vehicle for pat summation. (Her "little wit" may have its proper formal embod-

iment here in the absence of a more conventionally witty coalescence of sound and sense.) But the most important emblematic metrical point to note is the hypermetricality of the final line. Its seven stresses constitute the first (and, of course, only) instance of a true formal break in the poem. The quoted speech not only fails to realize the expectation that the pentameter and hexameter couplet will provide a satisfying sense of the pattern fulfilled but also actually breaks the mold. In a very basic, physical sense, the poem signals that this seemingly restricted and powerless voice nevertheless presents a serious challenge to conventional forms of organization, represented both by the stanza and by the poem's other, more conventionally poetic, voice. The difference between the Sailor's Mother's mind and affections and the mind and affections of her questioner is made a palpable, rhythmic reality. At the same time, the framing of these rhythmic differences in the same form suggests that the two ways of thinking and feeling are, properly understood, in dialectical relationship. Make the speaker's music the defining music of the poem, and the voice of the woman is reduced to a technical mistake. Hear the music of both voices as appropriate rhythmic embodiments of different "fluxes and refluxes" of passionate minds, and a different, more comprehensive, music may emerge—full of tension, and richer than either voice alone.

Any broad surview that emerges from "The Sailor's Mother," then, must issue from the reader's active participation in a dynamic poem made up of contrasts: abstraction and particularization; the heroic ancient spirit and the pathos of a simple beggar woman; the drive toward closure and the resistance to closure in the speech of the finally enigmatic figure. Wordsworth says in the Preface to *Poems* (1815) that "Poems . . . if they be good . . . cannot read themselves" (*Prose* 3:29). In "The Sailor's Mother" he depends on the presentation of dissimilar voices in similar forms to prompt the reader to work toward synthesis of the disparate elements of the poem. The activity of reading the poem finally binds speakers, poet, and reader together and functions as a proof of Wordsworth's assertion that the mind of the poet differs only in degree, not in kind, from that of ordinary men and women.[15] The stylistic clashes in "The Sailor's Mother" are best regarded, then, as instances of a strategy for the energetic representation of diverse minds in active interchange with the world and with one another.

A good deal of evidence exists to suggest that Wordsworth was conscious of the artistic uses of such metrical variety and dissimilarity and that he was concerned that this aspect of his technique and its principles

be understood. For example, in the note appended to "The Thorn" in editions from 1800 to 1805, Wordsworth says that the meter of the poem was selected not because of its appropriateness to the speaker's style and language but because of its ability to provide a contrast to them. Wordsworth's aim in "The Thorn" is to delineate a type of character that, though "sufficiently common" in his experience, had not, as of 1798, found sufficient literary expression. His speaker, whom he describes as "credulous and talkative" and "prone to superstition," is a man of "slow faculties and deep feelings." Although he has "a reasonable share of imagination," he is "utterly destitute of fancy." Such minds, Wordsworth says, tend to express themselves slowly, in words that they feel to be "impregnated with passion," whether or not those words are sufficient to convey the passion they feel (*PW* 2:512).

The challenge facing Wordsworth was how to portray the motions of such a mind with sufficient accuracy while simultaneously conveying pleasurable passion "to Readers who are not accustomed to sympathize with men feeling in that manner or using such language." Toward this end, he decided to employ a type of meter more "Lyrical and rapid" than would be strictly consonant with the voice he wished to portray. He wished to make the poem "appear to move more quickly" than its selection and arrangement of diction actually allows it to move: "It was necessary that the Poem, to be natural, should in reality move slowly; yet I hoped that, by the aid of the metre, to those who should at all enter into the spirit of the Poem, it would appear to move quickly" (*PW* 2:512–13).

The stanza that Wordsworth chose for "The Thorn," after an initial attempt at tetrameter couplets (see *PW* 2:240 app. crit.), is no more likely a choice than is the choice of an odic stanza for "The Sailor's Mother." It is an intricately rhymed, eleven-line structure formed by combining a variation of the ballad stanza (abc_4b_3) with a modified tail-rhyme stanza ($deff_4e_3gg_4$).[16] Although "The Thorn" marks the first use in English literature of a stanza of exactly this construction, stanzas similar to Wordsworth's had been used before, most notably by Gray in "Ode: on a Distant Prospect of Eton College" (1747) and "Ode on the Spring" (1748).[17] It is tempting to think that Wordsworth may in fact have had the example of Gray in mind when he developed this stanza. The fitting of the homely speech of a superstitious and "talkative" sea captain to a metrical frame recalling the elegant Gray has obvious ironic and revisionary possibilities, especially when it is remembered that Gray is a chief target of Wordsworth's arguments in the Preface. Gray is the poet whom Wordsworth places "at the head of those who, by their reasonings,

have attempted to widen the space of separation betwixt Prose and Metrical composition, and was more than any other man consciously elaborate in the structure of his own poetic diction" (*Prose* 1:133). One need not think specifically of Gray, however, to sense that the representation of the speaker's tale is designed to be pleasurably dissimilar both from the natural speech of such men and from the kind of speech that might conventionally find expression in such a metrical form.

The note to "The Thorn" demonstrates that Wordsworth expects of its readers the same sensitivity to the relation between meter and diction as he expects of readers of "The Sailor's Mother." In both poems the complex intertexture of feeling supplied by the meter is a chief means through which the poet leads the reader into physical relationship and sympathy with types of minds with which he or she normally would have little or no contact. A similar emphasis is present in his discussion in the 1800 Preface to *Lyrical Ballads* of his choice to write "Goody Blake and Harry Gill," which he calls "one of the rudest [poems] in the collection," both "as a Ballad" and in a "more impressive metre than is usual in Ballads" (*Prose* 1:150). Wordsworth does not say that the poem is designed to be more impressive than a ballad; he says that an important element in the conception of the poem was his choice to frame a rude ballad-narrative in a meter that the sensitive reader would feel to be more impressive than usual in the genre, both because of its inherent complexities and because of its literary-historical associations.

The *Lyrical Ballads* themselves contain sufficient contrast between the unusual use of this "impressive" meter and a more conventionally sanctioned use. It is, and ought to be, something of a shock, at least a gentle one, that "Lines Written near Richmond, upon the Thames, at Evening" (hereafter "Lines"), one of the most conventionally mellifluous poems that Wordsworth ever wrote, is cast in much the same mold as is "Goody Blake and Harry Gill":

> Glide gently, thus forever glide,
> O Thames! that other bards may see,
> As lovely visions by thy side
> As now, fair river! come to me.
> O glide, fair stream! for ever so;
> Thy quiet soul on all bestowing,
> Till all our minds for ever flow,
> As thy deep waters now are flowing.
>   ("Lines," ll. 17–24)[18]

> Oh! what's the matter? what's the matter?
> What is't that ails young Harry Gill?
> That evermore his teeth they chatter,
> Chatter, chatter, chatter still.
> Of waistcoats Harry has no lack,
> Good duffle grey, and flannel fine;
> He has a blanket on his back,
> And coats enough to smother nine.
> ("Goody Blake and Harry Gill," ll. 1–8)

The contrast provides a particularly good example of the kind of range that is characteristic of Wordsworth's versification. The only structural difference between the two stanzas is the placement of the augmented rhymes. Otherwise, Wordsworth relies entirely on diction, placement of pause, and punctuation to create, in "Lines," a poem in which the individual sounds and rhythms of the speaker's words are entirely and significantly fitted to the meter and, in "Goody Blake and Harry Gill," one in which every stylistic device seems calculated to underline the habits of mind that make the speaker's diction and syntax radically unfit for conventional metrical presentation.

In "Lines" a speaker, obviously a poet (he speaks of "other bards"), survives his position in the stream of time and literary history with a comprehensiveness of mind appropriate to the place, time, and subject (he not only remembers Collins but does so on the spot where Collins remembered Thomson).[9] Like the initial speaker of "The Sailor's Mother," his harmonious patterning of vocal sounds functions emblematically as well as expressively: the absence of tension between metrical pattern and realization functions almost as an element of characterization. He has mastered a number of conventional poetic techniques that indicate his right to call himself a "bard."

In "Goody Blake and Harry Gill," a speaker who is more like the speaker of "The Thorn" than of "Lines," at least in his credulity, does almost as much "chattering" as his subject's teeth. The frequency of such obvious concessions to meter as repetition (especially of his protagonist's names), cliché fillers ("it must be said," "as you may think"), and awkwardly colloquial contractions ("is't") helps to create a sense of this speaker as a village minstrel or balladeer with very different sensibilities from Thomson, Collins, and the young poet of "Lines." In fact, in a few places it is difficult to read metrically without wrenching normal pronunciations in a manner associated with doggerel. How, for example, ought the second line of the following to be pronounced?:

Yet still his jaws and teeth they clatter,
  s   s   s   +s   -s   s -s +s
Like a loose casement in the wind.
1.   ŏ B̄ ŏB   o B̄ o B
2.   B   ŏ   B
3.   ȯ B̄ ȯ   B

And Harry's flesh it fell away

The description above the line shows the problem: the ambiguity in relative stress in the first three syllables allows at least three realizations. Both 1 and 2 would be acceptable in most four-beat verse. The natural tendency to subordinate an adjective to the noun it modifies, however, tends to make number 1 a bit strained (it hints at a rare and disruptive triple offbeat), particularly given the kind of insistent ground rhythm that is apparent throughout the poem.[20] Number 2 is objectionable for the same reasons; it would be perfectly acceptable in more conversational, less robustly rhythmic, verse. In this context, however, it may seem too subtle, given the metrical set. This leaves the hyper-regular realization of number 3, which requires the line to be read exactly in the way that teachers of expressive and subtle pronunciation in poetry, from Gascoigne through Thelwall to the present day, eschew:

Like a loose casement in the wind
 ȯ B̄ ȯ B o B̄ o B

This is not to say that the third reading is the "correct" reading, but only that such a reading is possible (and even hinted at) given the rules of this meter, tendencies in the language, and the metrical set. In any sensitive reading it will vie with the less singsong possibilities as an element of the line's inherent optionality. Perhaps the best way to think about the tensions inherent in such a line is as an element in the presentation of a comic counterpart and contrast to the tensionless lines of the "bard" in "Written upon the Thames." The wide range of possibility in the realization of the line exposes, very much as do rhymes that hint at mispronunciation (July/truly), the medium of the poem and makes the telling inherently comic at the speaker's expense.

Such characteristics, along with the insistently paratactic syntax of the poem, define the speaker of "Goody Blake and Harry Gill" as a character whose mind, whatever its virtues, lacks the ability to "see the whole of what he is about to convey" except in a very schematic way.

There is no subtle, organically uninsistent subordination of parts to the whole here:

> And fiercely by the arm he took her,
> And by the arm he held her fast,
> And fiercely by the arm he shook her,
> And cried, "I've caught you then at last!"
>
> (ll. 89–92)

Wordsworth's acknowledgment in the Preface of the "blind association" of pleasure that a reader is wont to feel in reading poems written in the same or similar meter suggests that such widely various use of the same meter within a collection of poems is yet another way in which Wordsworth employs his principle of similitude in dissimilitude. The relationship between this poem and "Lines," like the relationship between the two speakers of "The Sailor's Mother" or between slow speech and rapid meter in "The Thorn," finally may work to encourage active comparison between those minds represented as aspiring to, and often achieving, imaginative "surviews" and those represented as variously focused on objects and events normally overlooked by the mind thus engaged. Such are the rhythms of the mind itself and of the society of which the individual forms a part.

These examples of Wordsworth's practical application of his theory of metrical opposition reveal a strong tendency toward metrical experimentation that would seem important to understand. This is particularly the case in light of evidence that these experiments spring from a specifically Wordsworthian motive that remains unaccounted for in the largely Coleridgean tradition of metrical analysis that has tended to dominate discussion of romantic versification. Wordsworth's metrical particularities and peculiarities are as deeply rooted in his own ideas concerning similitude in dissimilitude as Coleridge's are in his specifically organic theories. Proper understanding of the role that meter plays in Wordsworth's attempt to explore relationships among a wide range of types of mind—and among a variety of tendencies in the individual mind—will require a reexamination of the ways in which a use of metrical form is judged to be successful. It would be as useless as it is obviously wrong to judge the use of meter in the second half of "The Sailor's Mother" according to the same standards we use for the speaker of "Lines," especially when Wordsworth provides so many clues to the reader that his definition of successful metrical experimentation goes far beyond the desire merely to make his verse sound conventionally har-

monious or mellifluous. That Wordsworth can, and does, use the same stanza form for conventionally harmonious and unconventionally cacophonous effects in the same collection of poems—and even within individual poems—suggests that his understanding of pleasure as the product of the active perception of similarity in dissimilarity is a chief force, in theory and in practice, behind his variety of metrical styles.

In "The Concept of Meter: An Exercise in Abstraction," Wimsatt and Beardsley state that "it is just as important to observe what meter a poem is written in (especially if it is written in one of the precise meters of the syllable-stress [accentual-syllabic] tradition) as it is to observe what language the poem is written in."[21] The view of Wordsworth's metrical theory advanced in the first part of this study suggests that this statement is particularly applicable to Wordsworth's poetry. Wordsworth's distinction between the law of received metrical patterns ("the passion of metre," "the letter of metre," "the law of long and short syllable") and the actual embodiment of vocal sounds in temporal succession ("the passion of the subject," "the passion of the sense," "the spirit of versification") is presented in the critical prose not to recommend the entire subordination either of letter to spirit or spirit to letter but to call his reader's attention to the nature and extent of the powers exerted by each in the process of writing and reading poems.

The "complex end" of a poem, Wordsworth argues, always involves to some degree an active interchange between creative power and the conventional embodiments of power. The metrical frame, in this view, is an indispensable element contributing to the expressive ends of the poet; in addition, it frequently functions, through its complex relationship with the diction and syntax of the poem, not merely as a vehicle but as a trope. The process of bringing individual expression into relationship with conventional metrical patterns may be regarded both as analogous to and as an actual instance of the action and reaction, flux and reflux, of the mind and all forms of power within which and against which it acts. It follows, then, that an adequate perception of and response to the creative power exercised in any given poem must include a solid understanding of the nature of the power exerted by metrical convention in that poem. Reading Wordsworth metrically demands a Wordsworthian respect for the power that the metrical frame exerts, not in default of, but in conjunction with, powers of mind.

PART TWO

The Versification of Poems

3

"Words in Tuneful Order"

Wordsworth's Early Versification, *An Evening Walk* and *Descriptive Sketches*

GLITTERING VERSE

In book 5 of *The Prelude*, Wordsworth acknowledges that as a boy he was intensely susceptible to what he calls "glittering verse." By age thirteen (or "[t]wice five years," in the 1850 version), he says, his "ears began to open to the charm / Of words in tuneful order" and "found them sweet / For their own sakes, a passion and a power":

> And phrases pleas'd me, chosen for delight,
> For pomp, or love.
> (*13-Bk Prelude* 5.575–81).[1]

Wordsworth's discussion of this youthful passion for "words in tuneful order" expresses the same ambivalence toward the music of verse as does the description (in the appendix to the Preface to *Lyrical Ballads*) of meter as a "passport" to stylistic abuses. In both discussions Wordsworth combines a clear acknowledgment of the potential seductions of tuneful enchantment with considerable respect for the sheer power of verbal music. Wordsworth's early and undisciplined love of words for their "pomp" and sound led him to value poems that in his maturity he recognizes to be "false, and in their splendour overwrought" (l. 594).[2] But he also insists that the attraction to that splendour itself manifested "no vulgar power" (l. 595). On the contrary, the ability to derive "conscious pleasure" from "words themselves" (ll. 567–68) is an early expression of "that most noble attribute of man" (l. 597):

> That wish for something loftier, more adorn'd,
> Than is the common aspect, daily garb
> Of human life.
>
> *(13-Bk Prelude 5.599–601)*

The poet's early delight in language more lofty and "adorned" than that of common life is seen in *The Prelude* as evidence of an inherent tendency of the human mind toward the ideal, a tendency no more to be condemned than the childhood propensity to see meadow, grove, and stream as apparelled in celestial light. The suggestion here, also, is that the poet has become a poet in part because he has not lost that early sense of delight even as his ear has become more and more discriminating and more attuned to the "music of humanity" in all of its complexity. Youthful susceptibility to the elevated language of glittering verse is as essential to the foundation of the style of the mature poet as are early experiences of the glory of the commonplace in making up the mind of the mature and chastened man.[3]

In 1801 Wordsworth commented on the style of his own first substantial publications—*An Evening Walk* and *Descriptive Sketches,* both published in January 1793—in terms that invite comparison with the discussion of "glittering verse" in *The Prelude.* Writing to Anne Taylor, an admirer of the *Lyrical Ballads* who had expressed curiosity about how he had formed his style and opinions, Wordsworth suggests that she read the poems of 1793:

> You ask me if I have always thought so independently. To this question I am able to give you a satisfactory answer by referring you to two poems, which I published at the beginning of the year 1793. . . . They are juvenile productions, inflated and obscure, but they contain many new images, and vigorous lines; and they would perhaps interest you, by shewing how very widely different my former opinions must have been from those which I hold at present. (*EY,* 327–28)

An Evening Walk and *Descriptive Sketches* are anything but "independent" in thought and conception. In fact, they frequently read like tributes from the young poet to the poets on whom he was most dependent during the time he was forming his own style. Together, the two poems form a kind of mosaic of allusions, imitations, echoes, translations, and direct quotations and draw on hundreds of sources as various and far flung as Shakespeare and Erasmus Darwin, Virgil and Greenwood's "Poem on Shooting," *Ecclesiastes,* Beattie's *Minstrel,* and Goldsmith's

Traveller. Their "inflated" diction and syntax bespeak a mind a good deal more caught up in words "for their own sakes" than the Wordsworth of 1801 or 1802 would allow to be healthy.[4]

The verse form of *An Evening Walk* and *Descriptive Sketches,* the five-beat or heroic couplet, is without a doubt the least adaptable to independent thinking and expression of all verse forms in use in the later eighteenth century. Its dominance as the prescribed form for almost all narrative, epistolary, satiric, and descriptive verse from the late seventeenth century through the 1770s and beyond made it, as Donald Wesling says, a "class or *clique* phenomenon" unprecedented in English verse before or since.[5] (Robert A. Aubin's bibliographies list some 145 descriptive-topographical poems, in addition to *An Evening Walk* and *Descriptive Sketches,* written in heroic couplets and published in Great Britain and America between 1775 and 1795.)[6] Even more to the point, couplet style was by the end of the century firmly associated with and entrenched in the rationalist philosophy and aesthetics of the earlier century. To use the form was, to a degree, to subscribe to (or at least invoke) the ethics of the middle way, the aesthetics of antithetical structure and *concordia discors,* and the poetics of urbanity and decorum.[7] Rules governing the use of the form were codified to an extraordinary degree, down to the minutiae of the placement of pause and elision of extrametrical syllables. Pope's practice was generally acknowledged to have perfected the art of the couplet, as is evidenced in Johnson's declaration that "to attempt any further improvement of versification [beyond Pope's achievement] will be dangerous."[8] Small wonder that Blake consistently associated couplet poetry with mind-forged manacles and with birds (and people) singing in cages.[9]

The following quotation, a description of Chamouny in *Descriptive Sketches,* will give an idea of just how far from Wordsworth's mature style and versification these early poems are (instances of alliteration within verses are marked for comment below):

> Last let us turn to where Chamouny shields,
> Bosom'd in gloomy woods, her golden fields,
> Five streams of ice amid her cots descend,
> And with wild flowers and blooming orchards blend,
> A scene more fair than what the Grecian feigns
> Of purple lights and ever vernal plains.[10]

This is skillfully done, according to standards of verse composition that Wordsworth later would call into question. The semipersonification of

Chamouny and the woods that "bosom" the fields, the wordplay involved in the use of "bosom" as a participial adjective, the studied and learned reference to "Grecian" art as analogue and contrast—all make this "glittering" and artful verse with barely a hint of spontaneity. Neither the syntax nor the rhythms bear much relation to speech. The first verse goes so far as to wrench the natural pronunciation of "Chamouny" in conformity with the meter:

       -s +s -s
  Last let us turn to where Chamouny shields[.]
  B ŏ B o B o B o B

One of Wordsworth's many explanatory notes in the 1793 edition points out that this is a deliberate attempt to heighten the musicality of his poem: "This word is pronounced upon the spot Chàmouny, I have taken the liberty of reading it long ["changing the accent" in editions 1820-32], thinking it more musical" (104)." The fourth line contains a syntactic inversion for the sake of the rhyme. Five of six verses employ alliteration. Four of these five use the effect in a particularly studied manner, emphasizing, through balanced repetitions of sound early and late in the verse, the much-vaunted balance of the well-crafted pentameter line (Last let . . . Chamouny shields; with wild . . . blooming orchards blend; fair . . . feigns; purple . . . plains). The final verse seems particularly shaped by sound:

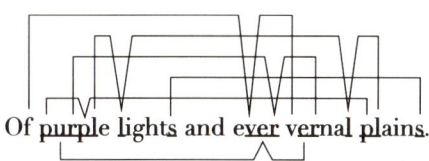

The repetition, coalescence, and interplay of the sounds p, l, r, and s and the internal rhyme of the syllables "pur," "er," and "ver" give the verse a feeling of an almost woven sonic integrity and unity, a unity that underpins the syntactic coordination of the two nouns and their two adjectives. These are, decidedly, "words in tuneful order."

Despite the differences between such verse and the kind of verse that Wordsworth would write and defend after 1797-98 or so (or, as will be argued here, in part because of them), Wordsworth continued to consider these poems as part of his corpus. In 1801, he saw a purpose to be served by having Miss Taylor read the early work in connection with *Lyrical Ballads*, which she admired chiefly for its "genuine simplicity" of style

(*EY*, 328); in 1815, he included revised excerpts from the two works in his *Poems*, and from 1820 through 1849–50 full-length versions of the poems appeared among the "Poems Written in Youth" in his collected editions. The versions in editions after 1815 are heavily revised, but they continue, even in revised form, to convey a sense of the wide differences in poetic taste and style of versification exhibited in the work of the youthful and the mature writer. Their inclusion suggests that Wordsworth continued to think of the poems, as he thought of his early susceptibility to overwrought poetry, as expressive of powers, habits, and tendencies that continued to affect the mature work, though in different ways than in his youth.[12] In the Preface of 1815, Wordsworth explains that the extracts from his juvenile work included in the collected *Poems* "seem to have a title to be placed here as they were the productions of youth, and represent implicitly some of the features of a youthful mind, at a time when images of nature supplied to it the place of thought, sentiment, and almost of action" (*Prose* 3:29). This, he says, is the period described in "Tintern Abbey," when natural "colours" and "forms" were

> An appetite, a feeling and a love,
> That had no need of a remoter charm,
> By thought supplied, or any interest
> Unborrowed from the eye.

To understand Wordsworth's mature metrical art fully, it is important to have an accurate sense of how such appetites find expression in verse, how they help to define and limit the mind expressed in the early work, and how this early verse is both similar to and dissimilar from the verse of Wordsworth's maturity.

"TAME IMITATION"

Understanding the relationship between the metrical style of the couplet poems of 1793 and the style of Wordsworth's mature work requires some appreciation of the technical achievement of the juvenilia that precedes *An Evening Walk* and *Descriptive Sketches*. None of this early verse really belies Wordsworth's own general assessment of his stylistic development: it was not until "my 28th year, though I wrote much, that I could compose verses which were not in point of workmanship very deficient and faulty" (*LY* 1:224). Some of it does, however, provide important evidence concerning the fundamental rules of metrical composition that Wordsworth

was taught to follow as a boy and that he would continue to follow throughout his career. And much of it suggests, despite its youthful deficiencies with regard to some of the many elements that Wordsworth would include under the term "workmanship" (precision or aptness of diction or figures and rigorous application of what he calls the "logical faculty," for example), that Wordsworth was in matters strictly related to meter and versification rather more accomplished at an early age than has been commonly supposed.[13]

The evidence of his first extant poem, the "Lines Written as a School Exercise at Hawkshead" (hereafter "School Exercise"), suggests that the fundamental tendencies of Wordsworth's metrical art were formed through habits of imitation instilled (or at least encouraged) during his school years. The "School Exercise," which commemorates the two-hundredth anniversary of the founding of Hawkshead grammar school, presents a vision of the "heavenly" "pow'r of Education," who rises before the musing schoolboy's eyes to deliver in "pleasing accents" a tribute to Archbishop Sandys, Hawkshead's founder. The poem was much admired by Wordsworth's teachers and fellow students, probably in large part because of its nearly perfect assimilation of the rules governing the closed couplet.[14] According to Wordsworth's own later assessment, it is a "tame imitation of Pope's versification, and a little in his style."[15]

Many of the couplets exhibit the rhythmic regularity, rapid pace, grammatical self-sufficiency, and syntactic balance associated with Pope's practice. Take, for example, the following description of the "Siren" Pleasure:

> Soon fades her cheek her blushing beauties fly
> B ŏ B
> As fades the chequer'd Bow that paints the sky.
> (ll. 97–98)[16]

And there are frequently even closer imitations of Pope's manner (and matter):

> Go to the world—peruse the Book of Man
> B ŏ B
> And learn from thence, thy own defects to scan
> (ll. 85–86)

Each of these couplets employs a rhythmic device that is a kind of metrical signature in Pope: a first line in which the first four syllables form a standard initial inversion group (+s -s -s +s; or a "trochaic" first

foot) and are followed by a definite pause and a second unbroken or less emphatically broken verse.[17] The inversion, and especially the fourth-syllable pause is one of the chief means through which Pope achieves his celebrated rapidity. The illusion of speed results from a psychological phenomenon frequently noticed in eighteenth-century prosodic manuals—that is, the tendency of a reader to equalize the time required to recite the two parts of a divided line. "When the pause falls on [read "after"] the fourth syllable," says Daniel Webb in *Remarks on the Beauties of Poetry* (1762), "we shall find, that we pronounce the six last [syllables] in the same time that we do the four first" (8).

Also contributing to the feeling of speed is the tendency of Pope's line to suggest an underlying four-beat—rather than a fully realized five-beat—rhythm. The pull of four-beat rhythm is very strong in all English verse. The early prominence of the four-beat line in Anglo-Saxon verse, its persistence throughout the history of the language, and its survival into the twentieth century give evidence of the strong psychological and physiological attractions of binary rhythm. In fact, five-beat verse may owe its adaptability to speechlike, conversational, or dramatic uses in large part to the fact that it may be felt as an escape from the powerful impulse to chant verse in the more fundamental, more songlike, four-beat rhythm.[18] Pope's ten-syllable line, strongly divided into two parts of four and six syllables each, will tend to encourage the emergence of the fundamental four-beat rhythm, again because of the psychological and physiological tendency to equalize the divided parts: the ear is "set" by the two strong beats before the pause and tends to adjust the final three beats accordingly, whether through suppression of one of the beats or by the leveling of all three (see Attridge 143ff). Note how Pope emphasizes typographically the four-strong-beat structure of the second line of the following couplet:

> But where's the Man, who Counsel *can* bestow,
> Still *pleas'd* to *teach*, and yet not *proud* to *know*?
> (*Essay on Criticism*, ll. 631–32)

Such devices obviously are a powerful means through which Pope's antithetical habits of mind find fluid and attractive rhythmic expression.

Wordsworth's use of the 4/6 structure in the couplet about the fleeting beauties of the "Siren" Pleasure quoted above shows a subtle ear for a device that produces an appropriate rapidity. In the following couplet, describing one kind of false education as a "vile wretch," he shows an understanding of how such rhythms may be used to embody antithetical patterns of thought (x marks a rhythmic pause):

> Nor that vile wretch who bade the tender age
> Spurn Reason's law and humour passion's rage.
> ò   B o   B (x)o   B o   B o   B
>
> (ll. 9–10)

The 4/6 division heightens the parallelism of the strong stresses on "Reason's law" and "passion's rage," just as Pope's line, quoted above, points up the parallel adjectives "pleas'd" and "proud" and the verbs "to teach" and "to know." The demotion of the verb ("spurn") in the first half of the line may even cause a slight sense of a similar demotion in "humour," emphasizing even more strongly the antithesis of Reason and Passion, law and rage. It hardly needs mention that the prosodic balance on display here cleverly, if conventionally, instantiates the very virtues embodied in the poem's majestically personified "pow'r of Education." The young Wordsworth, that is, already is predisposed to employ verse form as trope as well as frame: his ordered rhythms function emblematically as proof of the ethos of the speaker, showing that the power of Education has indeed informed her student's mind and work.

Another subtle effect that contributes to a sense of graceful ease in the "School Exercise" (and that survives in Wordsworth's mature verse) is the combined use of an initial inversion, a fifth-syllable pause, and a conjunction (or a preposition or other normally unstressed word) in the sixth position:

> Stern was her forehead, but a smile serene
> B   ŏ   B   o (x)B̄ o   B   o   B
> "Softened the terrors of her awful mein"

This is also an imitation of Pope or Popean practice. I estimate that about half of Pope's fifth-syllable pauses (which occur in about 7 percent of his lines, or in about 20 percent of those lines that employ pause) are followed by a conjunction, usually "and," in the sixth position:

> The Groves of *Eden,* vanish'd now so long,
> Live in Description, and look green in Song
> B   ŏ   B   o   B̄   o   B   o   B
>
> (*Windsor-Forest,* ll. 7–8)

The placement of the promoted syllable again allows the line to be felt as a sequence of four strong stresses. In the verse quoted from Wordsworth's poem, the Popean structure emphasizes the tempered demeanor

of Education—stern and smiling. Moreover, the spacing between the second and third strong stresses tends to encourage rapid pronunciation of the syllables after the pause, producing the feeling almost of a trisyllabic unit ("but a smile"; "and look green"). The effect, again as is appropriate to the subject, provides an appearance of escape from the rigid constraints of the decasyllabic and five-beat form, although the verse actually conforms strictly to the rules. Meter, like Education, supplies enabling restraints for youthful passions.

Wordsworth's management of the pause throughout the 112-line "School Exercise" is in fact a telling indication of his early ability to sense and imitate the minute particulars out of which a style is made. Standard eighteenth-century theory—which is actually little more than a description of the practice of Waller, Dryden, and, later, Pope—held that the pause ought to be limited strictly to one of three midline positions (after the fourth, fifth, or sixth syllable). Pope explains the principle in a letter of 1706 to Walsh: "Every nice Ear, must (I believe) have observ'd, that in any smooth *English* Verse of ten syllables, there is naturally a *Pause* at the fourth, fifth, or sixth syllable. It is upon these the Ear rests, and upon the judicious Change and Management of which depends the Variety of Versification."[19]

Earlier or later placement of the pause, if allowed too frequently, was considered a threat to the integrity of the line and a bar to the reader's ability to gain a strong sense of the metrical structure of the verse.[20] For the young Wordsworth, as for Pope, the midline pause, and the fourth-syllable pause particularly, is as much a structural element as are the rhymes or the number of syllables per line: in the "School Exercise," the pause falls after the fourth syllable in 45 percent of the lines that employ a pause, and 67.5 percent of the pauses fall after the fourth, fifth, or sixth syllable; in *Windsor Forest*, 47.1 percent of the pauses are fourth-syllable pauses, and 72.9 percent fall in one of the three midline positions.[21]

Other ways in which the "School Exercise" shows Wordsworth's early assimilation of eighteenth-century rules may be catalogued briefly. Placement of stress is extremely regular; that is, except for the use of a strong stress in the first position of a line (the standard "inversion" common throughout the history of the five-beat line), stresses tend to fall in the even positions, with very few instances of implied offbeat and pairing formations (what classical prosodists would call "medial inversion" or "trochaic or spondaic substitution"). Throughout the poem, individual sounds of words are marshaled skillfully: the rhymes are either perfect or conventionally acceptable ("driv'n" and "Heav'n" for example); alliteration and assonance (which eighteenth-century theory tended to

discourage as "accidental" and therefore no essential part of the structure of a verse) is carefully controlled; no hiatus or vowel-gaping occurs (that is, no awkward running together of vowel sounds over word boundaries, as in "the individual" or "the eternal").[22]

What Hazlitt calls Wordsworth's "chaunt" certainly has its beginnings in the young poet's imitation and internalization of the rhythmic and sonic habits of his predecessors. In an annotation made in about 1836 to the manuscript of Barron Field's *Memoirs of Wordsworth*, the poet claimed that "to this day" he would be able to "repeat, with little previous rummaging of my memory, several 1000 lines of Pope."[23] The "School Exercise" gives evidence that Wordsworth's memory was already well informed by couplet rhythm and couplet technique by 1785.

It remains to discuss what is perhaps the most pervasive and enduring of these subtle internalized habits. I have mentioned briefly above that Wordsworth seems to have been more careful throughout his corpus than are many of his contemporaries to maintain relatively tight restrictions on the total number of syllables per line, as well as on the number and placement of accented syllables. The early verse, from the "School Exercise" through *An Evening Walk* and *Descriptive Sketches* and beyond, shows clearly that Wordsworth was trained to regard legitimate verses as numerically strict and that he had at an early and impressionable age become adept in the use of various techniques for fitting his language to that strict numerical limit. The first four lines of the "School Exercise," as they appear in manuscript, provide a good example:

> And has the Sun his flaming Chariot driv'n
> Two hundred times around the ring of Heav'n,
> Since Science first, with all her sacred train
> Beneath yon roof began her heav'nly reign.—
>
> (ll. 1–4)

To ears accustomed to later nineteenth- and twentieth-century poetry, in which a great deal of variation in the number of syllables per line is permitted, the first verse quoted here has eleven—or even twelve—syllables, and loses nothing by being printed, as it was by De Selincourt, without the elision of the second syllable of "driven." It might be scanned thus:

```
                          +s-s-s +s (-s)
    And has the Sun his flaming Chariot driven
     o   B   o   B   o   B   o     B ŏ    B (o)
```

Trisyllabic "Chariot" would produce the effect that foot-based prosody calls "trisyllabic substitution"—an anapest for an iamb:

$$\smile\smile\,/$$
And has / the Sun / his flam / ing Cha/ riot driv(en)

"Driven" might be regarded either as a monosyllable or as a disyllable producing an unstressed (or "feminine") ending. To Wordsworth's ear, however, the entire verse would have been considerably more complex: it probably would have been regarded metrically as a perfect ten-syllable line, with "chariot" contracted by the blending of adjacent unstressed vowels to a disyllable (char-[jɒ]t) and "driven" shortened by elision to a monosyllable (as it is in the manuscript):

+s -s   +s
And has the Sun his flaming Cha<u>rio</u>t driv'n
 o B o B   o B   o   B o B

Similarly, "Heav'n" in the second verse and "heav'nly" in the fourth would be for metrical purposes monosyllabic and disyllabic, respectively. If the poem had been set in type in 1785, such signals of tension between metrical and phonetic systems would have been carefully marked (as indeed similar occurrences are in the 1793 editions of *An Evening Walk* and *Descriptive Sketches*) in accordance with conventional practices still common (though under attack) through the 1790s. In Dove Cottage MS 1 (and also, though less consistently, throughout the 1793 texts of *An Evening Walk* and *Descriptive Sketches*), Wordsworth shows a thorough grounding in all of the conventional practices of elision and contraction that had been codified and conventionalized in English verse from Chaucer through Cowper: for example, contraction ("ta'en" for "taken"), syncope of the penultimate vowel before intervocalic "r," "l," "n," or "m" ("past'ral" or "trav'ling"), and apocope ("th' east" for "the east").[24]

The question here is not whether or not Wordsworth or a reader would actually have pronounced, or even *could* pronounce, "chariot" and such words as disyllabic, or "Heaven" and "driven" as monosyllables; the point is that such words are regarded by poet and reader as *metrically* elided or elidable. Such words, that is, have in the kind of verse that Wordsworth learned as a boy a kind of dual existence, depending on whether the line is regarded as a real sequence of phonetic material or an ideal structure governed by number. Wordsworth would not substitute for "chariot" a word that did not at least admit the possibility of phonetic

contraction of the vowel in observance of the meter; he would not write something like "And has the sun his flaming vehicle driven." For the prosodist who insists on the relevance of strong stresses alone or of metrical feet in a definition of the line (for Thelwall or for Southey, for example), this option is at least theoretically no less admissible (ignoring for a moment the absurdity of the diction) than is "chariot driven": both create "anapests" substituting for iambs. Wordsworth, however, would exclude "vehicle" in such a position because it is not conventionally elidable.

Eighteenth-century poets were particularly fond of using such elidable syllables in the antepenultimate and penultimate positions in a verse. Wordsworth's use of such words in this position in the juvenilia amounts almost to a mannerism, suggesting that this may be one of the chief of those effects of "glittering verse" that he found so "sweet" in his early reading. The following examples, selected from the juvenilia nearly at random, show that the device occurs commonly in four-beat (which for Wordsworth is normally octosyllabic) as well as in five-beat verse:

> Awake, awake, and snatch the <u>slumb'ring Lyre</u>
> ("School Exercise," l. 109)
> I look'd Obedience the <u>Celestial</u> fair
> ("School Exercise," l. 111)
> To hear the <u>weltering</u> waves
> (*A Ballad*, l. 28)
> Still as I tread through <u>shadowy</u> maze
> ("Dirge Sung by a Minstrel," l. 42)
> Kissed with that rosy mouth <u>the inebriate</u> eyes
> (th'inbr[jɒ]t)
> (*Septimius and Acme*, l. 14)
> The oak its boughs and <u>foliage</u> twines
> (*Vale of Esthwaite*, l. 97)
> While hills o'er hills in <u>gradual</u> pride
> (*Vale of Esthwaite*, l. 113)
> As the soft star of dewy <u>evening</u> tells
> (Sonnet ... Helen Maria Williams, l. 11)
> Thro' bare grey dell, high wood, and <u>pastoral</u> cove
> (*EW*, l. 2)
> Or <u>desperate</u> Love could lead a <u>wanderer</u> there.
> (*DS*, l. 44)

A line from Wordsworth's unpublished "Sonnet Written by Mr ——— Immediately after the Death of his Wife" (c. March 1787) appears in Dove Cottage MS 4 [5 r] to bear a short-vowel mark over the penultimate syllable, presumably showing how the apparent extra syllable ought to be scanned:

> Of light and life upon a happier pole[.]

This effect was frequently singled out by commentators in the eighteenth century as one of the most beautiful and graceful effects possible in the pentameter line. Shenstone, for example, quotes Pope's "And pikes, the tyrants of the watry plains" (*Windsor Forest*, l. 146) and comments that "watry," which he describes as "almost a dactyl," is a "vast beauty" (*Works* 2:180).

As Shenstone's comment suggests, such use of elided or elidable syllables in a verse that poet and reader have agreed will be ten, and only ten, syllables is a potentially pleasurable source of complexity. At such places in a verse, speech rhythms and metrical constraints are most obviously felt to be working in and through each other—or interpenetrating, as Wordsworth will put it in the Preface to *Lyrical Ballads*. It finally matters little whether or not the "extra" syllables are actually pronounced in any one reading of the poem: if they are sounded they will be felt to be straining against the meter; if they are fitted to numerical restrictions, the meter will be manifested in the artificial pronunciation. What does matter is that the syllabic ambiguity makes the boundary between speech and metered language an element of the experience of the poem and potentially an element of meaning.

Such points of complexity in the verse are another of the means through which the strict rules of meter create a paradoxical sense of freedom from a merely univocal reading. The reader may feel himself curiously able to hear more than one realization. These basic techniques continue to play an important role in Wordsworth's mature verse—particularly in the blank verse—long after he frees himself from the more ephemeral and fashionable mannerisms that appear in his early verse as the natural consequence of his admiration of words for their own sakes. No matter how speechlike Wordsworth's diction and syntax become in some of the later verse, that verse is almost always written according to a system of strict numerical constraints (and even when it is not, the departure is significant because of the

usual observance of such constraints). The passionate speech of Wordsworth's verse is throughout the corpus as numerically regular and regulated as it is expressively independent and idiosyncratic. And it is no accident that the tensions between the two systems of organization—the passion of sense and the passion of meter—tend to surface in the mature verse in passages emphasizing the musical, orphic power of poetry and the poet. To take just two examples, in *The Prelude*, book 5, Wordsworth's praise of books as "only less . . . / Than Nature's self which is the breath of God" is impressively sonorous (and therefore the proper embodiment of a verse tribute to "numerous verse" conducted through figures of sound) to a large extent because it employs several elidable syllables (underlined):

> . . . all books which lay
> Their sure foundations in the heart of man,
> Whether by native prose, or <u>numerous</u> verse;
> That in the name of all inspirèd Souls,
> From Homer the great <u>Thunderer</u>, from the voice
> Which roars along the bed of Jewish Song:
> And that more varied and elaborate,
> Those trumpet-tones of harmony that shake
> Our shores in England; from those <u>loftiest</u> notes
> Down to the low and wren-like <u>warblings</u>, made
> For Cottagers and Spinners at the wheel,
> And sun-burnt <u>Travellers</u> resting their <u>tired</u> limbs,
> Stretched under way-side hedgerows, ballad tunes,
> Food for the hungry ears of little ones[.]
> (*14-Bk Prelude* 5.200–213)

Another thematic and expressive high point, the promise and hope of "active days urged on by flying hours,—" that concludes the "Glad Preamble," employs similar means toward similar ends:

> Days of sweet leisure taxed with patient thought
> Abstruse, not wanting <u>punctual</u> service high,
> Matins and vespers, of <u>harmonious</u> verse!
> (*14-Bk Prelude* 1.41–45)

In such passages, metrical tension reveals the ideal numerical structure that informs (and is challenged by) the infinitely variable and only partially quantifiable phonetic material of the verse.

"LIFE'S PURPLE TIDE": OTHER METRICAL EFFECTS IN THE EARLY VERSE

In the "School Exercise," the young Wordsworth demonstrates his ability to imitate many of the basic techniques upon which much eighteenth-century, and earlier, verse is founded and through which it achieves its characteristic music of carefully restrained energy. Other peculiarities of the early versification show the young poet's fondness for somewhat less subtle imitative or emblematic metrical effects and his willingness to experiment with more than one system of prosodic organization (and to more than one effect). In his first published poem, the hypersentimental sonnet "On Seeing Miss Helen Maria Williams Weep at a Tale of Distress" (1787), for example, Wordsworth shows a tendency to let the verse itself carry more than its share of the emotional burden. Watching Miss Williams weep in response to a sentimental tale, the speaker describes his own sympathetic response to her through images of flowing, swelling, and subsiding: "Life's purple tide" flows through every "thrilling vein":

> Dim were my swimming eyes—my pulse beat slow,
> And my full heart was swelled to dear delicious pain
>   (*PW* 1:269, ll. 3–4)

The sonnet proclaims and revels in what might be called the physiology of sympathy. The speaker offers himself as a kind of conduit for feeling that originates in a book and flows outward. Miss Williams's strong response to the "tale" proclaims her "virtue," which the speaker is certain will "shine bright" in times of genuine misery. The implication is, of course, that the speaker's feeling at second hand proves that he, too, possesses deep resources of feeling that will sustain him in his own impending night. The degree of the reader's own visceral response both to Miss Williams and to the speaker, then, presumably will offer important evidence concerning the reader's own strength of character.

Toward this end, the poem is metrically contrived to produce in the reader a sense of the very pulse of the speaker's experience. The first verse quoted here, for example, uses two metrical devices designed to produce the slow pace appropriate to tearful sympathy. The pause after the sixth syllable creates the illusion of slowing for the same reason that the fourth-syllable pause tends to suggest speed: the reader tends to feel that the second part of the line is equivalent in time of recitation to the first part. Wordsworth's use of four monosyllables after the pause also helps to create the desired pace, as the word boundaries create minute

pauses that are felt to be longer than the transitions between syllables in a polysyllabic word.

The placement of the syllable "beat" in an offbeat position also is effective:

$$\text{Dim were my swimming eyes—my pulse beat slow[.]}$$
$$\phantom{\text{Dim were my swimming eyes—my }}\text{-s +s s s}$$
$$\phantom{\text{Dim were my swimming eyes—my }}\text{o B ȯ B̄}$$

The demotion of stress on the syllable "beat" is felt as a source of tension in the line. It strains slightly against the natural rising rhythm, encouraging a greater sense of separation among the syllables "pulse," "beat," and "slow" than would be normal. Compare the effect that would result from the placement in the same position of a syllable less resistant than is "beat" to demotion:

Dim were my swimming eyes—my pulse was slow[.]
          o B   o B

Less tension, too, would have resulted had Wordsworth hyphenated "pulse-beat," making of it a disyllabic compound noun.

In the next verse, Wordsworth makes even more certain that the effect of slowing and swelling is felt on the pulses of his reader, as he swells the line to six beats and twelve syllables as both expression and emblem of the speaker's swelling heart:

And my full heart was swell'd to dear delicious pain
 o B̄ ȯ B o B o B oB o B

Such effects represent a clear departure from the mainstream couplet-verse devices on display in the "School Exercise," a departure signaled in the very choice of a form, the sonnet, which had only recently been revived—by the Della-Cruscans, Charlotte Smith, and other poets of melancholy sensibility—after a long period of virtual abandonment. Wordsworth's sonnet shows the young poet to have been as willing to experiment with forms stigmatized during the greater part of the eighteenth century as remnants of outlandish and barbarous Elizabethan expressiveness as he was to master the means through which Dryden and Pope tamed lawless enthusiasm and the English tongue.[25]

Wordsworth's most extensive poem before *An Evening Walk*, the long and uncompleted *Vale of Esthwaite*, employs a number of such devices

in the service of the aesthetics of expressive passion and direct physical sensation. The poem was begun perhaps as early as 1786 and was apparently still considered in progress as late as 1788 (*CEY*, 18–19).[26] In the *Vale of Esthwaite*, as in the sonnet on Helen Maria Williams, inward emotion, psychological states, and even ideas all tend to be represented in terms of physical sensation. Throughout the poem, the emphasis is on emotional changeability and on varieties of interaction between external stimuli and emotion, an emphasis that frequently finds expression in images of variable sound (particularly of flowing water):

> How sweet at Eve's still hour the song
> Of streams, the hills and vales among!
> Wide as the schoolboy's step the rill
> Drops from the near rock tinkling shrill;
> The Brook, scarce worth a bridge of stone,
> Soothes the lull'd ear with softer moan;
> A deep majestic murmur shews
> Where the slow solemn River flows;
> The torrent like the raving shore
> Swells the full choir['s] sullen roar.
>
> (*PW* 1:273)

This figurative language finds its appropriate rhythmic form in Wordsworth's choice and use of four-beat couplets, which aside from blank verse were the most inherently flexible verse form available to him. At least since Milton's "L'Allegro" and "Il Penseroso," the form was conventionally associated with the pleasurable similitude and dissimilitude that may arise from the use of identical metrical frames to express directly contrasting emotional states. And Milton's ability to produce a seemingly infinite variety of rhythmic patterns between the extremes of "Come pensive Nun, devout and pure, / Sober, steadfast, and demure" and "Come, and trip it as you go / On the light fantastic toe" was widely acknowledged as a metrical *tour de force* defining the inherent virtues of the form.

The many shifts of pace, disruptions of pattern, and even hypermetricality on display in Wordsworth's verse in *The Vale of Esthwaite* are obviously both emblematic of the speaker's ability almost to resonate physically with the external scene and expressive of his conscious joy or sorrow in relation to external nature. To take just one example, in one of the many soundscapes in the poem, the speaker begins by emphasizing the discord between his melancholic internal rhythms and the sound of a stream:

> Peace to that noisy brawling din
> That jars upon the dirge within
>
> (ll. 398-99)

He implores the stream to "cease," or at least to issue sounds more consonant with his internal "pain." The verse here appropriately and cleverly approximates in its pace and sonority a dirge:

> [thy] strain
> No more, as wont, can sooth my pain;
> Cease, cease, or rouse that sullen roar
> As, when a wintry storm is o'er,
> Thy rock-fraught heavy heaving flood
> Sounds dear, and creeps along the freezing blood.
>
> (ll. 402-7)

The long-vowel assonance throughout the passage creates the appropriate sonority: more / wont / or / roar / storm / o'er; Cease/ cease / heaving / dear / creeps / freezing. Pauses and repetition early in the passage tend to slow the pace. Most obviously, the use of the five-beat line at line 407 interrupts entirely the normal pattern of four-beat couplets, rounding off the passage and producing a marked pause, as would a hexameter in a Spenserian stanza or in a poem written in heroic couplets.

The reason for the rhythmic closure here becomes apparent in the second part of the passage, as the mood and the versification turn completely about. The speaker realizes in the midst of his melancholy dirge that the "merry" external sound is, after all, still "dear":

> 'Tis dear—and still with merry song
> Dash'd from the rough rocks lively leaps along.
> At sleepy noon what idler now
> Shall pore upon the willow bough?
> Upon thy bosom pleasure dancing,
> Still retreating and advancing,
> Still art thou dear, fond prattler, run,
> And glitter in to-morrow's sun.
>
> (ll. 408-15)

The speaker awakens from a doleful dream into the cheerful reality that was apparent all the time (note the emphatic repetition of "still") but to which his melancholy had made him deaf. The pause after the second

syllable in the first verse and the heavy emphasis required by the first syllable of the phrase "'Tis dear" emphasize the transition. The largely rising (or iambic) rhythm of the dirge (o B o B o B o B) has begun to shift to a more sprightly falling (or trochaic) rhythm ([o] B o B o B o B [o]), a shift that is complete in the couplet at lines 412–13:

> Upon thy bosom pleasure dancing,
> Still retreating and advancing[.]

In the second line of the quoted passage, a pentameter, alliteration on liquid consonants (rough rock; lively leaps along) produces a songlike contrast to the more staid pattern of the assonance in the line that ends the dirge. (Wordsworth uses a slightly revised version of this particularly felicitous line in *EW*, l. 120.)[27] The use of augmented rhymes in lines 412–13 (dancing/advancing), a device that Wordsworth almost always associates with fanciful and playful song (see, for example, "Written in March at the Foot of Brother's Water" or "The Kitten and the Falling Leaves"), completes the transformation of the speaker's rhythms from penseroso to allegro, all within a dozen or so lines.

The rhythmic movement from dirge to celebratory and "merry song" expresses and emblematizes the speaker's movement from preoccupation with the currents of his own melancholic mind to his openness to motion and music from without. The external "din" does not cease to sound even while the mind is in the act of imposing on it its own dirge. And the "merry song" indicating the opening of the speaker's mind to the influences of external objects is effective, insofar as it is effective, because it continues as a variation on the same basic metrical form as the dirge; that is, the gleeful song open to the influence of the "din" and the dirge that excludes it mingle palpably in the contrasting usage of the same verse form. The suggestion made by such verse is that the interactions of mind and nature explored in the poem as a whole are in fundamental ways vitally rhythmic. Internally motivated dirge and externally stimulated merry song vie for control, neither canceling the other. Together, the two strains make up and convey the complex pleasures of the youthful poet's mind.

The play of inner and outer rhythm here, like the similar emphasis in the "Sonnet" on bodily resonance as a source of sympathy, also tends to challenge the assumptions of more conventional landscape poetry of the period, in which natural phenomena more often than not are imaged as finally subordinate to an all-encompassing, intellectualized vision of unity.[28] Wordsworth's contrast of jarring songs provides no such

overarching unity; rather, it tends to function as an emblem of coexisting diversity of feeling, of thought, and of point of view. The implication here is that the possible songs are endless. One song does not subsume the other. Variety of voices, transitions between them, and relationships among them are chief ends of the versification.

As contrived as the "pulsing" verses of the sonnet to Helen Maria Williams are and as schematic as the contrast of dirge and song in the *Vale of Esthwaite* is, they exhibit important and enduring habits of mind that inform Wordsworth's art. The assumption that poetic passion produces pleasure in large part through an actual physical participation of speaker and reader in a bond of resonant sympathy survives in Wordsworth's mature verse, though it finds expression in increasingly more subtle ways. To compare, for example, the effect of rhythmic shifts and contrasts in the *Vale of Esthwaite* with the similarly expressive and emblematic rhythmic movements and transitions of "Tintern Abbey," or with the revolution of feeling and voice occurring in the transition from stanza 8 to 9 in the "Ode: Intimations of Immortality," is to see both how far Wordsworth was to develop from this relatively wooden use of metrical contrast and how fundamental such stylistic elements are to Wordsworth's desire to explore interrelations between the rhythms of mind and of nature. The emphasis of the art will change, but the conviction that the rhythm and sound of words themselves are powerful means through which a reader is moved to participate in sympathetic participation in the "fluxes and refluxes" of the impassioned mind remains an important part of Wordsworth's metrical art.[29]

THE "HARSH" VERSIFICATION OF *AN EVENING WALK* AND *DESCRIPTIVE SKETCHES*

By the time Wordsworth began working *An Evening Walk* and *Descriptive Sketches* into publishable shape, then, he was well into his fourteen years of apprenticeship to the Muse.[30] He had been engaged for some time in the habitual fitting of his thoughts to the "chains" of meter that he tells John Scott, in a letter of 1816, is absolutely essential to the education of a poet:

> If you have not practiced metre in youth, I should apprehend that your thoughts would not easily accommodate themselves to those chains, so as to give you a consciousness that you were moving under them and with them, gracefully and with spirit.... in nothing

is it more true than in composing verse that the nearest way home is the longest way about. (*MY* 2:285)

Nonetheless, one of the earliest and most persistent criticisms of the versification both of *An Evening Walk* and of *Descriptive Sketches* was that it is "harsh." The *Critical Review* of July 1793, for example, comments on the "obscurity" of *An Evening Walk*, which it said was "increased by a harshness in the construction and the versification." A month later, the same review notes of *Descriptive Sketches* that its "lines are often harsh and prosaic."[31] Coleridge, in a note to his "Lines Written at Shurton Bars" (1795) acknowledging a borrowing from *An Evening Walk,* praises Wordsworth's "manly sentiment, novel imagery, and vivid colouring" but must concede that his "versification is occasionally harsh" (*STCPW* 1:97). Coleridge had not materially altered this early impression as late as 1817, when he called attention to the "harshness and acerbity" in the "structure of the particular lines and periods" and in the "form, style, and manner" of *Descriptive Sketches* (*BL* 1:77). Twentieth-century views of both poems have continued to find the versification troublesome, usually arguing one or another modification of Emile Legouis's remark that there is something radically inappropriate about the use of closed couplets in descriptive poetry, particularly given Wordsworth's expressed intention to revise earlier models of description.[32] As has been noted above, conventions for the use of the couplet had been so codified by 1793 that any attempt to play with its boundaries was, as Johnson says, "dangerous." If ever there were a verse form that tended to import wholesale into a poem an entire system of conventional representation of feeling and thought, it is the heroic couplet in the eighteenth century.

In light of what has been said above about Wordsworth's ability to write technically correct verse (especially in heroic couplets) from an early age, the question of the "harshness" of these poems is particularly significant. It is unlikely that a poet who could write such conventionally and complexly correct verse as Wordsworth was able to write at age fifteen would be unable at twenty-two to recognize and mend metrical difficulties if he were so inclined. The stylistic harshness and acerbity, then, may reasonably be expected to have issued not from incompetence but from some deeper and more interesting source.

A quick overview of the versification *An Evening Walk* and *Descriptive Sketches* shows that it is in many ways as conventionally correct as is the versification of the "School Exercise." The couplets are, for the most part, closed, avoiding the harshness caused by open-ended or "broken" couplets, a stylistic mannerism that Wordsworth would later condemn

as the result either of artistic slovenliness or "affected imitation of our elder poets": "I have indeed, a detestation of couplets running into each other, merely because it is convenient to the writer;—or from affected imitation of our elder poets. Reading such verses produces in me a sensation like that of toiling in a dream, under the *nightmair.* The couplet promises rest at agreeable intervals" (*MY* 2:547). Verses are strictly limited, with very few exceptions, to ten syllables per line,[33] and Wordsworth employs a whole range of types of elision and contraction in perfectly conventional ways—including the use of elidable syllables at line endings—to fit his diction to the limits of the verse structure. Elisions and contractions are frequently indicated by spelling or punctuation, though not always consistently (and less consistently in *Descriptive Sketches* than in *An Evening Walk*):

> Mid' clust'ring isles, and holly-sprinkl'd steeps
> (*EW*, l. 14)
> Yet still, the sport of some malignant Pow'r
> (*EW*, l. 41)
> But doubly pitying Nature loves to show'r
> Soft on his wounded heart her healing pow'r
> (*DS*, ll. 13–14)
> A spot, that angles at the riv'let's feet
> (*EW*, l. 46)
> Bright'ning with water-breaks the sombrous gill
> (*EW*, l. 72)
> While chast'ning thoughts of sweetest use, bestow'd
> (*DS*, l. 29)
> Like Lightnings eager for th' almighty word
> (*DS*, l. 802)
> Slant wat'ry lights, from parting clouds a-pace
> (*EW*, l. 91)
> Ev'n so, by vestal Nature guarded, here
> (*DS*, l. 528)

And where elisions are not marked, they are obviously assumed: the verse, "Tower like a wall the naked rocks, or reach" (*DS*, l. 287), for example, must be read with "Tower" as a monosyllable or the line will not scan:

> Tower like a wall the naked rocks, or reach
> B o B̄ o B

Tow'r like a wall the naked rocks, or reach
  B   ŏ   **B**

The first option, above, is obviously inferior to the second.

Avoidance of hiatus is one of the more self-consciously classical aspects of neoclassical prosodic theory, and one might expect an early romantic poem to be harsh in its disregard for what the arbiter of eighteenth-century prosody, Edward Bysshe, calls "the first rule conducing to the Beauty of our versification": "The *e* of the Particle *the* ought always to be cut off before the words that begin by a vowel" (10). One example of such disregard does occur in *An Evening Walk*: "How busy the enormous hive within" (l. 143). The line appears in the 1836 text thus: "How busy all the enormous hive within" (l. 159). The insertion of "all" in the revised version points up the weaknesses in the 1793 form: "the" is required in 1793 to take a stress (or at least to be promoted). This is bad practice not only because it introduces a merely distracting discrepancy between semantic weight and metrical stress, but also because it makes very awkward any attempt to blend in pronunciation the final sound in "the" with the first syllable of "enormous." In the revised form, "all" takes the stress, sufficiently relieving "the" of emphasis and allowing it to be regarded, for metrical purposes, as contracted with "enormous": "th'enormous." Such lapses in the 1793 text are understandable, considering the fact that *An Evening Walk* and *Descriptive Sketches* contain more than 1,250 lines and that previously Wordsworth had published only a single sonnet. And on the whole Wordsworth's avoidance of clashing vowel sounds is as complete and as studied as even Bysshe could want it to be:[34]

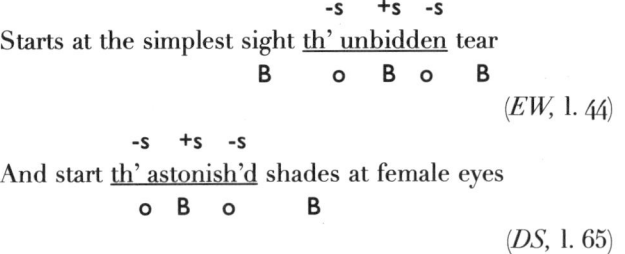

A few other peculiarities of the verse, especially in the earlier-written *An Evening Walk*, represent genuine metrical lapses. Here and there, adjectives give Wordsworth metrical trouble:[35]

Thence from three paly loopholes mild and small
B   o   B ô Bo   B   o   B   o   B

(*EW*, l. 335)

The initial inversion condition, which Wordsworth observes throughout *An Evening Walk* and *Descriptive Sketches* (as well as in his earlier and later verse), is left unfulfilled in this example. Monosyllabic adjectives in the third, offbeat, position of a verse employing initial inversion are common in pentameter verse:

Stoops her sick head, and shuts her weary eyes
B   ŏ   B

(*DS*, l. 222)

Mocks the dull tear of Time with deaf abortive sound
B   ŏ   B

(*DS*, l. 379)

. . . and o'er the void of heaven
Breathes the big clouds with vernal showers distent.
B   ŏ   B

(Thomson, "Spring," ll. 145–46)

Along the woods, along the moorish fens,
Sighs the sad genius of the coming storm[.]
B   ŏ   B   o

(Thomson, "Winter," ll. 66–67)

Wing'd with red Lightning and impetuous rage
B   ŏ   B   o

(*Paradise Lost* 1.175)[36]

The effect only works, however, when the adjective is followed immediately by the noun it modifies. In the example from *An Evening Walk*, the separation of "three" from "loopholes" neutralizes the natural tendency to subordinate the stress value of the adjective to that of the noun. The tendency to give the adjectives "three" and "paly" the equal stress appropriate to their equal syntactic functions promotes "three" to a full stress, ruining the meter.[37] Moving the second adjective makes the verse more conventionally acceptable and demonstrates the source of the problem:

Thence, from three loopholes [pale and] mild and small
B   ŏ   B   o   B   o   B   o   B

Wordsworth evidently was dissatisfied with the line, and in his 1794

revision of the poem (DC MS 9) he may be seen tinkering with its rhythm. An interlinear insertion in the manuscript suggests "And thence from" as an alternate reading for "Thence, from three." The revision would mend the line nicely:[38]

> And thence from paly loopholes mild and small[.]
> o B   o   Bo B   o
>
> (MS 9, l. 600)

The verse eventually becomes "Shedding, through paly loop-holes mild and small" in 1815 and following.

Much more frequent than these and a few other obvious lapses in technique, however, are instances in which Wordsworth's rhythmic patterns are not unmetrical but are uncommon in the couplet as his audience would have known it. The following passage, a revised version of some lines in the *Vale of Esthwaite* (ll. 95–98), will provide a good example of a kind of rhythmic complexity reviewers may have found troublesome:

> Now while the solemn evening Shadows sail
> On red slow-waving pinions down the vale,
> And, fronting the bright west in stronger lines,
> The oak its dark'ning boughs and foliage twines,
> I love beside the glowing lake to stray
> Where winds the road along the secret bay[.]
>
> (ll. 191–96)

The fifth and sixth lines are rhythmically about as simple and direct a realization of the meter as is possible (syntactic peculiarities of the kind evidenced in "beside . . . to stray" and "winds the road," aside). The first line employs initial inversion, and it and the fourth verse contain good examples of elided and elidable syllables in perfectly regular rhythmic sequence: "ev'ning," "dark'ning," "foli̱a̱ge" (fol-[jədʒ]). The second line employs the same effect that Wordsworth had used in the sonnet on Helen Maria Williams to achieve a slow pace in the phrase "my heart beat slow"—the placement of a semantically important, normally stressed syllable on an offbeat:

>   +s +s   +s
> On red slow-waving pinions down the vale
>   o B ȯ   B o

Here, the effect of the adjective in the third position is not as disruptive as it is in the example of "three paly loopholes," both because the initial inversion condition is not in effect and because the hyphen signals the demotion of "slow" as the first syllable in the single semantic entity "slow-waving." Instead of merely disrupting the rhythm, then, the placement of the syllable (and its length) has the effect of loading the line with greater emphasis than is usual. This effect, and the disruption of a strong rising rhythm caused by the demoted, and therefore still tension-producing, "slow" in the third position, acts imitatively to slow the pace of the line.[39]

The slowing produced by this verse leads immediately into the most disruptive rhythmic effect in the passage:

$$\begin{array}{cccc} \text{-s} & \text{-s} & \text{+s} & \text{+s} \end{array}$$
And, fronting the bright west in stronger lines
o B ŏ   B ô B o B o B

Stress-final double-offbeat formations occurring midline (the pattern employed here) are effective sources of rhythmic tension and disruption even in dramatic and Miltonic blank verse, in which they occur fairly frequently. This is the pattern, it may be remembered, that creates the sense of "dislocation" in the line from the "Old Cumberland Beggar" to which Wordsworth refers in the letter to Thelwall on the "passion of metre":

$$\begin{array}{cccc} \text{-s} & \text{-s} & \text{+s} & \text{+s} \end{array}$$
Impressed on the white road;— in the same line
ŏ   B ô B

In 1801, Wordsworth will justify such effects as expressive means appropriate to blank verse: the dislocation of the expected stress pattern of the line creates tension between the passion of the meter and the speaker's passion. Here, in *An Evening Walk,* the line certainly stands as an insistent challenge to normal expectations established by the use of the couplet and provides a marked contrast to the slow-paced line that precedes it. In any even moderately animated reading, the line will be distinguished sharply from the lines that introduce it: the double offbeat produces the illusion of speeding and slowing, as two syllables fitted to a single position are followed by two contiguous beats. The line ends, too, with a fairly strong rising rhythm, in contrast to the sense of suspension and slowing felt in "slow-moving pinions down the vale."

Read with the kind of attention to variety that energetic and expressive blank verse normally requires, the lines embody rhythmically an emo-

tional shift that occurs in consonance with the scene described. The speaker of *An Evening Walk*, like the speaker of *The Vale of Esthwaite*, fairly resonates with external nature as he places himself in a scene, the chief significance of which is the changeability of natural appearance. In heroic couplets, however, such effects are not part of the metrical set. As has been mentioned above, variety in the couplet prosody to which Wordsworth's readers would have been attuned is largely a matter of more subtle effects than the one Wordsworth employs here—mostly promotion and demotion of stresses and varied placement of pause in one of three midline positions. Double offbeats in any context other than as the fulfillment of the initial inversion condition occur rarely; nor are implied offbeats frequent. To a contemporary reader, Wordsworth's expressive effect would very likely be felt as harsh.

It is worth noting that the central image in the passage (the "dark'ning" boughs of the oak) is one that Wordsworth considered among the most significant in *An Evening Walk* (and, for that matter, in his early verse as a whole). The earliest version of the image appears in Wordsworth's hand, in prose, in Christopher Wordsworth's Hawkshead notebook, predating its use in the *Vale of Esthwaite*.[40] By the time Wordsworth dictated the Fenwick note to *An Evening Walk*, he had begun to think about the moment of perception described in the passage as something of a conversion on the road to Damascus:

> I recollect distinctly the very spot where this first struck me. It was in the way between Hawkshead and Ambleside, and gave me extreme pleasure. The moment was important in my poetical history; for I date from it my consciousness of the infinite variety of natural appearances which had been unnoticed by the poets of any age or country, so far as I was acquainted with them: and I made a resolution to supply in some degree the deficiency.[41]

I would argue that it is no coincidence that the lines that Wordsworth singled out as, in effect, the source of the poem's inspiration as well as a prime example of its aims—to awaken his reader to "infinite variety"—also are a source of difficulty in the verse. The rhythms of changeable natural appearance, as nature seems to the speaker to shape itself into "stronger lines," find appropriate expression in the speaker's reactive and changeable rhythmic pulse, from the slow languor of line 192 ("On red slow-waving pinions . . ."), to the rhythmically more impressive line under consideration here, a line that is felt to be emphatic precisely because it represents a departure from conventional practice. Wordsworth's attempt

to supply the "deficiency" of earlier landscape poetry here manifests itself not merely through the image itself but also through rhythmic indications of the impressionability of the speaker to the appearances he describes. The harshness stems from the fact that such shifts of expressive rhythm—which import into the poem a sense of a speaker in the process of reacting to the impressions described in the poem—traditionally are excluded from this kind of descriptive couplet verse in favor of those more subtle variations calculated to give evidence of a rationally composed mind engaged in a comprehensive overview of a fixed "scene."

Such tensions between the promise held out by the symbolic or exponential function of the verse and the actual expressive rhythms of the individualized speaker make this early verse difficult. They also make it an effective index of that tendency of the "youthful mind," as Wordsworth puts in the Preface to *Poems* (1815), to allow "images of nature" to supply to it "the place of thought, sentiment, and almost of action" (*Prose* 3:29). A telling—and characteristically passive—metaphor occurring later in *An Evening Walk* puts the issue succinctly:

> While, by the scene compos'd, the breast subsides,
> Nought wakens it or disturbs it's tranquil tides[.]
>
> (309–10)

In *An Evening Walk*, it is frequently the changeable "scene" itself that is represented as the maker or composer of the observing mind and its rhythms. Its ultimately gentle, beautiful effects find expression in the poem's transitions from day to night, sights to sounds, and—as in the conclusion of this passage about the "subsid[ing]" breast and its "tranquil tides"—in transitions from passages of metrical tension to passages marked by easy fulfillment of the metrical set and pleasingly harmonious alliteration and vowel music:

> The sugh of swallow flocks that twittering sweep,
> The solemn curfew swinging long and deep;
> The talking boat that moves with pensive sound,
> Or drops his anchor down with plunge profound;
> Of boys that bathe remote the faint uproar,
> And restless piper wearying out the shore;
> These all to swell the village murmurs blend,
> That soften'd from the water-head descend.
>
> (ll. 317–24)

Not a single implied offbeat, double offbeat, wrenched accent, deficient rhyme, or instance of hiatus intrudes. No syntactical structure overflows its metrical bounds. Each verse or couplet remains sonically and syntactically distinct until, in the final couplet, "all" blend into a single composed soundscape.

Whereas *An Evening Walk*, an "Epistle . . . from the LAKES of the North of England," attempts to represent the relatively gentle effects on the mind and heart of "the infinite variety of natural appearance," *Descriptive Sketches*, "Taken During a Pedestrian Tour in the . . . ALPS," delineates the rather more powerful and disruptive effects of the sublime. In *Descriptive Sketches,* the well-known passage of sublime description beginning "'Tis storm; and hid in mist from hour to hour" (ll. 332 ff) serves a function parallel to the "dark'ning boughs" passage of *An Evening Walk;* in each, Wordsworth seeks to contribute something original to the language of descriptive poetry by striving to embody a particular kind of complex interaction between the perceiver and the perceived. Wordsworth even makes public claims for the distinctiveness of the *Descriptive Sketches* passage, appending a long note to the 1793 text concerning the difference between descriptive writing that merely follows the "cold rules" of the picturesque and the bold passage at hand, in the composition of which he consulted no rules, but only "nature and my feelings" (72 n).

Once again, as in the "dark'ning boughs" passage of *An Evening Walk,* an aesthetically central passage is marked by a high degree of rhythmic disruption, and again that disruption takes the form of the "dislocating" effects of double offbeats and implied offbeats:

> 'Tis storm; and hid in mist from hour to hour
> All day the floods a deeper murmur pour,
> And mournfull sounds, as of a Spirit lost,
> Pipe wild along the hollow-blustering coast,
> 'Till the Sun walking on his western field
> ŏ   B ô B o   B̄ o B o B
> Shakes from behind the clouds his flashing shield.
>   (ll. 332–37)

The verse at issue comes at an important transitional point, as storm gives way suddenly to sunshine so brilliant that the mountains seem consumed in a "a mighty crucible," "like coals of fire" (346–47). Again, as in the example from *An Evening Walk,* the transition in natural appearances is marked in the poem's rhythm by a corresponding transition

in pace and structure. That Wordsworth clearly intended the contrast of dark and light, storm and sun, to be marked metrically and rhythmically is shown even more directly by his heightening of the effect in his revision of the lines in 1815:

> The sky is veiled, and every cheerful sight:
> Dark is the region as with coming night;
> But what a sudden burst of overpowering light![42]
> o   B   o B   o   B   o B o B   o   B

The initial double offbeat of 1793 gives way to a more direct statement of contrast, couched in structures—both the hexameter and the triplet—more obviously emblematic of an extreme shift in tone because of their break with the form. Moreover, the semantically contrastive rhyme (night/light) makes for a particularly abrupt sense of startling change, as the scene shifts from "coming night" to "overpowering light" within the compass of a single couplet. The argument might be made that Wordsworth's abandonment of the double-offbeat formation in the revised version implies that the original was insufficient to produce the required sense of contrast; nevertheless, the similarity between the *Descriptive Sketches* passage and the passage from *An Evening Walk* discussed above suggests that Wordsworth in 1793 considered the double offbeat in couplet form to be a source of rhythmic variety potentially equal in effect to the hexameter. In either case, it is worth noting that in the 1793 version, as in the parallel passage from *An Evening Walk*, Wordsworth employs means that strain against the metrical set in the interests of his overall aesthetic purposes. Descriptions of "infinite variety" hitherto unnoticed or of the sublimity of the Alps illuminated by the sun require extraordinary poetic means, even (or especially) at the minute level of the interpenetration of syntactical rhythms and metrical frame. Wordsworth, in both of these cases, depends on the regularity of the metrical set to provide the necessary sense of contrast to small variations in order to indicate the movements of a mind as it registers the impressions of that external nature it struggles to describe.[43]

Many of the minute characteristics of the versification of these two poems, particularly those that determine pace and rhythm, suggest that Wordsworth was in fact attempting to create a new kind of pentameter couplet, one that would allow presentation of a distinctive, even idiosyncratic, voice within the context of conventionalized habits of association. Coleridge senses the most pervasive of these characteristics when he comments, in *Biographia Literaria*, that *Descriptive Sketches* struck him as more demanding of the reader's attention than descriptive poetry had a

"right" to be: "The novelty and struggling crowd of images acting in conjunction with the difficulties of the style, demanded always a greater closeness of attention, than poetry, (at all events, than descriptive poetry) has a right to claim" (*BL* 1:77).

Frederick Pottle registered a similar consciousness when he noted long ago that the length of time one needs to read *An Evening Walk* is disproportionate to the number of lines, when compared with the equally long but relatively speedy *Windsor Forest* (*Idiom*, 105, 114). Much of this demand on the attention—and time—of the reader is of course due directly to the poem's frequently elaborate syntax, unfamiliar diction, and difficult and discontinuous imagery. Just as important in creating these demands, however, are difficulties stemming from metrical tension and experimental elements of Wordsworth's versification. Indeed, Wordsworth seems to have been as intent in these poems to create challenging and changeable, rhythmically varied and frequently slow-paced pentameters as he was in the "School Exercise" to assure that his conventionally correct verses would move with uniform grace and rapidity.

It will be recalled from the discussion of the "School Exercise" that the success of the young Wordsworth's imitation depends in large part on his grasp of two of the chief structural characteristics of Pope's couplets: the restricted placement of the pause in the three midline positions (in 67.5 percent of the verses that employ pause) and the frequent use (45 percent) of the fourth-syllable pause as a means of achieving balance and rapidity, through the suggestion of an underlying binary four-stress structure. The pentameter of *An Evening Walk* and especially of *Descriptive Sketches* marks a radical departure from these practices, as if Wordsworth were proceeding by ignoring as frequently as possible these structural constraints. The following table shows the distribution of the pause in Wordsworth's poems of 1793, compared with the distributions in *Windsor Forest*, Goldsmith's *Deserted Village* (to which Wordsworth's couplet poems frequently allude), and an early example of Coleridge's work in couplets, "Lines: On an Autumnal Evening," composed in 1793 and published in 1796 (*STCPW*, 51–54). Numbers describe the percentage of all lines containing a distinct pause, except in the category "unbroken," which gives the percentage of lines without a distinct pause in the total number of lines.

Wordsworth's liberal distribution of the pause throughout the line in both poems (and especially in *Descriptive Sketches*) distinguishes his practice sharply from the practice of Pope, Goldsmith, Coleridge, and even from his own earlier practice in the "School Exercise." This distribution, together with the relatively frequent use of two or even three

TABLE I
Distribution of Pauses after Syllables and Percentage of
Occurrence in Various Texts

Pause After Syllable	EW (%)	DS (%)	WF (%)	DV (%)	Lines (%)
1	7.6	6.6	1.8	1.8	3.1
2	15.3	17.9	10.0	3.5	12.5
3	2.9	7.0	-	1.8	3.1
4	18.8	17.5	47.1	44.1	43.7
5	8.2	7.4	20.0	12.9	12.5
6	15.9	9.5	5.6	17.0	-
7	2.4	1.4	0.6	2.4	3.1
8	1.8	2.8	1.3	0.5	-
9	0.5	3.2	-	-	-
Double	25.9	24.6	16.3	11.1	15.6
Triple	0.5	2.1	0.6	1.8	2.1
Unbroken	62.0	64.5	63.0	60.4	69.8

Midline pause (after fourth, fifth, or sixth syllable): *EW*, 42.9%; *DS*, 34.3%; *WF*, 72.9%; *DV*, 74%; *Lines*, 56.3%.

pauses in a line, in effect denies the pause any function as a defining characteristic of the meter or element of structure.[44] In *Descriptive Sketches* especially (in which a tendency nascent in *An Evening Walk* is, as the chart suggests, developed and emphasized), the use of pause outside of the middle positions, and in particular after the first or second syllable, is a direct challenge to standard practice, in which the midline pause acts as a natural rhythmic fulcrum.[45]

Such distribution of the pause does indeed demand "greater closeness of attention" than the metrical and generic contract would normally be thought to entail. This variety, and the tendency toward fairly frequent use of late pauses also accounts in large measure for the slow pace of the poems.[46] In dispensing with the midline break as a structural element, Wordsworth makes pause chiefly an expressive marker; it is not, as it is for Pope, a matter of metrical rule. Wordsworth will limit himself to the confines of twenty-syllable units with alternating stress, rhyming on every tenth syllable; he will not, however, allow his phrase length to be dictated by the usual rules governing the internal structure of the verses themselves. These internal structures depend on the emotion expressed. The result is a tense relationship between syntax and the larger kinds of patternings that the

verse employs, which in turn creates tension between this kind of rhythmic realization of pattern and the expectations of a readership versed in the usual means by which individual couplet verses are organized.

Wordsworth's practice in the couplet poems of 1793 leaves him free to employ all of the conventional devices of binary opposition that he had employed in 1785. But in the context of the various rhythmic realizations of meter in *An Evening Walk* and *Descriptive Sketches*, even conformity to the metrical set of the conventional couplet becomes an element of expression, indicative not merely of Wordsworth's mastery of the meter but of one particular kind of mental activity out of the many embodied in the various rhythms of the poems. Even absence of "dislocation" is expressive.

A good example of this occurs in *Descriptive Sketches*, lines 520-35, where Wordsworth inserts into his portrait of the Swiss mountaineer a brief sketch of the perfect contentment of "primaeval Man":

> Once Man entirely free, alone and wild,
> Was bless'd as free—for he was Nature's child.
> He, all superior but his God disdain'd,
> Walk'd none restraining, and by none restrain'd,
> Confess'd no law but what his reason taught,
> Did all he wish'd, and wish'd but what he ought.

The passage continues, suggesting that some of this Edenic ordered freedom still survives in the modern mountaineer (the final phrase quotes Smollett, "Ode to Leven-Water"):

> The native dignity no forms debase,
> The eye sublime, and surly lion-grace.
> The slave of none, of beasts alone the lord,
> He marches with his flute, his book, and sword,
> Well taught by that to feel his rights, prepar'd
> With this "the blessings he enjoys to guard."

These lines would be very much at home, at least rhythmically and syntactically, in one of the more conventional descriptive poems on which Wordsworth draws (they are in fact reminiscent in their general tenor and movement of Goldsmith's *Traveller*, especially lines 177-208). In seven out of ten lines that employ pause, the pause falls in a midline position; five of these are fourth-syllable pauses (these account for fully 10 percent of the pauses in this position in the entire 813-line poem).

The passage also employs antithetical syntactical and rhetorical means that are appropriate to the conventional couplet. In the verse "Walk'd none restraining, and by none restrain'd," the tendency of the fifth-syllable pause and the promoted conjunction to create a sense of balanced pairs of stresses emphasizes the repetitive wordplay, especially the polyptoton of restrained/restraining, and prepares for the impressive mingling of impulse and restraint in both subject and expression in the next couplet: "Confess'd no law but what his reason taught, / Did all he wish'd, and wish'd but what he ought." Wordsworth's speaker is prepared, when the occasion warrants, to employ a style that asserts and embodies the human potential to act boldly and to live contentedly within fixed laws. The basis for his praise of the Swiss mountaineer is the mountaineer's adaptation to a demanding set of circumstances; he has made a virtue of necessity. Duty has become one with wish; law and impulse are one. It is not surprising, then, that the antithetical rhythms of the "Spirit of Education" surface here. Wordsworth both praises and imitates the salutary dynamics of the mountaineer's life in what amounts to a kind of metrical and rhythmic purple passage.

But whereas in *The Traveller* all nationalities, all description, and all of the traveler's speech are finally brought under the unifying influence of a single antithetical style, Wordsworth's use of that style and its associations constitutes a kind of rhythmic allusion. In both *An Evening Walk* and *Descriptive Sketches,* passages emblematic of order, calm, and contentment are answered in other parts of the poems by passages (the oak which is seen "fronting the bright west in stronger lines" or the "'Tis storm" passage, for example) in which speech rhythms challenge the aesthetics of balance and containment. Wordsworth's various application of couplet form tends to assure that the verse pattern itself will not be overlooked as a mere transparent medium. Verse structure becomes a participatory element in expression, or a potential emblem of a mind-set toward nature, man, and society. The antithetical habit of mind, then, is shown to be one among many possible ways of proceeding, appropriate to the description of some kinds of relationships between mind and external nature.[47]

A further example from *An Evening Walk* will suggest another way in which metrical allusion and associations function in these poems. Early in the poem, the speaker identifies himself as someone who is returning to a familiar place where he had been happy. He describes that previous happiness in four lines that might serve as an emblem of the kind of manipulation of the metrical contract that occurs throughout both *An Evening Walk* and *Descriptive Sketches:*

> In youth's wild eye the livelong day was bright,
> The sun at morning, and the stars of night,
> Alike, when first the vales the bittern fills,
> Or the first woodcocks roam'd the moonlight hills.
>
> (ll. 23–26)

At first sight the couplets suggest in various ways that their rhetoric and rhythm do conform to expectations. The rhyme bright/night is a good example of the kind of alogical linking of logically opposed signifiers, an "amalgam of the sensory and the logical," that Wimsatt and others have described as the basis of distinctively neoclassical rhyme.[48] Similarly, the bipartite and parallel structure of the second line, with its juxtaposition of "morning"—which places an unstressed syllable just before the pause at the line's precise midpoint—and "night"—which is the last stressed syllable in the line before the end-line pause—balances strong and weak pauses in a way that echoes the sense, demonstrating a kind of technical virtuosity very much in line with expectations.

Both the logic and the rhythm of the third and fourth lines of the example, however, strain against the antithetical style of this first couplet. "Alike" in the first position of line 3 opens up the syntax, which at first seems complete at the end of line 2: the stars of night were in their own way as bright as the sun of morning. Coming on the heels of such a rhythmically and logically self-sufficient statement and set off from the line by the second-syllable pause, "Alike" seems at first to be a redundant and displaced word. Only when the reader is able to see the dual function of the word does "Alike" seem to fit, simultaneously modifying "sun" and "stars" in the first couplet and the two "firsts" of the second two lines, the first bittern and the first woodcocks. "Alike" thus strains against the implied closure of the bright/night rhyme and creates an unstable grammatical structure implying a fusion of the one and the many. The word "day," which seems at first to refer to the bright half of the twenty-four-hour cycle, becomes fused with its opposite; that is, "day" and "night," which in the couplet structure are nicely antithetical, become united grammatically into "livelong day." Likewise, the two "firsts"—one an adverb and the other an adjective—create a curious sense of fusion of discrete elements, as the speaker seems to suggest that it is difficult to distinguish which was first, morning or night, the first sound of the bittern or the first appearance of the woodcocks. Apparently, all was one to his "wild eye."

The problem—as both the couplet structure and the speaker's direct statements remind us—is that the speaker's eye is no longer

wild. The presentation of the imagery in a way that alludes to the conventional rhetoric of antithesis and clean categorical divisions, but does not conform to the demands of that rhetoric, becomes a kind of formal embodiment of the tension between the wild and the tame eye, between the landscape perceived as an interconnected and continuous fabric and as, potentially, a mere mass of little things. Rhythmic harshness comes from formal allusion to a habit of thinking, embodied in a characteristic style, which is almost immediately shown to be inadequate to the sense of relatedness that the speaker claims to feel and desires to convey.

The possibility of different ways of perceiving, of different "eyes" with the power to see, "infinite variety" in the everyday is suggested not through the kind of formal imitation of wildness that one sees, for example, in the Ossianic sublime poem (a kind that is finally more, not less, conventional than the kind of poetry that Wordsworth is writing here) but through the subtler means of exposing one kind of conventional structure—couplet rhetoric—as inadequate to comprehend the diverse range of the poet's perception and reflection. The speaker is represented as a man who recognizes that compensation for the loss of his early wild sense of the interconnectedness of night and day, firsts and lasts, the many and the one, must in his maturity be found through indirect means, through exploration of multiple ways of re-creating the lost sense of felt harmony. Couplet structure and couplet rhetoric become the means through which conventional boundaries of perception are simultaneously established and superseded. The tension that exists at that boundary expresses an impulse much more characteristic of later, romantic and postromantic, prosodic experiments than of late-eighteenth-century prosodic practice: it expresses a "hunger," in Donald Wesling's terminology, for an unprecedented voice spurred by the self-conscious recognition that the present stage of literary history is overwritten with precedents.[49] In other words, Wordsworth uses his convention-fraught medium to hint at a voice—an original organizing power behind the forms and images—that is discernible through, but not entirely contained by, that medium.

The end of *Descriptive Sketches* is perhaps the best indication that Wordsworth sensed at some level the potential richness of such emblematic and allusive use of the couplet. In lines 792–809 Wordsworth personifies "Conquest, Avarice, and Pride," "Death and Famine," "Oppression," "Machination," "Persecution," "Ambition," and "Discord," all of which are to be overwhelmed by Freedom's "waves" in order to prepare for "a lovely birth! / . . . another earth." Subject, verse form,

and the personified figures themselves all place the passage in direct and obvious relationship with the end of Pope's *Windsor Forest,* which itself draws on Dryden's *Annus Mirabilis,* and on the common source of all three poems, Virgil's Fourth Eclogue.[50] In *Windsor Forest,* "Father Thames" prophesies the coming of a Pax Brittanica, following the Peace of Utrecht, when "Unbounded *Thames* shall flow for all Mankind." Then "fair *Peace* shall stretch from "Shore to Shore / Till Conquest cease, and Slav'ry be no more." In Father Thames's vision, *Discord* will dwell in "Brazen bonds" with "Gigantick *Pride,* pale *Terror,* gloomy *Care,* / And mad *Ambition."* Also banished to "deepest Hell" will be *"Vengeance," "Persecution," "Faction," "Rebellion,"* and *"Envy."* Pope breaks off his "Flight," reminding himself that such themes, concerning as they do ultimate powers of Fate and the "thoughts of Gods," are out of place in his "unambitious" pastoral.

Generic and conceptual similarities between the ending of *Descriptive Sketches* and Pope's ending set up a context for more important dissimilarities, dissimilarities conveyed to a significant degree by rhythmic means. Pope's Thames personified speaks of its "swelling Tide" as a flowing and unifying force, a symbol of Britain's destiny to lead in the establishment of a world community unified by peaceful trade. As is appropriate to such a symbolic speaker, the voice of Thames is rhythmically—as it is for Denham in his much-admired, much-imitated couplet from "Cooper's Hill"—the very type of the neoclassical ideal of vigorous yet restrained expression: "Though deep, yet cleare, though Gentle, yet not dull, / Strong without rage, without ore-flowing full" (ll. 191–92). The Thames as a reconciling and harmonizing force is most clearly demonstrated in Pope's closing portrait of that "deepest Hell" to which the allegorical enemies of harmonious peace will be confined in the new order. The victory over "barb'rous *Discord"* and her associates is very much the victory of the arts of civilization over the forces of anarchy, and, as is appropriate, the whole is couched in terms that make it rather a pleasant picture of order restored:

> In Brazen Bonds shall barb'rous *Discord* dwell:
> Gigantick *Pride*, pale *Terror*, gloomy *Care*,
> And mad *Ambition*, shall attend her there.
>
> (ll. 414–16)

Discordia, properly bound, is an anti-Queen. In her proper place, she becomes a force of order, subordinating to herself Pride, Terror, Care, and Ambition, who become her attendants. Circumscribed, cast into the

"deepest Hell," the whole cacophonous lot of anarchic powers becomes part of the celebratory harmony expressed through the unifying rhythms of Thames's voice. Discord "dwell[s]" and Vengeance "retires." Pope's vision, and Pope's couplet, has a place for these forces.

Wordsworth's vision of the *novus ordo saeclorum* is rather more disruptive, confrontational, and open ended than Pope's.[51] Instead of the unifying Thames victorious, the passage invokes an unlocalized personification of "Freedom," whose power is imaged as "waves" with the potential to overwhelm or to "break" on the haunts of the discordant allegorical figures:

> Oh give, great God, to Freedom's waves to ride
> Sublime o'er Conquest, Avarice, and Pride,
> To break, the vales where Death with Famine scow'rs,
> And dark Oppression builds her thick-ribb'd tow'rs;
> Where Machination her fell soul resigns,
> Fled panting to the centre of her mines;
> Where Persecution decks with ghastly smiles
> Her bed, his mountains mad Ambition piles;
> Where Discord stalks dilating, every hour
> And crouching fearful at the feet of Pow'r[.]
>
> (ll. 792–801)

The powers at war with Freedom are still very much active presences at the end of the poem: they "scow'r," "build," "deck," "pile," and "stalk," among other things. These forces are not formulated as the *discordia* necessary to a conventionally pleasant *concordia discors:* they create real disharmony, and threaten still more. The power that will defeat them must overwhelm them, like the Nile, to bring forth a new order. Any and all attempts to fix the limits of the new order is, at this point, presumptuous, as any "sceptered child of clay" will find if he dares to stem the tide: he will be "Swept . . . from th'affrighted shore" and will "With all his creatures sink—to rise no more" (808–9).

As is appropriate to such a vision, the rhythms of the end of *Descriptive Sketches,* unlike those of *Windsor Forest,* do not suggest closure and completion. Wordsworth's couplets, like his images of active discord within a prayer for regeneration, remain tense and complex to the end. The run-on phrases in the first lines of couplets in lines 792 and 798, for example, followed as they are by eccentric or multiple pauses in the adjoining lines, tend to focus attention on the phrase, rather than the line, as the chief structural unit: "give . . . to Freedom's waves to ride /

Sublime o'er Conquest"; "Persecution decks with ghastly smiles / Her bed." At the same time, the rhymes and line endings do continue to exert an influence (as, in the letter to Thelwall, Wordsworth will insist they must do). Units of thought and sonic markers of metrical dimensions are in constant, imbalanced, play.

Perhaps more effective than any other rhythmic device in the frustration of closure is the abrupt ending of the poem and the shift in tone that signals it. Immediately following this rhythmically vigorous, intellectually expansive, and revolutionary vision of power that must overwhelm any and all restraining forces, Wordsworth ends the poem with a homely, four-line address by the speaker to his "friend." Note especially how the enjambed penultimate line denies the final couplet the epigrammatic, summarizing role that might be expected in this metrical frame:

> To night, my friend, within this humble cot
> Be the dead load of mortal ills forgot,
> Renewing, when the rosy summits glow
> At morn, our various journey, sad and slow.
>
> (ll. 810–13)

The allusion to the ending of *Paradise Lost* (which is also, of course, a beginning) is obvious:[52]

> They hand in hand with wand'ring steps and slow
> Through Eden took their solitary way.
>
> (Book 12, 646–49)

Adam's vision of the historical fulfillment of the prophesy of the seed involves a similarly triumphant expression of confidence in the ultimate restoration of harmony, mingled with consciousness that the fact of redemption nevertheless does not obviate the reality of the discord itself. The "sad steps" still must be made as the prophesy becomes realized through, and not despite, the slow and intricate turnings of human history. Wordsworth's coda effectively returns the poem to the horizontal plane, the world of space and time, after the expansive and allegorical Mt. Pisgah vision of lines 792–809. Its open-endedness, which is placed allusively in direct relationship to the order and closure of Pope's prophetic vision, engages and challenges the neoclassical version of universal harmony, issuing a Miltonic caveat: "But wisest Fate says no, / This must not yet be so" ("Nativity Ode," ll. 150–51). In such a complex vision, discord is both genuine discord and a prelude to harmony; it is not

merely order misunderstood or harmony misheard. The summits are "rosy," but the journey is long and steep. Stylistically, the several voices of various passions that sound in Wordsworth's poem are finally, and appropriately, unsubordinated. They exist in and by virtue of complex tension between themselves and a metrical frame that continues to promise unity of effect.

"A STRONG TINCTURE OF THE NORTHERN BURR"

Still another kind of peculiarity of the versification of Wordsworth's couplet poems offers a different but related sort of challenge to the associations and conventions of couplet prosody. The rhymes in both poems are fairly frequently deficient, and occasionally they are deficient in ways that make them obtrusively idiosyncratic. *An Evening Walk* contains the following pairs of consonance rhymes: stood/flood (65–66), woods/floods (125–26), fro/brow (135–36), wood/flood (431–32), road/abroad (87–88), road/broad (271–72), fro/brow (135–36), brow/throw (331–32), bow'r/floor (227–28), weight/height (251–52), share/afar (253–54), and look/broke (255–56). *Descriptive Sketches* contains fewer pairs (in a poem that is twice as long), but the number is still significant: o'er-broods/woods (9–10), bow'r/poor (31–32), air/afar (51–52), deplores/bow'rs (78–79), woods/floods (134–35), load/abroad (203–4), brow/below (225–26), boughs/repose (229–30), hour/pour (332–33), and lost/coast (334–35). Many of these rhymes occur in conspicuous positions, several of them in the final couplet of a verse paragraph.

Wordsworth would defend Dryden's frequent use of imperfect rhyme (compared with Pope's precision) in his conversations with Klopstock in 1798.[53] And some of the latitude that Wordsworth allows himself with rhyme is certainly due either directly to Dryden's influence or to the influence of later poets, John Dyer for example, whose practice is more Drydenesque than Popean. A number of these consonance rhymes, too, probably would be considered conventionally to be full rhymes for syllables that are rhyme poor (wood/flood and its varieties, for example).[54] Even taking such factors into account, however, several rhyme pairs in *An Evening Walk* and *Descriptive Sketches* continue to give evidence of a consistently idiosyncratic practice. For example, in *An Evening Walk* (ll. 87–88), Wordsworth rhymes "road" with "abroad"; in lines 271–72, he rhymes "road" with "broad." In *Descriptive Sketches*, "load" rhymes with "abroad" (ll. 203–4) and "coast" with "lost" (ll. 334–35). Helen Darbishire long ago pointed to the rhyme of "note" and "thought" in "I Heard a

Thousand Blended Notes," as an instance of Wordsworth's Cumberland accent, suggesting that the pronunciation would be "I heard thousand blended *nawts* [nɒts]." Ben Ross Schneider notes another indication of this pronunciation in Wordsworth's rhyming of "thought" with "remote" in an early translation from Catullus ("The Death of Starling," *PW* 1:263).[55] Similarly, in the *Vale of Esthwaite*, Wordsworth had rhymed "float" with "thought" (ll. 557–58). And "sought" rhymes with "remote" in a fragment in Spenserian stanzas written probably in 1795–96.[56] The rhymes in *An Evening Walk* and *Descriptive Sketches* that occur on this vowel sound suggest that Wordsworth may have been assuming the pronunciation [ɒ:] for [əʊ]: "rawd" for "road," a typical northern pronunciation of this vowel sound, commonly found in contemporary Cumberland dialect poetry (note the dialect spelling of "snow" as "snaw"):

> What can it be keeps him frae me?
> The ways are nit sae lang
> And sleet and snaw are naught at aw
> If yen were fain to gang![57]

A hint of dialect pronunciation may also be evident in other rhyme pairs, for example in the rhyming of "height" with "weight," in lines 251–52, a rhyme that suggests a bending of the pronunciation of "height" [haɪt] toward [heɪt], a vowel shift like the one indicated by northern dialect spellings of phonetically analogous words, as in the following, which appear in Anderson's *Cumberland Ballads:* "leyfe" for life, "neyce" for nice, "seyde" for side, "weyfe" for wife.[58]

In *Wordsworth's Cambridge Education,* Schneider suggests that Wordsworth's "strong tincture of the northern *burr*, like a crust on wine" (in Hazlitt's description), would have been a continual reminder to the poet that he was an outsider in Cambridge during his time there (1787–91). It was "certain," says Schneider, "to single him out for ridicule" and to "restrict his social sphere" (41). The presence of these rhymes, when taken along with the simultaneous allusion and resistance to conventional couplet structure and rhetoric, with the poem's obvious peculiarities of syntax (for which see Legouis's catalogue, mentioned above) and especially with the frequent use of diction rare enough or provincial enough to require explanatory prose notes ("gill," "intake," "pike," "sugh," and the like), suggests in yet another way that the young Wordsworth was at least as willing to distinguish the variable voices of his poems from the loco-descriptive tradition as he was desirous to establish a relation between his poems and that tradition. Wordsworth implies in a letter of

1794 to William Mathews that the poems were published—"huddled up," he says—at least in part in compensation for or as a justification of his refusal to distinguish himself within the institutionalized codes and forms of the University.[59] Appropriately, his metrical style gives evidence of his striving for an idiom and an accent that would suggest the independence and idiosyncrasies of a perceptively original outsider even (or especially) while he restricted himself to the confines of a verse pattern firmly resistant to anything idiosyncratic and to a genre that had conventionally taken generalized perceptions of "general nature" as its subject.[60] The poems that Wordsworth published in 1793, that is, present themselves as the work of a particular kind of man: he is a northerner with a distinctly original view of the "variety" of natural appearance that his predecessors have overlooked and a man of deep and sometimes unruly feeling for natural beauty and human suffering. At the same time, he is a man of various reading in some ancient and much modern literature and, as the title page of each of the poems proclaims prominently, a "B.A. / Of St. John's, Cambridge."

In *The Prelude*, book 6, Wordsworth looks back on his motives (in *Descriptive Sketches* especially) as involving a "fond ambition of my heart." This ambition, he says, impelled him to attempt to "chant" in praise of Alpine scenery, even though as a "youth" he was as yet "undisciplined in Verse" (*13-Bk Prelude* 6.600–605). In the letter to Mathews cited above, Wordsworth apologizes for having sent forth the poems in so "imperfect a state" (*EY*, 120). It would be a mistake, however, to take such statements as merely dismissive and to conclude as many commentators have done that the style that Wordsworth would develop in his maturity—the style that he describes in *The Prelude* as a "more melodious Song / Where tones of learned Art and Nature mix'd / May frame enduring language"—is formed entirely in reaction to or as the antithesis of this early, "glittering," and relatively unchastened style. One clearly and enduringly Wordsworthian element in the poems is their use of verse form and variety of versification to call attention to an active, organizing intelligence that expresses itself through the give and take of passion with linguistic and poetic forms. The peculiarities of this verse demand that attention be paid not only to the "thing / Contemplated . . ." but to "the Mind and Man / Contemplating":

> . . . and who and what he was,
> The transitory Being that beheld
> This Vision, when and where and how he lived—
>
> ("Prospectus," ll. 847–51)

The mind on display in *An Evening Walk* and *Descriptive Sketches* is young, ambitious for poetic fame, overawed by glittering phrases and rhythmic pomp, and more passively influenced by direct sensory impressions than is the Wordsworth whose later descriptive and discursive poetry will aim to express what the "blended might" of mind and nature might accomplish. It is also vigorous, complexly allusive, willing to engage in revisionary modifications of literary convention, intensely sensitive to modifications of perception under the influence of passion, and ambitious to create distinctive and impressive verbal music. In short, these early poems express the fluxes and refluxes of a particular kind of mind under particular circumstances.

When Wordsworth recommends these poems in 1801 to Miss Taylor, he claims them—for all of their dissimilarity from his more mature work—as parts of that work, expressive of a stage of development of the mind of the "transitory being" at work on *The Recluse*. They find their place in his corpus because they are—in spite of and because of their harshness—expressive of the effects upon the mind of an early passion for powerful and various sensual impressions, whether those impressions are natural sights and sounds or the sound and rhythm of words in tuneful order.

In addition to an early interest in the use of peculiarities of versification for expressive effects, *An Evening Walk* and *Descriptive Sketches* also demonstrate, albeit in exaggerated form, strong tendencies toward affective and emblematic versification. The juxtaposition of dissimilar voices in a single metrical frame and the use of conventional forms in unconventional ways are Wordsworthian trademarks. Such effects are grounded in part in his theory of poetry as a catalyst for, as well as an emblem and expression of, active perception and creation of relationship among disparate elements of experience. In Wordsworth's view, the poem does not stand aloof, quietly self-contained, enjoying its own perfections and symmetries. It does not enjoy a privileged status as something distinct in kind from all other forms of human communication and interrelationship (as it does for many contemporary and subsequent organic theorists whose work would influence so heavily the development of thinking about poetic style in England).[61] On the contrary, the "same human blood" flows through all such forms, and the poem is distinguished chiefly on the basis of a higher degree of organization and contextualization of its many elements, including its rhythmic and sonic elements. Accomplished metrical writing makes the good poem an order of words in time to which a reader will wish to return repeatedly, because the subtleties of the ordering continue to suggest that there is more in the

words than meets the eye, or the mind's eye, alone. An uncommon degree of organization brought to bear upon linguistic minutiae common to all discourse helps to provide pleasure by engaging the mind in the fundamentally poetic activity of discerning similitude in dissimilitude, through which it gains instruction in the nature of the organization and multiplicity of all perception.

An Evening Walk and *Descriptive Sketches* are structurally disunified poems. They read in parts like catalogues of sense impressions and responses, or like anthologies of fine phrases from Thomson, Beattie, Milton, and William Wordsworth, B.A. The use of a single and insistently regular verse pattern, however, provides an elementary kind of cohesion, asserting through rhythmic means the cohesiveness of the parts, however resistant to logical integration they may seem. The relationship between the fixed form and the loose structure of the poems functions as a kind of impetus to the reader to participate in fundamentally poetic activity, as he or she establishes points of contact among the seemingly disunified parts and discovers sources of variety within a verse form that seems at first so inflexible and invarious. Part of the reason *An Evening Walk* and *Descriptive Sketches* seem so harsh is that they demand, as Coleridge put it, more attention to such matters than this kind of poetry has a right to demand. But it is the intensity of the demand, not the demand itself, that makes the poems unlike what is to come in Wordsworth's mature style. That they make issues of coherence and relationship, unity and diversity so obviously and so insistently a dimension of their meaning is part of what makes them immature work; but the fact that they require attention to such elements makes the complexity of their music entirely characteristic of the poetry of Wordsworth's maturity.

Wordsworth's use in these poems of a language more elevated and more "adorned" than that of common life expresses the young poet's desire for "something loftier," for a kind of communication more adequate to his sense of the mind's vast power than is the idiom either of common life or of contemporary poetry. Beginning in 1797–98, Wordsworth's verse will take less insistently labored, less-elaborate outward forms, but it will continue to explore, through many "turnings intricate" the question of how far the language and sensuous forms of poetry can and cannot embody the conceptions of a "mighty Mind" whose home is "with infinitude" without swallowing up into an abstract, univocal, and static whole the "very world which is the world / Of all of us."[62]

4

Varieties of Rhyme
The Stanzaic Verse of the *Lyrical Ballads*

THE METRICAL VARIETY OF *LYRICAL BALLADS*

The tendency among commentators to dismiss as intrinsically uninteresting the prosodic features of Wordsworth's stanzaic verse, or to neglect those features entirely, originates in an evaluative assumption largely irrelevant to Wordsworth's own aims and practices. This assumption—that metrical interest resides chiefly or solely in overt innovation, insistent unconventionality, or expressive form breaking—underlies Saintsbury's extraordinary and influential dismissal of Wordsworth as the greatest English poet ever to have written prosodically negligible verse. The assumption is alive and well, too, in Robert Mayo's pronouncement that the *Lyrical Ballads* "could hardly be represented as more than a very limited prosodic experiment." Wordsworth's poems, says Mayo, "do not exhibit revolutionary or even surprising tendencies."[1]

The arguments pursued in the preceding chapters of this book have been designed in part to suggest that such familiarly romantic notions about prosody and verse form are not Wordsworth's assumptions. To say that Wordsworth's prosodic effects are "limited" because they exhibit few surface pyrotechnics may be helpful, but only if the aim is to distinguish them from those of poets such as Blake, Swinburne, or Whitman—who consciously seek in various ways to challenge or to redefine the principles on which the English poetic line had been written since Chaucer—or from those of Shelley, Tennyson, or Hardy, whose widely various and frequently original stanza forms constitute another kind of challenge to conventions of rhythmic and sonic organization. To stop with the observation, however, is to say very little that is germane

to Wordsworth's own aims and achievement within the limitations of the metrical tradition he accepts.

The stanzaic verse of *Lyrical Ballads* is representative of Wordsworth's practice throughout the corpus in that it achieves a significant variety of prosodic effects through subtle adaptation and reformulation of patterns firmly embedded in a four-hundred-year-old tradition. That Wordsworth tends not to break molds or dispense with traditional forms, either in *Lyrical Ballads* or throughout the corpus, is worth noting. Of the nearly nine hundred poems in the *Poetical Works* (1849–50), only nineteen are written in irregular forms, and almost all of Wordsworth's stanzas and verse forms either have precedents in earlier English poetry or are combinations or adaptations of traditional lines and stanzas.[2] But it is finally the minutiae of Wordsworth's "limited" experiment—an experiment that depends on tensions between new and old, strange and familiar, spontaneous impulse and fixed form, the syntax of "natural" expression and the organization of "art"—that demands attention if we are to hear Wordsworth's many voices. To approach the *Lyrical Ballads* with a sense of the subtleties made possible by strict adherence to the rules of accentual-syllabic verse (the subject of chapters 1 and 2), and with an appreciation of Wordsworth's own pervasive sensitivity to expressive, associative, rhetorical, and emblematic possibilities of verse forms embedded in an historical and cultural context (chapters 2 and 3), is to enable oneself to perceive the considerable extent to which these poems, both individually and as a collection, are powerful and challenging not despite their prosodic features (as is frequently assumed) but because of them. This approach may also suggest some of the ways in which Wordsworth's stanzaic verse throughout the corpus uses these conventional structures and their associations to advantage.

The 1798 first edition of the *Lyrical Ballads* is a study in contrasts. The book contains work by two poets who acknowledged that they held divergent opinions on fundamental questions of poetic theory, including the question of the nature and functions of meter. The title presented the contemporary reader with a perplexing juxtaposition of genres and with a vague distinction between "lyrical ballads" and "a few other poems." Subjects range from the midnight ride of an idiot boy to a poet's meditation on his past and present creative powers, from an impassioned monologue spoken by a dying Indian woman to a relatively prosaic conversation between a father and his son about the merits of Kilve compared with Liswyn farm.

Approached with attention to subtle distinctions, the collection is no less diverse prosodically. The stanza and versification of *The Rime of the*

Ancient Mariner (hereafter *Rime*), for example, sets that poem off from the remainder of the poems in the book as surely as does its archaic diction and its supernaturalism.[3] As the only poem in the *Lyrical Ballads* (in all of its editions) that employs consistently throughout its length techniques of versification in imitation of the prosody of popular balladry, it would be prosodically much more at home in Percy's *Reliques* than in the *Lyrical Ballads*. The $a_4b_3c_4b_3$ stanza used in the *Rime* is unique among the poems in the book, as is the pervasive use of double offbeats (two syllables between strong stresses, or "trisyllabic substitution"). Double offbeats help to create in the *Rime* the insistent, chanting pulse characteristic of genuine ballad rhythm: their use encourages a reader to compensate for the potentially disruptive effect of variable numbers of syllables between beats by equalizing both the degree of stress and the elapsed time between strong stresses. At the other end of the prosodic spectrum (and at the other end of the book) stands the remarkably subtle blank verse of "Lines Composed a Few Miles above Tintern Abbey," in which a wide range of speech motives—conversational, expository, didactic, and impassioned lyric—is embodied in a flexible and uninsistently structured medium, able to accommodate the rhythms of individualized speech and impassioned song alike.

Between these two prosodic extremes are twenty-one poems in twelve different verse forms. Five of these twenty-one (including three of the four contributed by Coleridge to the collection) are, like "Tintern Abbey," in blank verse. The remaining sixteen are composed in eleven different rhymed stanzas ranging in length from four to eleven lines. Three different forms of four-line stanzas appear in addition to the ballad stanza used in the *Rime* (for symbols used to describe stanzas here and throughout the present study, see page 16, "Descriptions of Stanza Forms"):

$a_4b_3a_4b_3$:
    "We Are Seven"
    "The Tables Turned"
  parts of:
    "Lines Written at a Small Distance from My House" ("To My Sister")
    "Lines Written in Early Spring"
    "Expostulation and Reply"
aba_4b_3:
    "Anecdote for Fathers"
  parts of:
    "Lines Written at a Small Distance from My House" ("To My Sister")

"Lines Written in Early Spring"
"Expostulation and Reply"

$a_4b_3a_4b_3$ (anapests):
"The Convict"

One poem, "The Idiot Boy" uses a five-line stanza in the form $abccb_4$, apparently invented by Wordsworth and used by him also in *Peter Bell* (composed 1798; published 1819).[4]

Three poems employ eight-line forms that are built by combining various modifications of a four-line stanza:

$a\_ba\_bcdcd_4$:
"Goody Blake and Harry Gill"

$aba_4b_3c_4d_{-3}c_4d_{-3}$:
"Simon Lee"

$ababcd\_cd\__4$:
"Lines Written While Sailing in a Boat at Evening"

A nine-line, Spenserian, stanza is used in "The Female Vagrant," an excerpt from *Salisbury Plain* (bulk of composition c. 1793–95; published as *Guilt and Sorrow* in 1842).

Two closely related variations of a ten-line stanza, apparently invented by Wordsworth, appear in three different poems. Again, as in the case of the eight-line stanzas listed above, these forms are built up of common and recognizable smaller units (couplets and quatrains):

$aabbcdcdee_4$:
"The Mad Mother"
"The Complaint of a Forsaken Indian Woman"

$aabbcde_4d_3ff_4$:
"The Last of the Flock"

In "The Thorn" Wordsworth uses the longest stanza in the collection. This eleven-line form ($abc_4b_3deff_4e_3gg_4$) is, like the ten-line forms, built from smaller substructures. As was noted in chapter 2, the stanza apparently was invented by Wordsworth, but bears some resemblance to certain odic stanzas found in mid- to late-eighteenth-century verse.

Such a number and variety of stanzas is correlative with and expressive of the collection's well-documented variety of poetic voices.[5] Ten poems seek to represent more than one voice, either through dramatic presen-

tation or quoted speech.[6] Three others ("The Nightingale," "The Tables Turned," "Tintern Abbey") identify an interlocutor, thereby placing the speaker of the poem in a context that makes his speech specific to an occasion, place, or relationship. Four of the poems are either mostly or entirely representations of women's voices ("The Mad Mother," "The Female Vagrant," "The Foster Mother," "The Complaint of the Forsaken Indian Woman"), and two more incorporate feminine voices into narrative or dialogue ("We Are Seven" and "The Idiot Boy"). Of the poems that presumably represent male voices, three are devoted to the speech of obviously dramatic or narrative characters—the *Rime*, "The Thorn," and "The Last of the Flock." These, along with the poems representing women's voices, make seven poems in all obviously undertaken for the purposes of exploring "fluxes and refluxes" of a mind or minds other than or in addition to the poet's own. The chief voices in at least six other poems are arguably presented as dramatic, whether they represent characters different from the poet or purposefully limited aspects of the poet's perceptions, feelings, and concerns: "Goody Blake and Harry Gill," "Simon Lee," "The Idiot Boy," "We Are Seven," "Anecdote for Fathers," and "The Convict." Multiplicity of form and perspective, it would seem, is an essential part of the texture of the collection.

Such multiplicity is also a predictable consequence of the attitudes toward poetic form and rhythm that Wordsworth may be presumed to have been developing throughout the mid- to late 1790s (in work on the *Salisbury Plain* poems, *The Borderers*, the *Ruined Cottage*, as well as in work directly toward *Lyrical Ballads*) and that he would set forth in detail in the 1800 and 1802 prefaces. The volume of 1798 clearly reveals its author's interest in using the resources of metrical art to embody movements of mind and relationships among diverse types of minds (or facets of a single variable mind) in a variety of situations. All of the poems in *Lyrical Ballads* are metered, and all (except for the *Rime*) obey the same general accentual-syllabic rules of metrical arrangement. At the same time each is significantly dissimilar from the others in the minutiae involved in the rhythmic and sonic realization of its metrical patterns. "Lines Written upon the Thames" and "Goody Blake and Harry Gill" are, as was pointed out in chapter 2, metrically very similar. The differences between their realizations of the metrical pattern—for example, in "Glide gently, thus forever glide" and "Like a loose casement in the wind"—are made evident (and measurable) through metrical similarity. That similarity and dissimilarity, along with the thoroughgoing operation of the principle in the similarity and difference at work in the relationship between the language of plain speech and of

metered verse, is all the difference that Wordsworth requires in order to produce "that sort of pleasure and that quantity of pleasure" that "a Poet may rationally endeavour to impart" (Preface to *LB; Prose* 1:119).

The preponderance of evidence suggests that the development of *Lyrical Ballads* (1798) as a collection was spurred at least as much by financial exigency as by purposeful art. Such an observation, however, does not at all undermine the argument that the book's stylistic diversity expresses a developing Wordsworthian poetic principle.[7] Whatever the mixture of financial worries, theoretical divisions of labor, and simple chance that finally determined the choices that made the book what it is, the poems make up, objectively, a formally diverse collection, exhibiting a range of significant variations on a simple set of prosodic rules and structures. Wordsworth's composition of the poems themselves, together with his part in having them published under the unifying description of the Advertisement, make the book a concrete expression of his attitudes concerning metrical art. This much having been said, however, Wordsworth's conscious interest in making his collection significantly diverse in metrical characteristics is certainly more clearly evident in 1800 than in 1798. In 1800, the principle of metrical similitude and dissimilitude is pursued with vigor, contributing substantially to the poems both as individual expressions and as parts in a growing poetic corpus that Wordsworth increasingly and self-consciously regarded as occupying an important place within the English poetic tradition.[8]

In addition to rearranging the contents of volume 1, dividing "Lines Written While Sailing in a Boat at Evening" into two poems—"Remembrance of Collins" and "Written on the Thames"—dropping his juvenile anapestic poem "The Convict," and adding Coleridge's lyric "Love" (in the stanza abc_4b_3), Wordsworth published in 1800 forty-one additional poems. Included among these new poems are thirteen in blank verse, the presence of which gives evidence of Wordsworth's growing interest and fluency in blank verse as his chief medium for a wide range of types of poems. The work in blank verse encompasses short and rhetorically conventional inscriptions, specimens of the narrative-lyrical-reflective verse of the kind that would eventually constitute *The Prelude* (in "There Was a Boy," for example), and long narratives and dramatic-narratives ("Michael" and "The Brothers"). Dorothy Wordsworth notes in a 1798 letter to Mary Hutchinson that Wordsworth had suddenly, during a period of intense work on *The Ruined Cottage*, begun to write with much greater "facility . . . as to the *mechanism* of poetry" (*EY*, 200): the blank verse of the 1800 *Lyrical Ballads* suggests through its sheer bulk and diversity that work on *The Prelude* in Germany (1798–99) had furthered

Wordsworth's mastery of the form that he would later call "infinitely the most difficult metre to manage" (*LY* 2:58).

These fifteen-hundred lines of blank verse pervade the second volume, appearing as if by design near the beginning, near the middle, and, emphatically (as in the 1798 volume), at the end. Blank-verse poems appear in volume 2 as the second, third, fourteenth, fifteenth, twenty-second, twenty-sixth, thirty-first, and thirty-sixth to forty-first (last) poems. In the revised order of volume 1, the six blank-verse poems are similarly seeded throughout: in 1798 they had fallen as the second, third, fourth, fourteenth, twentieth, and twenty-third (last) poems; in 1800, they occupy the third, sixth, seventh, fourteenth, seventeenth, and twenty-fourth (last) positions. That the blank verse tends also to be used in those of Wordsworth's poems in which a poet (rather than an Indian woman, an ancient mariner, or little Barbara Lewthewaite) is represented as speaking or narrating in his own person, suggests that these poems may be regarded as formal keynotes. They help to provide a kind of cohesion through periodic returns to a clearly recognized fixed form and to a voice easily associated with the unifying (but certainly not univocal) consciousness of the collection.

At the same time, this marked tendency toward formal cohesion is accompanied in the remainder of the second volume by a strong countertendency toward even more variety than is in evidence in the first volume. The twenty-eight rhymed poems in volume 2 employ sixteen different verse forms. Of these, only three are repeated from volume 1: (1) the four-line stanza $a_4b_3a_4b_3$ (after blank verse, the most common form in *Lyrical Ballads* as a whole) is used in "Lucy Gray" and in a number of poems that would henceforth be associated with one another as "Lucy poems"—"Strange fits of passion," "She dwelt among th'untrodden ways," "A slumber did my spirit seal"—and as "Matthew poems"—"The Two April Mornings" and "The Fountain"; (2) the five-line stanza of "Andrew Jones," a poem that is an overflow from composition on *Peter Bell*, in the same stanza as "The Idiot Boy" ($abccb_4$); (3) the eleven-line stanza of "The Thorn" ($abc_4b_3deff_4e_3gg_4$) used also in "The Idle-Shepherd Boys" and, with slight variation ($aba_4b_3cdee_4d_3ff_4$), in "A Fragment" (later "The Danish Boy").

The thirteen verse forms introduced in volume 2 of the 1800 collection are listed below. Note that Wordsworth's experiment here encompasses not only stanza pattern and rhyme scheme but also basic rhythmic pattern, as in the "trochaic" and "anapestic" verse:

Tetrameter couplets (and quatrains intermixed):
"A whirl-blast from behind the hill"

$abab_4$:
  "If Nature, for a favorite Child"
  "A Poet's Epitaph"
$a\_bc\_b_4$ (trochaics):
  "Song for the Wandering Jew"
$aabb_4$ (anapests):
  "The Two Thieves"
  "The Childless Father"
  "A Character"
  "Poor Susan"
$abab_5$:
  "Hart-Leap Well"
$aabb_6$:
  "The Pet-Lamb"
$a_4b_3cc_4b_3$ (anapests):
  "Written in Germany"
$aa_4b_3cc_4b_3$:
  "Ruth"
  "Three years she grew in sun and shower"
$aa_4b_3cc_4b_3$ (anapests):
  "Rural Architecture"
$a_4b_{-3}c_4b_{-3}dd_4ee_3$:
  "Ellen Irwin"
$ab_5c_4b_3c_5d_4d_3c_6$:
  "'Tis said, that some have died for love" (framed by a twelve-line stanza and a blank-verse ending)
$ababccd\_d\_4$ (trochaics):
  "To a Sexton"
$a_4b_3a_4b_3ccdee_4d_3$:
  "The Oak and the Broom"
  "The Waterfall and the Eglantine"

The two volumes of the 1800 edition of *Lyrical Ballads*, then, contain sixty-five poems written in twenty-five different verse forms. Excluding the eighteen poems in blank verse, the remaining forty-seven poems employ twenty-four different patterns. The extent of the formal variety of the collection may easily be gauged by comparison with Southey's *Annual Anthology* (1799), a collection of poems by various hands in which great stylistic variety would be expected: the anthology, although containing more than twice the number of poems composed in forms other

than blank verse (ninety-one), employs only six more verse forms (thirty) than are on display in *Lyrical Ballads*.[9]

From the standpoint of purely metrical concerns, the two chief movements in the 1800 revision and expansion may be seen as exhibiting a complementary tension; a unifying tendency is evidenced in the number of blank-verse poems and in the spacing of them throughout the collection, while at the same time the proliferation of various stanza forms provides a great deal of rhythmic and formal diversity, once again (as in 1798) serving in part to objectify a number of represented voices (the distraught lover in "'Tis said, that some have died for love," the child of the "Pet Lamb," the shepherd of "Hart Leap Well," for example). The range and variety of stanza forms tends to make multiplicity of expression itself an essential part of the experience of reading. At the same time, the sense of a pervasive authorial point of view, embodied in a recurrent form that functions as a rhythmic keynote, works against the impulse to read the collection as merely diverse. The collection is not an anthology but a significantly various and, as Wordsworth would have it, purposeful body of work. Beginning in 1807, of course, Wordsworth's interest in presenting his shorter poems as integral parts of a multiplex whole would find more obvious expression in the categories and classes he began to employ in *Poems, in Two Volumes* and later codified in *Poems* (1815) and subsequent editions. In the 1814 Preface to the *Excursion*, he would use the figure of a Gothic church to describe the relationship between the massive blank-verse *Recluse* and the many and various other poems. If *The Recluse* is the "body" of the church, says Wordsworth, then his other work may be regarded by the "attentive Reader" as so many "little cells, oratories, and sepulchral recesses" (*Prose* 3:5–6). Each poem is both an entity complete unto itself and also a part of the larger whole. The presence of so many variously shaped yet rhythmically related forms in *Lyrical Ballads* suggests that Wordsworth's impulses in this direction are already at work in 1800.[10]

In the following discussions of representative effects in the stanzaic poems of *Lyrical Ballads*, my chief purpose is to define and evaluate characteristic kinds of metrical complexity in relation to Wordsworth's overall concerns in the collection. The deceptively simple question that guides the approach to each example is *What does the choice of this meter and its particular use contribute to this poem?* Beyond this question, I have sought to trace some of the more important rhythmic and sonic means through which the poems of the *Lyrical Ballads* encourage the kind of active reading Wordsworth regards as indispensable to the full

experience and proper understanding of his poems. Given the absolute pervasiveness of the effects in which I am interested—no syllable is free from metrical arrangement—I of course make no claim to exhaustive analysis of even the most apparent of those effects that an impassioned recitation brings into play. My aim is to make explicit some of the complexity that such reading communicates implicitly in the interest of showing how metrical craft contributes to the enduring power of the *Lyrical Ballads*.

SPEAKERS FROM AFAR: LONGER STANZAS, MEDIATION, AND SYMPATHY IN "THE COMPLAINT OF A FORSAKEN INDIAN WOMAN," "THE MAD MOTHER," AND "THE THORN"

The purposes and effects of Wordsworth's stanzaic choices and uses are more apparent in some poems than in others. Some longer stanzas, for example, tend obviously to be used to mediate between a reader and poetic voices that are in one way or another likely to be regarded as particularly unusual or unsettling. In "The Last of the Flock," the narrator meets a man weeping "in the public roads" and, in making explicit his consciousness that the experience is unusual, marks the man and his tale as outlandish:

> In distant countries I have been,
> And yet I have not often seen
> A healthy man, a man full grown,
> Weep in the public roads alone.
>
> (ll. 1–4)[11]

In "The Complaint of a Forsaken Indian Woman," a culturally and geographically distant figure speaks out of a sense of intense and blank solitude. The speaker of "The Mad Mother" is presented as a distant figure not only because of her aberrant state of mind but also because she has come "from afar." In all three poems, speakers express profoundly painful thoughts and feelings in direct speech, whether through monologue (in the "Complaint" and "The Mad Mother") or through quotation in a narrative context ("The Last of the Flock"):

> My child! they gave thee to another,
> A woman who was not thy mother.

> When from my arms my babe they took
> On me how strangely did he look!
>   ("Complaint," ll. 31–34)

> —Where art thou gone my own dear child?
> What wicked looks are those I see?
> . . . .
> If thou art mad, my pretty lad,
> Then I must be for ever sad.
>   ("The Mad Mother," ll. 85–86, 89–90)

> God cursed me in my sore distress,
> I prayed, yet every day I thought
> I loved my children less[.]
>   ("Last of the Flock," ll. 86–88)

The poems are obviously related, then, in subject and presentation. The "Complaint" and "The Last of the Flock" are placed together in 1800 as the fourth and fifth poems in the collection; all three poems are classified as *Poems Founded on the Affections* in *Poetical Works*. The fact that the poems employ similar stanza forms suggests further that they are to be read as a group and that Wordsworth tended to regard this kind of stanza as especially suitable for direct expressions of unusually intense passions of loss and isolation. (The only other poem in *Poetical Works* to employ this stanza is "The Emigrant Mother" [published 1807], which represents the speech of another speaker "from afar," a French woman "dwelling upon English ground" in "a lonely Hamlet" who cares for an English child while she laments her separation from her own infant; this poem, too, appears among the *Poems Founded on the Affections*.)

The reasons behind Wordsworth's use of this metrical frame are in this case fairly easy to discern. As Wordsworth says in the Preface to *Lyrical Ballads*, poetic treatments of suffering, in order to effect the properly poetic purpose of establishing relations out of sympathetic feeling, must produce an overbalance of pleasure. Meter is an important—perhaps even the most important—means through which such overbalance may be produced: "There can be little doubt but that more pathetic situations and sentiments, that is, those which have a greater proportion of pain connected with them, *may be endured in metrical composition, especially in rhyme, than in prose*" (*Prose* 1:147; emphasis added). It is because of this power of meter, says Wordsworth, that a reader will read and, what is

more important, reread with pleasure intensely pathetic speeches in verse drama (Wordsworth's example is Shakespeare), whereas similar speeches in prose fiction (in *Clarissa*, for example) or prose drama (Edward Moore's *The Gamester*) will tend actually to cause pain and to discourage rereading. Even Shakespeare's "most pathetic scenes" never take his audience "beyond the bounds of pleasure." Wordsworth traces this power of meter to "small, but continual and regular impulses of pleasurable surprise from the metrical arrangement" (*Prose* 1:147).

The ten-line stanza that Wordsworth created for these poems presents itself, through its length and complexity of rhyme scheme (aabbcdcdee), as an obviously superadded, even schematic, frame. Constructed out of simple combinations (in couplets and quatrains) of the four-beat line, the stanza employs the most fundamental, common, and therefore (at least potentially) most rhythmically predictable and reassuring of all English lines. Such characteristics help provide what Wordsworth calls an "intertexture" of pleasurable feeling. The stanza is rhetorically useful as a means for bringing a reader into relationship with expressions of feelings with which he may be presumed to have no prior ground of sympathy and from which he may, under less carefully managed circumstances, recoil. The pleasure created by the rhythmic movement of syllables, by the sounds of words themselves, by the repetition and patterning of those sounds, and by the power of meter to place the passion at a suitable distance by "throw[ing] a sort of half-consciousness of unsubstantial existence over the whole composition" (*Prose* 1:147) help to make complexly pleasurable what might otherwise be disgusting or indulgently sentimental.

At the same time, the prosody of these stanzas—especially their particularly regular and insistent realization of the fundamental four-beat rhythm, their normally end-stopped lines, and their frequent use of repetition—tends to create an incantatory tone that makes the verse an expressively appropriate embodiment of characteristics of a mind under the influence of such feelings. The following, from the "Complaint," provides a good example:

> My fire is dead: it knew no pain;
> Yet is it dead, and I remain.
> All stiff with ice the ashes lie;
> And they are dead, and I will die.
> When I was well, I wished to live,
> For clothes, for warmth, for food, and fire[.]
> ("Complaint," ll. 11–16)

One of the chief functions of metrical art is of course the ability it gives the poet to build into the lines, through rhythmic tension and sonic patterning, a sense of the very physiology of a particular emotion (see the discussion of Wordsworth's "Sonnet on Seeing Helen Maria Williams Weep at a Tale of Distress," above). Whereas in prose the writer much more frequently must resort to descriptive language to direct attention to emotional overtones, the poet, and particularly the poet writing in the accentual-syllabic tradition, has means at his disposal for requiring and directing that "animated or impassioned recitation" of language without which Wordsworth says his poetry cannot properly be understood.[12] Speech organs may be more or less tense or relaxed, allowed to range freely among possible combinations of sound or constrained to a few repeated patterns. In the passage quoted above, the balance created by the division of three out of the first four lines into two halves of two beats each, the repetition of "dead" and "die," the pointed contrast and comparison between third- and first-person pronouns ("it is dead / I remain"; "they are dead / I will die") and between present and future—and present and past—verb tenses all create an insistent pattern based on binary opposition, expressing the intensity of the speaker's awareness of her own precarious position on the border between life and death. The phrases "My fire" and "stiff with ice" become, through patterned juxtaposition with the statements made by the speaker about herself ("I remain," "I will die"), applicable both to the fire and ashes themselves and to the speaker, whose own heat wanes and who will soon lie "stiff with ice." Alternately resigning herself to her death in solitude and kindling in her desire for one last means of human contact ("Too soon, my friends, you went away; / For I had many things to say" [ll. 49–50]), the movements of the mind are made palpable in the verse itself through tension between intensely painful sentiment and rhythmic, sonic, and syntactic order.

The artful patterning of this speech, then, may be seen as simultaneously a means for creating an effect necessary to poetic pleasure and an attempt to represent how mind and language act and react upon one another in a moment of intense suffering. The pleasure derived by the reader from the poetic representation of this mind in this set of circumstances is not different in kind from the speaker's own relationship to her own speech. The poem suggests that tensions between pleasure and pain played out through the medium of language are not merely elements of rhetorical craft, but are actually part of the means through which nature preserves the mind burdened by intense suffering. The poet's ability to embody such complexity of pleasure and pain—to allow a

reader to feel it in the very physical impulses of speech—is a chief means through which he may elicit sympathy for a speaker who is geographically, culturally, and emotionally distant from the English reader.

The double function, at once expressive and rhetorical, of Wordsworth's ten-line stanza would seem to make the form a particularly appropriate vehicle for the "Mad Mother." In that poem, the obviously wrought patterns created by meter and stanza form embody a monologue that the reader is to understand is intermittently spoken and sung:

> She talked and sung the woods among;
> And it was in the English tongue.
>
> (ll. 9–10)

Various devices of rhythm and stanza form aid the reader in imagining the monologue in the second through tenth stanzas of the poem to be—as literary representations of madness so often are—a broken song. The internal rhyme in the penultimate line of each stanza is the most obvious of these devices, providing at the end of each stanza a structural repetition insistent enough to allow it to function—almost—as a refrain:[13]

> My pretty <u>thing</u>! then thou shalt <u>sing</u>,
> As merry as the birds in <u>spring</u>.
>
> (ll. 59–60)

> If thou art <u>mad</u>, my pretty <u>lad</u>
> Then I must be forever <u>sad</u>.
>
> (ll. 89–90; emphasis added)

In the final stanza, the internally rhymed penultimate line also employs double offbeats:

> Now laugh and be gay, to the woods away!
> o B ŏ B ŏ   B o B
> And there, my babe; we'll live for aye.
>
> (ll. 99–100)

Double offbeats form a pattern quite common in song lyrics, in which musical accompaniment supplies the beats in relation to which the varying numbers of syllables in a line or phrase are performed. The rarity of this kind of variation in Wordsworth's verse (even in tetrameters) makes it particularly noticeable and effective. Here, it functions in con-

junction with the hint of a refrain to emphasize for expressive purposes the songlike patterns of the woman's speech.

It may be worthwhile to note that both of these devices make use of traditional and popular poetry and song in a way typical of Wordsworth throughout his work: they function to bring the "Mad Mother" into significant relation with oral and song traditions, while not submitting the poem's prosody and verse pattern to actual imitation of the practices of those traditions. Just as Wordsworth is interested in approximating the language of everyday speech while maintaining significant distance from it, so his tendency is in the *Lyrical Ballads* to allude to—suggest but not actually employ—the rhythms of popular poetry and song. The similarities between the "Mad Mother" and "Lady Anne Bothwell's Lament" (in Percy's *Reliques* [II.ii.13]) have often been remarked on;[4] both are written in stanzas of four-beat couplets, and both represent the speech of an abandoned mother to her "babe." But differences are as important as similarities in understanding the significance of the relationship. The writer of the Scottish song employs a refrain ("Balow, my babe, lye still and sliepe! / It grieves me sair to see thee weipe") in a song that is essentially a moral caveat ("I wish all maides be warnd by mee"). In Wordsworth's poem, the poet suggests rhythmically, through the shadow of the refrain structure and a hint of the prosody appropriate to song, a relationship between this speaker and the many abandoned women and suffering outcasts who haunt the song tradition. His decision not to employ throughout his poem the actual style and rhythmic characteristics of that tradition, however, allows him to pursue a considerably more complex exploration of the psychology of abandonment, grief, and maternal love than is common in popular song. Wordsworth's rhythms assist in the creation of a poem that suggests and simultaneously avoids a presentation of the woman merely as a negative moral exemplum; the poem demands much more active participation and therefore more genuine sympathy from the reader than would be desirable in the "Lament."

The particular kind and degree of madness exhibited in the speaker of "The Mad Mother" is expressed in part through the very fact of her lapses in and out of song. Her speech, which is every bit as patterned as that of the Indian woman in "The Complaint," tends to suggest sporadic attempts to create harmony where none exists, as if in the telling of her tale she gains some measure of comfort, even though she speaks only to deaf trees and her uncomprehending infant. As the speaker herself says, there is a use in measured language which only those who suffer intensely can know. Singing about sadness is often the best way to make it bearable: "And I am happy when I sing / Full many a sad and doleful

thing" (ll. 13–14). As in "The Complaint," Wordsworth organizes the speech and song of the mad mother in order to make it both an index of a mind and a source of pleasure in and of itself. The highly patterned use of alliteration and assonance, again suggestive of the lyrical nature of the speech, provides a particularly important counterweight to the painful substance of her words. (Brackets above the line mark occurrences of alliteration; those below mark instances of assonance:)

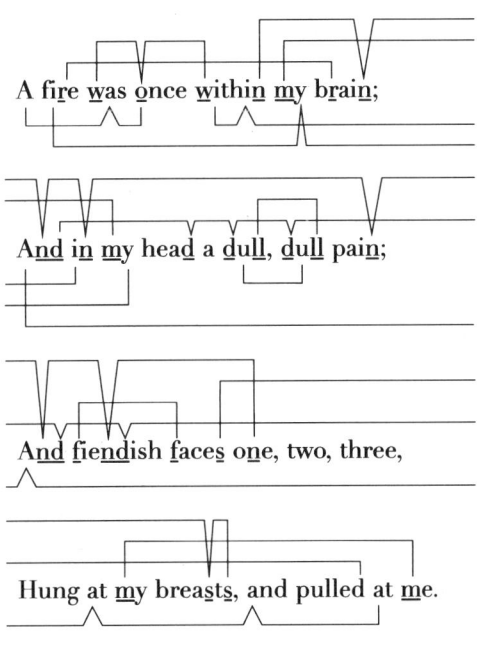

(ll. 21–24)

The expressive quality of the stanza (the appropriateness of its rhythmic and sonic patterns for a speaker who consoles herself through song) is thus meshed, as in the "Complaint," with the power of its artifice to temper for the reader the painful substance of the words. Meter and sound allow the reader and the mad mother to share a common ground of feeling: each is able to derive pleasure from "sad and doleful thing[s]" couched in measured language.

Another kind of attempt at rhythmic mediation between reader and speaker is Wordsworth's somewhat incongruous use in "The Thorn" of an eleven-line stanza that carries closer associations with odic poetry than might commonly be thought appropriate for the representation of the garrulous speech of a superstitious, repetitious, and intellectually

slow speaker. Wordsworth takes advantage of purely rhythmic means to maintain a semblance of dramatic fidelity to speech habits characteristic of such a man, while still providing the reader with a sufficient degree of pleasurable excitement. His strategy for accomplishing this is to employ a rhythmic pace and a degree of patterning in the rhythm and rhyme that create, at least on the surface, a mismatch with the poem's diction and syntax. The garrulous sea captain speaks in the stanzaic pattern of an Horatian ode.[15]

The chief means through which Wordsworth achieves his aims in "The Thorn" are simple yet powerful: the alternation of appeals to and departures from a fundamental and insistent rhythmic pattern. The stanza is in characteristic Wordsworthian fashion actually a kind of accretion or cento of component parts.[16] It begins, as do many of Wordsworth's longer forms, with a variant of the basic rhythmic structure of almost all popular poetry in English—the four-line stanza composed of four-beat lines. In the variant of this form used in lines 1–4 of each stanza of "The Thorn" (abc_4b_3), a pause substitutes for the fourth beat of the fourth line, marking an emphatic close to the structural unit:

> There is a thorn; it looks so old,
> o Bo B o B o B
> In truth you'd find it hard to say,
> o B o B o B o B
> How it could ever have been young,
> o B o Bo B o B
> It looks so old and grey.
> o B o B o B (o B)

The prevalence of the basic four-line, four-beat structure and its most common variants ($abcb_4$, abc_4b_3, $a_4b_3c_4b_3$) throughout the history of English poetry—in popular song and narrative as well as in more conventionally literary verse—suggests that it is closely linked with fundamental physical laws of speech production and perception of speech. For this reason, Malof calls the four-line, four-beat form "native" measure, distinguishing it from the various kinds of five-beat verse, rhymed and unrhymed, that have developed along more self-consciously literary lines. Attridge, who calls the structure the 4 x 4 stanza, sees it as an expression of the natural tendency of all speech to gravitate toward simple binary rhythms and hierarchies based on such rhythms.[17] The basic rhythmic unit of two syllables, one of which is perceived as more prevalent than the other, is itself binary. No matter how infinitely various the actual

phonetic content of the verse or passage, the individual rhythmic unit of the line (the foot, or the single realization of the offbeat-beat pattern) tends to be felt as a simple relationship between a generically strong stress and a generically weak stress. These binary groups tend, in turn, to be grouped in pairs. This is evident, for example, in the tendency of lines of four-beat popular verse and song to fall into dipodic rhythm. In dipodic verse or song, strong syllables in contiguous binary units (or "feet") are themselves read in relation to one another, with one assuming priority. The effect is common in nursery rhymes, in which the dipodic unit tends to be marked by rhyme (capital [+S] marks the relatively stronger stress in the dipodic unit):

+s -s   +S   -s +s -s   +S   +s -s   +S -s   +s -s +S
Every wife had seven sacks / Every sack had seven cats

Binary structures are also the rule in the standard line and stanza structures of the popular ballad. The basic line of popular balladry is actually a combination of two dipodic units (with four strong [+S] stresses per line), and the stanza itself is a rhymed couplet composed of these double-dipodic lines:

   +S   +s   +S   +s   +S   +s   +S
The kinge hee sterted forthe i-wys, And an angrye man was hee:

   +S   +s   +S   +s   +S   +s
Nowe, traytoure, thou shalt hange or drawe, And rewe shall thy
                                                                       +S
                                                                       ladie
("Sir Cauline," Percy's *Reliques,* I.i.4)

This structure is obscured in printed ballads, of course, by the convention of breaking the long lines into shorter lines, usually of four and three stresses ($a_4b_3c_4b_3$):

The kinge hee sterted forthe i-wys,	(a)
And an angrye man was hee:	(b)
Nowe, traytoure, thou shalt hange or drawe,	(c)
And rewe shall thy ladie.	(b)

The endurance of the four-line stanza in English poetry and song suggests a deep connection between this simple rhythmic form and a fundamental capacity to derive pleasure from the simple binary opposition of repeated yet distinguishable physical impulses.

Each of the stanzas of "The Thorn," then, begins by bringing into play, at the most minute levels of the physical experience of the poem, a most basic and familiar form of feeling. The native rhythm, as simple and natural as child's play, is expressively appropriate to this simple speaker, while at the same time it is rhetorically valuable by virtue of its pleasing familiarity. Having established this ground rhythm through the 4 x 4 form, each stanza of "The Thorn" then begins to play upon that powerful binary impulse:

$$+s \quad +S \quad +s \quad +S \quad +s \quad +S \quad +s \quad +S$$
There is a thorn; it looks so old, / In truth you'd find it hard to say,
$$+s \quad +S \quad +s \quad +S \quad \quad +S \quad +s \quad +S$$
How it could ever have been young, / It looks so old and grey.

The symmetrical, four-strong-stress couplet structure of lines 1–4 of each stanza is immediately modified by a five-line elaboration of and departure from that structure in the form $abcc_4b_3$. The asymmetricality of this structure creates tension between lines 5–9 and 1–4:

> Not higher than a two year's child,
> It stands erect this aged thorn;
> No leaves it has, no thorny points;
> It is a mass of knotted joints,
> A wretched thing forlorn.

This structure (which will be referred to as modified tail rhyme throughout the present discussion) is among the most common elements out of which Wordsworth's stanzaic verse is constructed. It is very close in structure and feel, for example, to the stanza ($abccb_4$) used independently in "The Idiot Boy" and *Peter Bell*. Variations of the structure form components of sixteen different stanzas in the *Poetical Works*.[8] As an expansion of the basic 4 x 4 stanza, formed by doubling the third line (the *c* rhyme), the tail-rhyme sections in the stanzas of "The Thorn" tend to create a sense of suspension of the impulses set in motion by the opening of the stanza. The effect may easily be felt by reading the quoted section above, omitting the "extra" line, and adjusting syntax:

> Not higher than a two year's child,
> It stands erect this aged thorn;
> No leaves it has, no thorny points;
> *It is a thing forlorn.

In the unrevised version, the extra verse provides a sense of brief escape from and return to a fundamental pattern.

Finally, the couplet that ends each stanza helps to give each internally various stanza a formal integrity, heightened by the use of roman numerals marking off the stanzas, that serves to set up the represented speech as a series of distinct repeated patterns, with a rhythmically familiar beginning, an elaborated middle, and a summarizing end. As Wordsworth's handling of the couplet rarely involves any appreciable tension in the realization of the metrical pattern, the effect is generally one of a return to simple and comfortable binaries, and in some stanzas even to more predictable, refrainlike, repetitive rhythms:

> It stands erect, and like a stone
> With lichens it is overgrown.
>
> (ll. 10–11)

> "Oh misery! oh misery!
> Oh woe is me! oh misery!"
>
> (ll. 65–66; 76–77; 252–53)

To a large extent, it is this division into distinct and various parts that helps make the stanza "more lyrical and rapid" than would be appropriate were the intent simply to use metrical arrangement expressively. By way of contrast, it may be noted that when Wordsworth uses this same stanza in volume 2 in "The Idle Shepherd-Boys" he neither establishes the ground rhythm of lines 1–4 as insistently as he does in "The Thorn" (or in "A Fragment," a poem similar in movement to "The Thorn") nor maintains as carefully the formal divisions among the parts that make up the stanza. A rhythmic effect as simple as a run-on line in the second line of the first quatrain establishes from the start of "The Idle Shepherd-Boys" a very different feel than is established by the end-stopped lines in the quatrains of "The Thorn":

> The valley rings with mirth and joy,
> Among the hills the Echoes play
> A never, never ending song
> To welcome in the May.
>
> (ll. 1–4)

As such enjambment is rare in the 4 x 4 form, the realization of the structure strikes one, in contrast to the four-square solidity of "The Thorn," as more

consciously artful, and perhaps more overtly playful. Similarly, in "The Idle Shepherd-Boys," boundaries between the five-line tail-rhyme section and the couplet are not as firmly observed as in "The Thorn":

> Into their arms the Lamb they took,
> Said they, "He's neither maim'd nor scarr'd"—
> Then up the steep ascent they hied
> And placed him at his mother's side,
> And gently did the Bard
> Those idle Shepherd-boys upbraid,
> And bade them better mind their trade.
>
> (ll. 93–99)

Note, for example, the effect of the strong pause after "side" (almost an end-stop) and the run-on line in the antepenultimate line. Such fluidity in the matching of syntax to line and rhyme boundaries is appropriate to the relatively sophisticated narrator of "The Idle Shepherd-Boys," whose considerable resources of diction and imagery establish to a large extent the poetic interest. Similar usage in "The Thorn" would undermine the rhythmic means through which the mediation between reader and speaker is accomplished, making of the stanza a less constant source of pleasurably patterned impulses than it needs to be, given the poet's aim to explore the habits of mind of a speaker with considerable deficiencies as a storyteller.

"The Thorn," as Wordsworth takes pains to point out in his note to the poem, is about telling a tale. The basic rhythm of the 4 x 4 stanza, carried on at length, may be appropriate for poetry of the "moving accident" but will not do in a poem so insistently about the interaction of mind and language, and about how feeling gives significance to action. The poem's chief focus is the mind of a speaker convinced, through his powerful response to a place and a story, of a mysterious bond between human suffering and the natural world. The power of such conviction and the dogged determination of the mind that professes it are what the meter must help to convey. In aiming to delineate the movements of mind exhibited by the speaker—fluxes and refluxes of a kind normally not regarded as appropriate for serious poetic treatment—Wordsworth is conscious also of his duty to give pleasure, to bring the outlandish subject of his poem into familiar relationship. His stanza conveys a feeling of the speaker's dogged persistence by continually appealing to an insistent rhythm. At the same time, departures from that fundamental and insistent rhythm provide the variety necessary to

maintain an overbalance of pleasure. Through the stanza form, then, Wordsworth allows the reader to feel on the pulses something of the processes through which the speaker of "The Thorn" builds up great things from least suggestions while also providing the distance necessary to an understanding of those processes.[19]

WORDSWORTH AND THE BALLAD STANZA
"EXPOSTULATION AND REPLY," "THE TABLES TURNED,"
AND THE LUCY POEMS

Wordsworth evidently considered the 4 x 4 ballad stanza ($a_4b_3c_4b_3$) to be severely constraining and potentially monotonous. In a note appearing in the 1800 edition of *Lyrical Ballads,* he calls the meter chosen by Coleridge for the *Rime* "unfit for long poems." Although Wordsworth asserts that Coleridge's handling of the stanza is "harmonious and artfully varied, exhibiting the utmost powers of that metre, and every variety of which it is capable," the clear implication is that even in Coleridge's hands, the stanza cannot be made to encompass the variety of effect that Wordsworth deems necessary to sustain interest.[20] The longest of Wordsworth's contributions to *Lyrical Ballads* in a 4 x 4 stanza ($a_4b_3a_4b_3$, $abab_4$, aba_4b_3) is the seventy-two-line "The Fountain." "Rob Roy's Grave" (composed 1805–6; published 1807) is the longest poem in any variant of the 4 x 4 stanza (abc_4b_3) in the entire *Poetical Works* (1849–50). At 120 lines, it is less than one-fifth the length of the *Rime.* Wordsworth's mistrust of the stanza for extended use suggests that his decision to remove the *Rime* from the prominent introductory position it had occupied in 1798 may have been motivated in no small measure by concerns that its prosodic characteristics would be mistaken as representative of the remainder of the volumes.

As has been mentioned briefly above, Wordsworth, unlike Coleridge, was not very interested in directly imitating the rhythmic movement of ballads. He preferred to establish a relationship to such poems through allusion to the fundamental rhythms of authentic balladry while maintaining subtle but effective rhythmic and structural distinctions between his stanzas and the basic $a_4b_3c_4b_3$ stanza (in accentual meter). Ballad subjects and speakers, such as those presented in "The Thorn," "Goody Blake and Harry Gill," the "Complaint," the "Mad Mother," or "A Fragment," for example, are always framed in stanzas obviously and designedly more impressive than would be common in Percy's *Reliques* or in the popular English and Scottish songs and tales Wordsworth knew so

well. In a note to "Ellen Irwin," Wordsworth calls attention directly to this tendency in his work: "As there are Scotch Poems on the subject in the simple ballad strain, I thought it would be both presumptuous and superfluous to attempt treating it in the same way; and, accordingly, I chose a construction of stanza quite new in our language" (Fenwick note; *PW* 3:443). The rhythmic dissimilarity between Wordsworth's balladlike poems and poems in the "simple ballad strain" is as important to Wordsworth as the connection of such poems with the ballad tradition.

Even in poems that do employ a variety of the 4 x 4 stanza common in the ballad tradition, Wordsworth's adaptation of stanza to subject, his handling of rhyme scheme (normally abab instead of abcb) line lengths (frequent use of the asymmetrical stanza aba_4b_3 instead of the simple bipartite structure formed by the regular alternation of four- and three-stress verses), and his use of syllabically regular verses set his stanzas apart from the prosody of authentic popular balladry or contemporary imitations of that prosody. None of the various four-line stanzas employed by Wordsworth in *Lyrical Ballads* may properly be labeled "ballad stanzas," though many bear outward resemblance to the "simple ballad strain." In fact, only one poem in Wordsworth's entire *Poetical Works* is written in the $a_4b_3c_4b_3$ ballad stanza. In that poem—"The Force of Prayer"—Wordsworth also uses accentualist techniques common to balladry (relatively frequent use of double offbeats or "trisyllabic substitution") with the result that "The Force of Prayer" presents itself, unlike Wordsworth's poems in the *Lyrical Ballads*, as obviously and self-consciously antiquarian.[21] Extant among the juvenilia not published by Wordsworth is a poem in the ballad stanza, a sentimental narrative written in 1787 about a death occasioned by unrequited love and called, appropriately enough, "A Ballad" (*PW* 1:265–67).[22]

The four-line, cross-rhymed stanzas, $a_4b_3a_4b_3$, and aba_4b_3 used by Wordsworth in "Expostulation and Reply," "The Tables Turned," "A slumber did my spirit seal," and in nine other poems in the *Lyrical Ballads*, then, are not "ballad stanzas," despite the consistent misidentification of them as such among Wordsworthians and prosodists alike.[23] The stanza is more firmly associated with lyric (and pastoral lyric)—from Spenser's July eclogue in the *Shepheardes Calender* to Herrick's *Hesperides* to the literary songs of Collins, Akenside, Chatterton, and Cowper—than it is with specifically popular narrative poetry.[24] To miss this fact of literary history is to risk applying inappropriate prosodic standards to Wordsworth's verse. For the post-Coleridgean (and heavily Coleridge-influenced) tradition of prosodic commentary,

the versification of the *Rime* is a milestone in a forward march of prosodic improvement and liberation. For Saintsbury, the prosody of the *Rime* is the "match that rekindled the torch of revived true English prosody" (*History of English Prosody* 3:60–61). Judged according to such progressive standards, what else can Wordsworth's own "ballad stanza" be but backward looking and unenlightened, a sign of a failure to liberate himself from the stultifying Continental influences that had dominated the eighteenth century?

To understand Wordsworth's careful use of the 4 x 4 stanza as a means for alluding to, assimilating, distancing himself from, or modifying elements of the ballad tradition to serve his own complex purposes is to begin to understand the metrical dimensions of the *Lyrical Ballads* on more Wordsworthian terms. It may be worthwhile, then, to trace in some detail the ways in which, and the purposes toward which, Wordsworth's stanzas depart, sometimes emphatically, from the kind of stanzas with which they are commonly identified. The companion poems "Expostulation and Reply" and "The Tables Turned" provide good examples of the kind of metrical subtleties that Wordsworth's four-line stanzas allow. As these poems are placed first in the 1800 collection in lieu of the *Rime,* and as at least part of Wordsworth's dissatisfaction with Coleridge's ballad as an introduction to the collection would seem to have been based on prosodic grounds, it will be appropriate to ask why Wordsworth may have regarded these poems as prosodically more suitable than the *Rime*.

It has been common in critical writing since the romantic period to equate loosening of specifically metrical restrictions with greater prosodic flexibility and versatility. The poet who follows the spirit of ballad prosody in counting strong stresses only, allowing variable numbers of syllables between strong stresses, operates under fewer rules than does the poet who maintains restrictions on both stresses and total syllables. The fewer the rules, the more free the poet; the more free the poet, the more various the verse.[25] It is arguable, however, that the strongest tendencies of the accentual prosody of the ballad tradition are toward greater, not less, restriction of possibilities of voice. Lines employing variable numbers of unstressed syllables between beats in general encourage strong emphasis on the predominant (normally rising) rhythm. Such rhythm lends itself to singsong (or at least to incantatory) recitation, as the reader is encouraged to group the varying numbers of syllables into roughly equal temporal units, marked by exaggerated stress on the ictic syllable or beat. The first stanza of the 1798 *Lyrical Ballads* is a classic example of the meter:[26]

> It is an ancyent Marinere,
>   And he stoppeth one of three:
> "By thy long grey beard and thy glittering eye
> "Now wherefore stoppest me?["]

As is appropriate in an introductory stanza, Coleridge introduces double offbeats in order to establish the metrical set:

> And he stoppeth one of three:
> ŏ   B   o   B   o   B

> "By thy long grey beard and thy glittering eye
> ŏ   B   o   B   ŏ   B(o)o   B

A reader can do relatively little to vary the basic rhythmic character of such verses. The double offbeat functions as a kind of metronome for the timing of stresses, and the one- or two-syllable groups between beats are felt to be equivalent in the amount of time that they require for pronunciation.[27] A fundamental pattern is immediately and unambiguously established, as is appropriate in a tale that posits an enchanting, even mesmerizing, relationship between a spellbound listener and a teller whose tale has become insistently patterned through compulsive repetition.

In contrast, Wordsworth's characteristic four-beat line, because it is accentual-syllabic, is not limited to a single predominant rhythmic tendency. A group of verses may employ rising (or iambic) rhythm, falling (or trochaic) rhythm, or a combination of the two. Note the subtle sense of a change of pace from the neutral or slightly falling rhythm of lines 1–2 to the stronger rising rhythm of the final two lines, in the following stanza:

> Books! 'tis a dull and endless strife,
> B   ŏ   B   o   B   o   B
> Come, hear the woodland linnet,
> B̄   ŏ   B   o   B   o   B   o
> How sweet his music; on my life
> ŏ   B   o   B   o   B̄   o   B
> There's more of wisdom in it.
> o   B   o   B   o   B̄   o
>   ("Tables Turned," ll. 9–12)[28]

The rhythmic variation, resulting from the initial inversion and the

implied offbeat formation in the first two lines, underpins the emotional transition from an injunction against books to praise of the linnet's music. The rhythmic transition would not be felt if the third line continued the pattern of inversion:

> Come, hear the woodland linnet,
> *Sweet is his music, on my life
> B   ŏ   B   o

The strong and insistent ground rhythm encouraged by accentual ballad prosody tends to limit the sense that there may be a range of possible realizations of the line; it also therefore tends to assert an identity between metrical form and the phonetic realization of the form (or between meter and rhythm). But Wordsworth's accentual-syllabic four-beat line is, just as surely as is its five-beat counterpart, a locus for potentially complex interaction of abstract pattern and variable realization. Such complexity makes possible—even may be said to require—a kind of active participation by the reader in the realization of the line in a way that is impossible in strict ballad prosody. Is there, for example, as clear a sense of a single "correct" or rhythmically required reading of the first lines of "Expostulation and Reply" as there is of the lines quoted above from the opening of the *Rime?*

> "Why, William, on that old grey stone,
> "Thus for the length of half the day,
> "Why, William, sit you thus alone,
> "And dream your time away?["]

The first verse alone contains at least three syllables that create tension between the phonetic material of the line and its abstract pattern ("Why," "on," "grey"):

> s   +s -s   s   s +s   s +s
> Why, William, on that old grey stone
> ó   B o   B̄ o B ó   B

"Grey" is relatively weakly stressed both because of the metrical demands and because of syntactic stress hierarchies (adjective - noun). The syntactic equivalence of the paired adjectives "old" and "grey," however, and the sonic similarities in the sequence of "long" vowels—"old," "grey," "stone"—may be felt to make "grey" somewhat resistant to the meter;

thus, it is marked here as a demoted syllable, a source of tension. "Why," as the syllable that sets the interrogative context of the poem, certainly must be felt to be more prominent than would be usual in the first position of a verse, yet the first syllable of "William" competes with it for the first strong stress. Such ambiguously placed syllables, including also the preposition "on" in a strong position, make the line open to a number of realizations. The first is stiff and schematic, but possible:

    -s +s -s +s -s +s -s +s
  Why, William, on that old grey stone
    o   B o B o B o B

Another might be more conversational, employing the initial inversion condition to subordinate "William" in an aside:

    +s -s -s +s -s +s -s +s
  Why, William, on that old grey stone
    B   ŏ   B̄ o B ȯ B

Still another—much more disruptive—reading might tend toward a more variably paced recitation, slow at both ends and rapid in the middle (because of the triple offbeat):

    +s +s -s -s -s +s s +s
  Why, William, on that old grey stone
    B ô B   ŏ   B ȯ B

The point here is that the verse presents itself as inherently open to variation. Its meter functions not to dictate a reading, but to provide a frame within which may be generated a certain limited number of more or less effective kinds of rhythmic subtlety, each potentially giving the substance of the speech a different emotional emphasis. The tension here between physical realization and the abstract pattern opens the poem, and the collection it introduces, to the kind of active reading that Wordsworth in the Preface of 1815 demands for all of his poems. Metrical tension awakens a "voluntary power to modulate" the "music of the poem" as the "spirit of versification" is felt to play with and against the "letter of metre" (*Prose* 3:29–30).

    This inherent variability or optionality contributes to meaning in a number of ways in Wordsworth's companion poems. In lines 21–24 of "Expostulation and Reply," for example, "William" makes a transition— or leap—from an introductory enumeration of facts concerning the

mechanism of perception ("The eye it cannot chuse but see / We cannot bid the ear be still") to a bold assertion that supersensual powers impress mind in a manner analogous to the way in which physical sensation impresses organs of perception:

> "Nor less I deem that there are powers,
> "Which of themselves our minds impress,
> "That we can feed this mind of ours,
> "In a wise passiveness.["]

(ll. 21–24)

Expressively, the strong rhythms of the unbroken lines 21–23 make the stanza unusually assertive. At a more subtle level, the stanza incorporates a number of indications of tension between its own supersensual pattern and the sensual realization of that pattern. For example, the word "power" is here (as it is frequently in Wordsworth) a locus of prosodic interest. As a triphthong or hypermonosyllable, it is too weak to occupy two metrical positions. Yet neither is it a true monosyllable. Wordsworth's use of the word here and throughout his work in metrical positions requiring a single syllable allows him to take advantage of a happy linguistic coincidence for symbolic purposes. The word that Wordsworth favors to describe the active force that binds all things, and through which the eternal and supersensual is manifested in the temporal and sensual, is itself an indicator of the tension between an idea of order (the poem's ideal form) and its realization. As more than a monosyllable, its placement as a monosyllable strains against the syllabic limits of Wordsworth's numbered line; as a conventional realization of a single syllabic position in verse, it confirms and objectifies the power of the metrical pattern to give shape to recalcitrant phonetic material. Here, its placement may be regarded as one of the many ways through which Wordsworth's verse calls attention—appropriately enough given the poem's subject—to the ways in which the power of truth is and is not embodied in the sensual medium of words. Such minute effects in a poem that presents itself as an order of words about the insufficiency of words to convey the spirit of natural order functions as a reminder that words, as words, are essentially fixed and dead. Without a reading inspired by the passion of the sense, and without the sense, gained through the experience of reading itself, of the give and take of mind and linguistic forms, these words would be no better than the "barren leaves" that are the appropriate expression of "dead men" in "Expostulation and Reply."

Another source of tension appears in the final verse of the stanza:

    -s-s   s   +s -s   s
    In a wise passiveness
    ŏ   B̄ ŏ B o   B̄

The pull that the word "power" exerts on the physical responses of a reader attuned to the metrical set is subtle; this example is less so. The stress-final double-offbeat structure (or pyrrhic-spondee group), the presence of just one fully stressed syllable ("wise" is metrically promoted because as an adjective it is subject to syntactic pressures that weaken its force relative to the noun it modifies), and especially the weak stress in the final position make the verse barely an adequate realization of the form. (Its metrical precariousness is reinforced, too, by the placement of the line at the end of an expressively confident and rhythmically impressive passage.) Such verses, and especially such promoted verse endings in emphatic positions (ends of stanzas, ends of poems), are characteristic of Wordsworth's metrical art:

    And bring no book; for this one day
    We'll give to idleness.
    o   B   oB o B̄
                          ("Lines [To My Sister]," 39–40)

    As blithe a man as you could see
    On a spring holiday.
    ŏ   B ŏ Bo B̄
                          ("The Two April Mornings," ll. 7–8)

    And oftentimes I talked to him,
    In very idleness.
    B o B̄
                          ("Anecdote for Fathers," ll. 19–20)

    And then my heart with pleasure fills,
    And dances with the Daffodils.
    B o B̄
                          ("I wandered lonely as a cloud," ll. 23–24)

    And I could wish my days to be
    Bound each to each by natural piety.
    B o B̄
                          ("My Heart Leaps Up," ll. 8–9)

Tennyson obviously found such rhythms a Wordsworthian signature. In May of 1835, he responded to a challenge by Fitzgerald "as to who could invent the weakest Wordsworthian line imaginable" with a pentameter in which a weak ending caused by a three-syllable word with the rhythm +s -s s ("passiveness," "holiday," "daffodils") occurs twice, once before the midline pause and again at the end:

> A Mr Wilkinson, (x) a clergyman.²⁹
> o Bo B o B̄   o B o B̄

In the example from "Expostulation and Reply," the "weakness" of the line is made especially evident through the promoted rhyme of impress/passiveness. Again, as with "power," the rhythmic context takes advantage of the physical qualities of a semantically significant word. The need to promote the third syllable of "passiveness" in order to supply the rhyme for the strong syllable "press" creates tension in the relationship between the two syllables, through which the word "impress" is felt to act physically—to impress itself—on the phonetic stuff of "passiveness." Or, in what amounts to much the same thing, the syllable that ends the stanza is unsettling because it is inadequate to the expectation of an equal-stressed rhyme. Either the stanza is felt to lack closure (and the physical stuff of the words betrays an inadequacy that belies the speaker's confident assertion) or its closure is felt to be emphatic (or overemphatic) because of the degree to which it involves the reader's physical impulses (and the speaker's confidence becomes the reader's own, manifested physically through assertive performance of the verse). Either way, a central idea at the heart of the poem—that power manifests itself in and through physical impressions for which one substitutes words at his own peril—is embodied in the verse itself. Such words are felt to be, like natural impulses, significant in part because of their ability to resist, almost successfully, abstract intelligence and its demand for univocal meaning.

The stanza structure commonly used in ballads, requiring as it does just one rhyme sound per stanza, tends also—like the characteristic line of balladry—to be regarded as less limiting than the two-rhymed form preferred by Wordsworth. Again, however, the tendency in the abcb stanza is toward greater, not less, uniformity in performance than is common in the abab form. The abcb stanza, which is structurally a couplet printed as a quatrain, tends to fall fairly regularly into a simple, binary pattern of organization, which in turn encourages relatively simple, coordinated, and repetitive syntactic structures. The example cited above from "Sir Cauline" will serve as well here:

> The kinge hee sterted forthe i-wys, / And an angrye man was hee:
> Nowe, traytoure, thou shalt hange or drawe, / And rewe shall thy ladie.

Coleridge's success in approximating these rhythmic and syntactic characteristics is obvious:

> The Sun came up upon the right, / Out of the Sea came he;
> And broad as a weft upon the left / Went down into the Sea.
> (ll. 83–86)

The cross-rhymed stanza, on the other hand, by virtue of the small additional complexity of a second rhyme sound, lends itself to various divisions. It may be used to imitate ballad long lines through enjambment of the first and third lines:

> Where are your books? that light bequeath'd / To beings else forlorn and blind!
> Up! Up! and drink the spirit breath'd / From dead men to their kind.

Here, in this speech by Matthew in "Expostulation and Reply," the balladlike rhythmic phrasing may serve to place witty emphasis on his presumably unintentional introduction of Gothic supernaturalism in the image of "dead men" breathing "to their kind."

The cross-rhymed stanza may also be employed as a four-part structure:

> And hark! how blithe the throstle sings!
> And he is no mean preacher;
> Come forth into the light of things,
> Let Nature be your teacher.
> ("Tables Turned," ll. 13–16)

This is a strikingly simple realization of the form: four independent clauses in four rhythmically discrete verses with little or no metrical tension. Such simplicity in the fitting of diction to the metrical frame may be felt as an element contributing to the effect of humorous lyricism in the passage ("no mean preacher"). Whatever the specific interpretation of its tone, however, the important point to note is how clearly this realization of the form differs from the other examples quoted here. Such

variety in the course of two companion poems in the same basic verse form must be felt to be an intrinsic element through which the poet is directing the affections of the reader toward the speakers and toward the intellectual content of his poems.

The most frequent kind of syntactic arrangement within Wordsworth's four-line stanzas creates a tripartite structure. In these stanzas, lines 1 and 2 typically contain independent clauses and are followed by pauses. Line 3 is enjambed:

> Enough of science and of art;
> Close up these barren leaves;
> Come forth, and bring with you a heart
> That watches and receives.
>
> (ll. 29–32)

Such use provides for a simple but potentially very effective rhythmic variation within individual stanzas and among groups of stanzas. In this example, the lengthening of the phrase in lines 3 and 4 corresponds to and expresses the shift from imperatives directed against actions ("enough," "close up") to an invitation to new experience ("come forth," "bring with you"). This invitation, constituting the final phrase of the poem, is both an opening (into experience) and a closing (of books and talk, of the stanza and the poem). The paradox of an end that is not an end is felt rhythmically, as the poem ends with a statement that overflows the line.

In all of the stanzas in the form $a_4b_3a_4b_3$ appearing in *Lyrical Ballads*, Wordsworth employs enjambment after the first line 30 percent of the time; he enjambs the third line in nearly 43 percent of these stanzas and always ends the stanza with a full stop. The second line is enjambed much more rarely than 1 or 3, in only about 12 percent of the stanzas. This infrequency is easy to understand. The stanza $a_4b_3a_4b_3$ (or $a_4b_3c_4b_3$) tends to be felt as a standard 4 x 4 or long measure quatrain ($abab_4$), with pauses substituted for realized beats in the second and fourth lines:

> The breezes blew, the white foam flew,
>   The furrow follow'd free: (x)
> We were the first that ever burst
>   Into that silent Sea. (x)
>
> (*Rime*, ll. 99–102)

Enjambed syntax over the second line frustrates the expectation of a strong pause and strains against a fundamental element of the stanza

structure. Such enjambment is therefore among the most disruptive effects possible in the form. As is the case with most unsettling and infrequently used prosodic effects, at least in the hands of a good poet, it may be assumed to be significant when it does occur:

> Sweet is the lore which nature brings;
> Our meddling intellect
> Mishapes the beauteous forms of things;
> —We murder to dissect.
> ("Tables Turned," ll. 25-28)

The uneasy effect caused by the tension between stanza form and the strong pull against the separation of subject and verb ("intellect / mishapes the beauteous forms of things") may be interpreted expressively, as a physical manifestation of the strength of the speaker's disgust for the dissecting intellect. It may also, or alternately, be regarded emblematically, as an insistent and obvious challenge to the arbitrarily imposed abstract dimensions of the form, presented as an instance of the speaker's protest against abstract forms in favor of experience and emotional impulse.[30] Such effects are decidedly uncharacteristic of the tradition of popular poetry to which the title of Wordsworth's collection and the superficial similarities of many of his forms make creative allusion. The key issue for the critic of Wordsworth's metrical style is to appreciate significant dissimilarities, as well as similarities, between his structures and rhythms and other possibilities.

The prosodic variety—and intrinsic optionality—exhibited in "Expostulation and Reply" and "The Tables Turned" tends to make these poems, to a large extent, dependent for their full effect on the reader's participation in and recreation of the dynamics of the speech of William and Matthew. Appropriately enough for poems about the relationship between physical impulse and apprehension of truth, the prosody of the poems thrusts to the foreground their physical texture, their rhythms, syntactic structures, and sonic patterns as intrinsic elements of meaning. Such effects suggest that the dialogue of Matthew and William is to be understood as being pursued only in part at the level of semantics and conventional signification. At a deeper, physical, level, the metrical arrangement incorporates powers residual in the physical nature of language itself, allowing the poems to create impressions through patterned sound and impulse in relation to an abstract idea of order. In other words, rhyme and rhythm here make palpable in the physical texture of the verse a key issue in the debate: if William (or

William Wordsworth) is to be convincing on the subject of the power of feeling, he must make his auditor(s) feel the truth of what he says. He must, as Wordsworth puts the issue in the fragmentary "Essay on Morals" written at Goslar, use words in such a way that they may speak to the body, incorporating themselves "with the blood & vital juices of our minds" (*Prose* 1:103).

When William attempts to sum up his position in "The Tables Turned," then, the reader attentive to the impulses of the verse will be in a position to take his meaning in a particularly complex way:

> One impulse from a vernal wood
> May teach you more of man;
> Of moral evil and of good,
> Than all the sages can.
>
> (ll. 21–24)

As the most straightforward realization of the basic 4 x 4 form in either "Expostulation and Reply" or "The Tables Turned," the stanza appeals more directly than any other stanza in either poem to those fundamental rhythmic patterns that have proven to be so deeply powerful, and lasting, in the English poetic tradition. This direct appeal to the powerful impulses of native meter is surely part of the reason why the stanza has been felt by generations of readers to represent a particularly apt summation of a Wordsworthian "creed." It speaks of the possibility of extralinguistic sources of meaning—and of the limitations of mere words addressed by and to the reasoning intellect—through language that has power in part through its ability to satisfy a basic sense of pattern that is independent of the semantic content of language. The physical resources of language, brought into relationship with these fundamental patterns, assert that a more-than-arbitrary relationship exists between these words and the things whereof they speak.

At the same time, it must also be noted that such an assertion also embodies in the poems an element of paradox central not only to "Expostulation and Reply" and "The Tables Turned" but also to Wordsworth's verse as a whole: that is, by asserting the relationship between this language and the language of the sense, or of "things forever speaking," the stanza perforce also asserts the distance between the two. The two impulses, toward a sense of the identity of language and nature and toward a recognition of the arbitrariness of language when compared with things, are in constant rhythmic relation to each other. The companion poems announce that Wordsworth's poetry will strive to bring

words to the test of things (or, in what amounts to the same thing, to fit words to patterns that will give lasting pleasure) in part by making the active reader constantly and creatively aware of the slippery relationship between words and things.

The reader who would take the words of Wordsworth's "credal" stanza—"one impulse from a vernal wood"—at face value, without attention to their rhythms or the rhythmic context in which they appear, would be playing Matthew's role, substituting mere words for the vital impulses in relation to which words have meaning and power to move. To understand these words as expressive of a speaker's energetically achieved and unstable position—arising out of an initially defensive response to a challenge, forming slowly, and taking shape through that speaker's own interaction with the words in which he expresses himself—is to see the difference between this kind of verbal injunction (and this kind of book) and the contents of the "barren leaves" that William tells Matthew, and William Wordsworth tells his reader, to close. What Wordsworth's William cannot say is indicated within the body of the poem itself through rhythmic variety and that prosodic optionality (even at the level of the syllable) that requires active participation by the reader in the speech impulses represented in the poem; what words inscribed on barren leaves exclude remains hidden from a hoodwinked reader. It is on this ground that Wordsworth's William charges intellect divorced from feeling with misshaping, dissection, and murder. If the shapes of language are not held in active relationship with the shape of things (the index of which in the literary work is the reader's pleasure), they will be free to misshape.

The placement of these prosodically simple yet subtly varied companion poems at the outset of *Lyrical Ballads* suggests that Wordsworth was also preparing his reader to approach the poems in the collection as a whole not merely through the eye of reason but also through minute impulses of the senses. The poems announce at the outset of the 1800 collection an intent to establish, even in work that employs what is perhaps the most common of all rhymed stanzas available to a poet in the late eighteenth century, a kind of active and demanding relationship among speaker, poet, and reader very different from that which Wordsworth seems to have thought could be effected even by "the utmost powers" of the fascinatingly regular meter of Coleridge's *Rime*. Wordsworth's companion poems promise rewards to the reader who will come forth, wisely passive, watching and receiving, into the light of words apprehended not merely as arbitrary signs but as things that have power to act with and against powers of mind.

Such attention is repaid in many different ways in the *Lyrical Ballads* (and for that matter throughout the *Poetical Works*), as all of the varieties of prosodic tension mentioned above—and more—are exhibited throughout the volumes. Among the most delicate of Wordsworth's prosodic effects, establishing some of the most subtle interrelations of mind and language in the collection, are to be found in those specifically lyric poems that employ the $a_4b_3a_4b_3$ stanza. In many of the poems employing these stanzas, Wordsworth seems especially intent to take particular advantage— for expressive, rhetorical, and emblematic purposes—of that sense of optionality in performance that is frequently allowed or encouraged by the fitting of language to strict metrical arrangement (compare the discussion of the first line of "Expostulation and Reply," above).

A case in point is the final stanza of "She dwelt among th'untrodden ways." How strongly must—or may—the word "could" be stressed, relative to "few" and "know" in the following verse?

       s s s
She *liv'd* unknown, and few could know
o B o B o B ȯ B
When Lucy ceas'd to be;
But she is in her Grave, and oh!
The difference to me.
             (ll. 9–12)

The rule of the octosyllabic line requires—indeed, insists quite strongly—that "could" not be strongly stressed. As the penultimate syllable in the line, and as the syllable preceding a rhymed syllable, it is felt to be especially restricted because line endings, especially in rhymed verse, are in large part what give the lines their distinctive character. (Wordsworth, as noted in chapter 1, was also particularly aware of line endings as important structural markers.)[31] This having been said, however, the fact remains that the syntactic relationship between "unknown" and "could know" seems to require a stress on "could" as a means for distinguishing (and relating) the conditions obtaining during Lucy's life and at the time of her death (emphasized here also by the italics on "liv'd"). If the second option is taken in performance, the line will be felt to end on a relatively unstressed syllable, an occurrence that creates tension in itself (as a violation of the metrical standard) and sets up further tension in the stanza as a whole, because the demoted syllable is also a rhyming syllable. If "know" carries a relatively weak stress, it forms with "oh!" in line 11 a kind of disruptive rhyme involving unequally

stressed syllables that William Harmon calls *"heterobaric."*[32] This difference in the stress values of rhyming syllables may account in part for the extremely powerful effect of the syllable "oh!" in the eleventh line. As a nonreferential indication of a purely expressive utterance, the syllable breaks syntactic boundaries; rhythmically, it is set off from the remainder of the line by strong pauses both before (in an unusual point in a four-beat line, after the sixth syllable), and after (line end). If the stanza is read in such a way that the syllable "oh!" is also felt to be in heterobaric relation to "know," such a rhyme would be still another means through which the syllable seems only partly assimilated into the poem's structure, as if the expressive demands of the situation actually at this point open up the form, releasing the syllable from the pattern (but without actually releasing it). The sound of the syllable, artfully placed in relation to other syllables, allows it to seem to have escaped the structure of the poem as literary artifact to speak directly to a reader.

Of course, one could, without violence to syntax or sense, recite "She dwelt among th'untrodden ways" in a manner that subordinated "could" to "know," in compliance with purely metrical demands. As has been noted throughout the present study, however, such a reading would only serve to reintroduce these tensions at a different level of apprehension. Indeed, if the meter is felt in a given recitation of the poem to be insistent enough to deny any more subtle rhythmic concession to the semantic contrast of "unknown" and "could know," or to force assimilation of the structurally embarrassing syllable "oh!" to a jog-trot rhythm that deemphasizes the late pause, it will still serve in its own way to emphasize these elements. To feel metrical demands overrule more subtle possibilities is, after all, to apprehend the possible subtleties even as they are assimilated to the regular form. The point is that the prosodic system that Wordsworth has chosen, and his most characteristic uses of that system, frequently introduce such tension among possible readings at important junctures in the poems.

The final verse of "She dwelt among th'untrodden ways" also shows Wordsworth taking advantage of a structurally important position to incorporate rhythmically a disturbing sense of open-endedness. As many commentators have noted, there is a strong general tendency in English poetic practice to equate full realization of the underlying metrical organization of a poem with a satisfying sense of closure; that is, poems are felt to end satisfactorily in part because their ending rhythms fulfill resoundingly a pattern that has been implicit throughout. One of the most celebrated cases of this effect is the ending of *Lycidas,* in which a deep sense of consolation and return to the salutary rhythms of everyday

life is effected in no small measure through Milton's use, after a sequence of variously irregular forms, of a concluding ottava rima stanza.³³ But the effect is prevalent also on a smaller scale. The couplets of Shakespeare's sonnets, for example, tend very frequently to exhibit a markedly greater degree of metrical and syntactic regularity than do the quatrains.³⁴ The end of "She dwelt among th'untrodden ways" is in this context obviously not in line with the general tendency:

> But she is in her Grave, and oh!
>   +s -s s
> The difference to me.
>   B o B̄ o B

Once again, as in the cases cited above—with "passiveness," "idleness," "piety"—Wordsworth uses a three-syllable word with the rhythmic form +s -s s to realize a beat-offbeat-beat sequence in a place where a fuller realization would be expected. It may also be worth noting that "difference" itself is a locus of metrical tension for another reason. In most contexts in Wordsworth's verse, the word would be subject to elision and would be considered metrically a disyllable: "diff'rence." Here, however, the meter requires full pronunciation; otherwise, the line collapses. Wordsworth seems to note just this point in a late copy that he made of the poem. In this manuscript, which contains a number of adjustments in punctuation and capitalization, the very syllable in question is underlined—"diff<u>e</u>rence"—emphasizing perhaps the need to retain it in performance (and acknowledging the fact that it normally would be elided).³⁵ Such expanded pronunciation of the word "difference," cuts against the metrical set (compare "th'untrodden" in the first line of the poem). It has the obvious expressive effect of slowing the pace of the line, thereby marking the emotional "difference" between the opening and closing of the poem. I would contend that these details, when taken together, create an unsettling sense of a speaker's failure to round off or close off his utterance. As individually minute as such effects are, they nevertheless form the chief prosodic means through which Wordsworth's poem embodies in its very physical structures the speaker's deep sense of a loss beyond the power of words to summarize or contain.

In "A slumber did my spirit seal," Wordsworth uses rhythmic means different from those employed in "She dwelt among th'untrodden ways" to create a very different feeling toward what is presumably the same instance of loss. In "A slumber did my spirit seal," the possibility of several tenable realizations of the final stanza may account in large part

for the poem's well-attested ability to evoke a feeling of almost elemental power. The tensions are felt especially in the first and third lines of the final stanza. Note the demoted and promoted syllables:

> No motion has she now; no force;
> ȯ B o B̄ o B ȯ B
> She neither hears nor sees;
>
> Roll'd round in earth's diurnal course
> ȯ   B   o   B   oBo   B
> With rocks and stones and trees!

The first verse might legitimately, if more disruptively, be read with an implied offbeat and a triple offbeat:

> No motion has she now; no force
> B ȯ B   ȯ̆   B   ȯ B

Such a reading would suggest a discrepancy between the motionlessness of the poem's subject and a disruptive emotive movement on the part of the speaker: the line in this realization is felt to begin slowly (emphasizing the long-vowel assonance of "*no mo*-tion"), increase in speed over the triple offbeat, and end slowly. The third verse also admits variety in the realization of the first two stresses:

>   s   +s
> +s   +s   -s +s
> Rolled round in earth's diurnal course

The first option, which subordinates "Rolled" to regular metrical demands, might express a certain monotony, suggesting a speaker who is beginning to give himself over to forces—manifested in the powerful binary rhythms of the 4 x 4 stanza itself—beyond his own power. The "spondaic" option, on the other hand, offers a slight sense of resistance to the insistent, leveling tendencies of the rhythm. Together, the options make the line itself resonant and suggestive of meanings beneath and beyond the signification of the words, as the two realizations embody the profound ambivalence of the poem itself and its speaker toward those "diurnal" powers working to level all human exertions of force.

The competing realizations may also contribute in no small measure to the sense that readers have long registered that somehow the final

lines of the poem seem to pick up the force that they seek to describe. A more accurate description would be that they make manifest in the relationship between abstract pattern and realization the dynamic tension between impersonal power and individual force that is the subject of the poem. In other words, "Rolled round in earth's diurnal course / With rocks and stones and trees," strictly speaking, cannot be said to imitate the rolling motion it describes; it can, however, bring into sympathy the physical impulses of a reader in such a way that he may feel in the approximation and departure from the basic 4 x 4 rhythm both the power of a force extrinsic to individual expression and the human impulse to resist or escape such power. The final verse itself is as full a realization of the metrical pattern as it is possible to have:

With rocks and stones and trees
o   B   o   B   o   B

The three concrete nouns are emphatically stressed in relation to the preposition and conjunctions. In comparison with the ending of "She dwelt among th'untrodden ways," the line provides rhythmic closure. Coming as it does, however, as the second part of the full phrase, its momentum and impetus is felt, in a way different from "She dwelt among th'untrodden ways," to be no less disturbing. It is, paradoxically perhaps, a verse in which the very lack of tension between pattern and realization is itself a residual source of tension.

The dialogue poems "Expostulation and Reply" and "The Tables Turned," then, announce at the outset of *Lyrical Ballads* (1800) that even the most ostensibly simple and predictable of Wordsworth's stanzas will reward careful attention to subtle tensions between the metrical frame and diverse realizations in actual sonic and rhythmic impulses. They announce, in short, that Wordsworth's "ballad stanzas" in *Lyrical Ballads* are not really ballad stanzas at all. Wordsworth uses the 4 x 4 stanza not as a vehicle for incantatory and spellbinding sustained narrative but as a familiar frame against which variable and volatile voices may be discerned. Whereas ballad prosody tends to exclude or minimize optionality and the "voluntary power to modulate" the "music of the poem," Wordsworth's 4 x 4 stanzas cultivate such complexity. Through these complexities Wordsworth is able to present the widely various speakers of "A slumber did my spirit seal," "The Tables Turned," "Anecdote for Fathers," "Lines Written in Early Spring," and "The Fountain," for example, all in a single, familiar, and conventionally restrictive metrical frame. Wordsworth's various adaptation of the stanza in *Lyrical Ballads* suggests that

the prosody of the poems in "ballad stanzas" may fruitfully be considered part and parcel of his expressed aim to illuminate the indwelling potential of whatever is most common and most familiar.

STANZAIC NARRATIVES: "RUTH," "HART-LEAP WELL," AND "THE IDIOT BOY"

Longer narrative poems in *Lyrical Ballads*—"Ruth," "Hart-Leap Well," and "The Idiot Boy," for example—also employ metrical means in ways that make attention to the "fitting of language to metrical arrangement" an important part of the experience of reading. In such poems, as in "The Thorn" or "Ellen Irwin," verse forms are employed that are distinguished—whether by stanza length and complexity, length of verse, or association with historical usage—from simpler, more stylistically transparent possibilities.

In "Ruth," Wordsworth achieves considerable rhythmic and sonic complexity through the use of a six-line tail-rhyme stanza: $aa_4b_3cc_4b_3$. This stanza, which has obvious structural similarities to the ballad stanza (it might be described as an $a_4b_3c_4b_3$ stanza with doubled first and third lines), had had by Wordsworth's time a considerably more various history of use than had the ballad stanza itself. Used both for lyrics and for narratives in Middle English, its strongest early associations are with metrical romances.[36] Chaucer's use of the stanza in *Sir Thopas* helped to establish a tradition of use for parodic, comic, or light verse (Gray's "Ode on the Death of a Favorite Cat," for example). In the later eighteenth century, the stanza had become increasingly popular as a serious lyric form (see Smart's "Song to David," Akenside's *Odes* [1.1, 1.5., 1.7, et al.], and Collins's "Ode to Pity," for example). Frequent use of the stanza in eighteenth-century translations and imitations of Horace's odes suggests that the alternation of pairs of longer lines with individual shorter lines was felt to be imitative of the similar alternation of longer and shorter verses in Horace's sapphic and adonic strophe. That Wordsworth understood the potential virtues of the stanza as a lyric form is documented by his own use of it in "Septimi Gades," an early adaptation of Horace, *Odes*, 2.6. The stanza also is used in *Lyrical Ballads*, in "Three years she grew in sun and shower" and "The Waterfall and the Eglantine" (ll. 51–56), as well as in eleven other lyric poems in the *Poetical Works* (including "Louisa" [pub. 1807], "September 1819" [pub. 1820], and "The Wishing Gate" [pub. 1828]).[37]

Wordsworth frequently troubled himself with theoretical problems

connected with the use of rhymed stanzas in longer poems. J. Payne Collier reports Wordsworth as saying that all "set forms" (by which Collier evidently means rhymed stanzas) are inferior to blank verse for "a poem of any continuance."[38] In a letter of 1816 to Southey, Wordsworth justifies his use of an "irregular frame" in the rhymed "Ode: The Morning of the Day Appointed for a General Thanksgiving," saying that short stanzas such as Horace's alcaics disallow "fervour and impetuosity," whereas long stanzas (he cites Spenser and the "Italian poets," presumably referring in the latter case to ottava rima) are "as apt to generate diffuseness as to check it" (*MY* 2:324–25). In "Ruth," the six-line form may be seen as an experiment in compromise. It is long enough to allow for some development of incident and thought but short enough not to require the poet to dwell on individual points in the narrative. At the same time, and as the history of the form as a lyric stanza suggests, intrinsic structural complexities—chiefly the alternation of couplets with the enclosed rhyme of the tails ($b_3cc_4b_3$)—allow sufficient flexibility in the relation of sonic to syntactic structures to accommodate varied effects within the set form. Smart seems to recognize just this potential for varied use of the stanza when he calls it in "A Song to David" (l. 18) a "wreath"—a structure of intertwined yet distinct rhythmic and sonic strands.

The tail-rhyme stanza used in "Ruth" is for these reasons preeminently suited to the poem's interplay, or interweaving, of circumstantial narrative and lyric passages. The lyric potential of the stanza is exploited especially in those sections of the poem in which the "Youth from Georgia's shore" tells his "tales" of the life that he and Ruth might share. Wordsworth's narrator says that these tales, told to Ruth among the enticements of a Marvelian *locus amoenus*—"in the green shade"—are "perilous to hear." The expressive use of the resources of his verse form helps Wordsworth to embody in these stanzas instances of the convincing—and perilous—power of the Youth's speech.

Some of the stanzas employ fairly straightforward expressive effects in direct quotation:

> ["]What days and what sweet years! Ah me
> Our life were life indeed, with thee
> So pass'd in quiet bliss,
> And all the while," said he "to know
> That we were in a world of woe,
> On such an earth as this!"
>
> (ll. 73–78)

The first verse creates a sense of being expressively charged not only because of the emphatic pause before and after the exclamation—"Ah me" (an exclamation point stands at line's end in *PW*)—but also because of the position of the adjective "sweet":

> What days and what sweet years! Ah me
> o B o B̄ ȯ B ȯ B

The effect—as I have had occasion to note elsewhere in this study—produces a sense of an ambiguous or hovering accent. Is the metrically promoted "what" felt to be more or less strong in comparison with the metrically (and syntactically) demoted "sweet"? If the parallel syntactic structure—"what . . . and what"—is felt to require emphasis (and therefore to level the stress of the second "what"), the line may be read with a fairly disruptive stress-final double offbeat (or pyrrhic-spondaic combination):

> What days and what sweet years! Ah me
> o B ŏ   B̄ ô B

Such a reading would give the verse a decidedly energetic and passionate feel, primarily through a contrasting sense of speed (in the third and fourth syllables) and slowness (in the final four syllables). But there is no compelling reason not to admit the first scansion above, also. The point is that the line, as is the case so frequently in Wordsworth, calls attention to itself as a text requiring for its full effect participatory performance with attention to the motives that drive the speech. Tension between the two realizations creates a minute sense of dislocation for the sake of feeling. Read with sympathy for the feeling that impels the verse, the ambiguity may be felt to be musical; otherwise, it risks being merely a source of awkwardness. That such lines are presented as having been musical to Ruth is an indication in part of the emotive force of the Youth, who "woo'd the Maiden" with "no feign'd delight," and in part of Ruth's participation, as a "reader" within the poem, in the emotions that shaped the words and dislocated the rhythm.

In other stanzas, chiefly those in which the narrator is engaged in paraphrase of the youth's speech, Wordsworth employs more complex sonic and rhythmic means to convey a sense of an enchanting power issuing not solely from what the Youth said but from the meanings of his voice. Some of these stanzas, including the example below, are among

the most prosodically interesting and effective lyric passages that Wordsworth had written to date:

> He spake of plants divine and strange
> That every day their blossoms change,
> Ten thousand lovely hues!
> With budding, fading, faded flowers
> They stand the wonder of the bowers
> From morn to evening dews.
>
> (ll. 49–54)

The second couplet is especially of interest. The falling rhythm, briefly suggested in the sequence "budding, fading, faded flowers," is frequently associated in Wordsworth's work with enchanted or enchanting speech or song. (The rhythm is used, for example, elsewhere in *Lyrical Ballads* for the "Song for the Wandering Jew," in which it helps to suggest the insistent power of the "trouble" that acts like a spell, binding the poem's subject to ceaseless motion.)[39] The impressive songlike quality of the couplet is reinforced by alliteration (fading, faded), by the *homoeoteleuton* of the participial endings, and by the delicate hint of augmented rhyme in the hypermonosyllabic "flowers" and "bowers." The rapid temporal sequence of "budding" through "faded" also suggests, through radically compressed allusion to a carpe diem motif, a gently imperative tone. The result is a stanza in which the spirit of carpe diem and the attractiveness of the Youth's enchanted world of promise may be felt directly and powerfully without intrusive mimicking of the external forms and formulae of more conventional representations of "perilous" and seductive speech. In other words, the reader catches the spirit of the youth's speech in the minutiae of the narrator's framing of his speech.

To the extent that the stanzas are effective as lyric poetry, then, they will work to implicate a reader's emotions, denying the comfortable, even voyeuristic sense of distance that carpe diem tends to allow. Through the flexibility of the tail-rhyme stanza, Wordsworth represents the Youth as able to create a powerful effect through passionate appeals to Ruth's best natural impulses. He "interwove" with images of the strangely beautiful place to which he will carry her "fond thoughts" of "a father's love" and the "tender ties" that bind the hearts of parents and children. He in effect promises Ruth her own dream: the union of human warmth (which her father, after his remarriage, has denied her) and a life in harmony with nature. This weaving of the enchanting but ill-fated dream is accomplished through the interweaving of words and images that make

the dream palpable to Ruth. And upon the power of the poet's words to make the beauty of that youthful dream palpable to the reader depends in large part on the reader's sympathy for the older, abandoned Ruth, whom the narrator has met among the Quantocks and for whom the dream has long been exposed as merely so many words.

The use of the five-beat line in the heroic or elegiac stanzas of "Hart-Leap Well" (abab$_5$) distinguishes the rhythms of that poem significantly from the fundamental rhythms of the 4 x 4 stanza. The pentameter is naturally a weightier and more flexible line than the four-beat line in which most of the stanzaic *Lyrical Ballads*—and most of the contemporary poems with which the *Lyrical Ballads* are usually compared—are written. Compare, for example, the effect of Wordsworth's lines with that of a stanza from Walter Scott's translation ("The Chase") of Bürger's "Der Wilde Jäger," a poem that appears to have been a source for "Hart-Leap Well":[40]

> Earl Walter winds his bugle horn;
>   To horse, to horse, halloo, halloo!
> His fiery courser snuffs the morn,
>   And thronging serfs their Lord pursue.
>   ("The Chase," ll. 1–4)

> "Another Horse."—That shout the Vassal heard,
> And saddled his best steed, a comely Grey:
> Sir Walter mounted him; he was the third
> Which he had mounted on that glorious day.
>   ("Hart-Leap Well," ll. 5–8)

Wordsworth's use of the five-beat line provides a rhythmic embodiment of the speaker's claim that his ends are different from those common in popular tales of "moving accident" designed to "freeze the blood." Strong associations between the five-beat line and heroic and other philosophically or sententiously serious verse make the line a signal or promise of a certain level of treatment of the subject. More immediately, the resistance of the line to the regularity and rapidity of performance that is encouraged by the 4 x 4 stanza distinguishes the poem's pace immediately and throughout its length from poems in which the chief focus is incident. In the stanzas quoted, both narrators focus on supposedly rapid action. But whereas "The Chase" uses rhythmic means to imitate the pace of the hunt, Wordsworth's stanza is conspicuously slow (note, for example, the effect of the pause after the sixth syllable in line 7). Imaginative time and real time, the pace of telling (and reading) and the pace of doing, are in

tension in Wordsworth's stanza in a way that they are not in the more directly imitative form. Such rhythms demand, and allow, a different kind of attention to the telling of the tale than is usual in such poetry.

The stanza itself also provided Wordsworth with two well-established traditions of use, the associations of both of which come into play in the overall design and movement of "Hart-Leap Well." As its two-branched history suggests, the rhythms and structures of this "heroic" or "elegiac" stanza had been found by Wordsworth's predecessors to be suited both to the narrative treatment of noble and ennobling human action and to reflection on the limits of human aspiration or the inevitable failure of human works and deeds. When Gray uses the stanza for "Elegy Written in a Country Churchyard," he takes advantage of the associations of the form, elegizing the mute and inglorious in a stanza most frequently used in the late seventeenth century to celebrate glorious human action and achievement (in Davenant's *Gondibert* and Dryden's *Annus Mirabilis*, to take just two examples).[41] The possible ironies inherent in the confluence of the two traditions apparently were not lost on Wordsworth, who presents "Hart-Leap Well" as two separate but related "rhymes." Part First narrates, without preliminaries or introduction, the events of the hunt, the building of the "pleasure-house" in commemoration of the "glorious day" (l. 8) on which Sir Walter hunted the Hart, and the naming of the place. Part Second deals, through dialogue, with attempts by a shepherd and the speaker to account for the natural gloominess of the place where the ruins of Sir Walter's handiwork are still barely apparent. This second "rhyme" ends with the speaker looking forward to the "milder day" when such monuments, which nature preserves to show us "what we are, and have been," will be allowed to fade entirely. Part First is, on the whole, a commemoration of Sir Walter's nearly superhuman exploits ("Such race, I think, was never seen before" [l. 16]; "—This race it looks not like an earthly race" [l. 27]); Part Second places those exploits and their issue in a natural and historical setting in which they are seen to be irreducibly and lamentably human.

Wordsworth's handling of the stanza in the two parts of the poem is also significantly differentiated. Part First uses the stanza to generate pleasurable interest in a tale of moving accident:

> Where is the throng, the tumult of the chace?
> The bugles that so joyfully were blown?
> —This race it looks not like an earthy race;
> Sir Walter and the Hart are left alone.
>
> (ll. 25–28)

As is appropriate to the narration of an old tale of a hunt that has passed into local memory with something of the status of myth, Part First also employs archaic stylistic touches: "And soon the Knight perform'd what he had said, / The fame whereof through many a land did ring" (ll. 79–80). The syntactic inversion and the somewhat dated Spenserian phrase "many a land" (elided to "man-[j]a land") tend to make the verse seem formulaic, as if the narrator were repeating an often-told tale (as indeed he will claim in Part Second he is). Diction and figures of speech, too, frequently strike the ear as out of keeping not only with the second part of "Hart-Leap Well" but also with the generally contemporary style of *Lyrical Ballads* as a whole (contemporary, that is, with the exception of the *Rime*). See for example, the use of "paramour" (l. 90), the description of Sir Walter as having "Made merriment" (l. 92) with the "dancers and the minstrel's song" (l. 91), and the use of the phrase "Ere thrice the Moon into her port had steer'd" (l. 81).

Part Second presents itself as a "simple song" piped "to thinking hearts" (l. 100). Cast in the form of a pastoral dialogue, its rhythmic movement is much more conversational and its general style more contemporary than Part First's. Note, for example, the effect of the pauses, marking off qualifying clauses ("for my part," "when I've been sitting") in the second and third lines of the following passage from the shepherd's speech:

> Some say that here a murder has been done,
> And blood cries out for blood: but, for my part,
> I've guess'd, when I've been sitting in the sun,
> That it was all for that unhappy Hart.
>
> (ll. 137–40)

Wordsworth's insistence on duality in the presentation of his "rhymes" suggests that the poem may fruitfully be regarded as a diptych. Two pictures representing different and related views of the same event are here contained in the same frame. The invitation to comparison, to understand one view in terms of the other, is made formally through the obviously different uses of the same verse form; it is also made more directly, through the speaker's insistence in making the issue of kinds of art—chiefly his own and that of Sir Walter's "cunning artist"—a subject of the poem.

The shepherd believes that the spot upon which Sir Walter built his pleasure dome is "curs'd" (l. 124) because of "that unhappy Hart" (l. 140). The great Lodge is gone, but the "cup of stone" that the architect had

fashioned and that "received the living well" remains. No animal will go near that "cup," however, and "oftentimes, when all are fast asleep, / This water doth send forth a dolorous groan" (ll. 133–36). The speaker of the poem, although agreeing that the shepherd is right to connect the spirit of the "doleful place" with the events of Part First, notes a "small difference" between his own and the shepherd's "creed." The "difference" to him is a matter of emphasis. Where the shepherd sees a curse, the speaker sees "sympathy divine" operating to teach a lesson. Nature here acts to preserve remnants of the ruined art of the "cunning artist" in order to show that such art eventually will be exposed for what it is: the monument raised to the glory of Sir Walter and his pleasures becomes in fact an ironic monument to unthinking and unsympathetic—and therefore ultimately powerless—man. The heroic becomes, through the processes of nature, the ironically elegiac.

The "cunning artist" consulted neither the genius of the place nor the spirit of the events that occurred there. If he had, he would have known that the pomp and splendor of a pleasure dome would be all out of keeping with the dell. In meddling with and trying to use to his own purposes the flowing "living well," symbolic of the dynamic powers and "sympathy divine" that the speaker senses, this artist makes of the spot an ironic monument to his own and his patron's vanity. The use of the figure of the cup of stone that "receives" the "living well" also suggests a relationship between Sir Walter's monument to his own pride and what the speaker calls the "ready arts" through which narrators of the "moving accident" "freeze the blood." The kind of poet who would make of the main tale of "Hart-Leap Well" itself a self-sufficient work—that is, who would rest content with Part First—would, in effect, merely mimic the "cunning" of Sir Walter's architect. His work, no less than the "pleasure dome," would itself be destined eventually to be a moldering testament to his own undeveloped powers of sympathy.

In the "milder day" that the speaker envisions, growing natural sympathies may indeed make artistic "blending" of pleasure in the suffering of another no longer intelligible (and no longer pleasurable). Until that day, however, it is no curse, but rather a blessing, to have reminders of the human capacity for such pleasures. Insofar as the stanza as it is used in Part First does in fact display considerable mastery of "ready arts" in a delineation of "moving accident," and insofar as its style may be regarded as a means for the aggrandizement of Sir Walter's hunt as some sort of supernatural quest, Part First is open to the charge of blending pleasure and pride (the narrator's and the reader's) with "sorrow" of a living creature. According to this interpretation of the stylistic texture of

the poem, the contrast between the archaic high style of Part First and the more elegiac (or at least dialogic and reflective) use of the stanza in Part Second is a means through which Wordsworth's poem attempts to establish, by active confrontation of "habits of association," a new sense of relationship between the "accident" of events and the permanent structures of thought and feeling that are, one way or another, made manifest in or through those accidents. The reader who responds to the optimistic strains of Part Second must do so warm from the chase and therefore with a sense, felt on the pulses, of the real and continuing presence of the passions and energies that are countered in the chastening "lesson" given there. The poem incorporates the very impulses that it seeks eventually to rectify, forcing a recognition at the level of minute and pleasurable rhythmic and sonic patterns that human pleasure and pride is indeed—and more frequently and more surely than it is pleasant to acknowledge—inextricably intertwined with sorrow of the meanest thing" (and not only the meanest) "that feels."[42]

Among the most prosodically interesting of Wordsworth's departures from the constraints of the 4 x 4 form is the five-line stanza in the form $abccb_4$ that he invented for "The Idiot Boy" (and used also in *Peter Bell*). This stanza, like the tail-rhyme stanza of "Ruth" and the $abab_5$ stanza of "Hart-Leap Well," bears a significant relationship to at least two different traditions of use. Paul Fussell, in *Poetic Theory and Poetic Form,* draws attention to similarities between Wordsworth's stanza and stanzas commonly appearing in popular "mad songs." Percy includes six of these songs in his *Reliques,* two of which employ the same rhyme scheme as "The Idiot Boy": Bishop Corbet's "The Distracted Puritan" (1648) and Tom D'Urfey's "The Lady Distracted with Love," from *Comedies of Don Quixote* (1694).

Fussell comments that the "stanza had for three centuries a distinct expressive advantage": "Like most fixed forms, it meant something in and of itself. It connoted immediately a happy, harmless, and verbally inventive brand of insanity" (140–41). Fussell does not discuss the issue of how and for what reasons a lyric form associated with mad speakers becomes in Wordsworth's adaptation an appropriate vehicle for a narrative spoken by a presumably sane, if often bewildered, narrator. Nor does he note the considerable differences between Wordsworth's stanza and the forms of the poems he cites as analogues. The mad songs in Percy actually employ a variety of poulter's measure; that is, a couplet composed of a six-beat line followed by a seven-beat line. One of the most common of English verse forms in drama and other serious verse of the earlier sixteenth century, poulter's measure survives beyond its heyday mostly in popular verse and hymnody, where it is normally found printed as a

four-line stanza, and is commonly known as "short meter" ($ab_3c_4b_3$). In the examples of mad song in Percy, the third line is further divided by an internal c rhyme into two two-beat verses, creating the five-line form ($ab_3c_2c_2b_3$). Here, for example, is a stanza from Bishop Corbet's "The Distracted Puritan," first as it is in Percy and then in long lines, showing its poulter's measure structure:

> They bound me like a bedlam
> They lash'd my four poor quarters;
>   Whilst this I endure,
>   Faith makes me sure
> To be one of Foxes martyrs.

      /   /   /   /   /   /
They bound me like a bedlam, they lash'd my four poor quarters
                                                    (6 beat)

     /   /   /   /   /   /
Whilst this I endure, faith makes me sure to be one of Foxes
                                                         /
                                                       martyrs.
                                                      (7 beat)

Despite all of the differences between Wordsworth's stanza and this kind of verse, however, Wordsworth's sensitivity to the "exponential" power of meter makes it tempting to think that he was encouraging, perhaps in a general way, a comparison between his poem and this tradition of "verbally inventive" song. Certainly, the possible allusion through form to a kind of verse in which the point is the gleeful presentation of idiosyncratic modes of perception has relevance to an assessment of the tonality of Wordsworth's narrator. It is not necessary to share Byron's condemnation of "The Idiot Boy" to see the shrewdness of his comparison, in "English Bards, and Scotch Reviewers," of its hero with its narrator: "all who view the 'idiot in his glory' / Conceive the bard the hero of the story" (ll. 253–54). There is indeed something of the idiotic (in the root sense of "singular," outside the bounds of publicly constituted reality and concern) in a narrator who finds in the adventures of Johnny, Betty Foy, and Susan Gale the substance for a narrative poem of four hundred lines. The connection between Wordsworth's stanza and mad songs, taken in combination with the narrator's frequent self-effacing asides concerning his power to narrate such "strange ad-

ventures" (l. 351), and his own statements about the "glee" with which he threw himself into the composition of the poem would suggest that similarities between Johnny's perceptions and the narrator's own are important, and intended, aspects of the poem as a whole.[43] If only in his predisposition to see in Johnny's two-line "story" something other and more important than mere misperception, the narrator of "The Idiot Boy" is a man with singular powers of perception.

Although the connection between the stanza used in "The Idiot Boy" and mad songs is an important one, other dimensions of the "exponential power" of Wordsworth's stanza are perhaps more important, and less dependent on specialized knowledge of a fairly recondite genre. The stanza used in "The Idiot Boy" (abccb$_4$) in fact bears a closer relation, structurally and rhythmically, to a five-line extension of the ballad stanza ($a_4b_3cc_4b_3$) than it does to mad songs. *The Rime of the Ancient Mariner* contains several stanzas in this form, a variant that Coleridge in all probability imitated directly from "Sir Cauline" in Percy.[44] Wordsworth's thematic, generic, and verbal echoes of the *Rime* in "The Idiot Boy" have often been noted.[45] A more pervasive kind of contact, in the similarity and dissimilarity of the prosodic forms of the two poems, has gone unnoticed. Compare, for example, the general structural similarities, and even the use of internal rhyme, in these stanzas:

> With throat *unslack'd*, with black lips *bak'd*
>   Ne could we laugh, ne wail:
> Then while thro' drouth all dumb they stood
> I bit my arm and suck'd the blood
>   And cry'd, A sail! a sail!
>
>   (*Rime*, ll. 149–53)

> But Betty's *bent* on her *intent*,
> For her good neighbour, Susan Gale,
> Old Susan, she who dwells alone,
> Is sick, and makes a piteous moan,
> As if her very life would fail.
>
>   ("The Idiot Boy," ll. 27–31)

Whereas the five-line form is used in "Sir Cauline" and *Rime* as an occasional departure from the normal cadence and structure of the poem for the purpose of introducing variety, in "The Idiot Boy" a "variant" stanza is employed as the pervasive metrical norm. In other words, Wordsworth's stanza transforms a structural departure or escape from

formal restriction into the standard measure of the entire poem. Such a description suggests that Wordsworth may have been using the stanza with conscious wit as the formal equivalent of the speaker's choice of an idiot for his subject: both subject and metrical form involve taking an aberration, something or someone singular, and making that aberration the measure of the fictional world created by the work. Just as Johnny's skewed perception throws new light, by comparison, on all of the perceptions contained in the poem, so the narrator's consistent use of an exceptional or aberrant form as a standard makes the entire question of singularity and its relationship to commonality an integral part of the minute formal elements of the poem.

As the foregoing considerations posit an audience capable of paying a good deal of attention to subtleties of poetic craft, it may perhaps be well to mention here that such an audience, capable of grasping this kind of formal play or formal wit, is envisioned by Wordsworth himself. In the Essay, Supplementary to the Preface (1815) Wordsworth describes his ideal readership as consisting of "those and those only who, never having suffered their youthful love of poetry to remit much of its force, have applied to the consideration of the laws of this art the best power of their understandings" (*Prose* 3:66). Of course, the reader of *Lyrical Ballads* does have close at hand, in the *Rime,* an example of the five-line stanza used as a variation. And parallels encouraging comparison between the two poems are everywhere apparent: "The Idiot Boy" is the only rhymed poem in the collection of comparable length to the *Rime;* it and the *Rime* are the only poems in *Lyrical Ballads* (1798) that are introduced by separate title pages; there are obvious structural similarities in the journey motifs of the two poems; and there are, of course, many verbal echoes of Coleridge's poem in Wordsworth's. A good example of these verbal echoes is the following, an obvious parody of the mariner's "Water, water, every where" (ll. 115, 117):

> In high and low, above, below,
> In great and small, in round and square,
> In tree and tower was Johnny seen,
> In bush and brake, in black and green,
> 'Twas Johnny, Johnny, every where.
> 							("The Idiot Boy," ll. 217–21)

The stanza alludes to the manner of ballad narrators not only through the echo of the *Rime* but also through the insistent use of such characteristic elements of ballad style as alliteration ("a̲bove, b̲elow"; "t̲ree and

tower"; "bush and brake") and syntactic coordination (there are six occurrences of "and" in these five lines).

All of these opportunities for comparison between "The Idiot Boy" and *The Rime of the Ancient Mariner* suggest that these formal aspects are intended to help establish a relationship between the voice of Wordsworth's narrator and the voice in Coleridge's poem. Through this comparison, Wordsworth connects the peculiar voice and subject of "The Idiot Boy" with the style and spirit of popular ballads of his day, but he does so on his own terms.[46] As has been noted above, nowhere in *Lyrical Ballads* does Wordsworth write in ballad style in a ballad stanza. When he does imitate the repetition, verbal stereotyping, and relatively heavy-handed prosody of ballads, he does so in stanzas that, like the stanza in "The Idiot Boy" or the eight-line stanza in "Goody Blake and Harry Gill," create a complex context within which the qualities of the voice narrating are put forward as an unavoidable and essential aspect of the poem's overall effect. In "The Idiot Boy," the stanza has a double-edged function. Its associational and physical aspects offer the poet the opportunity to create comic effects at the expense both of the characters and the narrator. For example, the similarities and differences between the "Idiot Boy" stanza and that used in the *Rime*, or in any serious ballad, suggest throughout the poem an element of self-importance or unwarranted *sprezzatura* in the narrator's character, as if he were showing through the form itself what he suggests directly in his asides to the "muses"—that the subject of his tale is too large and too significant to be contained within merely conventional constraints:

> I to the muses have been bound,
> These fourteen years, by strong indentures;
> Oh gentle muses! let me tell
> But half of what to him befel,
> For sure he met with strange adventures.
>
> (ll. 347–51)

Like Sidney's love-struck persona in the first sonnet of *Astrophel and Stella* ("Loving in truth, and fain in verse my love to show"), whose overabundance of passion requires him to use hexameter lines in a normally pentameter form, Wordsworth's narrator cannot contain himself within the four-line stanza usually employed for the type of poem that he is writing.

At other points in "The Idiot Boy," the emphatic use of repetition or of empty phrases to fill out lines (and even stanzas) suggests another

kind of strain contributing to the representation of the speaker as a man carried away by the importance of his tale:

> His heart it was so full of glee,
> That till full fifty yards were gone,
> He quite forgot his holly whip,
> And all his skill in horsemanship,
> Oh! happy, happy, happy John.
>
> (ll. 92–96)

Here the repetition of "happy" suggests what such repetition suggests for the speaker of "The Thorn": the speaker's "consciousness of the inadequateness of [his] own powers, or the deficiencies of language" to communicate a sense of the state of mind of the poem's singular hero (*PW* 2:513). The verse also, however, serves another of the several purposes of repetition mentioned by Wordsworth in his note to "The Thorn": it is evidence of the mind luxuriating in the consciousness that it has hit on a singularly appropriate — if imperfect — epithet.[47] The three "happys" express the speaker's own "glee" in the exercise of his craft, as he becomes caught up in his own story and the telling of his story. And, at least for a moment, he and Johnny are united by a shared emotion. Johnny forgets his "horsemanship"; the speaker forgets his craftsmanship, but each nevertheless proceeds along his way. Through such suggestions of relationship, the poem as a whole establishes strange and surprising connections between Johnny and his narrator, Johnny and the other speakers of *Lyrical Ballads,* and, finally, between Johnny and the readers of these poems.

The similarities and dissimilarities between the stanza used in "The Idiot Boy" and the ballad stanza assist Wordsworth in calling his reader's attention not only to the idiosyncrasies of his "gleeful" narrator but also to the ways in which his tale of the lone wanderings of an idiot boy is and is not like the ancient mariner's solemn tale of his own lonely journey. Wordsworth's creation of a comic voice for a narrative within these contexts suggests that he thought the two poems — "The Idiot Boy" and the *Rime* — like "Expostulation and Reply" and "The Tables Turned," would be richer for being paired. Both the mariner and the idiot boy have been "all alone," and each has returned to tell his tale. By creating in "The Idiot Boy" a voice that is only fully comprehensible in light of its relation to such voices as the mariner's, Wordsworth brings forth no less complex a question than the relationship between vastly different degrees of ability in exercising imagina-

tive power. Johnny's two-line story, that is, stands, through the medium Wordsworth's speaker's voice, in direct and pointed contrast to the magnificent symbolic universe of the mariner. In the Preface to *Lyrical Ballads*, Wordsworth says that a chief goal of his metrical experiments is to introduce the reader to an array of minds different from those normally met with in literature and to adduce sympathy for these by showing them to be different from preeminently "poetic" minds in degree rather than in kind. In presenting the idiot boy and the narrator who champions him in contrast to the mariner, Wordsworth pushes this experiment perhaps as far as it can go. And the degree to which a reader can derive pleasure from both poems—and can derive more pleasure from each because of their juxtaposition—is, from Wordsworth's point of view, a test of imaginative power.

WORDS FOR MUSIC: FORMAL PECULIARITIES AND METRICAL PLAY IN "THE REVERIE OF POOR SUSAN," "SONG FOR THE WANDERING JEW," "THE PET LAMB," AND "'TIS SAID, THAT SOME HAVE DIED FOR LOVE"

The playfulness evident in the versification of "The Idiot Boy" is by no means restricted to that poem alone, and serves as a reminder that those functions of metrical language that have formed the chief focus of the discussion above depend to a large extent on a conception of the poem as pleasurable play. Without the "as if" or gamelike quality that metrical language bestows on the language of a poem, without the sense of lines and stanzas as means for marking off the bounds within which the noise of everyday language becomes open to the infinitely various and meaningful patterns of combination and recombination that mark the physical form of an utterance as poetically significant, no more ostensibly serious function of verse would be possible. It all depends, as Wordsworth puts it in the Preface, on the "sense of difficulty overcome," the "blind association of pleasure" based on earlier experience with the play of rhythm and meter, and the "indistinct perception perpetually renewed" of language that both is and is not the language of everyday life. All of these forms of play contribute to the "complex feeling of delight" that is an indispensable source of power in all poetry, from the most "pathetic and impassioned" forms to those "lighter compositions," in which "the ease and gracefulness with which the Poet manages his numbers are themselves confessedly a principal source of the gratification of the Reader" (*Prose* 1:151).

One of Wordsworth's most eloquent affirmations of the passion of meter is the very fact of his incorporation, in all of his collections of poems from *Lyrical Ballads* (1800) through the final lifetime edition, of a number of poems in which "numbers" themselves are indeed a "principal source of gratification of the Reader." A survey of such works—in the common wisdom so un-Wordsworthian—might include, for example, "The Kitten and the Falling Leaves," "Written in March at the Foot of Brother's Water," "To the Cuckoo," "A Wren's Nest," "Yes, it was the mountain echo," a number of poems in *Poems, in Two Volumes* composed in a variety of stanzas imitated from Elizabethan and cavalier poets (see, for example, the three poems entitled "To the Daisy" and "The Green Linnet"), "To a Skylark" ("Up with me"), the "Power of Music," the "Hymn for the Boatmen," and "So Fair, so sweet, withal so sensitive." In all of these poems (and the list might be prolonged without difficulty to five or six times this length), Wordsworth may be seen to be taking to heart the sentiments of some favorite verses of Akenside's which he used as an epigraph to the *Yarrow Revisited* (1835) volume:

> —Poets . . . dwell on earth
> To clothe whate'er the soul admires and loves
> With language and with numbers.

In such poems, even more evidently than in others, Wordsworth demonstrates that his youthful love for words "in tuneful order" did not abate.

In the *Lyrical Ballads,* Wordsworth's more musical compositions are distinguished in general by his use of a verse form or rhythmic pattern that is more insistent than are the usual four- or five-beat lines in duple rhythms, generally rising or "iambic," employed in stanzas that rhyme in quatrains or couplets. The six anapestic poems in *Lyrical Ballads,* for example, announce themselves as words-for-music to a degree that no iambic poem can.[48] Because the consistent use of double offbeats between beats is not a feature of spoken language, there can be no mistaking the rhythms of these poems for the rhythms of speech. Such poems decidedly do not encourage much "voluntary modulation" on the part of a reader; on the contrary, they pointedly arrest or suspend those impulses, encouraged by other poems in the collection, toward active participation in the creation of the rhythms of the line.[49] The reader is asked in a sense to surrender to the fundamental four-beat rhythms of the song, much as the various figures in the 1806 anapestic poem "The Power of Music" surrender to a street "Orpheus," a fiddler who "sways"

a London audience with "harmony merry and loud." Such music unites its audience in a shared act of transformation: the noise of quotidian reality becomes music accompanied by natural sound:

> Oh blest are the Hearers, and proud be the Hand
> Of the pleasure it spreads through so thankful a Band;
> . . . .
> Now, Coaches and Chariots! roar on like a stream;
> Here are twenty souls happy as Souls in a dream[.]
>
> (ll. 29–30, 41–42)

In "Poor Susan," Wordsworth uses the simple pleasure of a repetitive measure, presumably with the same kind of pride that he notes here attends the fiddler's efforts, to describe (and to attempt to effect) a similar transformation through song of a city scene into a harmonious, dreamlike other world. The city-dwelling thrush that Susan has heard repeatedly for "three years" has power to enchant her. Its song transforms the unlovely London cityscape into a vision of the rural landscape in which she spent her childhood and from which she is now an "Outcast" (l. 17): "And a river flows on through the vale of Cheapside" (l. 8). The meter is, appropriately, enchanting in its own right:

> At the corner of Wood Street, when daylight appears,
> There's a Thrush that sings loud, it has sung for three years:
> Poor Susan has pass'd by the spot and has heard
> In the silence of morning the song of the bird.
>
> 'Tis a note of enchantment . . .
>
> (ll. 1–5)

Making no pretense to be an imitation of speech rhythms, the poem tends through its insistent rhythmic pattern to prize the diction away from its connection with the everyday. As chanted speech, it presents itself as emphatically less subtle and less urbane than does Wordsworth's more characteristic duple verse. Such rhythms are appropriate to the tone of the reverie itself—a wish for a return to the country and to childlike innocence; they also are appropriate to the speaker's role as a street Orpheus in his own right. The rhythms of his song are designed to lift the reader or listener out of the noise of talk and into the harmonies of music.[50]

Falling (or trochaic) rhythm, too, is used sparingly by Wordsworth in *Lyrical Ballads* (and throughout the *Poetical Works*) in poems for which

an insistent and relatively rigid rhythmic form is appropriate. As is the case with anapests, the trochaic is so firmly and decidedly distinguished from the rhythms of speech (it is a patterned reversal of the common rhythmic tendency of speech) that its distance from speech rhythm is perforce a constitutive element of the poem's content. That is, the fitting of language to meter that takes place when the metrical frame selected is a trochaic measure is so clearly a means for distancing the utterance from common speech that the transformation of the language out of its normal rhythm is presented as an element of principal importance.

In "Song for the Wandering Jew," for example, a large part of the expressive effect, and therefore (given its generic designation) of the meaning, depends on the power of meter to control recitation precisely. The song aims to express what the speaker calls the "trouble / of the Wanderer in [his] soul" (ll. 19–20). Rhetorically, the poem consists of a series of contrasts between the restless and displaced Wandering Jew and all of those creatures—Chamois, Sea-horse, Raven, Ostrich—that do, though they roam, swim, gambol, and run vagrant, have places of rest. Each stanza treats one creature, and each is structured roughly as an "although . . . nevertheless" statement (though the Chamois roams by day; yet it finds rest among the mountains), with lines 3–4 of each stanza answering lines 1–2. The rhythm of the stanzas plays on the deeply ingrained tendency in English speech to move from unstressed to stressed syllables. Frustration of that tendency tends to be felt as unsettling, as if the normal course of things has been suspended. The result in this case is an appropriate embodiment of the idea of perpetual motion and restlessness emphasized by the speaker:[51]

> Though the Sea-horse in the ocean
> Own no dear domestic cave;
> Yet he slumbers without motion
> On the calm and silent wave.
>
> (ll. 13–16)

Wordsworth heightens the unsettled effect of the falling rhythm through the use of enjambments after unstressed syllables in lines 1 and 3 of each stanza. Such enjambment tends to give the stanza the rhythmic feel of two fifteen-syllable, seven-beat long lines. This in effect creates a continual sense of rest denied: the rhyme and the physical presence of line endings at 1 and 3 hold out the promise of a place of rest, which the syntactical rhythms continually break. Thus Wordsworth's verse creates—again for the purposes of establishing a felt relationship between

a reader and another kind of outcast—a physical sense of the restlessness and "trouble" whereof his speaker sings.

Non-iambic rhythms are Wordsworth's preferred means, as they were for many of his predecessors and contemporaries, for poems in which the musical effect is of primary importance. Intrinsic characteristics— chiefly their rhythmic distance from speech rhythm—as well as traditions of association together make anapests and trochaics readily adaptable to and suggestive of musical lyric. But Wordsworth also occasionally uses a particularly unusual line or stanza form in generally iambic rhythm for poems in which the musical effect is of primary importance. "The Pet-Lamb," for example, uses a six-beat line unique in Wordsworth's poetical works—and very rare in English poetry—as a sign of and expressive vehicle for an equally unique voice.[52] The speaker of the poem, who has overheard a little girl imploring a tethered pet lamb with the words "Drink, pretty Creature, drink" (l. 2) is so taken by the girl's "tone" that he claims "almost" to have "receiv'd her heart into [his] own" (ll. 11–12). The poem continues as an overt instance of a kind of ventriloquism, as the speaker attempts to provide the "measured numbers" appropriate to express what the girl's look and tone seem to suggest she "would sing," "If Nature to her tongue could measured numbers bring" (ll. 19–20). The poem aims, that is, not merely to be descriptive of the child's perceptions and expression, but to be actually informed by them. Others of the *Lyrical Ballads*—"We Are Seven" and "Anecdote for Fathers," for example—incorporate the child's perspective through dialogue in which the simplicity of the child's answers serves as a contrast and corrective to adult sophistication of one sort or another. In "The Pet-Lamb" Wordsworth is attempting something very different: to give body to the meanings of the little girl's "look" and "tone" by writing a lyric that imitates the movements of the child's mind.

The main body of the poem consists of the "song" that is the result of this attempt. The song begins with simple expressions of childish perplexity over the lamb's restlessness, given the apparent sufficiency of present arrangements—"What ails thee," "Why pull so at thy cord" when all your wants are provided for?—but quickly develops in ways that hint gently at the little girl's growing unease. By lines 48 and following, she is beginning to ask questions of an entirely different order: are there "Things that I know not of" and "dreams of things which thou canst neither see nor hear"? The meanings conveyed by the little girl's voice, then, would appear to have been interesting to the speaker as an expression of complexity of emotion even in a relationship so ostensibly simple: her wishes for the lamb's complete happiness in

her care are mingled with a nagging sense of the impossibility of such perfect contentment.

Wordsworth confronts directly, and thereby makes problematic within the poem itself, the issue of the extent to which an adult speaker can in fact enter into and express the emotional state of a little girl. At the end of the poem, the speaker ruminates on the question of how much of the song is in fact expressive of the girl's "look and tone" and how much is the result of his own overlay of sentiment:

> As homeward through the lane I went with lazy feet
> This song to myself did I oftentimes repeat,
> And it seem'd as I retrac'd the ballad line by line
> That but half of it was hers, and one half of it was mine.
>
> (ll. 61–64)

Repeating the song "Again, and once again," however, he concludes at last that "more than half to the Damsel must belong," because "she look'd with such a look, and she spake with such a tone, / That I almost receiv'd her heart into my own" (ll. 65–68). The speaker's assertion here of his own conviction that he has succeeded in acting more as a conduit for the girl's own passions than as a shaping or imposing creator of those passions results from nothing more nor less than his repetition of the song itself. Through this curious device, Wordsworth suggests that he is willing to refer the question of the poem's authenticity directly to the poem's structures. That is, the speaker's claim—that the song itself satisfies any doubts he might have that he has indeed caught a "tone" (and therefore a movement of mind expressed in language) that is other than his own characteristic tonality and habit of mind—is to be proved for the reader exactly as it has been for the speaker himself—by listening to the verse.

It is chiefly in relation to this question that the singularity of the verse form and Wordsworth's handling of it are important. To put the issue simply, the poem is rhythmically so un-Wordsworthian that the rhythm itself substantiates the speaker's claim to be entering into another consciousness (or genuinely mingling that other with his own). The six-beat couplets are, as his frequent use of a pause after the sixth syllable or third beat in the line reveals, actually a variety of half (or short) meter ($abcb_3$) printed in long lines:

> The dew was falling fast, / the stars began to blink;
> I heard a voice; it said, / "Drink, pretty Creature, drink!"
>
> (ll. 1–2)

In such a meter, each half line is felt as a four-beat form with a strong pause substituted for the final (unrealized) beat. Accordingly, and as is appropriate in a poem in which the speaker attempts to re-create the child's own song, phrase lengths are severely restricted:[53]

> Rest, little Young One, rest—   (x)
> B   ŏ   B   o   B   (o B)
> thou hast forgot the day   (x)
> o   B   o   B   o   B   (o B)
> When my Father found thee first (x)
> ŏ   B   o   B   o   B   (o B)
> in places far away   (x)
> o   B   o   B   o   B   (o B)
>
>   (ll. 33–34)

The first and third half-lines quoted here also show a rhythmic effect—the double offbeat used without a compensatory implied offbeat—which by now will be recognized as uncommon in Wordsworth's verse. "The Pet-Lamb" in fact employs such effects more frequently than does any other poem in the *Lyrical Ballads* (with the obvious exception of the anapestic poems):

> Thy limbs will shortly be twice as stout as they are now,
> Then I'll yoke thee to my cart like a pony in the plough.
> ŏ   B   o B o B   ŏ   B o B o   B
>   (ll. 45–46)

Taken together, the short rhythmic phrases and the double offbeats contribute to make the verse of this poem pointedly unlike anything else in the remainder of the *Lyrical Ballads*. The speaker's very forms of feeling and habits of speech are presented as having been transformed by the experience of "almost" receiving the girl's heart into his own.

A final example from *Lyrical Ballads* will illustrate yet another way in which Wordsworth uses unusual or particularly musical verse forms innovatively and as a means to establish and define relationships among a speaker, the poet, and the reader. In "'Tis said, that some have died for love," Wordsworth uses an uncommonly elaborate verse form—an eight-line stanza in the form $ab_5c_4b_3c_5d_4d_3c_6$—to signal and to give rhythmic embodiment to a voice that is purposefully distinct both from other speakers in the collection and from the voice of a speaker (hereafter "the poet") who begins and ends the poem. This individuated voice is that of

a distraught lover, who "makes his moan" over the death of his "pretty Barbara":

> Oh! what a weight is in these shades! Ye leaves,
> When will that dying murmur be suppress'd?
> Your sound my heart of peace bereaves,
> It robs my heart of rest.
> Thou Thrush, that singest loud and loud and free,
> Into yon row of willows flit,
> Upon that alder sit;
> Or sing another song, or chuse another tree.
>
> (ll. 21–28)

This speaker's "feverish complaint," uttered "three years" after the death of the beloved, is rhetorically extravagant even by the generic standards of complaints. It is especially so in the context of *Lyrical Ballads,* which offers by way of contrast the understated simplicity of "A slumber did my spirit seal" and "She dwelt among th'untrodden ways" and the much more measured response to even greater devastation portrayed in "The Complaint of a Forsaken Indian Woman." In each stanza of "'Tis said," as in the stanza quoted above, the speaker implores, in rather stylized fashion ("Oh! move thou Cottage," "Roll back, sweet rill!"), some object in the landscape to be other than it is: he wishes oaks to be uprooted, murmuring leaves and waterfalls to be silenced, a Thrush to be displaced, a rill "chain'd," and a rainbowlike flowering eglantine to shed its flowers. In each case, the object or natural sight or sound that is scorned or rejected is one that in other contexts in *Lyrical Ballads* would offer the speaker comfort in his loss or relief from introspective torment. Cottage smoke, murmuring natural sounds, and flowing water evoke very different responses from the speaker of "Tintern Abbey." The "Thrush, that singest loud and loud and free" echoes the "thrush that sings loud" in "Poor Susan," where the bird's song transforms the dreary cityscape as if by enchantment. This speaker is, decidedly, out of tune.

The stanza chosen by Wordsworth marks the utterance as different from any other in *Lyrical Ballads* while it provides the opportunity to develop a broad-gestured and slightly mannered rhythmic context that is entirely appropriate to the extravagance of the rhetoric. The form stands out in the context of the *Lyrical Ballads* as the only example in the collection (and one of very few in Wordsworth's work as a whole) of a stanza that is neither historically precedented nor composed of recognizable shorter forms (normally variants and combinations of the

4 x 4 stanza). Unequal line lengths, combinations of cross- and enclosed rhymes, and asymmetricality make it also more complex than the average stanza in *Lyrical Ballads*. Its complexity is, in fact, of a kind more frequently encountered in stylized poetry in the courtly tradition than in poems about men who live "upon Helvellyn's side." In short, the stanza is as rhythmically overdone and as uncharacteristic of the *Lyrical Ballads* as a whole as is the speaker's imagery and rhetoric. This point becomes especially apparent when the stanzas are set in contrast to the conclusion of the poem, a blank-verse section in which the foregoing effusion is indicted as "feverish." The passage proves its point as much by rhythmic and stylistic example and contrast as by direct statement (note the rhythmic regularity and the late, slowing, placement of pauses):

> The Man who makes this feverish complaint
> Is one of giant stature, who could dance
> Equipp'd from head to foot in iron mail.—
> Ah gentle Love! if ever thought was thine
> To store up kindred hours for me, thy face
> Turn from me, gentle Love, nor let me walk
> Within the sound of Emma's voice, nor know
> Such happiness as I have known today.—
>
> (ll. 45–52)

Whereas in "The Pet-Lamb," Wordsworth's speaker had changed his rhythmic habits in response to and as an indication of an act of sympathy with the feelings of the poem's subject, here the dissimilar metrical forms of main body and frame (and the abrupt shift from one to the other) function both to link speaker and poet and to dissociate them. The metrical differences help to identify the strange music of the complaint as an expression of emotional pathology, mediated by a speaker who responds to his subject with a complex mixture of attraction and repulsion, sympathy and censure.

In this discussion of the stanzaic verse of the *Lyrical Ballads*, I have tried to show a few of the many ways in which specifically metrical effects work to make the experience of reading an active and constitutive part of what the *Lyrical Ballads* are, both individually and as a collection. Approached with attention to the kind of subtlety that Wordsworth would identify in detail in later prose comments, even a collection as ostensibly lacking in prosodic interest as is *Lyrical Ballads* may be seen to exhibit a wide and significant variety of accommodation between the

passion of the sense and the passion of meter. Complexity of relationship between the associations of a stanza and its adaptation in Wordsworth's corpus, rhythmic allusions to modes and kinds of verse other than those employed in the poem itself, choices of stanza forms that enforce for expressive and emblematic purposes rhythmic habits markedly different from the more usual patterns of the collection, various adaptations of similar verse forms to dissimilar expressive ends—all of these sources of prosodic tension and interest, and more, are on display in *Lyrical Ballads*. Moreover, the very presence in the collection of a significant range of metrical styles—from "Song for the Wandering Jew" to "Tintern Abbey," from the five-line comic narrative stanza of "The Idiot Boy" to the Spenserian stanzas of "The Female Vagrant"—may be recognized as an important manifestation of and appeal to the principle of similitude in dissimilitude, a principle fundamental to Wordsworth's definitions of poetry and of the poet.

    I have attempted to suggest, too, that the peculiarly Wordsworthian musicality of his stanzaic verse is, in fact, established in large part through its many kinds of accommodations between diction and meter—some conventionally fitting and sonorous, some designedly strained or awkward, some seemingly incongruous, but all expressive of a range of active passion and thought. The very qualities that have been conventionally identified (since the publication of *Biographia Literaria*) as evidence of Wordsworth's "inconstancy of style" and therefore of his weak grasp of the resources of his metrical art are among the chief sources of the poems' interest and power. Given Wordsworth's metrical theory—which will admit no ideal relationship between diction and meter and therefore will exclude no kind of diction and syntax on principle, merely because it may jar with the metrical form and with the expectations that writing in such meter may arouse—Wordsworth's practice should be expected to be no less unconventionally "inconstant" to a metrical ideal than it in fact is.

5

"Infinitely the Most Difficult Metre to Manage"
Characteristics of Wordsworth's Blank Verse

"PROOFS OF SKILL ACQUIRED BY PRACTICE"

Wordsworth considered his blank verse a consummate artistic accomplishment. In letters written in his middle and late years, he is quick to admonish correspondents who tend (like many twentieth-century commentators) to confound the painstaking fashioning of a powerfully original and various voice in blank verse with artless or "natural" expression. In a letter of 1831, Wordsworth warns William Rowan Hamilton not to be tempted by the seeming naturalness of blank verse into supposing that the effect of effortlessness takes no effort. Although there is no "cant" in Milton's claim to be "pouring easy his unpremeditated verse," Wordsworth tells Hamilton, it is "not *true* to the letter, and tends to mislead. . . . I could point out to you 500 passages in Milton upon which labour has been bestowed, and twice 500 more to which additional labour would have been serviceable: not that I regret the absence of such labour, because no Poem contains more proofs of skill acquired by practice [than does *Paradise Lost*]" (*LY* 2:454). Blank verse, Wordsworth writes to Catharine Grace Godwin, is "infinitely the most difficult metre to manage, as is clear from so few having succeeded in it" (*LY* 2:58).

Wordsworth certainly bound himself to a long apprenticeship in the craft of blank verse. Before the publication of the 1800 *Lyrical Ballads*, which contained thirteen new blank-verse poems, Wordsworth had published only some 230 lines in the form in three poems, all in the 1798 *Lyrical Ballads:* "Lines left upon a Seat in a Yew-Tree," "Old Man Travelling," and "Tintern Abbey." Between mid-1796, when he probably composed the fragment that Stephen Gill calls his "first significant use of

blank verse" ("The road extended o'er a heath," in DC MS 2),[1] and early 1800, after which the bulk of the thirteen new poems in *Lyrical Ballads* (1800) were begun, however, Wordsworth had amassed in manuscript a body of blank verse more than twenty times the size of his public output. These five-thousand-plus unpublished verses encompass dramatic, narrative, philosophical, autobiographical, descriptive, and lyric genres. They include work on *The Borderers*, early work on *The Prelude*, the "Prospectus" to *The Recluse*, "The Ruined Cottage," "Description of a Beggar," "A Night-Piece," and much more that would eventually find its way into print. By the time he published a substantial body of blank-verse poems in 1800, Wordsworth had been attending for some time and with impressive results to what he calls the "innumerable minutiae" on which "absolute success" in the art of poetry "depends" (*LY* 2:459).[2]

The few and "very simple" rules governing Wordsworth's practice in pentameters are set forth in the 1804 letter to Thelwall. After making explicit his claim that the passion of meter makes it "Physically impossible," even in blank verse, "to pronounce the last words or syllables of the lines with the same indifference, as the others, i.e. not to give them an intonation of one kind or an other, or to follow them with a pause, not called out for by the passion of the subject" (*EY*, 434), Wordsworth sets forth a "general rule" for the disposition of stresses: "1st and 2nd syllables long or short indifferently except where the Passion of the sense cries out for one in preference 3d 5th 7th 9th short etc according to the regular laws of the Iambic."[3] Finally, he offers this statement defining what he considers to be allowable variation within these rules: "I can scarcely say that I admit any limits to the dislocation of the verse, that is I know none that may not be justified by some passion or other" (*EY*, 434).

An additional set of remarks by Wordsworth, concerning the important issue of placement and variety of midline pauses, helps in constructing a more developed picture of Wordsworth's practical rules with regard specifically to blank verse. In a letter of 1816 to Robert Pearce Gillies, Wordsworth provides a rule of thumb while describing his own practice: "If you write more blank verse, pray pay particular attention to your versification, especially as to the pauses on the first, second, third, eighth, and ninth syllables. These pauses should never be introduced for convenience, and not often for the sake of variety merely, but for some especial effect of harmony or emphasis" (*MY* 2:343). Earlier in the same letter, Wordsworth had objected to Gillies's placement of pause in "The Visionary." He faults in particular a passage in which the line breaks after the sixth syllable in three consecutive verses and offers the general criticism that Gillies "frequently introduce[s] pauses at the

second syllable, which are always harsh, unless the sense justify them and require an especial emphasis" (*MY* 2:343).

The Wordsworth of 1816 might as well have been addressing the Wordsworth of 1793. It may be recalled that in the pentameter verse of *An Evening Walk*—and especially of *Descriptive Sketches*—placement of pause after the second syllable is a kind of stylistic mannerism and contributes to the sense of "harshness" that contemporary reviewers had sensed in the versification of Wordsworth's debut poems. Wordsworth's comments of 1816 show the poet had in his maturity come into broad agreement with the theory and practice of mainstream English tradition (most importantly with the practice of Milton) in which the pause in a five-beat line is in general restricted to the midline positions. (Wordsworth, however, extends the range of allowable normal pauses to include the seventh syllable.) As is common in Wordsworth's comments about meter and rhythm, he stresses variety of placement within these relatively strict confines, while again suggesting that he would allow almost any departure from the general rule as long as it were justified by the need for "especial emphasis" or by some "especial effect of harmony." As is the case with his discussion of "dislocation" in the letter to Thelwall, Wordsworth will exclude in theory no effect that may be justified in terms of the poet's chief duties: to express passion and to give pleasure. The only practices he will exclude prescriptively are those that might give the impression of caprice or inattention, because such impressions undermine the chief function of versification—to provide a normative "set" against which expressive impulses play. In terms of the discussion of the passion of meter pursued in the first chapter, Wordsworth's practical rules concerning the placement of pause reflect his concern that meter be manifested in the poem as a restricting presence or counterpassion, so that the passion of the sense may be made palpable through the dynamics of the relationship between the fixed form and infinitely variable realizations of that form.

According to Wordsworth's "rules," then, the blank-verse line is theoretically a ten-syllable unit with regularly alternating stress, a tendency toward internal structural balance, and a marked ending. This theoretical pattern (the passion of meter) exists, however, only in and through tense opposition with actual speech sounds and the passions that motivate them (the passion of the subject). This tension, the precise bounds of which Wordsworth consistently declines to define ("I can scarcely say that I admit any limits"), manifests itself chiefly in the interplay between an ideal and a real stress pattern (potentially causing "dislocation") and in ever-shifting relationships between metrical lines and variable phrases, achieved through enjambment (over marked terminations) and placement

of pause. A third source of tension also may be deduced from Wordsworth's comments and from his practices, the tension (and sense of optionality) produced by the fact that real speech sounds seldom fulfill unambiguously the numerical requirements of the ten-syllable line. Is "power" disyllabic or monosyllabic? Is it "heaven" or "heav'n"? Wordsworth's practice with regard to ambiguous syllables is less strict in his mature pentameters than in his juvenilia and in the couplets of *An Evening Walk* and *Descriptive Sketches*. As his definition of his "rules" suggests (and as his practice shows), however, he never abandoned his theoretical definition of the line as decasyllabic, nor did he adopt, as did many of his contemporaries and nineteenth-century successors, frequent "trisyllabic substitution" or variable offbeats as part of his metrical set. Wordsworth's numerical definition of the line implies that apparently extrametrical syllables ought to be recognized as potentially significant occurrences, not merely as grace notes or (in Thelwall's terms) "*appogiaturae*" to be resolved without tension in the normal course of the meter. Wordsworth's lifelong practice of using the tension between the numerical idea of the line and its actual sound is an important source of the liveliness and power of his blank verse.

The blank verse of the 1800 *Lyrical Ballads* shows that Wordsworth had by the late 1790s already begun to work within and through the general rules that he lays out in 1804 and 1816. Departures from the rules of syllable number and stress placement are, appropriately, rare. Only in "The Brothers" does Wordsworth employ a significant number of genuinely hypermetrical verses (verses containing more than ten syllables that do not also contain ambiguous or elidable syllables). And there the effect is clearly intended, as it marks a generic distinction between passages of direct dramatic speech (set off by the speaker prefixes "Leonard" and "Priest") and the narrative links between these speeches. Frequent use of unstressed "extra" final syllables (what Wordsworth calls a "trochaic ending")[4] is, of course, characteristic of dramatic blank verse and is a chief means through which such verse may be made to seem more conversational, less formal, than other kinds:

LEONARD.
These Boys—I hope
They lov'd this good old Man—

PRIEST.
They did, and truly,
o B o B o

> But that was what we almost overlook'd,
> They were such darlings of each other. For
> Though from their cradles they had liv'd with Walter,
>   o B o   B o
> The only kinsman near them . . .
>
>   ("The Brothers," ll. 237–42)

(Note in the example also the informal effect of the ninth-syllable pause in line 240, a placement that would be avoided in Wordsworth's nondramatic blank verse.) This kind of relatively loose blank verse is, for Wordsworth, appropriate only for passages of direct speech and occurs in his corpus regularly only in the dramatic passages of "The Brothers," in his tragedy, *The Borderers,* and in some passages of quoted speech in *The Excursion.* When true eleven-syllable verses with unstressed endings appear elsewhere, they may be considered to serve some extraordinary expressive or emblematic end.

Dislocations of stress pattern, except for "initial inversion," occur infrequently in the *Lyrical Ballads* of 1800 and are clearly related either to expressive motives or to aesthetic ends such as variety of pattern or pace. Among the most common kinds of dislocations other than initial inversion are the following (roughly in the order of their frequency of occurrence):

Stress-ûnal implied-offbeat pattern at the opening of a line
(midline stress-ûnal patterns are much less frequent)

>   . . . all at once,
> In one impression, by connecting force
> Of their own beauty, imaged in the heart.
> ŏ   B ô B
>
>   ("To Joanna," ll. 48–50)

Stress-initial implied-offbeat pattern at the seventh position
(or "fourth-foot inversion"—usually occurring after a strong
sixth-syllable pause)

> The world, and man himself, appeared a scene
> Of kindred loveliness: then he would sigh
> o B o B o B̄ ô B ŏ   B
> With mournful joy . . .
>
>   ("Lines left upon a Seat in a Yew-Tree," ll. 37–39)

Stress-ûnal implied-offbeat pattern other than at the opening of a line

> —Now, by those dear immunities of heart
> Engender'd betwixt malice and true love
> o   B   ŏ   B ô B   ŏ   B̄ ô B
> ("To Joanna," ll. 32–33)

*Stress-initial implied-offbeat pattern at the ûfth position
(or "third-foot inversion")*

> But I forget
> My purposes. Lay now the corner-stone
> o B   o B̄ ô B   ŏ   B
> As I requested
> ("Michael," ll. 413–15)

Because stress-initial implied-offbeat formations are rather disruptive of the metrical set, they tend not to occur earlier than the fifth position or, as Attridge puts it, "before the rhythm has had a chance to establish itself" (174). Implied offbeats in the third position (or "second-foot inversion") are indeed rare in Wordsworth's verse (and in English verse as a whole). Marina Tarlinskaja calculates that such effects account for only 4 percent of all "inversions" in Wordsworth (*English Verse,* 283, table 43). More will be said about Wordsworth's use of this source of tension below, in the discussion of "A Night-Piece." At present, it may be sufficient to note that where it occurs, this rare kind of dislocation may be expected, like the use of eleven-syllable lines with "trochaic endings," to mark some especially significant expressive or emblematic purpose.

A much more common and pervasive source of metrical variety and interest is Wordsworth's use of the less-disruptive effects of promotion or demotion of syllables. As these effects will be discussed in detail below in the course of analyses of individual passages and poems, I will limit myself here to a simple mention of one especially characteristic kind of demotion and one of promotion. Wordsworth is fond of using a relatively strongly stressed monosyllabic adjective in the third, offbeat, position. Placed in this position the syllable is felt to be in tense opposition to the meter and frequently produces a slowing effect. This probably results in large part from the strong pull in the metrical set against a third-syllable stress (for reasons mentioned immediately above):

> Some quaint odd play-thing of elaborate skill
>   o   B   ó   B
> ("Lines Written with a Slate pencil . . . Rydal," l. 17)

> . . . and often seems to send
> Its own deep quiet to restore our hearts.
>   o B ó B
> ("There is an Eminence,—of these our hills," ll. 7–8)

> The still, sad music of humanity
>   o B ó B
>   ("Tintern Abbey," l. 92)

Wordsworth's most characteristic kind of stress promotion involves the use of a normally unstressed preposition, article, or conjunction in a "beat" position. Very frequently, this promoted syllable, which has an effect opposite to the slowing effect of the demoted third syllable, falls in the sixth position. As the examples quoted above show, the effect very frequently occurs in those lines that contain a third-syllable demotion, where it seems to function as a kind of rhythmic compensation:

> Some quaint odd play-thing of elaborate skill
>   o   B̄ o B o   B

> Its own deep quiet to restore our hearts.
>   o B̄ o B   o   B

> The still, sad music of humanity
>   o B̄   o B o B

Such verses, in which an initial sense of slow weightiness is balanced by the diminution of stress and relative speediness of the line ending, are a Wordsworthian blank-verse trademark.

Wordsworth's placement of pause and use of enjambment in the blank verse of *Lyrical Ballads* also show him to be working in accordance both with his practical rules (as these would later be set forth in the letter to Gillies) and with his ideas about the function of meter in the accomplishment of the aesthetic ends of similitude in dissimilitude. Table 2 analyzes the distribution of pause in a sample of one thousand lines from *Lyrical Ballads*. It allows comparison of Wordsworth's mature practice

TABLE 2
Distribution of Pauses after Syllables and Percentage of
Occurrence in Various Texts

Pause After Syllable	EW (%)	DS (%)	LB[1] (%)	PL (Book I)[2] (%)	Task[3] (%)
1	7.6	6.6	2.6	0.2	1.6
2	15.3	17.9	4.8	4.9	4.3
3	2.9	7.0	5.9	4.5	7.6
4	18.8	17.5	13.2	24.2	23.7
5	8.2	7.4	13.5	16.6	11.3
6	15.9	9.5	16.8	27.0	21.0
7	2.4	1.4	12.1	10.7	12.7
8	1.8	2.8	3.8	4.9	4.1
9	0.5	3.2	0.3	0.5	0.4
Double	25.9	24.6	21.0	6.0	10.9
Triple	0.5	2.1	2.6	0.2	2.3
Unbroken	62.0	64.5	35.7	31.3	36.8

Note: Percentages are based upon the number of lines that employ pause; the percentage of unbroken lines relative to the total number of lines is given at the end of the table.

Midline pause (after fourth, fifth, or sixth syllable): EW, 42.9%; DS, 34.3%; LB 43.5%; PL, 67.8%; Task, 56%; Pause after fourth, fifth, sixth, or seventh: EW, 48.3%; DS, 35.7%; LB, 55.6%; PL, 78.5%; Task, 68.7%

1. The thousand lines analyzed were selected at random from LB (1800). They include "Lines Left upon a Seat in a Yew Tree" (66 lines); "The Brothers," ll. 1–164; "A Narrow Girdle of Rough Stones and Crags" (86 lines); "There Was A Boy" (32 lines); "Tintern Abbey" (160 lines); "The Old Cumberland Beggar," ll. 1–154; "Nutting" (55 lines); "Written with a Slate Pencil upon a Stone . . . upon One of the Islands at Rydal" (35 lines); "There is an Eminence,—or these our hills" (17 lines); "To Joanna" (85 lines); "Michael," ll. 1–146.

2. *Paradise Lost* sample (book 1) consists of 798 lines. The raw numbers for each position are as follows: after 1st = 1; 2d = 27; 3d = 25; 4th = 133; 5th = 91; 6th = 148; 7th = 59; 8th = 27; 9th = 3; double = 33; triple = 1; unbroken = 250.

3. *The Task* sample (book 1) consists of 770 lines. The raw numbers for each position are as follows: after 1st = 8; 2d = 21; 3d = 37; 4th = 115; 5th = 55; 6th = 102; 7th = 62; 8th = 20; 9th = 2; double = 53; triple = 11; unbroken = 284.

both with his own early work in pentameters (in *An Evening Walk* and *Descriptive Sketches*) and with two very different earlier uses of the form, each of which surely influenced Wordsworth's development—*Paradise Lost* and Cowper's *The Task*.

Pentameter couplets and blank verse, of course, have their own structures of organization, and it may be misleading to compare them here. But the table will help to show the extent to which Wordsworth's

five-beat line becomes a different kind of rhythmic structure in the years between 1793 and 1797–1800. Whereas in 1793 Wordsworth seems to have been striving through idiosyncratic placement of pause to distinguish the movement of his verse from that of predecessors and contemporaries, by the later 1790s he has accepted midline pause as an internal structural requirement of the five-beat form. Whatever will be distinctive about his verse will emerge within the context of certain enduring rhythmic patterns, inherent in the physical form of the verse itself (its tendency to break into a balanced 4/6, 5/5, or 6/4 structure), and sanctioned by earlier use.

Similarities in the placement of pause in Wordsworth, Cowper, and Milton suggest one of the reasons why the form is "infinitely the most difficult metre to manage." Blank verse may free the poet from the bondage of rhyming, but it imposes its own, more subtle, kinds of restraint at other levels of organization. There simply are not very many options for breaking a five-beat line without threatening its integrity as a line. At the same time, table 2 reveals some of the ways in which Wordsworth's verse in *Lyrical Ballads* does in fact distinguish itself rhythmically from the other samples: multiple pauses occur more frequently than is common in the nondramatic blank-verse tradition (this accounts for the relatively low percentages in each position under *Lyrical Ballads* compared with both Milton and Cowper); pauses are distributed fairly equally among the midline positions (that is, Wordsworth shows no clear preference, as do Milton and Cowper, for pauses after stressed syllables over pauses after unstressed syllables); and pauses fall almost as frequently after the seventh syllable as they do in the more conventionally acceptable positions, the fourth, fifth, and sixth syllables. Milton, although showing a similar tendency to eschew pauses after the second, third, eighth, and ninth syllables, definitely favors the fourth- and especially the sixth-syllable pause (he uses these two almost twice as frequently as he does the fifth- and seventh-syllable pause), and he uses the seventh-syllable pause less frequently than does Wordsworth. Cowper, whose blank verse is commonly cited as a forerunner of Wordsworth's because of its less Miltonically magisterial and more conversational movement, also shows a decided preference for pauses after even-numbered syllables. Cowper's preference for the fourth-syllable pause is perhaps a residual effect of his extensive early work in couplets (fourth-syllable pause being a trademark of eighteenth-century couplet verse). It also helps to account for the relative (and appropriate) lightness and rapidity of Cowper's line when compared with Milton's.

Another chief source of formal tension and variety in any blank verse is, of course, enjambment, which creates potentially meaningful kinds of interplay between syntactic structures and the metrical frame. Wordsworth's letter to Thelwall calls particular attention to line endings, as it asserts that the passion of meter is felt especially at line boundaries. At line ends, Wordsworth says, a minute sense of physical restraint must be felt, whether or not it is consonant with the rhythmic and syntactic manifestation of the passion of the subject. That is, a run-on line in good poetry does not invalidate the force of line endings; rather, it uses that inescapable force to effect.

Wordsworth uses run-on lines considerably less frequently than Milton but considerably more frequently than Cowper: 51.1 percent of the lines in the sample from *Lyrical Ballads* are enjambed, compared with 66.8 percent in *Paradise Lost* (book 1) and 36.6 percent in *The Task* (book 1).[5] Related to the issue of frequency of enjambment is Wordsworth's practice in the use of medial full stops (defined here as a midline pause, normally at the end of an independent clause and usually marked by punctuation stronger than a comma). Here, too, the three samples show important similarities and dissimilarities. In *Lyrical Ballads,* 14.1 percent (141/1000) of the lines surveyed contain a medial full stop, compared with 18 percent in the *Paradise Lost* sample (145/798) and 12 percent in the first book of *The Task* (93/770).

More revealing still is the ratio of medial full stops to all full stops. In Wordsworth's blank verse, 15.5 percent of the lines have full stops at line endings. Milton uses line-ending full stops in only 12 percent of his verses. In Cowper — again perhaps because of habits instilled through his writing of couplets — full stops correspond with line endings in 27.1 percent of the lines. The percentages of medial full stops relative to all full stops in the three samples, then, are 47.6 percent in *Lyrical Ballads,* 55 percent in *Paradise Lost,* and only 30.7 percent in *The Task.* Once again, Wordsworth's practice places him between the extremes of Milton's heavily enjambed style — in which the paragraph, not the line or the sentence, is the chief structural unit — and Cowper's more restrained style, in which the integrity of the line itself tends more often than not to be preserved.

These figures might easily be taken to suggest that the basic structure of Wordsworth's blank verse is a kind of compromise between the Miltonic and Cowperian, favoring the Miltonic. And such a conclusion would not be entirely wrong by way of a general description of Wordsworth's practice. Wordsworth does achieve greater interplay between metrical frame and syntax, line and phrase, than does Cowper. At

TABLE 3
Distribution of Pauses after Syllables and Percentage of
Occurrence in Various Texts

Pause After Syllable	*Tintern Abbey* (%)		*Michael* (ll. 1–146) (%)		*LB* Total (%)	
1	-		2.3	(2)	2.7	(17)
2	0.4	(5)	2.3	(2)	5.0	(32)
3	0.5	(6)	4.5	(4)	6.0	(38)
4	15.9	(18)	7.9	(7)	13.9	(88)
5	19.5	(22)	12.5	(11)	13.7	(87)
6	9.7	(11)	23.8	(21)	17.3	(110)
7	16.8	(19)	6.8	(6)	12.4	(79)
8	0.4	(5)	5.7	(5)	3.8	(24)
9	-		-		0.4	(2)
Double	21.2	(24)	32.9	(29)	22.1	(140)
Triple	0.3	(3)	1.1	(1)	2.7	(17)
Unbroken	29.4	(47)	39.7	(58)	36.6	(366)
Enjambed	55.6	(89)	44.9	(67)	51.1	(511)

Note: Numbers in parentheses give the total number of occurrences of pause in each position.

the same time, he allows the counterpassion of the frame to manifest itself (through greater end-stopping and conformity of phrase and line) more frequently than does Milton. And Wordsworth does distribute the pause more equably among the midline positions than does either Milton or Cowper. A closer look at the *Lyrical Ballads* sample, however, reveals an important way in which Wordsworth's practice is not adequately described as a compromise between seventeenth-century and eighteenth-century habits. In both Milton and Cowper, the tendencies of the larger sample provide, by and large, an accurate reflection of individual passages within the sample: that is, Milton's clear preference for late pause and frequent enjambment and Cowper's clear preference for early pause and infrequent enjambment tend to be in evidence throughout the samples. In the selection from the *Lyrical Ballads*, however, the tendency toward moderation suggested by the figures turns out to be a statistical fiction, an average of a very wide variety that does not accurately describe any one part of the sample. Any given passage of Wordsworth's blank verse may be as frequently end-stopped and line-conscious

as Cowper, as frequently enjambed and paragraphed as Milton, or virtually anywhere in between. It all depends on the expressive and aesthetic ends of the poet, on who is represented as speaking, about what, in what genre, to whom, and under what circumstances.

Table 3 allows comparison of Wordsworth's enjambment and placement of pause in two parts of the one-thousand-line sample—"Michael" and "Tintern Abbey"—with the total for the entire sample.

Different kinds of poems apparently require very different kinds of verse. In the narrative poem "Michael," Wordsworth's blank verse is characterized by unbroken lines (39.7 percent is an extremely high percentage),[6] by a clear preference for pauses after stressed syllables (especially after the sixth), and by relatively infrequent enjambment. The very high frequency of unbroken and syntactically self-contained lines contributes substantially to the effect of simplicity in "Michael":

> He had not pass'd his days in singleness.
> He had a Wife, a comely Matron, old
> Though younger than himself full twenty years.
> She was a woman of a stirring life
> Whose heart was in her house . . .
>
> (ll. 80–84)

Here and throughout the poem, syntactical and metrical structures tend to be commensurate much more frequently than in Wordsworth's blank verse as a whole. As a result, there is relatively little complexity in the interplay of the passion of the meter and the passion of the sense.

In "Michael," the clear preference for one placement of pause (and that one late in the line) also helps to create, through the appearance of a relatively easy fit between passion and metrical scheme, a simplicity of expression appropriate to the story of a man who does not "wear fine clothes" (letter to Charles James Fox; *EY*, 315). The sixth-syllable pause tends to make a five-beat line appear to move slowly. And the frequent use of a single pause tends to make the pause itself seem an element of structure, as opposed to an element of expression:

> Nor should I have made mention of this Dell
> But for one object which you might pass by,
> Might see and notice not. Beside the brook
> There is a straggling Heap of unhewn stones;
> And to that place a Story appertains,

> Which, though it be ungarnish'd with events,
> Is not unfit, I deem, for the fire-side
> Or for the summer shade. It was the first,
> The earliest of these Tales . . .
>
> (ll. 14–22)

Note in particular how both of the midline full stops in the passage occur in the sixth position (nine of the fourteen midline full stops in the sample passage fall in this position also). In such verse, the favored midline position comes to be felt as only slightly less an element of structure than is the length of line. The placement of pause, that is, is properly an element of the "general rule" governing the verse, rather than a disruptive exception. It produces not expressive tension but a sense of pleasing variety appropriate to a narrative founded on deep, not volatile, feeling and presented for the delight of a "few natural hearts" and for the sake of those "youthful Poets" who will be the narrator's "second self" when he is gone. The rhetorical gesture here, as in "Hart-Leap Well," suggests a kind of preexisting bond among poet, tale, and reader. The rhythmic characteristics of the verse may be regarded as a chief means for incorporating this bond into the tale. Wordsworth offers few surprises in "Michael," few twists and turns of passion or expression. The rhythm of his verse functions not so much as an overt challenge to preexisting habits of association but as a gentle reinforcement of salutary combinations of thought and feeling that the speaker assumes are at his disposal. This is the voice of the village storyteller, telling to effect a tale that instantiates commonly acknowledged kinds of power; it is not the voice of the bard creating new combinations of thought and feeling.

"Tintern Abbey" departs from the averages of the sample almost as sharply as does "Michael," but in very different, even idiosyncratic, ways. Whereas "Michael" restricts the distribution of pause, "Tintern Abbey" disperses it evenly and widely in positions four to seven. Whereas the line is broken in "Michael" much less frequently than in the sample as a whole, in "Tintern Abbey" it is broken much more frequently. "Tintern Abbey" employs enjambment in 4.5 percent more of its lines than does the sample; "Michael" in 6.2 percent fewer. Such devices in "Tintern Abbey" are as appropriate to the expressive ends of a poem, the versification of which Wordsworth called "impassioned music" (*PW* 2:517), as is the verse of "Michael" to a "history / Homely and rude" (ll. 34–35). Pause is not, in the following passage, chiefly a structural source of

pleasant variety. It is an expressive index of the tension inherent in the act of a mind engaged in complex processes of thought and feeling:

> We see into the life of things.
>   If this
> Be but a vain belief, yet, oh! how oft,
> In darkness, and amid the many shapes
> Of joyless day-light; when the fretful stir
> Unprofitable, and the fever of the world,
> Have hung upon the beatings of my heart,
> How oft, in spirit, have I turned to thee
> O sylvan Wye! Thou wanderer through the woods,
> How often has my spirit turned to thee!
>   (ll. 50–58)

The paragraph break falling after the eighth syllable, the triple pause in the second full verse, and the double pause (including a second-syllable pause) in the seventh line quoted all help to create the impression of a mind engaged in a process of discovering—and making—the meanings it articulates, rather than of a speaker reciting a tale the general course of which is known in advance. Phrases are allowed to take their own shape, expressing and emblematizing through tension between metrical and syntactic structures the fluxes and refluxes of the speaker's mind.

Such features of the verse call attention to the minutiae of expression to a greater degree than is usual, or welcome, in narrative verse. Note, for example, the parallel repetition, with significant syntactic and rhythmic variation, in the seventh and ninth lines of the quoted passage:

> How oft, in spirit, have I turned to thee
> o   B(x)o B o(x) B o B   o B
> O sylvan Wye! Thou wanderer through the woods,
> How often has my spirit turned to thee!
> o   B o B̄   o B o B   o B

The rhythmic effectiveness of the minute change in phrase may easily be felt merely by repeating the lines, in either form, without the variation:

> How oft, in spirit, have I turned to thee
> O sylvan Wye! Thou wanderer through the woods,
> How oft, in spirit, have I turned to thee!

> How often has my spirit turned to thee
> O sylvan Wye! Thou wanderer through the woods,
> How often has my spirit turned to thee!

Even more revelatory of the power of Wordsworth's repetition is the unsatisfactory effect resulting from a reversal of the repeated lines:

> How often has my spirit turned to thee
> O sylvan Wye! Thou wanderer through the woods,
> How oft, in spirit, have I turned to thee!

The unsettling nature of this rewritten version probably results from the expectation that endings, even verse paragraph endings, will resolve tensions, not introduce them. In Wordsworth's original version, the final line is indeed a more neatly satisfying, less complex realization of the scheme than is the first. Even the reduction of stress on the auxiliary verb ("has") contributes. Whereas the pause in the first line allows "have" to take a full stress, in the final line the absence of a pause gives the line four primary stresses. The result is a faster paced verse that also takes advantage of the deep-seated physical pull of the four-beat, binary rhythm around which all five-beat verse plays. Its approximation of the feel of a four-beat verse contributes to its ability to function as a grounding, stabilizing influence on the paragraph as a whole.[7] Such effects help to underscore and embody the speaker's assertions, to give physical proof that the progressive regeneration of power he professes to feel is in fact under way. Rhythmic strength expresses and emblematizes the poet's sense of regeneration upon his return to the sources of his power.

Of interest, also, is the way in which the lines call attention, through their similarity, to the very subtle but philosophically central difference between the content of the two phrases; namely, the question of the extent to which the reinvigoration of the speaker's power, celebrated in the poem, is a result of the self-motivated "turning" (and returning) of the "I" and the extent to which it is a result of an influence other than and perhaps superior to the "I." In short, has the speaker himself turned, or has he been turned? By repeating the phrase in rhythmically similar and dissimilar forms—one that expresses, in a broken line, the speaker's assertion of power (I have turned), the other that acknowledges, in a single unbroken line, the primacy of the "spirit" in the act of restoration (my spirit has turned)—Wordsworth embodies in an essentially lyric mode what might be called the motivating (and paradoxical) tension

underlying the entire poem. An assertion of a free and spirited, self-motivated turn out of the course that necessity seems to have dictated and an assertion of the speaker's belief that finally it was not in fact a free and self-motivated turn are matched, rhetorically and rhythmically, not as antithetical statements but as two variations on the same theme. In such places, the passion of the sense and the passion of meter overlap and interpenetrate in complex ways. Such interpenetration tends to focus attention on the medium itself, justifying Wordsworth's assertion that the poem might have been called an ode chiefly on the strength of its "impassioned music."[8]

Another telling—and effective—difference between the blank verse of "Michael" and that of "Tintern Abbey" is evident in the use of midline full stops. In the "Michael" sample, only fourteen full stops fall in midline positions, compared with thirty-three at line ends (14/47; or 29.8 percent); "Tintern Abbey" contains twenty-seven medial full stops, and only fourteen full stops at line ends (27/41; or 65.8 percent). The difference in Wordsworth's practice in the two poems—and especially the differences between each poem individually and the *Lyrical Ballads* sample totals—are a fair index of just how various Wordsworth's rhythmic practice can be. In the total one-thousand-line sample, the percentage of medial full stops relative to total full stops is 47.2 percent (143/303). Wordsworth's preference for end-line full stops in "Michael" is nearly as marked a deviation from this average as is the opposite preference for midline full stops in "Tintern Abbey."

In "Michael," the frequent coincidence of full stops with line endings is another of the many ways through which Wordsworth creates that sense of easy recitation of event that is the proper form of communication between his storyteller and the sympathetic audience. Where metrical and expressive structures are commensurate—where line endings mark units of thought—the poet foregoes one of the chief means at his disposal for creating complexity and tension:

>   UPON the Forest-side in Grasmere Vale
>   There dwelt a Shepherd, Michael was his name,
>   An old man, stout of heart, and strong of limb.
>   His bodily frame had been from youth to age
>   Of an unusual strength: his mind was keen,
>   Intense, and frugal, apt for all affairs,
>   And in his Shepherd's calling he was prompt
>   And watchful more than ordinary men.
>
>   (ll. 40–47)

The effectiveness (and distinctiveness) of Wordsworth's quite deliberate reduction of rhythmic complexity and tension may be appreciated by comparing it with the very different effects that issue from Southey's attempts in the 1790s to create a blank-verse style appropriate to "homely and rude" tales. In *Hannah*, for example, a work frequently grouped on the basis of style with Wordsworth's plainer blank-verse poems of the late 1790s,[9] midline full stops account for fully 70 percent (21/30) of total full stops, and twenty-seven of the fifty-one lines in the poem are enjambed (52.9 percent). The rhythmic effect of such verse is the very opposite of the effect achieved in "Michael":

> [I]t was one,
> A village girl; they told us she had borne
> An eighteen months strange illness; pined away
> With such slow wasting as had made the hour
> Of Death most welcome—To the house of mirth
> We held our way, and, with that idle talk
> That passes o'er the mind and is forgot,
> We wore away the hour.
>
> (*Hannah*, ll. 5–12)

Southey avoids commensurability of phrase and metrical unit as surely as Wordsworth favors it. Whereas Wordsworth achieves simplicity of expression through devices that reduce tension between the metrical frame and the expression of the speaker (allowing in the process a certain latitude in diction, phrasing, and figures without violating the decorum of his tale), Southey seems intent on compensating for unremitting homeliness of diction and syntax through the use of rhythmic means that create such tension. This is not the place to debate the relative merits of Southey's and Wordsworth's versification. It may be worthwhile to note here, however, that from Wordsworth's point of view Southey's passage of circumstantial narrative (like his own in the passage quoted from "Michael") lacks the kind of passion that would justify all of this overflowing of physical boundaries and challenging of the integrity of the line.

Wordsworth's practice in "Michael," in *Lyrical Ballads* as a whole, and indeed throughout the *Poetical Works* shows that he tended to reserve such verse—heavily enjambed and with frequent midline full stops—for poems or passages of poems in which the play of the speaker's emotions is of the essence. Such verse is not used merely to give a kind of counterbalancing rhythmic license or formal status to poems on homely subjects. In *Lyrical Ballads,* the only poem approaching Southey's in the

frequency of enjambment and use of midline full stops both is "Tintern Abbey," in which the practices clearly are employed in the service of expressive and emblematic ends.[10] The passage in the poem in which these devices appear most frequently is, predictably, the conclusion, in which the voice of the speaker expresses his hope and faith that the fleeting glimpse he has had of the permanent integrity of his experience will not wholly pass away:

> Nor, perchance,
> If I should be, where I no more can hear
> Thy voice, nor catch from thy wild eyes these gleams
> Of past existence, wilt thou then forget
> That on the banks of this delightful stream
> We stood together; and that I, so long
> A worshipper of Nature, hither came,
> Unwearied in that service: rather say
> With warmer love, oh! with far deeper zeal
> Of holier love. Nor wilt thou then forget,
> That after many wanderings, many years
> Of absence, these steep woods and lofty cliffs,
> And this green pastoral landscape, were to me
> More dear, both for themselves, and for thy sake.
>
> (ll. 147–60)

Upon the assertion that this deeply personal experience is in fact communicable to his companion (and, by implication, to posterity) rests to a significant degree Wordsworth's entire poetic project. Appropriately, the stylistic resources used in the service of the assertion are extraordinary, even within the context of this most prosodically complex of the *Lyrical Ballads*. Of the fourteen lines that make up this passage, ten are enjambed (64.3 percent; the ratio in the poem as a whole is 160/89, or 55.6 percent); six full stops occur in midline positions, compared with only one (the final stop) at the end of a line (compared with 27/14 in the poem as a whole). The effect of the ending, rhetorically, is that of a single powerful assertion of the power of remembrance, continually augmented and revised: "Nor, perchance," "rather say," "Nor wilt thou then forget." The effect of its prosodic character is to embody in the physical experience of reading (and hearing) the tension between assertion and revision—or the sense of confident summation tending toward closure—and the countertendency toward an open-ended avowal of the inability to fix the meaning of the occasion. The extraordinary degree of complexity in

the interplay of metrical frame and syntax serves extraordinarily complex ends. Such passages, expressive of a complex interpenetration of thought and feeling, demand to be internalized more than simpler passages do, to be felt and remembered in all of their physical details. Such a demand is appropriate, because to a considerable degree the meaning of the passage is dependent on the reader's participation (along with the interlocutor) in the experience of just this kind of interpenetration and on his or her remembrance of the complexity of thought and feeling that is the motivating tension in the poem.

The only other passage in "Tintern Abbey" that approaches the ending in the degree to which metrical and syntactic units are in opposition is the beginning. In lines 1–23, fourteen lines are enjambed (60.9 percent) and five of six full stops are medial (83.3 percent; compare 65.8 percent for "Tintern Abbey" as a whole; 47.2 percent [143/303] in the *Lyrical Ballads* sample). This coincidence in tendency in the first twenty-three and the final fourteen lines may in fact help to account for the full sense of closure produced by the final lines, even though their rhythmic character is unconventional for an ending; that is, although the final fourteen lines do not fulfill the usual expectations of closure—that at endings tension between meter and rhythm, scheme and realization will be reduced—they suggest a kind of completion by means of a return to the rhythmic characteristics of the beginning. More important for present purposes, however, are the different ends to which similar metrical means are employed in the two passages. In the conclusion, the tension between line and sentence as competing forms of organization is primarily an expressive indicator; in the opening, such tensions are more directly emblematic and are especially related to generic considerations.

As the length of the introductory verse paragraph itself makes a statement concerning its speaker's ambitions and powers, it needs to be considered whole:

> Five years have passed; five summers, with the length
> Of five long winters! and again I hear
> These waters, rolling from their mountain-springs
> With a sweet inland murmur.—Once again
> Do I behold these steep and lofty cliffs,
> Which on a wild secluded scene impress
> Thoughts of more deep seclusion; and connect
> The landscape with the quiet of the sky.
> The day is come when I again repose
> Here, under this dark sycamore, and view

>   These plots of cottage-ground, these orchard-tufts,
>   Which, at this season, with their unripe fruits,
>   Among the woods and copses lose themselves,
>   Nor, with their green and simple hue, disturb
>   The wild green landscape. Once again I see
>   These hedge-rows, hardly hedge-rows, little lines
>   Of sportive wood run wild; these pastoral farms
>   Green to the very door; and wreathes of smoke
>   Sent up, in silence, from among the trees,
>   With some uncertain notice, as might seem,
>   Of vagrant dwellers in the houseless woods,
>   Or of some hermit's cave, where by his fire
>   The hermit sits alone.
>
>   (ll. 1–23)

This paragraph accomplishes a type of fusion of subject and style of versification that is pointedly unlike anything else in the *Lyrical Ballads*, either in blank verse or rhyme. The speaker, in his graceful synthesis into a harmonious whole of disparate elements of the scene, attempts and accomplishes more than any other speaker in the collection. His imaginative fusion of past and present, landscape and sky, motion and stillness, natural wildness and circumscribed domesticity into a complexly unified picture of the landscape demonstrates exactly the type of mental activity that Coleridge implicitly singles out in *Biographia Literaria* as the force behind Wordsworth's most impressive manner: "He [the poet, described in *ideal* perfection] diffuses a tone, and a spirit of unity, that blends, and (as it were) *fuses,* each into each, by that synthetic and magical power, to which we have exclusively appropriated the name of imagination" (*BL* 2:15–16). The verse paragraph—and the poem as a whole—depicts a man possessed of a "prospectiveness of mind" or a "surview" through which he is able to "foresee the whole of what he is to convey." This foresight allows him "to subordinate and arrange the different parts [of his speech] according to their relative importance, as to convey it at once, and as an organized whole" (*BL* 2:58).

Wordsworth's marshaling of the resources of rhythm and sound in the passage is, appropriately, designed to assert the speaker's comprehensive powers. The paragraph consists of four sentences, each describing in its main clause a distinct aspect of the speaker's perception: "I hear," "I behold," "I . . . repose / . . . and view," "I see." These sentences become progressively longer and more complex. The first is a compound sentence of thirty-seven syllables; the second employs a compound sub-

ordinate clause and is forty-three syllables long; the third sentence contains sixty-five syllables and uses three verbs, a subordinate clause, and three prepositional phrases; the fourth has eighty-one syllables and is a series of three dependent clauses each completing the main clause "I see." Within these sentences, the placement of the pause is extremely varied but tends to fall late more often than early in the line. Nearly a third of the lines contain more than one pause (seven of twenty-three), and in the remaining lines the pause falls variously after the third (once), fourth (once), fifth (twice), sixth (five times), and seventh (three times) syllables. The multiple pauses tend to create the effect of a spontaneous, conversational tone while the tendency toward late placement tends to produce a slow pace.

As the speaker makes more and more connections among details, progressively building up to a unified whole, his method of describing becomes progressively more capacious. The careful, slow, and patient composition of a landscape complete unto itself finds its appropriate expression in the speaker's amassing of his words in slowly paced, progressively longer and more complex formal structures. The whole is unified in large part through the repetition of key sounds (particularly by the repetition, four times, of the word "again") that function (to expand on Wordsworth's metaphor of metrical writing as "fitting") as threads running through the paragraph, helping to make of the separate phrases a unified whole. The repetition of the consonant h—to take just one of many instances that might be used to illustrate this pervasive management of sounds—is a particularly important means through which Wordsworth underpins and patterns his speaker's expression. The sound is used sparingly in early and middle portions of the paragraph: "I *h*ear" (l. 2), "be*h*old" (l. 5), "*H*ere" (l. 10), "*h*ue" (l. 14). It is nevertheless sounded frequently enough to call attention to its presence as an important element in the structure of the paragraph. When, in lines 15–23, the sound becomes (along with s and w) a dominant consonant sound, it functions, as does the repetition of "again," to unify the paragraph. The amassing in the end of the paragraph of key sounds used sparingly in previous verses parallels the steady increase in the length of sentences and works to reinforce the paragraph's creation of a voice that seems to gain power as it progresses. Wordsworth thus underpins his speaker's ability to build great things from least suggestions, ensuring that his reader will have aural, as well as cognitive, evidence of that power.

In a poem that attempts to create a monument to the power of time to create as well as to destroy, this subtle building up of discrete phrases into a unified verse paragraph produces an effect more important than

mere harmony of sounds for the sake of harmony. The stitching together of these sentences, effected in large part through the tendency of repeated sounds to work against the onward temporal succession of the sounds of words, is an instance of, as well as a vehicle for, the speaker's imaginative fusion of past and present into a single scene. Just as the speaker creates through images and figures of speech a representation of the ability of imagination to hold intellectually separable elements in harmonious suspension, so the repeated sounds (particularly those of the insistently repeated word "again"), by eddying back upon themselves, give structure to the temporal succession of the words. The thread of repeated sounds and syllables helps Wordsworth, in Ezra Pound's terms, to cut a form in time,[11] making the paragraph a union of temporal and spatial organization analogous to those described elsewhere by Wordsworth through such figures as the "speaking monument" of *The River Duddon* (3.3). The paragraph is not merely a description of a result of imaginative perception; it is an active instance of imaginative process.[12]

The opening paragraph of "Tintern Abbey" is extraordinarily complex not only in comparison with the verse of "Michael" or with the stanzaic poems of *Lyrical Ballads* and the *Poetical Works* but even within the context of Wordsworth's blank verse as a whole. It therefore stands out not merely as a powerfully expressive use of language (though it is that, of course) but as an emblem of (and proof of) the operation of those very powers that the poem is engaged in attempting to define and assert. The heightened formal qualities of the passage function to elevate and foreground the medium itself in such a way that the powers of the poet as poet are made a subject of the poem in a particularly insistent way. These are, after all, "*Lines* Written . . . above Tintern Abbey." The poet's powers as a writer, as composer of internal and external landscapes in words, are as surely on display as are his capacities to think, feel, and remember. If "Michael" gives us the poet as storyteller, rehearsing a well-known tale, this announces the poet as shaper of hitherto unapprehended experience, giving body to the previously unarticulated through the music and mystery of verse. The blank verse of the poem is appropriately formal, lyrical—magisterial. Its elevated style presents it as a masterpiece, in the sense of a work of art undertaken in part to provide "proofs of skill acquired by practice."

In a poem about the ability of poetry to respond powerfully to loss, such proofs of the speaker's control over the resources of his art are constitutive of meaning in a precise way: the formal composition of the lines, presented as having issued spontaneously from a state of height-

ened passions, is a kind of instance of the speaker's paradoxical claim that his life to date has been (like the "wanderer" Wye) both perfectly free and powerfully determined. Will and necessity, spontaneity and pattern, passionate expression and the poet's duty to shape expression into pleasurable poems are bodied forth in the very speech impulses and patterned sounds of the verse.

In the first chapter, I suggested that Wordsworth's is an aesthetic based not so much on unity as on significant diversity, the end of which is the presentation of as wide a variety of poetic speakers as may be pleasurably encompassed by the synthetic and sympathetic mind. Wordsworth's complex and odic blank verse in "Tintern Abbey" is effective in part because of intrinsic tensions employed to effect and in part because, within the context provided both by rhymed poems and by the less formally complex, less passionate and elevated blank verse in the collection, it is extraordinary. Conversely, the presence of the blank verse of "Tintern Abbey" in *Lyrical Ballads* helps to bring out more strikingly the different relationship among speaker, subject, and audience that results from the formal simplicity of "Michael." In "Michael," the poet who is capable of the heightened verse of "Tintern Abbey" sets aside some of the devices of composition at his disposal in order to single out one among many sources of his power; in "Tintern Abbey," the poet who is capable of the austerity of the verse of "Michael" provides a stylistically all-encompassing instance of the full power of the mental river into which the tributary represented in "Michael" flows.

"Michael" and "Tintern Abbey," then, represent two effectively dissimilar adaptations of the same verse form to Wordsworth's purposes in *Lyrical Ballads:* the "fitting" of language to metrical arrangement for the purpose of delineating, and encouraging sympathetic participation with, a range of types of minds or of individual minds under various circumstances and influences. And they are only two of many different kinds of blank verse in a collection that includes the dramatic blank verse of "The Brothers" (and of Coleridge's "The Foster-Mother's Tale" from *Osorio*), the Cowperian verse of "Poems on the Naming of Places" (see especially "There is an Eminence, of these our hills," and "To M.H."), and the highly rhetorical and sententious verse, anticipatory of the Wanderer's speeches in *The Excursion,* of "The Old Cumberland Beggar" (especially its peroration).

Wordsworth's blank-verse variety is clearly apparent even within individual poems in *Lyrical Ballads.* The 1800 version of "Animal Tranquillity and Decay, a Sketch," for example, draws on prosodic means to present

a pointed and abrupt change of focus and tone on the part of the speaker. (The poem in this regard anticipates the kind of purposeful dissonance that has been discussed above in connection with "The Sailor's Mother.") In "Animal Tranquillity and Decay," as in "The Sailor's Mother," a speaker comments on the appearance of a person he meets on the road, drawing from that appearance a general preliminary impression. The "mein and gait" of the sailor's mother make her "stately" and dignified; the old man's "face, his step / His gait" form "one expression":

> ... every limb,
> His look and bending figure, all bespeak
> A man who does not move with pain, but moves
> With thought—He is insensibly subdued
> To settled quiet.
>
> (ll. 4–8)

The physical expression of the man, his demeanor and his movements, have a language of their own that "bespeaks" his character. The speaker, who may be regarded as a kind of translator into words of these outward signs and actions, finds in his subject an embodiment of one who has been "by Nature led" to a "peace" that he describes as "perfect." The exercise of patience throughout a long life has become so habitual to the old man as to "seem a thing, of which / He hath no need" (ll. 11–12).

The speaker sums up his impression with an implicit contrast between himself (the "young") and his subject:

> ... He is by nature led
> To peace so perfect, that the young behold
> With envy, what the old man hardly feels.
>
> (ll. 12–14)

The artful antithesis of the speaker's summation—its balance of the concerns of young and old, of the intense interests of "envy" and the supposed disinterestedness of the old man—is typical of the whole of the character sketch. Throughout the sketch, the speaker sets up balanced contrasts between free will and necessity, activity and passivity (the practice of patience leading to a state in which it seems that no patience is needed), and gain and loss (tranquility and decay).

These contrasts are couched in the first fourteen lines in highly patterned, prosodically subtle language. The opening "sketch" is in

fact structured as a kind of blank-verse sonnet.[13] It begins with discrete facts about the man's appearance (the birds do not "regard" him; he "travels on"; his "face, his step, / His gait" form "one expression"), continues with reflections on patience and the meanings of the old man's appearance, and ends with a summation neatly contained in the lines quoted above. The turn from description to reflection occurs, as would be expected in a poem in sonnet form, midway through line eight, dividing the first fourteen lines into a neat binary structure, octave and sestet.

Within this larger pattern are many other patterns, all of which tend to present the speaker as adept in the habits of formal composition requisite to the kind of exemplary character sketch he has undertaken. A higher than normal incidence of enjambment (eight of fourteen lines; 57.1 percent) and midline full stops (four of six full stops are medial) help make the sketch as rhythmically impressive as any of the blank verse in the collection. These characteristics also help account for the sense of closure at the end of line 14, where the full stop is prepared for by the slowing effects of the pauses after unstressed syllables in lines 13 and 14 and by the use of the demoted third-syllable adjective in line 13:

> To peace so perfect, that the young behold
> o B ȯ B o(x) B̄ o B o B
> With envy, what the old man hardly feels.
> o B o(x) B̄ o B ȯ B o B

Note, too, how the promotion of "that" and "what" in the two lines produces the effect of four strong beats per verse, drawing on the stabilizing effect of native measure and thereby contributing to the sense of binary structure on which sonnet form depends.

The sketch also achieves a kind of unity through frequent repetition of verbal sound—particularly alliteration, internal rhyme, and homoeoteleuton. The repetition of third-person pronouns ("he," "his," and "him") throughout the first fourteen lines (ten times) gives sonic evidence of the speaker's insistent and minute focus on his subject. The repetition of initial *p*, from "peck" (l. 2) to "pain" (l. 6) to "patience" (twice, in ll. 10 an 11) to "peace so perfect" supplies a thread of sound underpinning the key transformation of the old man into an example of perfection. The final two lines achieve their sonnetlike summarizing power in part through the rhyme of "behold" and "old" that links lines 13 and 14.

An instance of line-ending homoeoteleuton is particularly significant:

> . . . He is one by whom
> All effort seems forgotten, one to whom
> Long patience has such mild composure given,
> That patience now doth seem a thing, of which
> He hath no need.
>
> (ll. 8–12)

The juxtaposition in the final feet of successive verses of "by whom" and "to whom" and the repetition of "patience" in lines 10 and 11 call attention through prosodic minutiae to an overarching thematic concern: the relationship between the old man as one who acts and as one who is acted upon. He is both an agent "by whom" effort has been forgotten through long exercise of patience and a creature of necessity "to whom" nature has "given" peace by leading him to his present state. Taken together, these various kinds of formal pattern help give the first fourteen lines an intense feeling of formal coherence. The sketch is as perfect a reconciliation of opposite or discordant qualities as ever Coleridge could want to see and hear.

Then comes the abrupt downfall.[4] Lines 15–21 (end) of the poem suggest prosodically and otherwise that here, as in "The Sailor's Mother," the perfect "sketch" can only achieve its internal perfection and harmony through the exclusion of the subject himself. When the speaker asks the old man "whither he was bound" on his "journey" (note again, in the pun on "bound," the speaker's confidence in his ideal of the perfect relationship between self-determination and necessity), he receives an answer that speaks only of disharmonies and disruptions of peace and contentment, of war and an old father's loss of a son:

> he replied
> That he was going many miles to take
> A last leave of his son, a mariner
> Who from a sea-fight had been brought to Falmouth,
> And there was lying in an hospital.
>
> (ll. 16–20)

Line 18 provides the first metrical dislocation in the poem (there is in ll. 1–17 not even an initial inversion), and it comes in a particularly disruptive position:

A last leave of his son, a mariner
o   B ô B   ŏ   B   o   B o B̄

Such second-foot inversions, as has been mentioned above, are extremely rare because they are so dangerous to the metrical character of the line. The promoted ending of the line continues the effect of ill-fitting meter and rhythm and prepares for a further departure from the metrical set in line 19, where Wordsworth introduces an eleven-syllable line with a "trochaic" ending (a dramatic pentameter):

Who from a sea-fight had been brought to Falmouth
            o   B   o B   o

In short, Wordsworth could not have made the shift in kinds of blank verse more abrupt. Even the 1798 version, in which these lines are presented as quoted speech instead of paraphrase, is not as disruptive as is this change of pace in the voice of the speaker himself. It is as if the speaker's very recollection of the effect of the old man's unanticipated response has produced an emotional deflation affecting his powers of expression. He goes from blank-verse master to stammerer in meter as he recounts the excruciatingly prosaic answer of his erstwhile poetic and perfectly contented subject. The concluding passage is utterly devoid of figures of speech (even "going many miles" makes prosaic the "journey" in the speaker's question) and uses no word or arrangement of words that would be out of place in the barest matter-of-fact speech. Wordsworth shows through stylistic dissonance that, whatever the speaker has captured of his subject, his conventionally unified sketch (in ll. 1–14) is just that—a sketch. The concluding lines effectively break open the sketch, challenging the very aesthetic principles on which it is based and suggesting that the quotidian reality that is the old man's existence must challenge (as must all human existence) the well-intentioned but ultimately inadequate attempt of art to represent it as "something loftier" and "perfect."[15] The ear cautions speaker and reader alike to see more clearly. The voice of the old man, like other voices of other men and women encountered by chance in Wordsworth's poetry, admonishes the speaker, bringing him back to the "very world." Through such means Wordsworth implies that the poetry that can adequately comprehend that "very world" is a poetry in which the desire for earthly perfection and the life lived in time and space struggle for dominance in the very music of the poem.

The range of styles within "Animal Tranquillity and Decay" is admittedly more striking and more productive of prosodic dissonance than is

usual in Wordsworth's blank-verse poems. In fact, the last seven lines were not retained by Wordsworth in reprintings of the poem in collected editions from 1815 through 1850. Whether Wordsworth judged that the juxtaposition of metrical styles was too dissonant (at least for the ears of his readers, if not for his own) or whether he decided that the internal tensions between youth and age, tranquillity and decay couched in the easy rhythms of the fourteen-line sketch were themselves sufficient to give the summation the desired effect of a too-perfect and too-neat closure, it is difficult to say. What is clear, however, is that the principle behind such widely various use of the same or similar metrical forms is in evidence throughout Wordsworth's corpus. The presence of such diversity and such range in the blank verse of *Lyrical Ballads* (1800) suggests that a chief attraction of (and source of difficulty in) blank-verse composition is the opportunity it affords for the juxtaposition of diverse (even extreme) realizations of the same metrical pattern. The presence, for example, of the last seven lines of "Animal Tranquillity and Decay," the first twenty-three lines of "Tintern Abbey," the dramatic blank verse of "The Brothers," the homely narrative verse of "Michael," and the marmorial "Lines left upon a Seat in a Yew-Tree," all in Wordsworth's first substantial collection, make complexity of voice itself an issue of primary importance. In the more or less tense reconciliation of the discordant qualities of regularity and departure from pattern, in the easy or difficult fitting of phonetic material to abstract and predetermined forms, and in the fluidity or turgidity of the mind as it is expressed through the physical operation of speech reside a fundamental and infinitely complex kind of meaning in Wordsworth's corpus.

WORDSWORTH'S "BEST SPECIMENS": "A NIGHT-PIECE" AND "YEW-TREES"

According to Henry Crabb Robinson, Wordsworth considered "A Night-Piece" (composed probably January 1798; published 1815) and "Yew-Trees" (composed 1804, 1811–14; published 1815) his "best specimens of blank verse."[16] Given Wordsworth's characteristic precision of statement, such a description may be considered an invitation to consider this pair of poems, both of which appear in Wordsworth's collected works as Poems of the Imagination, as together containing in small much of what is vital in and characteristic of Wordsworth's most intensely lyrical and imaginative blank verse.[17] A close focus on these two relatively short poems also will provide an opportunity to delve into some of the more minute levels of prosodic organization in Wordsworth's blank verse.

Whereas the first section of this chapter focused chiefly on Wordsworth's habits in placement of pause and use of enjambment, this section will be concerned more immediately with significant instances of rhythmic dislocation, the structural integrity of individual verses, and patterns of assonance and alliteration.

In "A Night-Piece," a speaker describes a "pensive traveller" who experiences an unexpected and intensely pleasurable moment of vision brought about by the breaking forth of the moon and stars from a thick cloud cover.[18] The dynamics of the poem give it a clear four-part structure: an emotionally neutral beginning, in which the speaker describes a poetically unpromising overcast night (ll. 1–7); a rising action, as the traveller is "startled" by a rift in the clouds, and his eye, which has been "bent earthwards," now is directed toward a "Vision" of "The clear Moon, and the glory of the heavens" (ll. 8–13); an emotional peak, in which the vision is described (ll. 14–21); and a falling action, as the traveller's mind, "not undisturbed" by the "delight" it feels, "slowly settles into peaceful calm" (ll. 23–26).

Wordsworth says that he composed the poem extempore on the road between Nether Stowey and Alfoxden, and in DC MSS 15 and 16 it bears the title "A Fragment," appropriate to the sense of unpremeditated overflow that the poem attempts to imitate. The versification is in fact as clear an instance as Wordsworth's corpus affords of powerfully expressive and affective blank verse. The volatile and shifting verse rhythms and patterns of sound function primarily to convey the impression that the speaker of the poem is actually, in the process of composition, under the influence of the intense and delightfully disturbing emotions that the poem recollects. These elements of versification in turn serve to encourage the sympathetic participation of a reader in the dynamics of tension and release appropriate to the emotions expressed in the poem. The finished poem, that is, presents itself not merely as an account of the vision but as an invitation to the reader to participate in a reenactment of its emotional content and structure.

The first part of the poem contains virtually no metrical complexity, and therefore no metrical tension, apart from initial inversion (ll. 2, 3, 7), some promotion and demotion of stresses, and three instances of elidable syllables (underlined):

```
                —The sky is overcast
                    o  B  o  B o B
  s  -s -s +s  -s      +s
  With a continuous cloud of texture close,
   B̄   ŏ   B   o     B   oB   o   B
```

Heavy and wan, all whitened by the Moon,
B ŏ   B ȯ   B o   B̄ o   B
Which through that veil is indistinctly seen,
 o   B   ȯ   B o B o B   o B
A dull, contracted circle, yielding light
o B   o   B   o B   o B   o   B
So feebly spread that not a shadow falls,
o B   o   B   o   B o B   o   B
Chequering the ground, from rock, plant, tree, or tower.
B   ŏ   B   o   B   ȯ   B   o   B

Even the variant structures — for example, the promotion of the initial syllable in the second line and the formation thereby of a relatively weak initial inversion pattern (the ubiquitous +s -s -s +s) — are appropriate to the nearly emotionless calm of the opening. Indeed, the line seems to be designedly gentle when compared with an earlier version (in DC MSS 15 and 16):

With a close veil of one continuous cloud
ŏ   B   ô B   o B   o B   o   B

(Butler and Green, 276; 500–501)

Here, the relatively more disruptive stress-final pairing (-s -s +s +s) and the implied offbeat produce a kind of metrical tension, implying complexity of emotion, that Wordsworth evidently came to feel was out of place at this point in the poem. The revised version provides a more neutral metrical unit that will help provide in lines 1–7 the basis for an important contrast between the rhythm of the opening and the considerably more complex rhythmic patterns in the central two sections of the poem. Similarly, the list of nouns in line 7, in which "plant" is placed in an offbeat position between the semantically equivalent "rock" and "tree," tends toward a leveling of stress values and a concomitant diminution of the rhythmic pulse and pace.

In part 2, increasing metrical complexity in the form of double and implied offbeats corresponds to increased emotional activity, as the plodding traveller is startled by the illumination of the previously dull and darkened landscape:

At length a pleasant instantaneous gleam
o   B   o   B o   B̄ o B o   B
Startles the pensive traveller as he treads
B   ŏ   B   o   B o   B̄ o B

His lonesome path, with unobserving eye
o B o   B   o B̄ o B o B
s +s -s   -s   +s +s
Bent earthwards; he looks up—the clouds are split
ȯ B   ŏ   B ȯ B o   B o   B
Asunder,—and above his head he sees
o B o   B̄   o B o B o B
The clear Moon, and the glory of the heav<u>e</u>ns.
o   B ȯ B   ŏ   B o B̄ o B

(ll. 8–13)

Line 11, as the scansion clearly shows, contains a particularly disruptive instance of a stress-final double-offbeat pattern interrupted by a strong third-syllable pause. Although the metrical set encourages the four-syllable group to be considered as a whole (with the implied offbeat compensating for a double offbeat), this realization sharply splits that normal pattern asunder. An even more unsettling challenge to the metrical set occurs in line 13, with an instance of an effect that has been labeled the *diabolus in prosodia* (or the metrical equivalent of music's diminished fifth, or "devil's," interval)—second-foot inversion.[19] The expressive and emblematic effects of the prosodic breaks in these lines are sufficiently obvious. The "gleam" breaks forth, jolting the "unobserving" traveler, the speaker, and the reader out of the well-beaten, earthbound, and continuous path. It transforms the familiar and predictable into something extraordinary and celestial. There is no more familiar path for the voice to take than the pentameter, and there are few disruptions more threatening to the form itself than the kind Wordsworth introduces here.

The challenge to the metrical set initiated in this second part of the poem develops in part 3 into a realization as close as Wordsworth comes in his pentameter to a genuine departure from "the regular rules of the iambic" and from his own rules concerning placement of pause. Here Wordsworth takes advantage of a number of devices—chiefly enjambment, multiple midline pauses (including pauses in eccentric positions), and effective placement of polysyllabic words—to continue and develop the effect begun in part 2 of extraordinarily energetic speech rhythms. The use of short phrases in this passage is especially effective, as it reproduces in performance the very motions of the speech organs appropriate to the visionary experience. The scene is literally breathtaking:

There, in a black blue vault she sails along,
B   ŏ   B ȯ   B   o   B o B

>   Followed by multitudes of stars, that, small
>   B   ŏ   B o   B̄ o   B (x) o(x)   B
>   And sharp, and bright, along the dark abyss
>   o B (x)o   B (x)o B   o   B   o B
>   +s -s   s   s
>   Drive as she drives;—how fast they wheel away,
>   B   o B   o (x) o   B   o   B   o B
>   Yet vanish not!—the wind is in the tree,
>   o B   o   B   o B   o B̄ o   B
>   But they are silent;—still they roll along
>   o   B   o   B o   B   o B o B
>   Immeasurably distant;—and the vault,
>   o B o B̄ o B   o   B̄ o   B
>   Built round by those white clouds, enormous clouds,
>   ȯ   B   ŏ   B ô B   o B   o   B
>   Still deepens its unfathomable depth.
>   ȯ   B o B̄   o B o B̄ o B
>
>   (ll. 14–22)

The phrase "Drive as she drives" is in the context of Wordsworth's metrical set an astounding departure. The second-foot inversion is disruptive enough; a sequence of four consecutive atypical syllables occurring at the beginning of a line threatens to break the back of the meter. In this case, the combination of strong enjambment before and a midline full stop after the atypical sequence helps to neutralize its disruptive tendencies. The enjambment and the unconventional pattern do, however, tend to prohibit rapid or rhythmically regular pronunciation and make the full stop after "drives" as emphatic as possible. All of this works to emphasize by way of extreme contrast the rapidity and regularity of the second part of the next full phrase, in which the speaker reaches an emotional peak in the contemplation of a vision of profound permanence vested in eternal motion, of infinity and containment both: "how fast they wheel away / Yet vanish not."

Part 4, introduced by an echo of the transition that began the movement from lesser toward greater metrical complexity ("At length . . ."), concludes the poem with a return to the rhythmic regularity and longer phrases of the opening:

>   At length the Vision closes; and the mind,
>   o B   o   B o B o   B̄ o   B
>   Not undisturbed by the delight it feels,
>   B   ŏ   B   ôB̄   ŏ   B   o   B

Which slowly settles into peaceful calm,
o B o B o B̄ o B   o B
Is left to muse upon the solemn scene.
o B   o   B   o B   o   B   o   B

Only the phrase "not undisturbed by the delight" disturbs the return of realized stresses to their theoretically proper places. The hint of a very rare triple offbeat caused by the placement of the preposition "by" in a beat position is a ripple in the calm that Wordsworth achieved in revision. In DC MSS 15 and 16, the line appears thus:

Not undisturbed by the deep joy it feels
B   ŏ   B   ŏ   B ŏ B o B

Introducing the contrast between "delight" and the "peaceful calm" to which the disturbance gives way, Wordsworth also achieves a rhythmic flurry appropriate to the contrast he obviously wishes to make in the structure of the experience between the heightened emotion of the vision and the deeper calm to which it gives way. Elsewhere in this concluding passage, and especially in the two final rhythmically unbroken lines, the prosodic regularity of the opening section returns, marking the slow subsidence of the speaker's emotions after the "Vision closes."

Contributing to the sense of fulfillment and closure, too, is a slow gathering of alliteration, especially on the sounds [z] and [s] and the sonorant consonants *m, l,* and *n:*

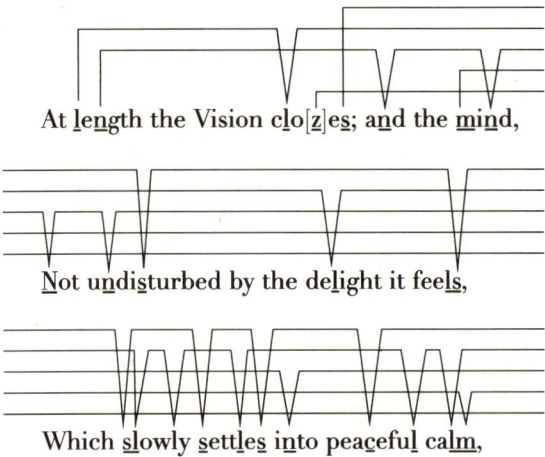

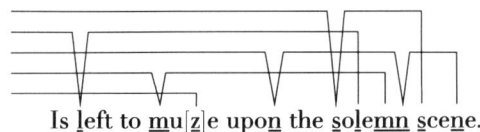

Is left to mu[z]e upon the solemn scene.

Also contributing is the repetition at the end of the final two lines of the rhythmic pattern **+s -s / +s** (/ = word boundary)—"peaceful calm," "solemn scene"—in which the first two syllables form a disyllabic adjective and the last a monosyllabic noun. The effect, a repetition of identical rhythmic and syntactic forms with different sounds, might be called a "stress-contour rhyme." More will be said below about this pattern in the discussion of the ending of "Yew-Trees," including evidence that Wordsworth acknowledged its use and effectiveness in Milton. At present it may be sufficient to note that the identical grammatical and rhythmic structure at the end of successive lines is as close as one can come in blank verse (short of a Shakespearean scene-ending couplet, that is) to the sense of closure supplied by a couplet in rhymed verse.

The four-part poem, brief enough to be apprehended as a single rhythmic, sonic, and syntactic whole, proceeds, then, from rhythmic simplicity to extreme complexity and back, giving at the end a sense of return to the beginning, but with a difference. The rhythmic regularity that in the beginning was appropriate to the experience of the "unobserving eye" is now the embodiment of feeling appropriate to the eye disturbed and then made quiet and solemn by an intervening vision of a sublimely immeasurable abyss in which action and stasis, sound and silence, are one. The structure helps convey through the very rhythmic impulses of the poem a sense that the state of mind embodied at the end of the poem is not different in kind from—and in fact is inextricably connected with—the common and everyday operations of mind with which the poem began. The delight produced by the vision, in other words, is the effect of the whole movement from and return to the everyday and is intended to produce a sense of the potentially heightened significance of—or the "glory" in—the common. Physically, the poem departs sharply from and returns completely to the common rhythms of the metrical set, creating through the process a new sense of the potential richness of that constraining set of conventional expectations.

"A Night-Piece" is impressive and effective in large part because its clearly individuated voice finds expression by means of an extraordinary degree of strain on the metrical set. The versification of "Yew-Trees," the

other half of Wordsworth's "specimen," is founded on a very different relationship between expressive impulses and metrical restraints, the passion of the subject and the passion of the meter. Indeed, the prosodic dissimilarity of the two poems suggests that extreme variety—even contrariety—is precisely what the poems, as "specimens" of blank verse, were intended by Wordsworth to exhibit.

In contrast to the speaker of "A Night-Piece," the speaker in "Yew-Trees" is, as has frequently been noted in recent criticism of the poem, curiously impersonal and unindividuated. In "Yew-Trees," differences between the single ancient yew, the "pride of Lorton Vale," and the "fraternal four" of Borrowdale—which form an "umbrage" "not uninformed by Phantasy"—spark a meditation that tends to deflect attention away from the speaker and toward the relationship itself and its implications.[20] The poem seems almost to exist to provoke and sustain consideration of relationships between the one and the many, individual act and communal gathering, historical individuals ("Umfraville or Percy") and timeless allegorical figures, war and "united worship," pride and "fraternal" feeling, substance and shadow. Its pleasures, it might be said, are more purely intellectual than are the more immediate and sense-induced "delights" of "A Night-Piece." Indeed, Lee Johnson has gone so far as to argue that at its deepest levels of organization, the pleasures of "Yew-Trees" are the pleasures of geometrical contemplation.[21]

The speaker of "Yew-Trees" recedes, as Theresa M. Kelley puts it, with the effect of foregrounding tensions between the sublime otherness of singularity and the beauty of containment.[22] Appropriately, then, the prosody and music of the poem depend relatively little on the most disruptive kinds of variation—dislocations of stress pattern—and more on subtleties of phrasing of a kind that tend to reveal the abstract metrical underpinnings of the language, placement of pauses, and patterning of vowel and consonant sounds. The rhythmic pulse remains relatively constant throughout.

In "A Night-Piece," five of twenty-six lines employ implied offbeat and pairing formations (-s -s +s +s, or +s +s -s -s). Only three such formations occur in the thirty-three lines of "Yew-Trees." Their sparing use calls special attention to them, not so much as indications of the speaker's passion (although they are that) as places of particular conceptual importance pointing emblematically toward thematic concerns. The first two instances occur at the very beginning:

    There is a Yew-tree, pride of Lorton Vale,
    o B o B   o B   o B o B

Which to this day stands single, in the midst
ŏ   B ô B   ŏ   B o B̄ o   B
Of its own darkness, as it stood of yore[.]
ŏ   B ô B   o   B o   B o B

The first of the two stress-final formations is the more disruptive because of the relative weakness of "this." As an adjective it would normally be expected to be subordinated to the noun it modifies.[23] An alternative scansion might merely promote "to" and demote "this":

Which to this day stands single, in the midst
o   B̄ ŏ B   ŏ   B o B̄ o   B

This option would make the beginning of the line rhythmically more regular, but it would fail to give expression to the contrast, which becomes clear only in the next line, between "this day" and the phrase "as it stood of yore." At issue here is not how to fix the line by a prescriptive rule of pronunciation; the point is to notice that the lines have built into them at this (early) point a kind of rhythmic complexity that demands a fairly high level of attention to relationships between semantic and nonsemantic details. A good instance of metrical complexity used for emphasis, the uncertain stress value of "this" and the dependence of the syllable on contrasting syllables in the next verse, assures that the relationship between past and present, which is a chief focus of the poem, is felt in the very physical structure of the line. The voice must register the contrast between the syllables "this day" and "of yore" in order for the lines to have metrical integrity.

The only other instance of dislocation in "Yew-Trees" occurs at a point of similar conceptual importance. This time, the effect is somewhat more complex:

But worthier still of note
o   B   o   B   o B
Are those fraternal Four of Borrowdale,
o   B   o B o   B   o   B o B̄
Joined in one solemn and capacious grove[.]
B   o B ô B   ŏ   B o   B
B   o B ô B o   B̄   o B o   B
B   ŏ   B o   B̄   o B o   B

As the alternate scansions show, the line is difficult to account for according to Wordsworth's own strict requirements. "One" must be

emphasized in any meaningful realization of the verse. Juxtaposed with "four," it is acted on semantically very much as "this" is by the implied contrast in "days of yore." (Note, here, however, that the double adjective, compared with the demonstrative adjective plus noun formation in the second line, is not affected as strongly by syntactic stress hierarchies.) But how can a reading give "one" its due without either producing a jarring triple offbeat (option 1) or realizing six stresses in a ten-syllable line (option 2)? Both of these options are possible but are unusual given the metrical set (whether that set is defined as "Yew-Trees," Wordsworth's blank verse, or English nondramatic blank verse as a whole). And both would leave the initial inversion condition unfulfilled. The third scansion shows a way in which initial inversion conditions could be fulfilled — by regarding "one" as demoted — but this is precisely what any reasonable reading would want to avoid.

Again, the absolute stress value of "one" is not the issue. The point is that a powerful and legitimate set of expectations based on the tradition of accentual-syllabic verse and the local conditions of Wordsworth's blank verse (that the line will have five stresses; that the initial inversion and double offbeat conditions will be fulfilled) is being challenged. The reason behind the difficulty may be the speaker's wonderment (an expressive indication) or the poet's desire to emphasize, as in the earlier example, a conceptual point or both. What is certain is that a metrically sensitive reading of the verse calls attention to the juxtaposition of "four" and "one," embodying in the physical structure of the verse the thematically important issue of unity and multiplicity.

Aside from these three rhythmically complex lines at two different points in the poem, and aside from several commonplace instances of initial inversion formations, "Yew-Trees" contains virtually no further rhythmic dislocation. Variety of versification is accomplished by the relatively more subtle means of promotion and demotion of stress, length of phrase, placement of pause, and patterning of alliteration and assonance.

Fourteen of the thirty-three lines in "Yew-Trees" (42.4 percent) are unbroken, and none of its lines contains more than one pause. Both of these characteristics are much more pronounced in "Yew-Trees" than is usual in Wordsworth's blank verse: in the sample of one thousand lines from *Lyrical Ballads* (1800), fewer than 37 percent of the lines are unbroken, and about one-quarter contain double or triple pauses. Unbroken lines tend, of course, to emphasize the abstract and formal metrical pattern underlying the verse more frequently than do broken, dramatic lines. The occurrence of double and triple pauses in five of twenty-six

lines in "A Night-Piece," for example, is a chief means through which Wordsworth creates the sense of growing emotional complexity:

> There // in the black blue vault she sails along,
> Followed by multitudes of stars // that // small
> And sharp // and bright // along the dark abyss
> Drive as she drives // how fast they wheel away,
> Yet vanish not! // the wind is in the tree[.]
>
> (ll. 14–18)

By comparison, the impressiveness of a similarly important passage of description in "Yew-Trees" depends less on rhythmic interruption and more on a sense of formal integrity and order manifesting itself through the physical stuff of the speaker's language. This effect is produced in part by the high frequency of unbroken lines in the passage and in part by the use of words requiring, or at least inviting, elision:[24]

> But worth*ie*r still of note
> Are those fraternal Four of Borrowdale,
> Joined in one solemn and capac*iou*s grove;
> Huge trunks!—and each partic*ula*r trunk a growth
> Of intertwisted fibres serpentine
> Up-coiling, and invet*e*rately convolved[.]
>
> (ll. 13–18)

"Worthier," "capacious," and "inveterately" are clearly and easily elidable. One effect of such elisions is, of course, to foreground the line as a unit governed by tight restrictions on numbers of syllables. Here, to put the point in terms relative to the issue of line integrity, the elisions may be regarded as a pleasant coincidence of optional pronunciation and the pressure for conformity that the metrical scheme of the whole line imposes on its individual parts. The elisions seem natural enough in pronunciation, so the hint of elision in conformity to metrical requirements is not obtrusive. The effect created is that of slightly heightened and formalized natural pronunciation—an instance, perhaps, of what Hazlitt calls Wordsworth's "chaunt."

"Particular," on the other hand, would seem to be more difficult to account for in the metrical scheme. The consonant combination c + vowel + l is subject to rules of elision in earlier English verse: Bridges includes "articulate," for example, in a list of words that he judges are regularly regarded as elided for metrical purposes in *Paradise Lost*.[25] But any

attempt to fit "particular" in actual pronunciation into a three-syllable space surely requires a much greater sense of shoe-horning its recalcitrant phonetic stuff into the meter than does the much more natural pronunciation of "inveterately" as a four-syllable word. Without such fitting, however, the line would have a double offbeat without an implied offbeat to offset it:

    Huge trunks!—and each particular trunk a growth
    ȯ   B   o   B   oB ŏ   B   o   B

Such realization of the metrical pattern is, of course, perfectly allowable in late-eighteenth- and early-nineteenth-century blank verse. And Wordsworth himself, though a strict syllabist in his early training, later shows a tendency to be slightly less strict in his management of syllables. But the fact remains that such effects are not frequent in Wordsworth, early or late. The problematic "extra" syllable alternately may be regarded as an instance of what Attridge calls delayed compensation. That is, the double offbeat of the seventh position compensates for an implied offbeat elsewhere in the line, perhaps between the first and second syllables:

    Huge trunks!—and each particular trunk a growth
    B ô B   o   B   oB ŏ   B   o   B

This option, however, as in the similar example in the immediately preceding line ("Joined in one solemn . . . "), introduces six beats in the line. And it may be remembered from the discussion above of "this day" that, in general, syntactical stress hierarchies will tend to subordinate the adjective "huge" to the noun "trunks."

It seems best, then, to think of "particular" as, for metrical purposes, a three-syllable word. This does not mean that the reader must actually pronounce the elision (or that the poet himself would have done so, or even that it is physically possible to do so): it means that a fully informed reading of the line in the context of Wordsworth's metrical set will involve a sense of the delicate tensions that work to make "particular" an extraordinarily interesting word. As a word that both does and does not fit the rhythmic structure of the line, it stands out to the ear as a recalcitrant bit of phonetic material. Such words seem almost to require two kinds of apprehension simultaneously, one that subsumes the word according to the requirements of harmonious poetic numbers and one that allows it a "natural" pronunciation that does not quite fit.

That the metrically interesting word "particular" appears in the midst

of a description of the relationship of parts to wholes, of individual "fibres," "inveterately convolved," and the one "huge" trunk they form (which is itself only one of four that make up the single "pillared shade") is no accident. Similar sonic and rhythmic peculiarities occur in such conceptually important places throughout Wordsworth's poetry. The use of "powers," discussed above in connection with "Expostulation and Reply," is one good example. Another occurs in the midst of what may be Wordsworth's most resoundingly confident and imaginative assertion of the possibility for perfect community among perfectly distinct individuals—*Home at Grasmere*, lines 149–51. There, Grasmere Vale is described in grand summation both as an "Abiding-place of many Men" and as a perfect unity:

> A Whole without dependence or defect,
> Made for itself and happy in itself,
> Perfect Contentment, Unity entire.[26]

Wordsworth's fondness for phonologically complex or rhythmically ambiguous words at points where, conceptually, the demands for closure are most insistent has been noted above in the discussion of promoted rhymes in stanzaic verse. Here, "entire," as a word that may be described as hovering between a monosyllabic and disyllabic pronunciation, concludes the four-square statement of assurance of perfection with a lingering ghost of a sound that resists easy inclusion in the metrical scheme. Its tension perfectly embodies the conceptual tension residual in the assertion of the decidedly individual speaker (none other than William Wordsworth, poet) that he is a perfectly assimilated member of the community.

Granted, the leap from such minute elements of poetic composition to such grand and central preoccupations of Wordsworth's poetry of the imagination is a large one. It is, however, one that Wordsworth invites. In the Preface to *Poems* (1815), Wordsworth draws attention to the shaping and creative power of imagination, claiming that it is manifested chiefly in relationships between "numbers" and "unity": "The Imagination also shapes and *creates;* and how? By innumerable processes; and in none does it more delight than in that of consolidating numbers into unity, and dissolving and separating unity into number—alternations proceeding from, and governed by, a sublime consciousness of the soul in her own mighty and almost divine powers" (*Prose* 3:33). As Christopher Ricks has remarked, the phrase "consolidating numbers" "cannot but bring to mind the other sense of *numbers,* 'harmonious numbers,' that poetic imagination which consolidates numbers into

unity by creating poetic numbers within poetic unity."²⁷ Ricks's argument focuses on Wordsworth's use of complexly ambiguous line endings and enjambment—what Paul Sheats calls Wordsworth's skill in maintaining a "delicate equilibrium between process and stasis"—in order to claim in part that Wordsworth's blank verse gains much of its power from its ability to embody in its movement just this kind of tension between parts and wholes, between numerous single verses and the one poem of which they are integral parts.²⁸ Wordsworth's blank-verse line endings, he suggests, frequently function as a "type or symbol or emblem" of the poet's "commitment to those ample relationships which yet do not swamp or warp the multiplicities which they accommodate. No fragmentation into separateness; but also no dissolution within a greedily engrossing unity" (3). This concern on Wordsworth's part commits him to a kind of verse in which the "separate line of verse must not be too simply separate, and yet it must have its individuality respected" (3). In the following passage from *The Prelude,* says Ricks, the lines both "are about—and supremely evoke—the impossibility of stopping short":

> and oftentimes,
> When we had given our bodies to the wind,
> And all the shadowy banks, on either side,
> Came sweeping through the darkness, spinning still
> The rapid line of motion; then at once
> Have I, reclining back upon my heels,
> Stopp'd short, yet still the solitary Cliffs
> Wheel'd by me, even as if the earth had roll'd
> With visible motion her diurnal round.
> *(13-Bk Prelude* 1.479–87)

Such verse suggests that "there can be no cutting off the sequential, and the verbal sequences themselves tell their tale" (5).

The contribution of unbroken lines and elisions to the sense of the distinctness and integrity of the individual verses in "Yew-Trees" already has been suggested. The complexity of "particular," on the other hand, may be seen as a part of the artistic impulse in the opposite direction—that is, as a challenge to the line as the determining unit of organization. The most prevalent and obvious means through which the blank-verse line is both defined and challenged is, of course, enjambment, which occurs more frequently in "Yew-Trees" than in the average passage of Wordsworth's blank verse: nineteen of thirty-three (or 57.6 percent) of

the lines in "Yew-Trees" are enjambed, compared with 51.1 percent in the *Lyrical Ballads* sample, and only 38 percent in "A Night-Piece" (ten of twenty-six). The ending of the poem—one of the most elaborately sonorous passages in all of Wordsworth's verse—is a good example of the interconnection (or serpentine intertwisting) of the numerous verses into a single unified whole:

> ghostly Shapes
> May meet at noontide—Fear and trembling Hope,
> Silence and Foresight—Death the Skeleton
> And Time the Shadow,—there to celebrate,
> As in a natural temple scattered o'er
> With altars undisturbed of mossy stone,
> United worship; or in mute repose
> To lie, and listen to the mountain flood
> Murmuring from Glaramara's inmost caves.
>
> (ll. 25–33)

I am chiefly interested here in the prevalence of those sonic and rhythmic characteristics of individual verses that depend for their full effect on juxtaposition with other verses. Enjambment in five of the nine lines is obviously one of these, as is the wide variety in the placement of pauses in lines following enjambments. A less-obvious but no less effective device is similarity and dissimilarity in the stress contour and sound of line endings—the effect that has been called stress-contour rhyme in the discussion of the final "couplet" of "A Night-Piece."[29]

Wordsworth's consciousness of and interest in such effects is shown by his mention of a particularly interesting example of stress contour similitude in dissimilitude in Milton. Pointing out "some of the artifices of versification by which Milton produces so great an effect," Wordsworth cites the following from *Paradise Lost* (II.486–88):

> ... pining atrophy,
> Marasmus, and wide-wasting pestilence,
> Dropsies and asthmas, and joint-racking rheums.

Wordsworth reportedly commented that "the power of the final 'rheums' is heightened by the 'atrophy' and 'pestilence'" occurring at the end of the two preceding verses.[30] Certainly there is a kind of semantic rhyme in the example: the three kinds of disease, different

and similar, placed in a formally important position, help to give the final word added force by virtue of accretion. But Wordsworth also was likely to be remarking on a specifically rhythmic source of emphasis here. The phrases "pining Atrophy" and "wasting pestilence" have identical grammatical forms and stress contours (/+s -s/ +s -s -s/), and both require promotion of the third syllable of the noun to the status of a secondary stress for full metrical realization of the line. They produce therefore relatively weak endings, bordering on falling rhythm, and thereby help to emphasize by contrast the rhythmically strong and rising "Joint-racking rheums." In addition, the placement of "rheums" after a two syllable adjective—"racking rheums"—makes the ending even stronger. (The use of "racking" as the second element in a compound also contributes to the contrast.) Milton's passage uses the "passion of meter" to effect. "Rheums" is felt to be powerful in part because the minute physical tensions that exist at line boundaries even in blank verse allow it to be placed in rhythmic contrast to the semantically similar nouns that precede it.

The conclusion of "Yew-Trees" draws on this opportunity, though admittedly in a less-obvious way, in the placement of "Skeleton" and "celebrate." These offer rhythmic contrast to the final four lines, three of which have the now familiar grammatical and rhythmic form: "mossy stone," "mountain flood," and "inmost caves." The relatively weak realization of the metrical scheme in those lines ending with the pattern +s -s -s (or +s -s s)—"Skeleton," "celebrate"—and the use of the semantically weak (and enjambed) "o'er" in the following line tend to deemphasize the singleness of individual lines and to set up and reinforce the very strong conclusion, in which the unbroken and rhythmically regular final line grounds the whole. The coupletlike effect of "mountain flood" and "inmost caves" also assists in creating the profound sense of closure in this passage, as does the similar rhythmic effect marking the ending of "A Night-Piece."

Perhaps the most important element of versification contributing to the sense of interconnection among the concluding verses is the management of assonance and alliteration. The texture is closely woven, giving the passage an almost Spenserian luxuriance of sound. Among the most obvious examples of sound patterning is the remarkably persistent repetition of long *o*. It resonates from "o'er" to "stone" to "repose" (all in the important final positions of verses) and is finally picked up—as are many of the sounds in this final passage—in the last line with "inmost." This long *o* contributes in the final verse to an extraordinary

example of vowel music in which the restriction and repetition of the vowels, in conjunction with the heavy use of sonorant consonants in "Murmuring" and "Glaramara" contribute substantially, through a kind of sonic undertone, to the poem's sense of the power that rolls through all things.

This effect is not, as might be supposed, dependent on onomatopoeic effects. "To lie and listen to the mountain flood / Murmuring from Glaramara's inmost caves" sounds no more like a mountain flood than does any other combination of vowels and consonants. Its power is felt because of the minute, physical sense that a reader will have when he or she participates sympathetically in the reenactment of the patterned tension and release of the speech apparatus necessary to an impassioned pronunciation of these words. The reader will feel, consciously or unconsciously, whether reading aloud or silently (but metrically and with animation, of course), that vowels—the free-flowing column of air that provides the breath out of which articulate speech is shaped—here predominate over and are facilitated by the relatively weak resistance of the consonants (many of which are in fact semivowels—[y], [w], and [r]). The effect thus produced by the relatively unimpeded vowels may be regarded as a means for giving embodiment in language to the feeling that the powerfully inarticulate murmuring stream produces in a sympathetic listener. The ending in two "long" vowels (actually one long vowel and a diphthong)—"inmost caves"—would also seem to contribute to this sense of the passage as a stream of words organized as much by powerful nonsemantic forces too deep for words as by specifically semantic requirements of intelligibility and referentiality.

Alliteration, too, functions in these final lines primarily as a means for preparing the way for the sonic and rhythmic fulfillment of the final line, or line and a half. As in "A Night-Piece," Wordsworth here favors the consonant sounds *s, l, m, n,* and *r.* Of all of the consonant sounds from "to celebrate" to "inmost caves," only five are not repeated at least once (and many are repeated at least twice). Significantly, all five of these unrepeated sounds—the *ng* of "murmuring," the *f* of "from," the *g* of "Glaramara," and the [k] and *v* of "caves"—all occur for the first time in the final verse, while at the same time repetition of a few consonants increases toward the end: "*l*ie and *l*isten" "*m*ountain / *M*ur*m*uring . . . Gla*ram*ara's . . . in*m*ost." The lines exhibit a growing concentration of vowel sounds and consonant sounds alike (brackets above the line mark occurrences of alliteration; those below mark instances of assonance):

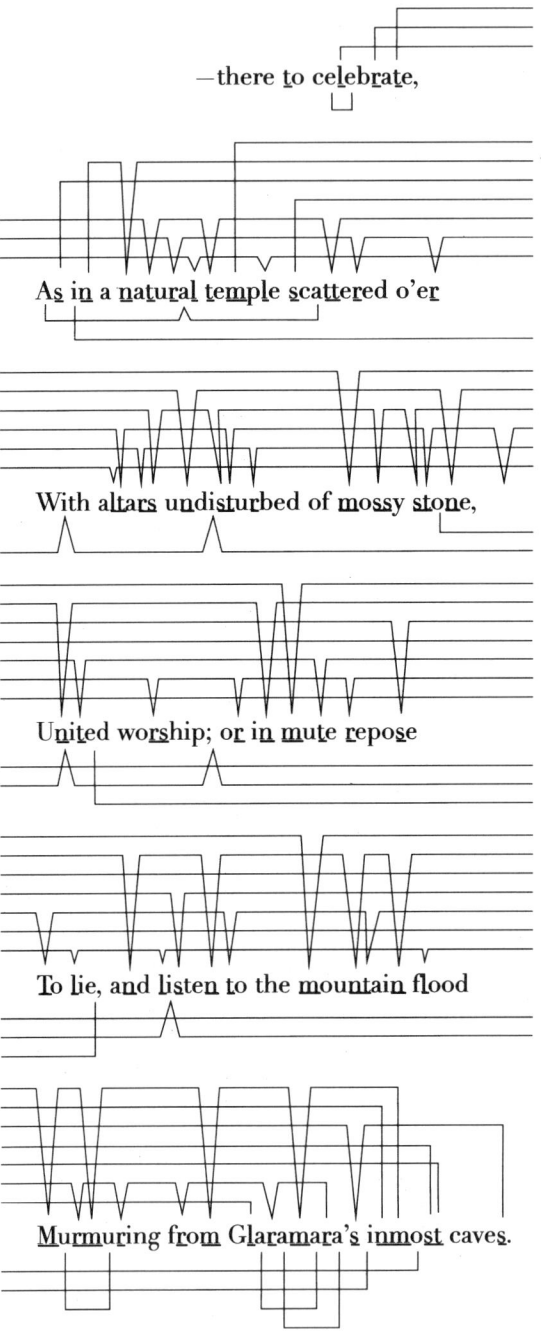

But this concentration is only one of two movements; repetition of a few sounds is simultaneously countered by the introduction of new consonant sounds (none of the marked sounds are anticipated in the densely woven lines that precede these lines):

>   or in mute repose
> To lie, and listen to the mountain flood
> Murmuri<u>ng</u> <u>f</u>rom <u>G</u>laramara's inmost <u>c</u>a<u>v</u>es.

The result is an extraordinary effect of concentrated power with a residual hint of single and individuated sounds that remain unencompassed by the overall pattern of the passage. The consonants of the final syllable in particular—"caves"—detach it emphatically from the sonic pattern of the whole. Thus the poem, which is so powerfully focused on issues of the relationship of the many and the one, ends with a syllable that admits of varying interpretations: is it the appropriate sound of closure and coherence, or a sonic hint of an opening, of something that resists inclusion into the scheme? Again, as with the example of "entire" in *Home at Grasmere*, the prevalence of sonic or rhythmic ambiguity at key points such as this allows Wordsworth to embody in the very viscera of the verse artistic and intellectual tensions fundamental to his poetry, particularly to the poetry of imagination. If the imagination may be defined as the faculty that makes one out of many without violence to the many—or that makes wholes in which the parts are both distinctly individuated and fully incorporated—then such minute effects of the versification are best regarded as instances of the operation of that power, as well as means for describing it.

"Rarely is any Wordsworth text innocent of other Wordsworth texts." Eric Walker's apt phrasing of what is by now a critical commonplace applies as surely to issues of metrical similitude in dissimilitude as it does to better-trodden topics in Wordsworth studies.[31] "Yew-Trees" provides a specimen of Wordsworth at his most sonorously impressive. Its rhythmic regularities and deep sonic structures give the work a feel of almost sculpted wholeness and indivisibility. Its conclusion comes as close as does any passage of Wordsworth's verse to a Tennysonian abandonment of the individualized speaking voice to the abstract harmonies and relationships of pure vowel music. "A Night-Piece," which immediately precedes "Yew-Trees" in the Poems of the Imagination (in *Poems* [1815]), is a specimen of Wordsworth's blank verse at its most expressively dislocated. Nowhere in Wordsworth's blank verse do more and more kinds of rhythmic disruptions occur in so short a space. No

passage of blank verse more successfully conveys a sense of spontaneous overflow of emotion through skillful suggestions of an individual escape from superimposed structures of metrical form.

Wordsworth's grouping of the poems together in his *Poems* and in his comments to Henry Crabb Robinson suggests that in the end the marmoreal verse of "Yew-Trees" and the volatile and elastic verse of "A Night-Piece" are to be recognized as representative of complementary impulses. By juxtaposing them, Wordsworth suggests that in his blank verse every escape implies a return, every point of tension implies release from tension, every concession to the passion of the meter implies a departure motivated by the passion of the subject. Every fixed realization of a line, in short, implies all of the possibilities that must be excluded in the realization of the line. Taken to its logical conclusion, the aesthetics on which Wordsworth's metrical art is founded implies that every line of blank verse potentially resonates with every other one, producing endless and endlessly dissimilar echoes of the same immutably fixed form. The prosodic power of Wordsworth's blank verse depends on the reader's sensuous apprehension (and abstract conception) of this infinite diversification of the same and coalescence of the infinitely diverse.

ASSOCIATIVE FUNCTIONS OF BLANK VERSE: WORDSWORTH, MILTON, AND THE MILTONIC

Thus far, I have been concerned for the most part with characteristic expressive and emblematic functions of Wordsworth's blank-verse rhythms and structures. An adequate understanding of the issues involved, however, also requires some consideration of the historical associations of blank verse, associations that make the form particularly well suited to explorations of relationships between the personal voice and echoes of the past, the voice of one poet and the voice of that "nature that exists in [all] mighty poets." As the most malleable of regular accentual-syllabic verse forms, blank verse offered Wordsworth the most flexible means for developing and presenting his own voice in all of its complexity. At the same time, iambic pentameter verse carries the heaviest weight of associative power (as "exponent or symbol") of any form in English. Its very malleability, its adaptability to idiosyncrasies of use, has also made it historically impressionable.

One significant and somewhat paradoxical result of this impressionability is that particularly powerful and idiosyncratic uses of blank verse tend to become so closely connected with the form itself as to seem the

self-evidently natural way for it to be used. Thus, when Samuel Johnson warns that blank verse tempts the poet to greater extravagance in the use of syntactic distortion and more frequent departure from simple expression than does rhymed verse, he is equating Milton's particular use of the form with the form itself. A comment made by Cowper in 1784 nicely summarizes this tendency in the blank-verse tradition. Writing to John Newton, Cowper objects to criticism of his blank verse on the grounds that it is insufficiently like Milton's and Thomson's. "Milton's manner was peculiar," says Cowper, "so is Thomson's":

> He that should write like either of them, would in my judgment, deserve the name of a Copyist, but not of a Poet. Blank verse is susceptible of a much greater diversification of manner, than verse in rhime. And why the modern writers of it have all thought proper to cast their numbers alike, I know not. Certainly it was not necessity that compelled them to it. I flatter myself however that I have avoided that sameness with others which would entitle me to nothing but a share in one common oblivion with them all.[32]

The most formally variable form is in practice the most rigidly undiversified. In *The Task*, of course, Cowper did to some extent achieve his goal of diversifying the tradition and thereby influenced not only Wordsworth (who acknowledged his debt to Cowper in a MS note to "Thoughts, Suggested on the Day Following, on the Banks of the Nith" [published 1842]) but also Coleridge, Lamb, and a whole generation of writers.[33] Wordsworth's own task in 1797–1820 or so (that is, until his own verse in its turn began to seem to younger writers the self-evidently natural way to write blank verse) would also require him to work directly against, and with, the conventionalized sonic and rhythmic "sameness" that R. D. Havens attributes to "idolatry" of the Miltonic.[34]

Wordsworth's well-known description of Milton's "voice" in "London 1802" puts in significant figurative terms the kind of power that Milton's verse seemed to embody:

> Thou hadst a voice whose sound was like the sea.
>
> (l. 10)

Wordsworth here is of course not referring solely to Milton's specifically prosodic qualities. His identification of the Miltonic voice with elemental natural power, however, does suggest the degree to which he regarded Milton's verse as having accomplished in its own way what he wished to

accomplish. Milton's artful management of fixities and fluidity, unity and multiplicity, restraint and freedom makes the very physical stuff of his verse nearly as self-evidently powerful as is nature itself. Wordsworth's figure also suggests that the Miltonic could be, in a practical sense, as overwhelming as the sea.

As I argued in chapter 1, Wordsworth took very seriously the power of verse forms to become associated with a particular usage or set of stylistic characteristics. Wordsworth, like Cowper before him, may have regretted this fact of the history of taste, but he could neither deny it nor ignore its consequences. What this means is that Wordsworth's own blank-verse style had to be developed and, ultimately, presented within the context of Milton's achievement and example.

The Miltonic is a constant presence in Wordsworth's blank verse not only because of conventional associations but for more immediate and practical reasons. We know from various sources—and especially from the evidence of Wordsworth's own rhythms—that he had hundreds of lines of Milton by heart. Milton was for Wordsworth not merely an external and intellectualized standard of style—a certain percentage per paragraph of syntactic inversions, enjambed lines, latinate and polysyllabic words—to be alluded to or not, by choice, as the occasion warranted. Miltonic rhythm and phrasing had to be for the boy and young man who could recite long passages of *Paradise Lost* a fully internalized presence informing his own patterns of speech and recitation. Milton's measures were for him felt in the blood and along the heart—and in the lungs and speech organs as well.

Metrical and rhythmic imitation of or allusion to Milton, then, is always an extremely complex matter in Wordsworth. What precisely is the difference, after all, between the internalized Miltonic voice that echoes "like the sea" and all of the figuratively analogous natural "voices" through which Wordsworth seeks to represent the specifically extraliterary (even extralinguistic) sources of his intellectual and emotional strength? Milton's verse is for Wordsworth the proper embodiment of the "mighty nature" that exists in some few poets. Its complex and diverse music bestows on mere words characteristics analogous to those the poet habitually associates with the workings of nature. Milton's music is perfectly distinct and individuated. In Cowper's terms, it is "peculiar."[35] At the same time—and this is what distinguishes it from the "glittering verse" to which Wordsworth was so attracted in his early youth (and which he wrote in his early work)—such verse strikes the ear as never merely personal and singular.[36] Great verse, like a powerful natural phenomenon, presents itself as a distinctly individuated manifestation of uncontainably extraindividual

power. As book 5 of *The Prelude* sets out to attest, such verse had power to act on the young Wordsworth with a force comparable to that which he elsewhere attributes to the influence of the Derwent, the "sound like thunder," the sea itself, and all other phenomena through which one may feel "whate'er there is of power in sound."[37]

One important aspect of this complex relationship between Wordsworth and Milton has been convincingly set forth by Judith W. Page, who singles out for discussion several specifically "metrical allusions" to Milton in *The Prelude*.[38] These metrical allusions function, according to Page, in a way similar to a particular kind of verbal allusiveness described by James K. Chandler—by creating "intentional representation[s] of unconscious influence."[39] In other words, the Miltonic rhythmic strain functions as evidence in the midst of "spontaneous" utterance of the internalization of previous poetic influence and therefore is able to represent deep "workings of the unconscious mind" (292). Milton's rhythms, Page argues, are as much a source of enduring power in Wordsworth's imagination as are the memories that make up the "spots of time" passages in *The Prelude*. The surfacing of these rhythms in Wordsworth's work are "tributes to the power of meter which Wordsworth acknowledges in his prose writings" (293).

Page shows how Milton's metrical style haunts Wordsworth's imagination in book 1 of *The Prelude*, where Wordsworth's speaker struggles with doubts about his capacity to write a poem rivaling Milton's own. Frequent syntactic inversion ("With meditations passionate from deep / Recesses in man's heart") is, of course, the chief signal of Miltonic influence. Another more subtle means is the use of a fairly rare and peculiarly Miltonic kind of enjambment; that is, enjambment that falls within a phrase. This occurs three times in fewer than one hundred lines in *The Prelude*, book 1:

> The Poet, gentle creature as he is,
> Hath, like the Lover, his unruly times;
> His fits when he is neither sick nor well,
> Though no distress be near him but his own
> Unmanageable thoughts.
>
> (*13-Bk Prelude* 1.146–50)

> I settle on some British theme, some old
> Romantic tale, by Milton left unsung[.]
>
> (ll. 180–81)

> With meditations passionate from deep
> Recesses in man's heart, immortal verse
> Thoughtfully fitted to the Orphean lyre[.]
>
> (ll. 233–35)

These effects, argues Page, show that Wordsworth "habitually and customarily associates Miltonic rhythms with grand achievement" (293). Miltonic rhythms, then, are the proper embodiment of Wordsworth's spontaneous expression of anxiety concerning his own achievement and aims.

Because her focus is specifically the psychology of Wordsworth's metrical allusions, however, Page finally wishes to argue that these Miltonic rhythms are always, or primarily, evidence of Wordsworth's anxiety of influence, a kind of rhythmic burden that he must cast off (or a demon to be "exorcised") in the search for his own more natural and genuinely Wordsworthian rhythms (293–94). My own view is that Wordsworth's original use of internalized and naturalized Miltonic rhythm includes this dimension but is in fact much more various and more pervasive than Page's thesis suggests.[40] Considered with regard to specifically metrical issues, the Miltonic voice is not best regarded as always, or even usually, antagonistic. Its rhythms are in many cases not opposed to Wordsworthian spontaneity or expressive naturalness but are actively complementary to it. Thus, in certain situations (*Prelude* book 1, for example) the particular activity of mind being instanced (Wordsworth's creation of a distinct autobiographical self) may find proper expression through antagonism to the Miltonic. In other situations, however, Wordsworth's complex purposes will involve incorporations of, contrasts with, undercuttings of, or even a kind of appropriate passivity before the Miltonic. Another way to put this is that as long as Wordsworth retains his own memory of and physical response to Milton's power and continues to write in blank verse, the Miltonic may be channeled, but it cannot be ignored (or "exorcised" or cast off). Its undersong is as persistent as the undersong of the Derwent.[41]

The versification of "Yew-Trees," for example, has appropriately been called "Miltonic" in large part because of lines such as the following:

> Huge trunks!—and each particular trunk a growth
> Of intertwisted fibres serpentine
> Up-coiling, and inveterately convolved,—
>
> (ll. 16–18)

The polysyllabic adjectives and adverb, the enjambment, and the syntactically impressive delayed placement of the Miltonic "serpentine" all serve to call attention to the verse as being as baroquely "convolved" as the subject of the description. Such verse would be perfectly at home in Milton's description of Eden—that *locus* of unity in multiplicity—in book 4 of *Paradise Lost*. In Wordsworth's corpus, however, these rhythms and syntactic peculiarities make the passage stand out as one kind of verse among many. The lines therefore present themselves as a kind of allusive purple passage, distinctly more musically impressive than usual.

I use "musical" here in the sense in which O. B. Hardison, Jr., uses it in *Prosody and Purpose in the Renaissance* to describe Milton's peculiar ability to seem to incorporate in the very texture of his verse powerful extrasemantic forces (an ability that Wordsworth strives to develop on his own terms). Such effects pervade *Paradise Lost,* providing sustained aesthetic evidence of the poet's Orphic or prophetic function:

> Like Homer, [Milton] begins by commanding the epic Muse to sing; and the infinitely varied music of the song continues until the departure of Adam and Eve from Paradise at the end of book 12 of *Paradise Lost*. Since the Muse sings of "things invisible to mortal sight," the poem is, among other things, a powerful reassertion of the ancient theory that poetry is constitutive and that its power comes to it through music.[42]

Distortions of speech order are signs of the informing power of Urania's celestial harmonies, which bend the lowly English language to forms outside and beyond those appropriate to merely communicative, imitative, or psychologically expressive purposes.

In Wordsworth's corpus, such effects frequently occur within contexts in which the process of imaginative reformulation, through which the prosaic and everyday is elevated into a song of supersensual significance, is precisely the point of the verse. For all of the musical grandeur of the "intertwisted fibres serpentine," the subject is—pointedly—not the tree of the knowledge of good and evil. It is a stand of yew trees in an actual place with the homely and decidedly English name of Borrowdale. Such interpenetrations of Miltonic celestial music and native English subjects function in the service of a familiar Wordsworthian task. They help to substantiate the claim that the commonplace, imaginatively apprehended, can be as impressive to the mind as any of the more conventionally grand subjects of earlier poetry. Chanting of Borrowdale yews in Miltonic strains while remaining decidedly within the realm of things

visible to mortal sight, Wordsworth juxtaposes through the music of his verse the "groves elysian and fortunate fields" and an actual spot that in the clear light of the noontime sun has power to lift the speaker to a vision of more than earthly power.

The complexity of Wordsworth's use of the associational power of his blank verse to create Miltonic contexts for his own different aims is a subject worthy of a book of its own. For present purposes, it may be sufficient to suggest some of the more important of Wordsworth's tendencies in this regard through a metrical analysis of his most direct statement of his aims relative to Milton's, the "Prospectus" to the *Excursion*. As is appropriate to so important and comprehensive a manifesto, the versification of the passage is itself an attempt to instantiate the powers that it describes and celebrates.

From a conventional point of view, the "Prospectus" is among the most stylistically uneven passages in all of Wordsworth's blank verse. It has lines of extreme grandeur in which Wordsworth draws on Miltonic music as evidence of his own status as a transcriber of celestial harmonies or as bardic singer of things unattempted yet in prose or rhyme:

> For I must tread on shadowy ground, must sink
> Deep—and, aloft ascending, breathe in worlds
> To which the heaven of heavens is but a veil.
> All strength—all terror, single or in bands,
> That ever was put forth in personal form;
> Jehovah—with his thunder, and the choir
> Of shouting Angels, and the empyreal thrones,
> I pass them, unalarmed.
>
> (ll. 28–35)[43]

The passage is both extremely passionate and, prosodically, extremely regular and taut. Promotion and demotion of syllables, variation of polysyllabic and monosyllabic words, and varied placement of pause create all of its rhythmic interest. Enjambment (note the Miltonic midphrase enjambment of the first line), syntactic displacement (especially suspension of the subject and verb "I pass" in the second sentence), the high percentage of easily elidable words (shadowy, heaven, heavens, personal, th'empyr*ea*l), and of course the diction itself all help to create the effect of steadily mounting power, flowing in response to the speaker's invocation, in the immediately preceding lines, of Milton's Urania, "or a greater Muse, if such / Descend to earth or dwell in highest heaven!"

232 • THE VERSIFICATION OF POEMS

At the other end of the scale are passages such as the following, in which elements of Miltonic rhythm persist—in enjambments and some syntactic traits, for example—but are in uneasy combination or at cross purposes with other elements—especially the repetitious and philosophically abstract diction and the disruptive parenthetical phrases:[44]

> ... while my voice proclaims
> How exquisitely the individual Mind
> (And the progressive powers perhaps no less
> Of the whole species) to the external World
> Is fitted:—and how exquisitely, too,
> Theme this but little heard of among Men—
> The external World is fitted to the Mind;
> And the creation (by no lower name
> Can it be called) which they with blended might
> Accomplish:—this is our high argument.
>
> (ll. 62–71)

"Exquisitely," "progressive powers," "external World," "individual mind," "species"—such diction gives evidence of a mind under the influence of a different motive force than that which informed the passage of high inspiration and aspiration quoted above. The parentheses, asides, and qualifications ("perhaps no less"; "by no lower name") express a mind concerned with a kind of philosophical explicitness that is difficult to accommodate in the context of chanted "spousal verse." The physical evidence of the tension is easy enough to document in the rhythmic complexity of several key lines:

```
            +s -s[s] -s
How exquisitely the individual Mind
  o   B o B̄ o  B   oB o  B
(And the progressive powers perhaps no less
  B̄    ǒ   B  o   B    o B   o B
Of the whole species) to the external World
  ǒ      B ô B o B̄   o  B  o    B
Is fitted; and how exquisitely, too—
 oB  o B̄   ǒ  B o B̄  oB
 or     ǒ    B ô B
```

The word "exquisitely" stands out rhythmically in both of its occurrences, and of course its repetition calls particular attention to it. The pronun-

ciation required by the meter—+s -s [s] -s—in both cases realizes a beat with a very weakly stressed syllable, almost producing the effect of a triple offbeat. In the first occurrence of the word, the added complexity of the elision of "th'individual" creates a shadow of even a fourth consecutive weak syllable. These elements, taken together with the second elision in "individual" make the verse an extraordinarily complex—one might be tempted to say "exquisite"—realization of the metrical scheme. The use of a stress-final pairing formation in line 65, and arguably in line 66, is, as has been noted, characteristic of more conversational verse than this. It helps here to give the parenthetical structure the rhythm appropriate to a sotto voce insertion.

The most disruptive rhythmic structure in the cited passage occurs in the next line, which is itself a syntactically disruptive parentheses:

    Theme this but little heard of among Men—
    ò   B   o   B   o   B ŏB ô B

The final four syllables constitute a rhythmic structure but little heard among readers of English verse. The pattern -s /-s +s/ +s, in which the middle two syllables are contained within a word boundary, is singled out by prosodists as a rare—or even, according to some systems, a disallowed—feature of five-beat verse. Whether it is called a "juncture inversion" caused by "autonomous polysyllables" (as it is by Tarlinskaja) or a "stress-final pairing with linkage" (as it is by Attridge), it has been avoided throughout the history of English pentameter with remarkable consistency. Only twenty-four clear examples of the pattern are recorded in Tarlinskaja's sample of thirteen thousand lines of pentameter verse from Spenser to Swinburne.[45] So disruptive is the formation that it has been common among prosodists to explain it away by means of a theory of "recession of accent," or shifting the accent forward for metrical purposes to the first syllable of the disyllabic penultimate word. The editors of the Norton edition of *The Prelude* provide a good example of the usual way of accounting for this anomaly in a footnote to another instance of linkage, in book 1, line 336:

                             the soul
Remembering how she felt, but what she felt
 -s   -s   -s   -s
Remembering not, retains an obscure sense
 ŏ   B ô   B
Of possible sublimity

                                      (ll. 334–37)

The footnote directs the reader to shift the accent to the first syllable of "obscure" and notes that "Milton too sometimes stresses the first syllable" (J. Wordsworth et al. 82 n. 2). Theories of recession of accent, however, only beg the question. The most compelling evidence that Milton (or Wordsworth in imitation of him) intended recession of accent on "obscure" (or "among") is the offense that the ear (or, more accurately, the speech apparatus) takes when confronted with such a metrically dislocating rhythmic structure:

> Encamp their Legions; or with obscure wing.
> (*Paradise Lost* 2.132)

Whether the word is pronounced "ob-*scure*" or "*ob*-scure," the reader is left with evidence of tension between speech and meter. Robert Bridges leaves the issue open with regard to Milton's practice, describing the rhythmic character of such phrases as "doubtful" and venturing the opinion that Milton tended to exclude such effects from later verse because of its tendency to unsettle the rhythm (*Milton's Prosody*, 28–35). Attridge's conclusion on this point is probably the best; that is, that these metrical anomalies are instances of a "balance of tensions created by deliberate (and unavoidable) mismatching of metrical form and linguistic structure" (268). They are, in other words, irreducibly and inherently troublesome features that call a great deal of attention to the fact of the poet's craft in fitting language to aesthetically dictated formal structures.

For all of these reasons, a reader attentive to rhythm cannot but register a sense that this latter passage is considerably less conventionally harmonious than is the verse surrounding it. Here, the signs of fitting recalcitrant language to metrical form are so clearly audible—and are especially so because of the juxtaposition of the passage with the more conventionally harmonious verse of lines 28–35—that it seems justified to inquire whether or not such various use of metrical form may have some expressive or emblematic value. The question is especially of interest because the relatively inharmonious passage is placed in a position of extreme importance, culminating as it does in the announcement that "This is our high argument."

The "Prospectus" is, of course, as much about the ways in which Wordsworth wishes to distinguish himself from Milton as it is a claim of poetic fraternity with him. (Indeed, as Cowper's comment above suggests, the fraternity of effective blank verse writers must be a fraternity of strongly distinct individuals.) A phrase represented by Wordsworth as

direct quotation from Milton subtly sums up an important difference relevant to a discussion of the two poets' verse harmonies. In *Paradise Lost*, book 7, Milton prays to Urania (as the muse of astronomy, the source of the poem's invisible and celestial harmonies) to find her audience by singing through him. Milton's music is figuratively not his own:

> Still govern thou my song,
> Urania, and fit audience find, though few.
> (*Paradise Lost* 7.30–31)

Wordsworth invokes Milton by misquoting him even before he makes any mention of the Muse. Wordsworth's act boldly appropriates for himself the power to "give utterance in numerous Verse" to his "fair trains of imagery," "feelings of delight," "affecting thoughts," and "dear remembrances":

> Of Truth, of Grandeur, Beauty, Love, and Hope—
> . . . .
> I sing; "fit audience let me find though few!"
> (ll. 14, 23)

The inserted phrase "let me" in a line that claims a close similarity between Wordsworth's and Milton's aims nicely expresses the ambivalence of Wordsworth toward the Miltonic. For one thing, it shows that the Miltonic is not for Wordsworth (as the Authorized Version is for Milton in *Paradise Lost*, for example) a sacred text inviolable to creative appropriation and revision. Furthermore, if *The Recluse* is to be a poem asserting the creativity, as well as the receptivity, of the individual "Mind of Man," then its music must result from a fitting of the kind of power represented in Milton's poem by Urania to diction that is expressive of the fluxes and refluxes of the individual human mind. Wordsworthian power of song, in short, will work not only by fitting the language of common humanity to "number"; it will also fit those numbers to the variety, idiosyncrasy, and volatility of human speech. This is not to suggest of course that Milton did not do something of the same in his verse. All good poets struggle in the accommodation of language to number. The point is that Wordsworth is announcing himself in the "Prospectus"— and is giving examples in the verse of the "Prospectus"—to be in the act of drawing the boundaries differently than they were drawn by Milton. Milton's English under the influence of heavenly order—what Johnson called, appropriately for the present discussion, his "Babylonish dia-

lect"—will not be Wordsworth's English. Wordsworth reserves the right to draw when appropriate on Miltonic sources of power, but he will not limit himself to them.

From this point of view, then, the conventionally inharmonious passage about fitting and being fit may be regarded as a point at which the verse itself makes such fitting an issue. The overtly philosophical language here, needed by the poet to attempt to introduce his theme "but little heard of among men," resists incorporation into the "song" in such a way that one cannot but be attentive to two contrary impulses at work. One impulse foregrounds the language as different from that usually heard in such contexts; the other informs the ear that this language, after all, does fit; that is, it can indeed be sung, though doing so may stretch the reader's conventional sense of what is appropriate to be sung. Or the tension might be regarded as an element of expressive use, depicting a speaker who holds passionately the abstract ideas that the diction expresses. In submitting such diction to the organizing patterns of the song, especially in the context of other passages that are more conventionally harmonious, Wordsworth's verse seeks to humanize ideas, to give physical realization to notions. The poet of *The Recluse,* he claims, can sing philosophically.

These metrical poles finally may be regarded as instances of the large claims of the "Prospectus" itself. Wordsworth is claiming through example that the work to which these lines form an overview and introduction will have—must have, in order to be the poem therein described—a music of its own, one appropriate to its extreme ambition. Just as the Miltonic landscape marks boundaries beyond which Wordsworth's muse must fly or sink, so Miltonic blank-verse rhythm marks one great example of the possible fitting of the English language to metrical arrangement. Wordsworth's own versification, to be appropriate to his song of the unfathomable human mind, must be free to accommodate language that may strain its conventional arrangements almost to the breaking point. The harmonies of Wordsworth's verse, in other words, will issue from the poet's juxtaposition of a considerably more various range of stylistic elements than is usual in the English grand style.

As is the case in the arguments mounted by Wordsworth in the Preface to *Lyrical Ballads,* or in his claim that he can accept almost unlimited "dislocation" in his blank-verse line, the "Prospectus" effectively asserts (and like "A Night-Piece" and "Yew-Trees" provides an instance proving the assertion) that the poet will accept no limitations beyond those which are necessarily entailed in his choice of a conventional verse form. According to this view and to this aesthetic principle, stylistic unevenness

or inconstancy to a single ideal of metrical realization becomes a chief means for embodying Wordsworth's extraordinary ambition: to accomplish on his own terms a poetic task comparable to Milton's own. And those passages or transitions in which Wordsworth's verse seems to be least Miltonic may be seen finally as instances of Wordsworth at his most truly Miltonic. Insofar as these passages express stylistically his independence from Milton within a context that directly invites comparison, they embody Wordsworth's understanding that the recovery of ancient liberty from various kinds of "modern bondage" is the task of every great poet. It is what Cowper means when he says that he believes that he has escaped the "common obscurity" of all of the imitators of Milton. It is part of what we mean when we say that Wordsworth's blank verse introduces a distinctive voice into English poetry.

Conclusion
On the Power of Sound

When Wordsworth first included "On the Power of Sound" in a collective edition of his poetry, he gave it pride of place as the last of the Poems of the Imagination. "On the Power of Sound" (composed 1828–29; published 1835) is, among other things, a poet's apologia—a defense, in mythic terms, of a life dedicated to "fitting" the English language to the requirements of "numerous verse." It suggests in grandly comprehensive terms how pervasively important metrical art is in the corpus as a whole.[1]

Wordsworth's apology is magisterial both in statement and design. A formal "Argument" (rare in Wordsworth's *Poetical Works*) stands at the head of the poem, mapping out with matter-of-fact bluntness an outrageously broad thematic sweep. The poem is to range from consideration of "The Ear" itself (imagined "as occupied by a spiritual functionary") to "the destruction of the earth and the planetary system," the "survival of audible harmony, and its support in the Divine Nature, as revealed in Holy Writ." In the course of the poem, Wordsworth's treatment ranges from natural sounds "acting casually or severally" ("The little sprinkling of cold earth that fell / Echoed from the coffin-lid"), to the "power" and "Origin" of music ("Orphean Insight!"), to the "Pythagorean theory of numbers and music, with their supposed power over the motions of the universe" ("By one pervading spirit / Of tones and numbers all things are controlled"), and finally to the Voice of voices, the originating creative Power that "to Light gave Being" and that "shall finish doubt and dim foreseeing, / And sweep away life's visionary stir." Sound is imaged in scores of forms in the poem. Encompassing "whispers" and "shrieks," lion's roar and lamb's bleat, Wordsworth's catalogue of sound images reads like a recapitulation of the basic vocabulary of his lifelong concern for "whatever there is of power in sound." Cuckoos, nightingales, the "hungry barkings" of the eagle, "headlong streams and fountains," the "lowing mead," and "forest hum of noon," sounds and echoes of the hunt, bells and knells of

all kinds, Hosannas and requiems, the "blackening clouds" that "in thunder speak of God," milkmaids' song, lullabies, patriotic hymn, "babe's first cry," and "voice of regal city / rolling a solemn sea-like bass" all find place in the fourteen-stanza poem.

The task that Wordsworth's speaker sets for himself is an enormously large and daunting one: to discover a "scheme," a "scale of moral music" whereby this vastly varied world of natural sound—figuratively "wandering Utterances"—might be comprehended as an organized whole. Wordsworth strives to imagine something like a harmonic system or a grammar of natural sound, some system of correspondence and difference through which this "vast . . . compass" and "swell of notes" might be saved, translated into articulate signs. With such a scheme or scale at his disposal, the Orpheus-like poet would be able to sound a chord sufficient to release from the oblivion of dim and fading memory all that he has most dearly loved in the mighty living world of eye and ear.[2] Is there any possibility, the poet asks in stanza 11, that these "Powers" that "survive but in the faintest dream / Of memory" might be given a more permanent form?:

> O that ye might stoop to bear
> Chains, such precious chains of sight
> As laboured minstrelsies through ages wear!
> O for a balance fit the truth to tell
> Of the Unsubstantial, pondered well!
>
> (ll. 172–76)

The answer to this wishful question comes, significantly, in the form of a rhetorical fiat. In stanza 13 Wordsworth finds the scale and the "chains of sight" he needs through an act of "representation" (Wordsworth's word, in the "Argument") of all sounds "under the form of thanksgiving to the Creator." Through a leap of imagination, "wandering Utterances" and dying echoes of voice become melody, harmony, and text in a vast "hymn / Of joy" that articulates nothing less than the full significance of being in time and space:

> Break forth into thanksgiving,
> Ye banded instruments of wind and chords;
> Unite, to magnify the Ever-living,
> Your inarticulate notes with the voice of words!

The key transition (or transition in key) from the tone of longing wishfulness in stanza 11 ("O for a balance fit the truth to tell / Of the Unsubstantial") to

the resoundingly affirmative hymn of thanksgiving of stanzas 13 and 14 ("Break forth into thanksgiving . . . !") comes in the stanza that was, in fact, the earliest composed part of the poem. "Wandering Utterances" are transformed into purposeful notes through an act of representation of all sounds as agents of harmony, a representation made possible by the introduction in stanza 12 of the Pythagorean "mystery." The speaker asserts in the bluntest possible terms—and with as imperious a manner as that of a conductor raising his baton before an unruly orchestra (or of Prospero conjuring the actors in his masque)—that "all things" are intermeasurable (or, poetically speaking, "controlled") according to a single system of correspondence. Vastly different and individuated concrete "things" turn out, mysteriously, to be modalities of a single substance and as such are intermeasurable through an abstract language of "tones and numbers":

> By one pervading spirit
> Of tones and numbers all things are controlled
> As sages taught, where faith was found to merit
> Initiation in that mystery old.
>
> (ll. 177–80)

Alfred North Whitehead has discussed the Pythagorean insight—in terms incidentally useful for grasping the central issues and tensions of Wordsworth's argument—as either the "luckiest of lucky guesses" in the history of Western thought or as "a flash of divine genius penetrating to the inmost nature of things."[3] Pythagorean understanding of the numerical underpinning of reality provides for Whitehead the basis of a powerful critique of the mind/matter split and its resultant "fallacy of misplaced concreteness." In defining reality as essentially vibratory and periodic, the Pythagorean tradition allows for an understanding of "things"—of material "reality" itself—as having no existence except as a "streaming" of activity unfolding in space and time. What appear to be steadily existing, permanent phenomena are, properly comprehended (without the "film of familiarity"?), just as surely vibratory manifestations of underlying power as are sounds, which we know to be explainable as "the outcome of vibrations in the air":

> A steadily sounding note is explained as the outcome of vibrations in the air: a steady colour is explained as the outcome of vibrations in ether. If we explain the steady endurance of matter on the same principle, we shall conceive each primordial element as a vibratory ebb and flow of an underlying energy, or activity. (35)

According to such a view, each "primordial element will be an organized system of vibratory streaming of energy." The notion of a universe of steadily enduring things definable in terms of simple location gives way to a universe of musiclike waves, in which each "thing" may be perceived as an activity among other activities: "Accordingly there will be a definite period associated with each element; and within that period the stream-system will sway from one stationary maximum to another stationary maximum—or, taking a metaphor from the ocean tides, the system will sway from one high tide to another high tide." "This system," Whitehead continues, "is nothing at any instant." In a way directly analogous to the sounding of a note of music, the system "requires its whole period in which to manifest itself" (35).

To translate this into the figures of "On the Power of Sound," Wordsworth, in appealing to Pythagorean "tones and numbers," leaps to a vision of the entire created world as infinitely diversified modulations of the central activity of creation. That activity is represented as a voice:

> As Deep to Deep
> Shouting through one valley calls,
> All worlds, all natures, mood and measure keep
> For praise and ceaseless gratulation, poured
> Into the ear of God, their Lord!
>
> (ll. 204–8)

"All" ultimately manifests itself as sound to the ear of God and, by implication, to the ear of godlike imagination. This is because sound is of all things in the created universe the most directly communicative of the essentially periodic nature of the "primordial element." The sound of the cuckoo frozen at any one instant simply is not the cuckoo's song. To be what it is, it requires its "whole period in which to manifest itself." It becomes a "thing" identifiable as such to sense only through its full unfolding in space and time, from initial attack to final decay. Whereas the eye has a disconcerting (and tyrannous) tendency to assert the independence from the whole of its objects of perception, giving the world of sight an appearance of permanence that misrepresents its essentially vibratory and periodic existence, the ear knows the world to be continually resonant of the time in which it was created and pregnant with the time that will undo it. The insistent transitoriness of the experience of sound opposes the tyranny of the eye, moving the mind eventually out of the merely "visionary" (and its tendency toward static

misrepresentation) into an experience of something more directly communicative of the fundamental *activity* of creation:

> A Voice to Light gave Being
> To Time, and Man his earth-born chronicler;
> A Voice shall finish doubt and dim foreseeing,
> And sweep away life's visionary stir[.]
>
> (ll. 209–12)

The Pythagorean "lucky guess" (or is it "divine insight"?), then, is in Wordsworth's poem the poet's enabling fiction. It allows him to represent the entire created world as a manifestation of an essentially poetic activity: the continual articulation of the silent one into the vocal many and the reconsolidation of the many into the one. This key Poem of the Imagination thematizes on a grand scale what Wordsworth defines in the Preface to *Poems* (1815) as the primary operation of the imagination (and one that has been discussed above as a key to understanding his metrical art). The imagination "shapes and *creates*," says Wordsworth, "delight[ing]" especially in a process of "consolidating numbers into unity, and dissolving and separating unity into number." These alternations proceed from, "and are governed by, a sublime consciousness of the soul in her own mighty and almost divine powers" (*Prose* 3:33).[4] The power of sound is the best emblem for the power of imagination because imagination perceives "all things" as the ear perceives the world of sound: as a vastly diversified articulation in time of an essential unity.

The implications of Wordsworth's representation of sound in "On the Power of Sound" and the connections between its argument and the treatment of sound elsewhere in the corpus are numerous and complex enough to have warranted extended study in their own right.[5] Mary Jacobus reads the poem as Wordsworth's attempt to redeem the "personal lyric" of *The Prelude* from time and death through recourse to the "WORD," defined here as "voice transcendentalized as Logos."[6] "On the Power of Sound" is for Jacobus the "optimistic, orthodox Christian sequel to the Arab dream [in *Prelude*, book 5], revised not to foretell 'Destruction to the children of the earth' but rather to prophesy salvation of and through the Word" (157). Jacobus's reading suggests that Wordsworth's poem, though perhaps psychologically necessary, involves a degree of anxious revision of earlier (more courageous or more authentic) positions. The same kind of suspicion is certainly present in John Hollander's historical reading, according to which "On the Power of Sound" is an "imaginatively dangerous remythologizing

CONCLUSION • 243

of natural music."[7] The poem is "dangerous" according to Hollander because its rhetorical movement into the Pythagorean "mystery" threatens the very source of Wordsworth's strength—his insistence on the primacy of the "very world" of sounds over the music of the spheres. Insofar as Wordsworth's mythologized overview tends to diminish the importance of the haunting presence *in* sound, it threatens what is strongest in Wordsworth's earlier resistance to myth and to the tendency of myth to mute the actual sound of the lived human life. In "On the Power of Sound," says Hollander, Wordsworth remythologizes the music of the spheres "*via*, but not terminating in, the fabulous power of what is . . . mundane." Through this process, Hollander claims, "even 'the still, sad music of humanity,' become[s], for the sound that lies as far behind language as it does beyond music, but phonetic shadows" (79).

Reading "On the Power of Sound" in the way that I have set forth above—as an insistently mythologized, quasi-autobiographical defense, an apologia for his metrical art—however, allows for a different, more integral and less sinister, view of its relation to the rest of Wordsworth's work. To put the issue simply, the audacity of Wordsworth's rhetoric in "On the Power of Sound" is matched by (and conveyed through) the obvious singularity of the poem's formal means. The poem announces itself in all sorts of ways not so much as the last word on the subject but as a particularly strong word of advice to listen attentively to impulses that pervade the music of the corpus as a whole.

A metrical reading notes first of all that the stanza form and sonic patterns make the poem unlike anything else in Wordsworth's corpus. As I noted in the discussion of "The Thorn" in chapter 4, Wordsworth's longer stanzas (ten lines or more) are with one exception "centos," or amalgamations of recognizable smaller forms, usually quatrains, couplets, and tail-rhyme sections.[8] The exception is the stanza used in "On the Power of Sound," which seems to be designedly resistant to being broken down into components. The sixteen-line stanza is the most complexly patterned, structurally integrated stanza in Wordsworth's poetical works. The rhyme pattern $a_{-3}ba\_bc_5dcdef_4e_5gf_4gh_5h_4$ both suggests and frustrates attempts by the ear and eye to discern clear divisions of quatrains or couplets. Stanzas contain very few variations from the pattern. There are no variations in rhyme and only eight departures (in 224 lines) from the standard metrical pattern.[9] Within stanzas, patterns are present that are more minute than are able to be shown in schematic form; for example, line 13 of each stanza (with two exceptions) is a catalectic tetrameter, a seven-syllable verse suggesting a falling or trochaic rhythm in the midst of an otherwise iambic poem. Yet for all of this complexity of rhyme and

meter (and perhaps, paradoxically, because of it), the verse pattern tends to give the initial impression of spontaneous irregularity. Any verse pattern longer than sonnet length, especially when it employs varied line lengths and provides no clear subdivisions in rhyme pattern, will appear irregular at first sight. Wordsworth seems to heighten this appearance through enjambment and midline pauses (note the emphatic exclamation point in line 3) in the opening lines of the poem:

> Thy functions are ethereal,
> As if within thee dwelt a glancing mind,
> Organ of vision! And a Spirit aërial
> Informs the cell of Hearing, dark and blind;
> Intricate labyrinth, more dread for thought
> To enter than oracular cave[.]
>
> (ll. 1–6)

In fact, the compositional history suggests that the stanza originally was a creature of spontaneous overflow. Judging from De Selincourt's *apparatus criticus*, the germ of "On the Power of Sound" is a set of lines composed for and rejected from "The Triad," an irregularly rhymed poem (composed 1828). The lines—beginning "The Heavens, whose aspect makes our minds as still"— correspond to lines 181–92 of "On the Power of Sound," the fifth to sixteenth lines of stanza 12 in the published poem. Later, Wordsworth added another set of verses rejected from "The Triad" to the head of this group. These lines correspond to lines 177–80, or the first four lines of stanza 12:

> By one pervading spirit
> Of tones and numbers all things are controlled
> As sages taught, where faith was found to merit
> Initiation in that mystery old.[10]

The stanza thus created stood as the introduction to a five-stanza version of "On the Power of Sound" (De Selincourt's MS A), with subsequent stanzas presumably written in conformity with the sixteen-line form created through revision. A form arrived at through accidents of revision, then, becomes the most rigorously formal stanza in Wordsworth's corpus. More to the point that I wish to pursue here, a stanza that gives an appearance of being organized primarily in accordance with the exigencies of the moment turns out to manifest a rather elaborate underlying pattern. A free impulse issues in a fixed scheme,

an overflow manifests order, the passion of the sense expresses itself in a system of "tones and numbers."

Wordsworth's theme and versification both make the emblematic significance of the poems' physical pattern more obvious than is common in Wordsworth's corpus. In stanza 13, for example, Wordsworth's representation of the infinite variety of natural sound "under the form of" a single hymn of thanksgiving is marked by a number of metrical minutiae that together make the activity of unifying the linguistic many into an integral whole an important part of the experience of reading. For example, Wordsworth employs strong enjambment at the midpoint of the stanza (end of line 8), a place where the rhyme scheme suggests a natural division and where most of the stanzas employ full stops:

> Nor mute the forest hum of noon: 6
> Thou too be heard, lone eagle! freed 7
> From snowy peak and cloud, attune   8
> Thy hungry barkings to the hymn   9
> Of joy   10
> (ll. 198–202)

Another, more subtle, example is the use of apparently extrametrical syllables in the thematically central line 196:

> Unite, to magnify the Ever-living,
> Your inarticulate notes with the voice of words!
> (ll. 195–96)

Here, as in a similar example from "Yew-Trees," the placement of "inarticulate" and "with the voice" is, for the ear practiced in hearing Wordsworth's verse, a challenge to fit the language to the metrical scheme, to unite this verse with the system of stress and number that governs all of Wordsworth's verse. The syllables admit of elision but (like "particular" in "Yew-Trees" [l. 16]) do not go gentle into a metrically induced oblivion:[11]

> Your inartic'late notes wi'th' voice of words!
> o B oB o B   o   B   o B

In a poem that thematizes the relationship between naturally unique and individuated occurrences of sound and a system of "tones and numbers" comprehending all such occurrences, such minutiae offer concrete instances of sound that may be heard not as exclusively one *or* the other

but as both. Twelve syllables of natural speech pronunciation are metrically ten. The activity of fitting the individual instance to the controlling pattern exercises powers of articulation and consolidation both.

Wordsworth's stanza in "On the Power of Sound" expresses and emblematizes the activity of unification through and in diversification in yet another way. As has been noted, the stanza is without precedent either in Wordsworth's corpus or in English poetry in general. At the same time, however, it is suggestive enough of sonnet form to invite comparison with what may be the single most readily recognizable rhymed form both in the corpus and in the tradition. The rhyme scheme suggests, but does not quite conform to, sonnet quatrain and couplet divisions. Moreover, the total metrical length of the sixteen lines in the stanza is exactly equivalent to the metrical length of the sonnet: each has, typically, seventy metrical beats. The relationship seems especially apparent and significant when "On the Power of Sound" is considered within the contexts of Wordsworth's corpus and his career. The *Poetical Works* contains more than five hundred sonnets; therefore, to know Wordsworth's verse is to be fully attuned to the structure and movement of the sonnet. During the years when "On the Power of Sound" was drafted and revised, Wordsworth's preferred form, especially for longer and more important themes, was increasingly the sonnet sequence, in which numbered sonnets function as stanzas (or almost so) in a longer work (note here, too, the numbering of stanzas in "On the Power of Sound").

Wordsworth's stanza in "On the Power of Sound," then, may be regarded as an attempt to fashion out of the sonnet tradition a form "more interwoven and complete / To fit the naked foot of Poesy."[12] Considered as such, the experiment is interestingly of a piece with his thinking about the sonnet in the 1820s and 1830s. During this period, Wordsworth is writing sonnets on the sonnet, including "Scorn not the sonnet, critic" and "There is a pleasure in poetic pains" (both composed in 1827). These deal overtly (as does the much earlier written "Nuns Fret Not") with issues that I am suggesting are more covertly present in "On the Power of Sound": the poet's commitment to work in strictly controlled verse forms and the pleasures and rewards of doing so. This is the period, too, during which Wordsworth makes his well-known comments to Alexander Dyce about the sonnet, comments that reveal a great deal about the attractions that sonnet form so obviously held for him.[13] Praising Milton for his refusal to submit to the divisions—either merely "arbitrary" or, at best, binary—encouraged by the Italian form, Wordsworth defines the "excellence of the Sonnet" as consisting mainly in a "pervading sense of intense Unity." He goes on to say, a "little fanci-

ful[ly]," that he is "much in the habit" of looking on the sonnet not "as a piece of architecture, making a whole out of three parts," but as "an orbicular body,—a sphere—or a dew-drop" (*LY* 2:604-5).

A "pervading sense of intense Unity" would seem to have been on Wordsworth's mind, and such unity seems to be the goal of the stanza used in "On the Power of Sound." Although most of the stanzas divide syntactically in half at line 8, the differences between the patterns of lines 1–8 ($a_{-3}ba\_bc_5dcd_4$) and lines 9–16 ($ef_4e_5gf_4gh_5h_4$) are sufficient to frustrate any easy sense of a binary structure. In fact, the appearance of asymmetricality creates a sense that the eighth-line division does not divide the poem into equal parts. Short of actually counting syllables and metrical units, it is difficult to register the fact that lines 1–8 and lines 1–16 each contain precisely the same number of metrical beats (thirty-five).[14] Again, the appearance of no particular order manifests in its "full period" an underlying order. Contrarily, numerical regularity finds expression in and through the appearance of unique occurrences.

Many such incitements to emblematic reading occur in the minutiae of the verse in "On the Power of Sound." Their prevalence, taken along with the overt themes of the work, constitutes an open invitation to a reading of the poem as emblematic of an important function of Wordsworth's metrical art as a whole. As a late poem, placed prominently in a centrally important category of the *Poetical Works*, the poem's image of a world of diffuse and varied sound unified by the ear of imagination cannot but bring to mind Wordsworth's hopes and fears for his own "wandering Utterances," the poems that make up the *Poetical Works*. Dora Wordsworth's response to the poem speaks volumes about the context in which the formidable task of this poem's composition was undertaken and pursued: "We all think there is a grandeur in this Poem," she writes to Edward Quillinan in November 1829, "but it ought to have been in the 'Recluse' and Mother on that account but half enjoys it" (see *LY* 2:309-10 n. 4).

In 1814, Wordsworth could be satisfied with a figurative description of his "minor poems" as forming the "little cells, oratories, and sepulchral recesses" of an (as yet) unfinished concrete expression of thanksgiving— the metaphoric "gothic church" of the Preface to *The Excursion* (*Prose* 3:5-6). As long as *The Recluse* remained the great work that was to be done, each of the parts had a place within that work, and *The Recluse* itself would take its place in a larger whole among the works of Chaucer, Spenser, Shakespeare, and Milton. Hundreds of shorter efforts were guaranteed continued life by virtue of their inclusion within the greater

work. In 1828–29, when the plan of the all-inclusive *Recluse* was a rapidly fading dream (at least as originally conceived), Wordsworth begins to emphasize a different kind of figure.

Asserting the claims of the musical over, or in tense opposition to, the architectural as an adequate figure under which to represent the unity of his work, Wordsworth redirects attention away from the visual image of what might have been (an image in which the unsheltered cells and oratories are doomed to ruin) and encourages aural apprehension of the work on its own terms, as nothing more (or less) than what it is—a body of work to which a prelude is the appropriate form of introduction. In Wordsworth's metrical art, each sound, syllable, word, verse, stanza, or verse paragraph is represented as simultaneously an expression of spontaneous impulse and a fulfillment of a single controlling system of organization. Each is neither one nor the other but both. Wordsworth's poetic voice is neither wholly bound to common speech nor wholly free to revel in its own harmonic relationships, aspiring to a celestial music beyond the mire of human complexity. It is a third thing—sung speech or spoken song, able to accommodate a "vast . . . compass" of "fittings" of the two systems of organization to each other. The creative "voice" of Wordsworth's verse exists in the active tension between the syntax of passion and the passion of meter, "True to the kindred points of Heaven and Home."[15]

"On the Power of Sound" suggests that this aesthetic principle at the heart of Wordsworth's metrical art may be extended imaginatively to the corpus as a whole. The "wandering Utterances" that constitute the corpus itself—the odes, elegies, meditations, narratives, didactic poems, political sonnets, hymns, songs, and the vast compass of diverse voices that find expression in common measure and blank verse, sonnets, cento stanzas, four- and five-beat couplets, and the rest—stand on their own, each reflective of the particular impulses and accidents of its composition. At the same time, the ear of imagination may hear all of these as infinitely varied modulations of a single activity. Heard within the full period of their unfolding, they may be understood as magnificently and diversely articulated expressions of a single system of "tones and numbers."

> One song they sang, and it was audible,
> Most audible, then, when the fleshly ear,
> O'ercome by humblest prelude of that strain,
> Forgot her functions and slept undisturbed.
> *(14-Bk Prelude 2.416–19)*

Notes

INTRODUCTION

1. Letter of 17 December 1836 from Barron Field to Wordsworth, quoted in Ernest De Selincourt, ed., *The Letters of William and Dorothy Wordsworth, The Later Years, Part III, 1835–1839*, 2d ed., rev. Alan G. Hill (Oxford: Clarendon Press, 1982), 355 n. 4 (hereafter cited as *LY* 3).

2. Stephen Gill, *William Wordsworth: A Life* (Oxford: Clarendon Press, 1989), 312–13. Field's copy of Wordsworth's *Poems* (1815), which records in minute detail Wordsworth's revisions in subsequent editions of the *Poetical Works*, is held at the Wordsworth Library, Grasmere. See also Barron Field's *Memoirs of Wordsworth*, ed. Geoffrey Little (Sydney: Australian Academy of the Humanities, 1975). Little's notes include Wordsworth's annotations to Field's MS. Letter of 17 December 1836 from Field to Wordsworth, quoted in *LY* 3:355 n. 4.

3. *Rhyme's Reason: A Guide to English Verse*, enl. ed. (New Haven, Conn.: Yale University Press, 1989), 1.

4. See *The Pedlar*, MS M, ll. 100ff. (MS copied about 6–18 March 1804): "Oh! many are the Poets that are sown / By nature, men endued with highest gifts, / The vision and the faculty divine, / Yet wanting the accomplishment of verse" (James Butler, ed., *The Ruined Cottage and The Pedlar* [Ithaca, N.Y.: Cornell University Press, 1979], 391). The lines eventually form the basis of *The Excursion*, Book First, ll. 77ff. Many of Wordsworth's comments about poetry and poetic craft touch upon this distinction between a natural or "silent" poet and the poet who is also an artist in verse, capable of organizing language in enduring forms. Wordsworth discusses the product of such organization as instances of "sensuous incarnation" of poetic power, in the "Essay Supplementary to the Preface" of 1815 (*The Prose Works of William Wordsworth*, ed. W. J. B. Owen and J. W. Smyser [Oxford, 1974], 3:65) (hereafter cited as *Prose*). See, for example, *The Fourteen-Book Prelude*, ed. W. J. B. Owen (Ithaca, N.Y., 1985), 13.264–74 (hereafter cited as *14-Bk Prelude*)—in *The Thirteen-Book Prelude*, ed. Mark L. Reed (Ithaca, N.Y., 1991), 12.264–74 (hereafter cited as *13-Bk Prelude*)—and Wordsworth's tribute to his brother John, the silent poet, in "When to the Attractions of the Busy World," in *The Poetical Works of William Wordsworth*, ed. Ernest de Selincourt and Helen Darbishire (Oxford, 1940–49), 2:118–23 (hereafter cited as *PW*). Jonathan Wordsworth discusses the complexities of the silent poet and Wordsworth's figurative discussion of poetic incarnation in "As with the Silence of the Thought," in *High Romantic Argument: Essays for M. H. Abrams*, ed. Lawrence Lipking (Ithaca, N.Y.: Cornell University Press, 1981), 41–76. See also Stephen K. Land, "The Silent Poet: An Aspect of Wordsworth's Semantic Theory," *University of Toronto Quarterly* 42 (1973): 157–69.

5. Chief among these exceptions are listed below. Some of these works focus on an aspect of Wordsworth's metrical theory or practice in the midst of treatments of a broader range of topics. Some of them are more specialized treatments of a particular element of the topic under consideration in this study. I wish here to acknowledge my indebtedness to these

works: On Wordsworth's theoretical position and its relation to the history of English prosodic thought, W. J. B. Owen, *Wordsworth as Critic* (Toronto: University of Toronto Press, 1969); Judith Page, "Wordsworth and the Psychology of Meter," *Papers on Language and Literature* 21 (1985): 275–94; Donald Wesling, *The New Poetries* (Lewisburg, Pa.: Bucknell University Press, 1985); and Dennis Taylor, *Hardy's Metres and Victorian Prosody* (Oxford: Clarendon Press, 1988). On the *Lyrical Ballads*, Stephen Parrish, *The Art of the "Lyrical Ballads"* (Cambridge: Harvard University Press, 1973); Mary Jacobus, *Tradition and Experiment in Wordsworth's "Lyrical Ballads"* (Oxford: Clarendon Press, 1976); John E. Jordan, *Why the "Lyrical Ballads"?* (Berkeley and Los Angeles: University of California Press, 1976); and Don Bialostosky, *Making Tales: The Poetics of Wordsworth's Narrative Experiments* (Chicago: University of Chicago Press, 1984). On Wordsworth's stylistic development, Paul Sheats, *The Making of Wordsworth's Poetry, 1785–1798* (Cambridge: Harvard University Press, 1973). On the blank verse, Christopher Ricks, "A Pure Organic Pleasure from the Lines," *Essays in Criticism* 21 (1971): 1–32; Marina Tarlinskaja, *English Verse: Theory and History* (The Hague: Mouton, 1976); Lee M. Johnson, *Wordsworth's Metaphysical Verse: Geometry, Nature, and Form* (Toronto: University of Toronto Press, 1982). On the sonnets, Lee M. Johnson, *Wordsworth and the Sonnet*. *Anglistica*, vol. 19. (Copenhagen: Rosenkilde and Bagger, 1973). On various aspects of Wordsworth's musicality in relation to English poetic traditions, John Hollander, especially in *Images of Voice: Music and Sound in Romantic Poetry*, Churchill College Overseas Fellowship Lectures, No. 5. (Cambridge: W. Heffer and Sons, 1970); *Vision and Resonance: Two Senses of Poetic Form* (New York: Oxford University Press, 1975); and *Melodious Guile* (New Haven, Conn.: Yale University Press, 1989). My study, *Numerous Verse: A Guide to the Stanzas and Metrical Structures of Wordsworth's Poetry*, Studies in Philology, Texts and Studies Series (86, iv) (Chapel Hill: University of North Carolina Press, 1989), provides a comprehensive descriptive catalogue of Wordsworth's verse forms.

6. John Hollander pointed out as early as 1970 the difficulty of apprehending the metrical forms of English romanticism through the eyes and ears of its "devouring offspring, Modernism." See Hollander's "Romantic Verse Form and the Metrical Contract," in *Romanticism and Consciousness*, ed. Harold Bloom, 181–200 (New York: Norton, 1970). Recent examples of continued interest in the topic are Timothy Steele, *Missing Measures: Modern Poetry and the Revolt against Meter* (Fayetteville: University of Arkansas Press, 1990) and David Perkins, "How the Romantics Recited Poetry," *Studies in English Literature, 1500–1900* 31 (1991): 655–71. Perkins's article, which appeared after the arguments pursued here were long developing, gives an overview of work that promises eventually to cover several of the topics that I claim here are insufficiently treated in romantic criticism. Perkins's conclusions—that the romantic period is a period of "transition" in attitudes concerning verse recitation, that "Romantic recitation was far more musical than we now conceive" (665), and that criticism of the romantic period may well benefit from closer attention to the sources and effects of this "sensuously appealing" art than has been paid in recent years—are all consonant with the arguments and aims of this study.

7. Perkins, "How the Romantics Recited Poetry," 655.

8. For a recent discussion of the influence of such developments on dramatic performances of Shakespeare's blank verse (and for an informative attempt to supply a means for distinguishing Shakespeare's metrical aesthetic from our own), see George T. Wright, *Shakespeare's Metrical Art* (Berkeley and Los Angeles: University of California Press, 1988).

9. See Robert Alter, *The Pleasures of Reading in an Ideological Age* (New York: Simon and Schuster, 1989), esp. 23–48 and M. H. Abrams, "How to Do Things with Texts," in *Doing Things with Texts*, ed. Michael Fisher, esp. 293–96 (New York: Norton, 1989) for discussions of the losses in subtlety and "literary tact" that can and frequently do result from the theoretical collapsing of literary and nonliterary language into the single category "discourse."

10. Coleridge's remarks on Wordsworth's stylistic "inconstancy," in *Biographia Literaria*;

or, *Biographical Sketches of My Literary Life and Opinions*, ed. James Engell and W. Jackson Bate (Princeton, N.J.: Princeton University Press, 1983), 2:121–26 (hereafter cited as *BL*), are echoed throughout the tradition of commentary on Wordsworth as artist. See, for example, Matthew Arnold's 1879 preface to the *Poems of Wordsworth:* "In [Wordsworth's] seven volumes the pieces of high merit are mingled with a mass of pieces very inferior to them; so inferior to them that it seems wonderful how the same poet should have produced both" (*The Complete Prose Works of Matthew Arnold*, ed. R. H. Super [Ann Arbor: University of Michigan Press, 1973], 9:42). Such attitudes are obviously behind Saintsbury's claim that Wordsworth's corpus is distinguished by "amazing inequality" of style, an inequality that Saintsbury traces directly to the "uncertainty of his prosodic grip." See *A History of English Prosody* (London: Macmillan, 1906–10), 3:71.

11. Evidence concerning Wordsworth's memorization of verse is conveniently summarized in W. K. Thomas and Warren U. Ober, *A Mind For Ever Voyaging: Wordsworth at Work Portraying Newton and Science* (Edmonton: University of Alberta Press, 1989), esp. 14–16. For extended discussions of the poetic use to which Wordsworth's put his prodigious memory, see (in addition to Thomas and Ober) Edwin Stein, *Wordsworth's Art of Allusion* (University Park: Pennsylvania State University Press, 1988).

12. On the issue of metrical "framing," see chapters 1 and 2, and Hollander, "Romantic Verse Form": "Romantic metrical theory, as informal a body of thought as it is, finally avows the emblematic, framing, defining role of metrical format as consistently as does that of Whitman, Hopkins, or some of the poets of our own day" (200).

13. See my *Numerous Verse*, "Introduction" and the Catalogue, passim.

14. William Hazlitt, "Lectures on the English Poets, VIII: On the Living Poets," in *The Complete Works of William Hazlitt*, ed. P. P. Howe (London: Dutton, 1930–34), 5:162. Evidence of the survival of this assessment of romantic prosody may be found in Carl Woodring, *Politics in English Romantic Poetry* (Cambridge: Harvard University Press, 1970). Although Woodring says he finds it "personally hard to assert that the French Revolution exerted pressure for a renovation in prosody," he goes on to assert that "a new freedom entered English prosody with the romantic generation, a freedom that brought relaxation, if not revolution, as in the free substitution of trisyllabic feet within a basic iambic meter. The new freedom cracked the regular prosody of the Popian couplet, broke open the Bastille of the closed couplet itself, gave new life to stanzaic forms that had not been exercised for a century, and created . . . a great variety of new stanzaic forms" (11).

15. On the prevalence (and deleterious effects) of a progressive, developmental model in historical discussions of metrical styles, see Paul Fussell, *Theory of Prosody in Eighteenth-Century England*, Connecticut College Monograph No. 5, 1954, esp. 161–63. "Next to a natural ear able to distinguish the rhythm of a waltz from that of a march," says Fussell, "a healthy suspicion of the validity of the idea of progress in the arts seems to me to be the metrical historian's and theorist's most useful stock in trade" (161). Fussell calls for a "re-alliance" of prosodic study with "the sense of history" (163).

16. See, for example, Alicia Ostriker, *Vision and Verse in William Blake* (Madison: University of Wisconsin Press, 1965) in which romantic prosodic styles are divided cleanly into "liberal" and "conservative." According to Ostriker, Blake's genuinely liberal originality provides the exception to the rule that "liberal practice in versification limped far behind liberal theory" (24) until at least as late as the composition of *Christabel* (30).

17. Among recent attempts to reassess and to challenge the applicability of Coleridgean categories to Wordsworth's verse, I have found Don Bialostosky's adaptation of M. M. Bakhtin's dialogic theories particularly congenial in a general way. In Bialostosky's recognition of an important dimension of pleasurable play of voice in Wordsworth, and in his emphasis upon the poem as an entity that is capable of resisting under the proper circumstances a stifling univocal effect, I find support (and, in some instances, a context) for my

own specifically metrical and historically oriented approach. See Bialostosky's *Making Tales* and *Wordsworth, Dialogics, and the Practice of Criticism* (Cambridge: Cambridge University Press, 1992).

18. Bysshe's *The Art of English Poetry* (London, 1702, 1705, 1708, with many reprintings thereafter) has been called "very likely the most influential prosodic handbook ever written" (Brogan 242). A. Dwight Culler, "Edward Bysshe and the Poet's Handbook," *PMLA* 63 (1948): 858–85, provides a detailed treatment of Bysshe's influence, as does the same author's introduction to the Augustan Reprint Society edition (No. 40) of the first part of Bysshe's work, *The Art of English Poetry* (1708; Los Angeles: William Andrews Clark Memorial Library, 1953). Wordsworth owned a copy of the 1710 issue of Bysshe's book. See Chester L. Shaver and Alice C. Shaver, *Wordsworth's Library: A Catalogue Including a List of Books Housed by Wordsworth for Coleridge from c. 1810 to c. 1830* (New York: Garland, 1979), 44.

19. For Johnson's comments, see his "Life of Pope," in *Lives of the English Poets*, ed. George Birkbeck Hill (Oxford: Clarendon Press, 1905), 3:251. For the fullest recent discussion of Augustan "period style" and its implications for romantic prosody, see Wesling, *New Poetries*, esp. 29–85. This topic will be taken up in detail in chapter 3.

20. See Wordsworth's letter to Charles Henry Parry: "People's ears have however lately become accustomed to that freer movement, which I am not so likely to be reconciled to, as a younger Reader" (*LY* 4:89–90). See also Mary Moorman, *William Wordsworth: A Biography. The Later Years, 1803–1850* (Oxford: Clarendon Press, 1965), 572 n. 1.

21. William Hazlitt, "My First Acquaintance with Poets," in *Complete Works* 17:118–19.

22. On the difficulties of re-creating a "period style," and on the multiplicity of styles exhibited in the "transitional" romantic period itself, see Perkins, "How the Romantics Recited Poetry."

23. Attridge's system, in giving appropriate attention both to a normative pattern of expectation (or "metrical set") and the actual physical content of verses, is designed to steer between "the Scylla and Charybdis" that destroy many prosodic arguments: that is, it resists both "identifying metre with the actual physical characteristics of particular utterances (a rock against which musical scansion and instrumental measurements run the risk of being dashed)," and the "danger of abstracting metrical structure too far from the spoken language (a whirlpool which generative metrics finds it hard to avoid)." The system instead relies upon the "fundamental nature of language rhythm itself: a sequence of controlled variations in the release of energy, experienced both physiologically and psychologically, which underlies all our speech activities." Derek Attridge, *The Rhythms of English Poetry* (London: Longman, 1982), 312.

24. "Stress" and "nonstress" (or "unstress") are used here and throughout the study as relative terms; that is, they distinguish the prominence of individual syllables in a sequence in relation to other syllables in a sequence. The use of "stress" implies no distinction among the various elements contributive to this articulatory or acoustic prominence. For the purposes of this study, a "stress" may result from relative prominence of pitch, duration, loudness, or any combination of the three. The word does not imply, as it does for some commentators, loudness or intensity alone. "Syllable" is employed throughout the study to mean "the smallest *rhythmic* unit of the language." Debates about the precise phonetic nature of the syllable are for the purposes of metrical scansion largely beside the point. See Attridge, *Rhythms of English Poetry*, 60–67.

25. Attridge's "base rules" allow an offbeat to be realized by one or two unstressed syllables (161). The issue of whether or not Wordsworth's verse allows two-syllable offbeats in any other circumstances than as part of an "initial inversion" or an "implied offbeat" formation, is taken up in detail in chapters 1, 3, and 5.

26. The rules in this section are summarized from "The Rules of English Metre," chapter 7 of Attridge, *Rhythms of English Poetry*, 158–213.

27. References are to book and line.

28. *Studies in Philology* 84 (1987): 365–93.

I. SIMILITUDE IN DISSIMILITUDE

1. References to the Preface to *Lyrical Ballads* (hereafter cited as *LB*) are, unless otherwise noted, to the text of 1850 as it appears in W. J. B. Owen and J. W. Smyser, eds., *The Prose Works of William Wordsworth* (Oxford: Clarendon Press, 1974). The 1850 text has been chosen because it includes Wordsworth's 1802 additions, many of which focus upon metrical issues.

2. See *Prose* 1:184 for analogues to Wordsworth's statement in eighteenth-century aesthetics. Owen and Smyser point in particular to parallels in Francis Hutcheson, *Inquiry into the Original of our Ideas of Beauty and Virtue* (London, 1726), Adam Smith, "Of the Nature of that Imitation which takes place in the Imitative Arts," in *The Works of Adam Smith* (London, 1811), Sir Joshua Reynolds (*Discourse* 11), Joseph Priestley (*Oratory*), and James Beattie, *Essays on Poetry and Music* (London, 1779). See also Coleridge's discussion of imitation (as opposed to copying) as dependent upon the "interfusion of the SAME throughout the radically DIFFERENT, or of the different throughout a base radically the same" (*BL* 2:72).

3. On the "passion of the subject" (Ernest De Selincourt, ed., *The Letters of William and Dorothy Wordsworth, The Early Years, 1787–1805*, rev. Chester L. Shaver, 434 [hereafter cited as *EY*]), see the discussion of Wordsworth's letter of 1804 to Thelwall, below.

4. For a recent discussion of the importance of such "overdetermined" language in literary art see Robert Alter, *The Pleasures of Reading in an Ideological Age* (New York: Simon and Schuster, 1989), esp. 82–83.

5. Although Thelwall's "Introductory Essay" (from which I quote here) apparently was not published until 1812, parts of the *Selections for the Illustration of a Course of Instructions on the Rhythmus and Utterance of the English Language* (London, 1812) were in circulation, as course materials, well before this date, and Thelwall may be presumed to have been elaborating the ideas in the "Introduction" during the time of his correspondence with Wordsworth. See Thomas Stewart Omond, *English Metrists: Being a Sketch of English Prosodical Criticism from Elizabethan Times to the Present Day* (Oxford: Clarendon Press, 1921), 125–28.

6. For a representative discussion of Wordsworth's metrical theory as based on a view of meter as superficially ornamental, see Owen, *Wordsworth as Critic*, 125–27. For an example of the survival of this assumption, see Ernst Häublein, who calls Wordsworth's attitudes "superficial" and "unorganic" (*The Stanza* [London: Methuen, 1978], 6).

7. The letter was not published until 1967, which helps to explain why it has not received the critical attention it deserves. Other than my own citation of the letter in *Numerous Verse* (6), I am aware of only two published uses of the quotation: Perkins, "How the Romantics Recited Poetry" (658, 663) and Stephen Gill, *William Wordsworth: The Prelude*, Landmarks of World Literature (Cambridge: Cambridge University Press, 1991), 29–30. Perkins uses Wordsworth's comments in the course of an argument, much broader in scope than is mine, concerning differences in performance of verse in the romantic period and in the twentieth century. Gill cites the passage in his very useful short discussion of the verse of *The Prelude* (chapter 2). He emphasizes (following Ricks, "Wordsworth: 'A Pure Organic Pleasure from the Lines'") the constant interplay and tension in Wordsworth's blank verse between syntactic structures and "the properties of *printed* verse, which are perceptible only to the eye."

8. The general tendencies, if not the complex specifics, of this development in romantic prosodic theory and practice toward greater expressive loosening of metrical rule are summarized by Omond, *English Metrists;* Saintsbury, *History of English Prosody;* Fussell, *Theory of Prosody;* Ostriker, *Vision and Verse,* and Taylor, *Hardy's Metres.* Tarlinskaja, *English Verse,* provides the statistical analysis to support this assessment of tendencies.

9. The quotation copied in DC MS 14 is from Richard Payne Knight, "The Progress of Civil Society" (1796). See Duncan Wu, *Wordsworth's Reading 1770–1799* (Cambridge: Cambridge University Press, 1993), 81–82. Wu provides a text of the note, from which the following excerpt is drawn: "Dr. Johnson observed, that in blank verse, the language suffered more distortion to keep it out of prose than any inconvenience to be apprehended from the shackles & circumspection of rhyme.... This kind of distortion is the worst fault that poetry can have; for if once the natural order & connection of the words is broken, & the idiom of the language violated, the lines appear manufactured, & lose all that character of enthusiasm & inspiration, without which they become cold & vapid, how sublime soever the ideas & the images may be which they express" (Wu, 82).

10. For the importance of subordination of meter to grammar in the development out of the romantics of modern metrical styles, see Wesling, *New Poetries,* chaps. 1 and 2.

11. Taylor wishes to argue in *Hardy's Metres* that Wordsworth and other romantics failed to understand meter as abstraction—as a law in dialectic interplay with the variety of speech rhythm—but erred on the side of "variety for its own sake" because of their revulsion from the too-strict and mechanical metrical "law" of their immediate predecessors (15–17). It remained for the Victorians, specifically Coventry Patmore and Hardy, to grasp fully the implications of meter as abstraction. As the present discussion suggests, I do not agree with Taylor's assessment of Wordsworth's prosodic sense (which Taylor acknowledges sometimes approaches the goal attained by the Victorians) as merely "impressionistic" (17). Wordsworth's discussion of "the passion of meter" (overlooked by Taylor) is nothing if not an acknowledgment of dynamic interplay between contrary systems of organization. In a separate article, "Hardy and Wordsworth," *Victorian Poetry* 24 (1986): 441–54, Taylor notes that Hardy developed a key assumption concerning the "mimetic" function of meter that he found in Wordsworth; that is, that "through meter and rhythm the poem can model the interaction of mind and world" (451).

12. Wordsworth's use of "long" and "short" is, of course, imprecise (see comments on "stress" and "unstress" in the Introduction, above). It is also entirely characteristic of the period, and is to be expected from a poet whose primary training in prosodic terminology would have come through study of classical, chiefly Latin, verse, in which duration is of chief prosodic importance. Wordsworth's use is consistent throughout his life (see, for example, the prose "Advertizement" to *The White Doe of Rylstone* and *LY* 2:30). The usage, however, implies no tendency actually to regard difference in duration alone as the salient feature of English verbal rhythm. (Wordsworth does not consider himself to be writing in quantitative meters.) "Stressed" and "unstressed" may be substituted for "long" and "short" in Wordsworth's descriptions without misrepresenting his theoretical position.

13. For the importance of Thelwall, see Omond, *English Metrists,* 115, 125–28. As T. V. F. Brogan, *English Versification, 1570–1980,* 223, points out, most if not all of what is important to or representative of prosodic trends in Thelwall's work is anticipated by Joshua Steele, in *Prosodia Rationalis* (London, 1779). But see Omond's discussion of a possible line of influence from Steele through Thelwall to Coleridge's *Christabel* meter.

14. See the quotation on Thelwall's title page, from Shaftesbury: "Milton and Shakespeare have restored *the antient Poetick Liberty,* and happily broken the Ice for those who are to follow them; who, treading in their Footsteps, may, at leisure, polish our Language, *lead our Ear to finer Pleasure, and find out the true Rhythmus, and harmonious Numbers, which alone can satisfy a just Judgment, and Music-like Apprehension.*"

15. See Edwin Guest, *A History of English Rhythms* (1838; reprint, London, 1882). Guest cites Thelwall as a purveyor of the "fashionable opinion" that elidable syllables in earlier verse "may be pronounced without injury to the rhythm." The extent to which Thelwall (and other "fashionable" romantic prosodists) are willing to go in scanning even Dryden and Pope with variable numbers of syllables per line is, for Guest, extreme. As will be shown

below, it would also have been so for Wordsworth, although Guest includes Wordsworth and Coleridge both among those who have "countenanced this error" (175–76).

16. Here I speak of course not of the specifics of Thelwall's system, but of the general issue of its treatment of syllables. Other, more directly influential, romantic commentators and practitioners justify variable syllable counts on other grounds. Southey, for example, advocated free "substitution" of trisyllabic feet in disyllabic measures through analogy with a classical model (any "iambic" foot may be filled with an "anapest"). See Southey's letter to Wynn, 9 April 1799, in *Selections from the Letters of Robert Southey*, ed. J. W. Warter (London, 1856), 1:69. Coleridge, of course, developed one of the most influential accentual alternatives to syllable-counting verse in *Christabel*, in which "accents" alone determine the metrical form of the line, and in which the total number of syllables per line may vary freely from four to twelve. On the importance of the treatment of syllables in reading older English verse, see Edward R. Weismiller, "Metrical Treatment of Syllables," in *The Princeton Handbook of Poetic Terms* (Princeton, N.J.: Princeton University Press, 1986), 145–46 and Wright, *Shakespeare's Metrical Art*, esp. 151–54. Wright calls the issues involved in the performance or omission of extrametrical syllables "notoriously treacherous" (151).

17. See Steele, *Missing Measures*, 55–68.

18. See Note on Scansions and Prosodic Terminology in the Introduction for the use of "marriage" as descriptive of the interaction of meter and rhythm. Borrowed form Attridge, the term is of course particularly apt for a discussion of Wordsworth, who so frequently describes the interaction of mind and nature as a figurative "marriage."

19. For a discussion of meter and other schemes as potential tropes, see Hollander, *Melodious Guile*.

20. On the issue of metrical form as symbolic of the ideal or the metaphysical in Wordsworth's verse, informing and countering the "natural," see Lee M. Johnson's treatment of large-scale "geometrical" patterns in Wordsworth's verse (*Wordsworth's Metaphysical Verse*). Geometrically based metrical patterns, like geometry, provide "a mathematical ordering of the external universe—a union of abstraction and concreteness that, in a way poetically parallel to Newton's, is not restricted to one individual's subjectivity but possesses a logic which may be tested and shared by others" (51). The extent to which I am in agreement with many of Johnson's arguments (particularly those asserting the seriousness of Wordsworth's commitment to metrical art) will be sufficiently obvious. My objections to his arguments center chiefly on how this interpenetration of ideal form and particularized concrete instance is experienced in the act of reading. Whereas Johnson requires a reader to recognize geometrical proportions (the "golden section," for example) underlying some extended passages of blank verse, I argue that the tensions between metaphysical and physical, ideal and real, abstract and concrete, external and internal, are pervasively manifested in the actual physical texture of the verse, insofar as it continually strikes the reader or listener as simultaneously governed by number and rule and open to seemingly infinite free play and variation. Johnson does touch upon these topics in his chapter 4, "The Art of Conceptual Form."

21. See, for example, Ted Hughes's comments on the subject: "I think it's true that formal patterning of the actual movement of verse somehow includes a mathematical and a musically deeper world than free verse can easily hope to enter. *It's a mystery why it should be so*" (See Häublein, *Stanza*, 11–12).

22. Hazlitt, "My First Acquaintance with Poets," 118–19.

23. See Fussell, *Theory of Prosody*, esp. 53ff., 97.

24. William Cockin, *The Art of Delivering Written Language* (London, 1775), 135.

25. Joseph Addison, *The Spectator*, no. 285 (26 January 1712), in *The Spectator*, ed. Donald F. Bond (Oxford: Clarendon Press, 1965), 3:13. For other arguments and analogies justifying the power of meter to improve language, see Fussell, *Theory of Prosody*, esp. 53ff., 97.

26. John Dryden, "Essay of Dramatic Poesy," in *The Essays of John Dryden*, ed. W. P. Ker (Oxford: Clarendon Press, 1926), 1:107.

27. Edward Manwaring [Mainwaring] *Stichology* (London, 1737), 74.

28. See Wordsworth's comments on "manufactured" verse in the Alfoxden notebook, quoted above (note 9).

29. For parallel comments on the operation of linguistic trickery in prose (specifically in the prose of Godwin and others who attempt to "lay down rules for the actions of Men"), see Wordsworth's fragmentary "Essay on Morals" (*Prose* 1:103–4).

30. See Coleridge, *Lectures 1808–1809: On Literature*, ed. R. A. Foakes (Princeton, N.J.: Princeton University Press, 1987), 1:494–95; Emerson, "The Poet," in *The Collected Works of Ralph Waldo Emerson* (Cambridge: Harvard University Press, 1983), 3:6–7.

31. The main lines of the standard critical dichotomy between these two schools of thought are conveniently summarized by Fussell (*Theory of Prosody*) and by Wesling (*New Poetries*, esp. 34). It is important to keep in mind that these attitudes were becoming increasingly polarized during the years when Wordsworth was beginning to publish: "To the conservatives [Augustan prosodists], the process [of the making of a poetic line] was genuinely one of construction, of fitting existing materials into a preconceived plan; to the liberals [romantic period prosodists and their predecessors], the process was one of organic "creation," in which the plan gradually evolved as the created work took shape" (Fussell, *Theory of Prosody*, 48).

32. The comment appears in J. Payne Collier's preface to Coleridge's *Seven Lectures on Shakespeare and Milton* (London, 1856), lii.

33. For comments on this poem as a *locus classicus* of organic metrical theory, see Fussell, *Theory of Prosody*, 48 n. 43 and "Some Observations on Wordsworth's 'A Poet!—He hath put his heart to school,'" *Philological Quarterly* 37 (1958): 454–64.

34. It has perhaps not been sufficiently noted by Wordsworthians that Wordsworth's call for the language of real life is one in a long history of attempts to redress perceived imbalances between the language of discourse and the language of art. As Barbara Herrnstein Smith puts it in reference to these periodic movements, poetic revolutions are always fought over the issue of the *relationship* between the dictates of art and of natural discourse; it is only in critical discourse that the two strands in this relationship are held as separable. See *Poetic Closure* (Chicago: University of Chicago Press, 1968), 30 and n. 23.

35. Tom Moore, *Tom Moore's Diary*, ed. J. B. Priestley (Cambridge, 1925), 185. In this passage Moore also reports that Wordsworth spoke of "the immense time it took him to write even the shortest copy of verses,—sometimes whole weeks employed in shaping two or three lines, before he can satisfy himself with their structure."

36. Wordsworth later reuses the substance of these comments in a letter to Sir William Maynard Gomm (16 April 1834), in which he makes explicit the connection between his dedication to his craft and the distinction made in *The Excursion* (book 1, ll. 77ff.), between the Poet and "Poets that are sown / By Nature" yet "[want] the accomplishment of verse" (*LY* 2:704).

37. In speaking of diction chiefly as the product of passion, I am of course speaking in relative, not absolute, terms. In fact, Wordsworth's theory of the relationship between diction and expression is based on the same kind of paradoxical unity of competing aspects as underlies his metrical theory. See Land, "Silent Poet."

38. Preface to *Poems*, 1815; *Prose* 3:26–27.

39. Hollander, *Vision and Resonance*, 136.

40. For an example of this critical assumption, see Ann Williams, *Prophetic Strain* (Chicago: University of Chicago Press, 1984), 166–67. Williams argues that Wordsworth attempts to create in "fictive discourse" an "illusion" of "natural discourse" (the terms are Barbara Herrnstein Smith's, in *On the Margins of Discourse*). This "interest in appearing to dissolve

the margins of discourse," says Williams, "may also throw light on Wordsworth's insistence that poetry uses 'the language really spoken by men'" and may "illuminate his somewhat inept discussion of the function of meter." See also James C. McKusick, *Coleridge's Philosophy of Language,* Yale Studies in English, 195 (New Haven, Conn.: Yale University Press, 1986), where Wordsworth's discussion of meter in the Preface to *LB* is characterized as an attempt to "extricate" himself from the "embarrassment" posed by "the evident artifice of poetic meter" to his theory and practice of "natural" poetry (113).

41. Evidence of Wordsworth's interest in, and respect for, the power of bad poetry to please surfaces frequently, and reinforces my contention that a main concern of his metrical art is to explore the ways in which poems work to oppose (but not to overpower) the "bigotry" of unanalyzed and passive taste. See, for example, the "Appendix" to the Preface to *LB:* "It would not be uninteresting to point out the causes of the pleasure given by extravagant and absurd diction . . ." (*Prose* 1:162). Henry Crabb Robinson reports that Wordsworth spoke to him in March 1808 of his intention to write an essay on the pleasure produced by bad poetry. Wordsworth was still interested in this topic as late as September 1808, when he remarked that either Coleridge or he himself would write the essay (Mark L. Reed, *Wordsworth: The Chronology of the Middle Years, 1800–1815* [Cambridge: Harvard University Press, 1975], 378, 395) (hereafter cited as *CMY*).

2. METRICAL TENSION AND VARIETIES OF VOICE

1. Although most treatments of the disagreements between Coleridge and Wordsworth on this score have tended to assert the shortcomings of Wordsworth's thought, Wordsworth's differences with Coleridge have been treated sympathetically (though with emphases and conclusions different from those of this book) by Parrish, *Art of the Lyrical Ballads* (esp. 14–24), Johnson, *Wordsworth's Metaphysical Verse* (esp. 188–91), Bialostosky, *Making Tales* (esp. 51–54), and Page, "Wordsworth and the Psychology of Meter."

2. A letter to Sotheby of July 1802 in which Coleridge complains of this difference of opinion with Wordsworth, suggests that the issue was a fundamental and long-standing source of disagreement between the two poets: "*Metre* itself implies a *passion,* i.e. a state of excitement, both in the Poet's mind, & is expected in the Reader—and tho' I stated this to Wordsworth, & he has in some sort stated it in his preface, yet he has [not] done justice to it, nor has he in my opinion sufficiently answered it." *Collected Letters of Samuel Taylor Coleridge,* ed. Earl Leslie Griggs (Oxford: Clarendon Press, 1956–71), 2:812 (hereafter cited as *STCL*).

3. For evidence that Wordsworth in many cases heightened in revision effects that Coleridge had singled out in *Biographia Literaria* as "disharmonious," see Eric C. Walker, "*Biographia Literaria* and Wordsworth's Revisions," *Studies in English Literature, 1500–1900* 28 (1988): 569–88. See also Walker's "Wordsworth's 'Haunted Tree' and 'Yew-Trees' Criticism," *Philological Quarterly* 67 (1988): 63–82, which argues in part that "much of the energy of Wordsworth's poetry is often generated in the exchange" between different levels of style and language (79).

4. For an analysis pertinent to these concerns, arguing that Wordsworth's poetry seeks to embody a range of expressive peaks and valleys even at its most admittedly autobiographical, see Mark L. Reed, "The Speaker of *The Prelude,*" in *Bicentenary Wordsworth Studies in Memory of John Alban Finch,* ed. Jonathan Wordsworth (Ithaca, N.Y.: Cornell University Press, 1970), 276–93.

5. John Jones, *The Egotistical Sublime: A History of Wordsworth's Imagination* (London: Chatto and Windus, 1954), 84–85. On "the structure of distinct but related things that is the world of Wordsworth," see 33ff.: "[Wordsworth] is not in revolt against the Great Machine,

the master-image of eighteenth-century science and philosophy. Only the phrase is unwordsworthian. . . . he would prefer something more supple, like 'this universal frame of things.' His complaint is that nobody has as yet observed its component parts with sufficiently devoted care, or experienced fully the power and beauty of its movement."

6. Ll. 19–24; quotations from "The Sailor's Mother" are from the 1807 text as it appears in Jared Curtis, ed., *Poems, in Two Volumes and Other Poems, 1800–1807* (Ithaca, N.Y.: Cornell University Press, 1983), 77–78.

7. For the influence of Prior's "Ode," see Earl R. Wasserman, *Elizabethan Poetry in the Eighteenth Century*, Illinois Studies in Language and Literature, 32 (Urbana: University of Illinois Press, 1947), 104–6.

8. The title of Gray's ode on first publication in Dodsley's was "Hymn to Adversity." Mason restored Gray's MS title, "Ode . . ." in 1775. Wordsworth refers to the poem as an "Ode" in the I.F. note to "Ode to Duty." (Curtis, *Poems, in Two Volumes*, 407.)

9. Quotations from Coleridge's poems, as well as dates of composition, are from *The Complete Poetical Works of Samuel Taylor Coleridge*, ed. E. H. Coleridge (London: Oxford University Press, 1912) (hereafter cited as *STCPW*). The dates of composition of the two poems in question here are presented by the editor as conjectural.

10. Several recent treatments of "The Sailor's Mother" have dealt fruitfully with the issue of its stylistic contrasts. In "Wordsworth's Dialogic Art" (1989), Bialostosky makes the poem a test case for understanding Wordsworth's thoroughgoing commitment to a "dialogic" poetics, based upon complex interplay of voices. He also discusses the poem in *Making Tales* (136–38) and in *Wordsworth, Dialogics, and the Practice of Criticism* (67–73). See also Gene W. Ruoff, "Wordsworth on Language: Toward a Radical Poetics for English Romanticism," *Wordsworth Circle* 3 (1972): 204–11. Though none of these treatments centers on specifically metrical issues, each tends to support my arguments concerning Wordsworth's keen interest in complex and theoretically unlimited kinds of metrical "intertexture."

11. For definitions of "initial inversion condition" and other metrical terms used in this chapter, see Note on Scansions and Prosodic Terminology in the Introduction.

12. See the note on "Descriptions of Stanza Forms" for "consonance rhyme" and "promoted rhyme" (as well as for "augmented rhyme," used below).

13. Wordsworth's revision of this line for *PW* (1827) suggests that part of the awkward effect may have been unintended: "From bodings, as might be, that hung upon his mind." Nevertheless, while the revision introduces, in the word "hung," an element of imaginative diction lacking in the first version (picking up and extending the implications of the "burden"), it does so, I think, without homogenizing the rhythmic and metrical texture of the poem (the double pause remains). See the "Preface" to *Poems* (1815), for Wordsworth on the imaginative power of the verb "to hang" (*Prose* 3:31).

14. Coleridge is speaking here (chapter 17) without specific reference to "The Sailor's Mother": "For *facts* are valuable to a wise man, chiefly as they lead to the discovery of the indwelling *law*, which is the true *being* of things, the sole solution of their modes of existence, and in the knowledge of which consists our dignity and our power."

15. On distinctions of "kind" and of "degree" compare Preface to *LB*: "Among the qualities . . . enumerated as principally conducing to form a Poet, is implied nothing differing in kind from other men, but only in degree" (*Prose* 1:142).

16. "Tail rhyme" refers to a class of stanzas distinguished by their use of rhyming lines (or "tails"), interposed between two or more *pedes* (usually couplets or triplets). Variations on the most common form of tail rhyme ($aa_4b_3cc_4b_3$), the "romance six" used in many medieval metrical romances, play an important role in Wordsworth's stanzas. *PW* (1849–50) contains twenty-seven poems in tail-rhyme stanzas and an additional twenty poems in stanzas (such as that used in "The Thorn") that incorporate modified tail-rhyme sections. See my *Numerous Verse*, 57–60 and Appendix II.

17. Wordsworth's stanza differs from Gray's chiefly in its use of an additional line and of unrhymed lines (three of eleven lines in each stanza have no rhyme). Both stanzas, however, are built up from the same basic stanza forms (ballad stanza and tail-rhyme), a practice uncommon before Gray. Wordsworth uses a stanza identical to Gray's ($a_4b_3a_4b_3ccdee_4d_3$) in "The Oak and the Broom" and "The Waterfall and the Eglantine" (both 1800). A closely related stanza ($abb_4a_3ccdee_4d_3$) is employed in "Elegiac Verses, in Memory of My Brother, John Wordsworth" (1805; pub. 1842).

18. "Lines Written near Richmond . . ." (1798) was divided in *LB* (1800) into two poems: "Lines Written While Sailing in a Boat at Evening" and "Lines Written near Richmond upon the Thames" ("Remembrance of Collins"). The stanza quoted is the third stanza of the 1798 poem; it became the first stanza of "Lines . . . Richmond" in 1800. The texts cited here and in the quotations from "Goody Blake and Harry Gill" are the 1798 Reading Texts in James Butler and Karen Green, eds. *Lyrical Ballads, and Other Poems, 1797–1800* (Ithaca, N.Y.: Cornell University Press, 1992), 104–5, 59–62.

19. Wordsworth's title makes obvious reference to Collins's "Ode on the Death of Mr. Thomson," which when published carried this announcement: "The scene of the following STANZAS is suppos'd to lie on the Thames near Richmond." Wordsworth's stanza, ababcd_cd_$_{4'}$ bears an obvious relation to the form used by Collins in his "Ode" ($abab_4$). Wordsworth alludes directly to Collins's "Ode" in ll. 29–40 and note.

20. On the "stress hierarchies," which enforce (among other things) the rhythmic subordination of adjectives to nouns, see Attridge, *Rhythms of English Poetry*, 67–70.

21. William Wimsatt and Monroe Beardsley, "The Concept of Meter: An Exercise in Abstraction," in *The Structure of Verse: Modern Essays on Prosody*, ed. Harvey Gross, 168 (New York: Ecco Press, 1979).

3. "WORDS IN TUNEFUL ORDER":
WORDSWORTH'S EARLY VERSIFICATION, *AN EVENING WALK* AND *DESCRIPTIVE SKETCHES*

1. References are to book and line.

2. Commentators have variously identified the poems and poets to which Wordsworth here refers. DeQuincey identified Gray and Goldsmith as among the favorites that Wordsworth and John Fleming "chaunted" for two hours at a time while strolling around Esthwaite. Havens and others have assumed that the passage refers to Dryden and Pope, but the kind of poetry described here—"airy fancies / More bright than madness or the dreams of wine" (ll. 591–92)—makes this unlikely (see Raymond Dexter Havens, *The Mind of a Poet* [Baltimore, Md.: Johns Hopkins University Press, 1941], 401–2). The editors of the Norton *Prelude* suggest Macpherson's Ossian translations, based on Wordsworth's imitation and echoing of these in the *Vale of Esthwaite*, but the references to "verses" in l. 589 suggests otherwise, as Macpherson's work is written in rhythmic prose. (Jonathan Wordsworth et al., eds., *The Prelude 1799, 1805, 1850* [New York: Norton, 1979], 182 n. 1.)

3. Compare Coleridge on such susceptibilities as necessary to a great poet (he is discussing Shakespeare's early verse): "The delight in richness and sweetness of sound, even to a faulty excess . . . I regard as a highly favorable promise in the compositions of a young man. 'The man that hath not music in his soul' can indeed never be a genuine poet." He goes on to say that incidents, thought, interesting feeling and the "art of their combination or intertexture in the form of a poem" may be learned by a man of talent: "But the sense of musical delight, with the power of producing it, is a gift of imagination . . . . It is in [this] that 'Poeta nascitur non fit'" (*BL* 2:20).

4. Emile Legouis's catalogue and discussion of the stylistic peculiarities of *EW* and *DS* is still enormously helpful. His list of some twenty characteristics includes archaisms ("broke"

for "broken"); intransitive verbs used transitively ("I gaze / the ever-varying charms," *EW,* ll. 17–18); irregular suppression of the article; "violent suppression of an auxiliary" ("They not the trip of harmless milkmaid feel," *EW,* l. 226); suppression of the verb; use of words in an obsolete sense; Miltonic inversions of subject and verb ("Starts at the simplest sight th'unbidden tear," *EW,* l. 44); imitation of Latin ablative absolute; "inversion of the direct pronominal object, with all the characteristics of one of Milton's Latin constructions." Emile Legouis, *The Early Life of William Wordsworth,* trans. J. W. Matthews (New York: Dutton, 1932), 134–35.

5. For the fullest recent discussion of the "period style" of the Age of Pope, and its implications for romantic prosody, see Wesling, *New Poetries,* esp. 29–85.

6. *Topographical Poetry in XVIII-Century England* (New York: Modern Language Association of America, 1936), 297–391.

7. For a survey of these issues, see William Bowman Piper, *The Heroic Couplet* (Cleveland: Case Western Reserve University Press, 1969).

8. Johnson's comments appear in his "Life of Pope" (*Lives of the English Poets* 3:251).

9. Ostriker identifies the "great cage" in which Har and his captived birds sing in *Tiriel* (plate 3, ll. 10–25) as Blake's description of Augustan verse (*Vision and Verse,* 21). In the "Public Address," Blake condemns Pope for his "Metaphysical Jargon of Rhyming," a failure of execution that is among "the Most nauseous of all affectation & foppery." In the same work, Dryden's rhymes are acknowledged to be preferred by "Stupidity" over Milton's verse because of their "Monotonous Sing Song Sing Song from beginning to end" (*Poetry and Prose,* 565, 570).

10. *DS,* ll. 680–85. All quotations from the 1793 text of the poem are from the Cornell University Press edition, ed. Eric Birdsall (1984).

11. The revision of "reading it long" to "changing the accent" is a good example of the imprecision in (and interchangeability of) prosodic terminology mentioned above (chapter 1, note 12).

12. Averill's description of the poems as "portraits of the young poet's mind" is apt. I am in disagreement, however, with his elaboration of the significance of the portraits as "emblems of a dead self that is the object at once of condescension and of nostalgia" (*EW,* 16). I find Wordsworth's attitudes much more inclusive of this earlier self than the terms "condescension" and "nostalgia" would suggest. As has been argued in chapters 1 and 2, Wordsworth would not, I think, make as clean a distinction as would Averill (or Coleridge) between what Averill calls "intrinsic" poetic merit and the merit of a poem as an index of a particular kind of insufficiency of perception and expression, presented for the purpose of comparison with other (and perhaps more comprehensive and steadily focused) kinds of mental activity. See James Averill, ed., *An Evening Walk* (Ithaca, N.Y.: Cornell University Press, 1984).

13. For Wordsworth's broad definition of "workmanship," see his letter to Maria Jane Jewsbury, 4 May 1825 (*LY* 1:343); for his listing the precise operation of the "logical faculty" among the signs of workmanship, see his letter to W. R. Hamilton, 24 September 1827 (*LY* 1:545–46).

14. For Wordsworth's reputation as a writer of verse among the boys at Hawkshead, see the query, variously reported, of the older schoolfellow whom James A. Butler has called the "first Wordsworthian": "I say, Bill, when thoo writes verse dost thoo invoke t'Muse." (Butler, "The Muse at Hawkshead: Early Criticism of Wordsworth's Poetry," *Wordsworth Circle* 20 [1989]: 140.) Another version of the incident quotes the older boy thus: "How is it, Bill, thee doesnt write such good verses? Doest thee invoke Muses?" (See Reed, *CEY,* 291).

15. Christopher Wordsworth, *Memoirs of William Wordsworth* (London, 1851), 1:10. For a discussion of Wordworth's diction in relation to Pope's *Dunciad,* see Abbie Findlay Potts,

Wordsworth's Prelude: A Study of Its Literary Form (Ithaca, N.Y.: Cornell University Press, 1953; Octagon Books, 1972), 33–38.

16. All quotations from "School Exercise" are from Dove Cottage MS 1, which differs in several instances of punctuation and capitalization from the text as it appears in *PW*.

17. The comma after "thence" in l. 86 in Dove Cottage MS 1 seems out of place; *PW* omits it.

18. See Attridge, *Rhythms of English Poetry*, 124. On the fundamental importance and staying power of the four-beat line in English verse, see Attridge (chapter 4) and Joseph Malof, *A Manual of English Meters* (Bloomington: Indiana University Press, 1970), esp. chap. 4. In his Introduction (1830) to the *Lay of the Last Minstrel*, Sir Walter Scott argues that the four-stress line is "so natural to our language, that the very best of our poets have not been able to protract it into the verse properly called Heroic, without the use of epithets which are, to say the least, unnecessary."

19. Alexander Pope, *Correspondence of Alexander Pope*, ed. George Sherburn (Oxford: Clarendon Press, 1956), 1:23.

20. See *Rambler*, No. 90, in which Johnson argues that parts of a verse containing fewer than three syllables are "in danger of losing the very form of verse." The poet, therefore, ought to restrict himself whenever possible to "only five pauses" (after syllables three through seven) in pentameter verse (2:111). Evidence that Wordsworth was conscious of these rules as rules (and was not merely operating according to the evidence of his ear) may be seen in the letter of 1816 to Robert P. Gillies — Ernest De Selincourt, ed., *The Letters of William and Dorothy Wordsworth, The Middle Years, Part II, 1812–1820*, 2:343 (hereafter cited as *MY* 2, followed by the page number[s]), quoted at length and discussed in chapter 5, below.

21. The percentages cited there and throughout this study are based on my own counts, unless otherwise noted. They are presented here with qualifications, because the placement of a pause, especially in unpunctuated lines, is often a matter of interpretation. As a hedge against subjectivity, I have employed a very strict method, and have defined as "unbroken" almost all lines in which the pause is not indicated by a mark of punctuation. Following this approach, I define some 60 percent of the verses in most heroic couplets (Pope's included) as "unbroken," even though an impassioned reading might actually require pauses in many of these unpunctuated lines. The percentages cited throughout this study are based on the number of lines containing pause, not on the total number of lines. This and subsequent tables are offered, then, not as definitive descriptions but as comparative indices of large tendencies. My indebtedness to Walter Jackson Bate for various aspects of the approach of this chapter will be obvious to anyone familiar with *The Stylistic Development of Keats* (New York: Modern Language Association, 1945). My counts are not comparable to his, since his tabulations assign pause to all but the most obviously unbroken lines.

22. M. L. Barstow [Greenbie] singles out this aspect of the early verse for comment: "Wordsworth was always careful to avoid hiatus — more careful than most poets of the nineteenth century, to whose ears it was less offensive than the poets of the preceding century felt it to be." *Wordsworth's Theory of Poetic Diction* (New Haven, Conn.: Yale University Press, 1917), 74 n. 3.

23. Field's text at this point quotes Hazlitt, who charges that Wordsworth unfairly slighted Dryden and Pope, "whom, because they have been supposed to have all the possible excellencies of poetry, he will allow to have none." Wordsworth calls the charge "monstrous." See Field's *Memoirs of Wordsworth*, 37 and n. 43.

24. These most common kinds of syllabic reduction are conveniently summarized in Bysshe's *Art of English Poetry*. Weismiller recommends using the blanket term "elision" for all of these techniques, while adding a number of other kinds to the list: for example, coalescence of contiguous vowels when the first is stressed (monosyllablic "prayer" and disyllabic "piety," for example); *O* or *U* assimilated or converted to consonantal [w] before

a vowel ("echoing"/ ec[w]ing; "shadowy"/ shad[w]y); blending into a single syllable a final syllabic liquid or nasal and a vowel beginning a following word ("river of"; "open his"). See Weismiller, in Preminger, *Princeton Handbook*, 145–46.

25. See Stuart Curran, *Poetic Form and British Romanticism* (New York: Oxford University Press, 1986), esp. 29–39. Curran notes the outpouring of "sonnets of sensibility" in the 1780s (of which Wordsworth's is one), and especially the importance of Charlotte Smith's *Elegiac Sonnets* (1784). For Wordsworth's admiration of Charlotte Smith see *PW* 4:403.

26. The poem was never published by Wordsworth in full; an "Extract" appears in editions, 1815 ff. See *PW* 1:270–83, for a text of 569 lines pieced together from three MSS.

27. Coleridge also was fond of this line. He slightly misquotes the line as it appears in *EW* ("Dash'd down the rough rock, lightly leaps along") in the MS to "Songs of the Pixies": "Dash'd o'er the rough rock, lightly leaps along," and he seems to be recalling it in *Lines to a Beautiful Spring in a Village* (1794). See Averill, *Evening Walk*, 44.

28. Thomson, for example, tends to find the diversity of the seasons neither important in itself nor a challenge to the harmony he everywhere perceives. His poem, unlike Wordsworth's, proceeds through continuous finding of what he set out to find: *order* in variety. See William Langhorne, Fable X of "Fables of Flora," for an assessment of Thomson that emphasizes his blank verse as a vehicle for a vast intellectual vision of "truth resistless, beaming from the source / Of perfect light immortal" against which "Vainly boasts / That golden broom its sunny robe of flowers." Langhorne contrasts this vision with the octosyllabics of William Hamilton of Bangour, in which "Whatever charms the ear or eye," no matter how various, may be included. (Dr. Robert Anderson, ed. *Works of the British Poets* [London: John and Arthur Arch, 1795], II:264–65.)

29. Because my primary concern in this chapter is limited to Wordsworth's early published verse (especially *EW* and *DS*), because so much of the work before composition of these poems is translation (and therefore presents special problems), and because much of the very early work is not yet available in adequate scholarly editions, a full consideration of the juvenilia would be impractical here. On matters relating to style in Wordsworth's juvenilia see Sheats, *Making of Wordsworth's Poetry.* Greenbie, *Wordsworth's Theory of Poetic Diction*, is informed by its author's acute sensitivity to verse rhythm and for that reason is still most helpful. On stylistic and metrical characteristics of Wordsworth's translations from the Latin, see the series of works on this subject by Bruce E. Graver: "Wordsworth's Translations from Latin Poetry" (Ph.D. diss., University of North Carolina, Chapel Hill, 1984); "Wordsworth and the Language of Epic: The Translation of the *Aeneid,*" *Studies in Philology* 83 (1986): 261–85; "Wordsworth's Georgic Beginnings," *Texas Studies in Language and Literature* 33 (1991): 137–59.

30. Throughout this chapter, *EW* (composed probably 1788–89) and *DS* (composed 1791–92) are discussed as if they were contemporaneous, despite the earlier composition of the former poem. Their simultaneous publication and Wordsworth's usual linking of them in conversations and letters suggests that the poet tended to think of the two poems as similar enough in style to be read and discussed in tandem. For Wordsworth's "apprenticeship," see the tongue-in-cheek reference in "The Idiot Boy": "I to the Muses have been bound / These fourteen years, by strong indentures" (ll. 337–39).

31. *Critical Review,* n.s. 8 (July 1793), 347; n.s. 8 (August 1793), 472–73.

32. Compare Hugh Blair, for whom rhyme and expressive "vehemence" are at odds: "The constraint and strict regularity of rhyme, are unfavourable to the sublime, or to the highly pathetic strain. . . . It is best adapted to compositions of a temperate strain, where no particular vehemence is required in the Sentiments, nor great sublimity in the Style" (*Lectures on Rhetoric and Belles Lettres* [London, 1785] 3:110). For twentieth-century variations on the argument, with specific reference to Wordsworth's couplet poems, see Legouis, *Early Life of William Wordsworth*, 128–33; Geoffrey Hartman, "Wordsworth's *Descriptive Sketches* and the Growth of a Poet's Mind," *PMLA* 76 (1961): 519–27 and *Wordsworth's Poetry 1787–1814* (New

Haven, Conn.: Yale University Press, 1964), esp. 110–15; and Frederick A. Pottle, *The Idiom of Poetry* (Ithaca, N.Y.: Cornell University Press, 1946), 129–30. But see also Sheats, who argues briefly that the couplet is not, at least in *EW*, an "aesthetic error," but the "most obvious vehicle for a demonstration of poetic skill" (*Making of Wordsworth's Poetry*, 50 and 262 n. 9).

33. *EW* employs two twelve-syllable, six-beat (hexameter) verses (ll. 186, 206); three hexameter lines appear in *DS* (ll. 105, 379, 653).

34. In his mature verse, and in revisions of *EW* and *DS*, Wordsworth tends to avoid hiatus less through typographical means and more through avoidance of phrasings that would require elision.

35. Another example appears at *DS*, l. 137:

    Heard, by star-spotted bays, beneath the steeps[.]
    B o B ô B o B o B o B

36. References are to book and line.

37. The same difficulty arises in l. 3 of "Sweet was the walk along the narrow lane" (*PW* 1:290), a sonnet written 1789–92; published in 1889:

    +s +s   +s
    Shagged with wild pale green tufts of fragrant hay[.]

38. Averill, ed., *An Evening Walk*, 248–49. All quotations from the MSS of *An Evening Walk* and from the 1793 text of the poem are from this edition.

39. This is the same effect that Pope achieves with the well-known line in the *Essay on Criticism*, "And ten low words oft creep in one dull line." The effect may be understood as stemming from a lack of subordination of stresses. The offbeats are all realized by words that tend to require stress. Wordsworth draws upon these means again in *DS*, l. 593: "To pant slow up the endless Alp of Life."

40. See Z. S. Fink, ed. *The Early Wordsworthian Milieu. A Notebook of Christopher Wordsworth with a Few Entries by William Wordsworth* (New York: Oxford University Press, 1958). The passage in question, dated 1784–85 by Fink, appears on page 5 of the notebook:

    As when the moon as she
    . . .
    raises her orb above the Horizon
    rests upon the Branches of some
    tall Oak, which grows upon
    the summit of the Horizon

41. Averill, *Evening Walk*, 54 and 54 n. to ll. 193–94.

42. Birdsall, *Descriptive Sketches*, 70 app. crit.

43. Sheats discusses the challenge of Wordsworth's description to *concordia discors* theories (*Making of Wordsworth's Poetry*, 61ff.).

44. Blair warns about the disruptiveness of this effect: "There are some, who, in order to exalt the variety and the power of our Heroic Verse, have maintained that it admits of musical pauses, not only after those four syllables, where I assigned their place [after the third, fourth, fifth, and sixth], but after any one syllable in the Verse indifferently, where the sense directs it to be placed. This ... is the same thing as to maintain that there is no pause at all belonging to the natural melody of the verse; since, according to this notion, the pause is formed entirely by the meaning, not by the Music. But this I apprehend to be contrary both to the

nature of Versification, and to the experience of every good ear" (*Lectures on Rhetoric and Belles Lettres* 3:108–9).

45. Several of these early pauses occur in the second line of a couplet after a run-on first line and an initial inversion, and thus challenge further the structural integrity of the couplet. See, for example, *Evening Walk*, 305–6: "Or the swan stirs the reeds, his neck and bill / Wetting, that drip upon the water still."

46. For the connection between speed of performance and early or late placement of pause, see the discussion of the psychological tendency to equalize the time required to read the two unequal parts of a divided line (noted above in connection with the "School Exercise").

47. For a discussion of the pervasive influence of *The Traveller* on *DS*, see Potts, *Wordsworth's Prelude*, 131–48. Potts suggests that technical problems posed by Goldsmith's antithetical and analytic style are central to Wordsworth's use of the poem in *DS*.

48. W. K. Wimsatt, Jr., *The Verbal Icon* (Lexington: University of Kentucky Press, 1954), 166.

49. See Wesling, *New Poetries*, esp. 18–22.

50. Sheats notes the Virgilian ending (*Making of Wordsworth's Poetry*, 73–74), but refers to the couplets of *DS* as "still-conventional." Birdsall points out the echo of "Windsor Forest" in the Cornell edition of *Descriptive Sketches*, 116 n. to ll. 792–809.

51. Theresa Kelley has recently called attention to the conclusion of *DS* as perhaps the most unabashedly sublime passage in Wordsworth: after the 1790s, says Kelley, "Wordsworth would never again offer so unequivocal a celebration of the sublime." See *Wordsworth's Revisionary Aesthetics* (Cambridge: Cambridge University Press, 1988), 3ff. Kelley also notes in Wordsworth's passage an echo of Thomson's celebration of Britannia, in *The Seasons* ("Summer," ll. 423–310); see p. 3 and 209 n. 5.

52. The echo is noted by Birdsall, *Descriptive Sketches*, 116 n.

53. For Wordsworth's notes on this conversation, see *Prose* 1:91–98 and *BL* 2:205.

54. For "consonance rhyme" and other terms from William Harmon's "Rhyme in English Verse: History, Structures, Functions," *Studies in Philology* 84 (1987): 365–93, see Note on Scansions and Prosodic Terminology in the Introduction.

55. Darbishire, *The Poet Wordsworth*, 8–9; Ben Ross Schneider, Jr., *Wordsworth's Cambridge Education* (Cambridge: Cambridge University Press, 1957), 41.

56. The Spenserians are in Dove Cottage MS 2, printed by De Selincourt as XVI (b) in *PW* 1:293–95; see Stephen Gill, ed. *The Salisbury Plain Poems of William Wordsworth* (Ithaca, N.Y.: Cornell University Press, 1975), 290–92.

57. Robert Anderson, "The Impatient Lassie," in *Ballads, In the Cumberland Dialect* (Alnwick: W. Davison, n.d.), 32.

58. When the pronunciation of "height" changed from that suggested by the survival of the "ei" in its stem [*het*] to modern [*haıt*] is uncertain, and "height" does appear as a rhyme for "weight" in late-seventeenth- and early-eighteenth-century verse (see Dryden, "Epilogue to the Second Part of the Conquest of Granada," ll. 15–16: "None of 'em, no not *Jonson*, in his height / Could pass, without allowing grains for weight"). The *OED*, however, suggests that [*haıt*] was the most common pronunciation at least from the sixteenth century (as Milton's spelling "hi*ghth*" suggests) and all of the examples that I have been able to gather suggest that standard eighteenth-century pronunciation would have been [aı], as in these couplets from Pope and Cowper:

> He said, and clim'd a stranded lighter's height
> Shot to the black abyss, and plunged down-right.
>
> (*Dunciad*, book 2, ll. 287–88)
>
> Duly, as ever on the mountain's height
> The peep of morning shed a dawning light.
>
> ("Charity," ll. 260–61)

59. See Wordsworth's letter of 23 May 1794 to William Mathews: "It was with great reluctance that I huddled up those two little works [*EW* and *DS*] and sent them into the world in so imperfect a state. But as I had done nothing by which to distinguish myself at the university, I thought these little things might shew that I could do something" (*EY*, 120).

60. Sheats comments in his discussion of Wordsworth's Hawkshead period that Wordsworth, living in a region that attracted more than its share of descriptions, would have been sensitive from an early age to the gap between the landscape as it is known to someone who lives in it—someone whose mind and affections had been formed through active interchange with it in all its variety—and that landscape as it appeared in guides and literary descriptions. Living in the Lake District, says Sheats, would have given Wordsworth "daily instruction in the relationship between word and thing" (*Making of Wordsworth's Poetry*, 22).

61. For the development of these tendencies from Alexander Baumgarten's *Philosophical Reflections on Poetry* (1735) through the New Critics, see M. H. Abrams, "From Addison to Kant: Modern Aesthetics and the Exemplary Art," in *Doing Things with Texts*, 159–87, esp. 173–83.

62. *13-Bk Prelude* 8.69; 6.539; 10.725–26.

4. VARIETIES OF RHYME: THE STANZAIC VERSE OF THE *LYRICAL BALLADS*

1. Robert Mayo, "The Contemporaneity of the *Lyrical Ballads*," *PMLA* 69 (1954): 516–17. For Saintsbury's dismissal of Wordsworth's verse (*History of English Prosody* 3:74), see the Introduction to this book.

2. See my *Numerous Verse*, passim and esp. 8–13.

3. Richard Payne, in "'The Style and Spirit of the Elder Poets': The *Ancient Mariner* and English Literary Tradition," *Modern Philology* 75 (1978): 368–84 suggests that the diction and placement of the *Rime* are calculated to make the issue of style itself—and particularly the function of stylistic variety—a singularly important aspect of the reader's experience of the collection as a whole. Payne finds it "downright startling" to consider the "composite" style of the *Rime* (with its mingling of Chaucerian idiom, Renaissance neologism, and modern northernisms) and of *LB* as a whole (with its introductory poem so dissimilar stylistically from what is to follow), in relation to the similarly composite stylistic texture of Percy's *Reliques*.

4. The similarities observed by Fussell (*Poetic Meter*, 140–41) between this stanza and a stanza appearing in seventeenth- and eighteenth-century "mad songs," will be discussed below in connection with "The Idiot Boy."

5. Among the several studies that emphasize Wordsworth's representation of various kinds of speech as central to his aims in *LB*, I am most indebted to Parrish, *Art of the Lyrical Ballads;* Frances Ferguson, *Wordsworth: Language as Counter-Spirit* (New Haven, Conn.: Yale University Press, 1977), esp. 11–34; and Bialostosky, *Making Tales.*

6. These ten are the *Rime of the Ancient Mariner,* "Foster-Mother's Tale," "The Female Vagrant," "Anecdote for Fathers," "We are Seven," "The Last of the Flock," "The Mad Mother," "The Idiot Boy," "Expostulation and Reply," and "Old Man Travelling."

7. For the circumstances of the composition and collection of the 1798 edition, see Mark L. Reed, "Wordsworth, Coleridge, and the 'Plan' of the *Lyrical Ballads*," *University of Toronto Quarterly* 34 (1965): 238–53. Neil Fraistat provides a convenient summary of arguments for and against the integrity of the collection in *The Poem and the Book* (Chapel Hill: University of North Carolina Press, 1985), 49–53.

8. See Gill, *William Wordsworth* (184–90), for an account of Wordsworth's careful preparation of the 1800 volume. Gill suggests that Wordsworth was concerned with the minutest matters of arrangement and appearance; e.g., on "18 December Wordsworth was worrying

about the shape of the volumes . . . . He insisted, too, on how *Michael* should be printed, that is, on the actual appearance of the type at certain points" (185).

9. Of 114 poems in the *Annual Anthology* for 1799, twenty three are written in blank verse. The remaining ninety-one poems employ thirty different forms.

10. As early as May 1798, Coleridge had told Joseph Cottle that the idea of separate publication of the individual poems in what was to be *LB* (1798), without Coleridge's contributions, was "decisively repugnant & oppugnant" to Wordsworth, as the resulting collection would "want variety" (*STCL* 1:411–12). N. Stephen Bauer sees evidence of Wordsworth's strong preference for collective presentation of his works throughout his career in the poet's resistance to publishing in anthologies or annuals: "As he wrote more and more," writes Bauer, "Wordsworth came to see his poems working together in two ways: first, shorter poems with similar characteristics combined to form single longer poems (something he encouraged by classifying the poems, beginning as early as the edition of 1800); and second, all the combined groups then united to create a single, gigantic Poem. . . . For his poems to affect the reader the way Wordsworth desired they must be read together[.]" See "Wordsworth and the Early Anthologies," *Library*, 5th ser., 32 (1972): 37–45.

11. This and all quotations from the *Lyrical Ballads* are from Butler and Green, *Lyrical Ballads, and Other Poems*. Unless otherwise noted, the text cited is the Reading Text of *LB* (1800) or, in the case of passages appearing in 1798 and unchanged 1800, the Reading Text of *LB* (1798). Where the text of a poem published in 1798 has been changed in 1800, I have inserted the 1800 changes from the editors' app. crit.

12. For "animated and impassioned recitation," see the preface to *Poems* (1815), *Prose* 3:29.

13. Only one poem in the entire *PW* employs a true refrain: "The Seven Sisters," a poem composed in 1800 and published in the *Morning Post* on 14 October 1800. It first appears in Wordsworth's collected works in *Poems in Two Volumes* (1807). See my *Numerous Verse*, 95.

14. See Parrish, *Art of the Lyrical Ballads*, 122. For a convenient overview of sources and analogues, see Patrick Campbell, *The Lyrical Ballads of Wordsworth and Coleridge: Critical Perspectives* (London: Macmillan, 1991), 118.

15. For the relationship between this stanza and the stanza used by Gray in "Ode: on a Distant Prospect of Eton College" (1747), and "Ode on the Spring" (1748), see the discussion of "The Thorn" in Chapter 2.

16. Wordsworth published in 1835 a cento made up of a stanza each from Akenside and Beattie, with a transitional couplet from Thomson, saying in a note to that compilation that he "sometimes indulge[d]" in the "harmless" practice of "linking together, in his own mind, favourite passages from different authors" (*PW* 4:396). The second stanza of this cento takes a form $(aab_4c_3b_4c_3d_4e_3d_4e_3)$ that would not seem out of place among Wordsworth's original ten-line stanzas. The "Cento" suggests that the habits of mind indulged by Wordsworth in his "harmless" cento making also informed his selection and creation of his most distinctive longer stanzas. All but one of Wordsworth's longer stanzas (ten to twenty lines) in *PW* are built up from recognizable smaller stanzaic units or couplets. The one exception is the sixteen-line stanza used in "On the Power of Sound" $(a_{-3}ba\_bc_5dcdef_4{}_5gf_4gh_5h_4)$, discussed below, in the Conclusion to this book. See my *Numerous Verse*, 12.

17. Malof, *Manual of English Meters*, esp. chap. 4; Attridge, *Rhythms of English Poetry*, esp. 80–96.

18. For tail rhyme, see Chapter 2, n. 16.

19. In the course of a discussion with different aims and concerns from mine, Paul Sheats provides some useful comments on Wordsworth's stanza and on the issue of "inconstancy of style." See "'Tis Three Feet Long and Two Feet Wide': Wordsworth's 'Thorn' and the Politics of Bathos," *Wordsworth Circle* 22 (1991): 92–100.

20. For the text of Wordsworth's note, see Butler and Green, *Lyrical Ballads, and Other Poems*, 791. In a letter of December 1814 to Gillies, Wordsworth criticizes the versification of

Hogg's *The Haunting of Badlewe* (1814) in terms that give further evidence of his relatively low opinion of ballad metrics: Hogg's poem, says Wordsworth, is "harsh and uncouth," and Hogg himself is "too illiterate to write in any measure or style that does not savour of balladism" (*MY* 2:179–80).

21. "The Force of Prayer," first published in *Poems* (1815), appeared soon thereafter as part of a note to *The White Doe of Rylstone*, itself in part a retelling of a tale found in Percy ("The Rising in the North"). Wordsworth's use of "The Force of Prayer" as an explanatory note to another poem imitates an antiquarian editorial convention (employed by Percy, for example), and suggests that the poem represents a self-conscious experiment with the ballad as a historical form. With regard to the issue of Wordsworth's general unwillingness to break with traditional accentual-syllabic practice, see the prose "Advertizement" to *The White Doe* (DC MS 61, drafted and abandoned probably between 2 December 1807 and 3 January 1808). There, Wordsworth's abortive attempt to explain the principles of his meter gives evidence that he was uneasy about the relatively frequent use of double offbeats (or "trisyllabic substitution") in the poem. See Kristine Dugas, ed. *The White Doe of Rylstone; or, the Fate of the Nortons* (Ithaca, N.Y.: Cornell University Press, 1988), 185–203, esp. 201–2. A similar attitude toward accentual verse is apparent in the titling of a poem by Dorothy Wordsworth in *PW*; the poem ("Loving and Liking"; *PW* 2:102–3) is called "Irregular Verses" because it employs accentualist prosody (and is, therefore, irregular in comparison with the large majority of other poems in the collection).

22. But even in the case of "A Ballad," the regular eight- and six-syllable verses suggest that Wordsworth's balladry was filtered through a more consciously literary tradition of sentimental poetry and was not influenced directly by popular songs and tales. Wordsworth also used the stanza in some work composed probably between November 1796 and June 1797 and eventually published as part 2 of Coleridge's unfinished poem "The Three Graves" (see Reed, *CEY*, 27; *PW* 1:308–12). All of the verses in Wordsworth's contribution to the poem are syllabically regular; Coleridge's parts 3 and 4, published in *The Friend* (No. 6, 21 September 1809) employ double offbeats, though less frequently than in the *Rime*.

23. Paul G. Brewster's 1938 assessment continues to suffice for many commentators: it was in "ballad stanza form, meter, and rhyme," says Brewster, that the ballad had its "greatest influence" on the poetry of Wordsworth ("The Influence of the Popular Ballad on Wordsworth's Poetry," *Studies in Philology* 35 [1938]: 611). Herbert Hartman misidentifies the cross-rhymed 4 x 4 stanza used in one-third of the Goslar poems as the "most characteristic stanza form of the Percy collection" ("Wordsworth's 'Lucy' Poems: Notes and Marginalia," *PMLA* 49 [1934]: 135). T. V. F. Brogan's article on "Ballad Meter" in the *New Princeton Encyclopedia of Poetry and Poetics* (Princeton, N.J.: Princeton University Press, 1993) provides a good overview of the complexity involved in taxonomies of this stanza. See 118–20. On distinctions between the stanza aba_4b_3 (and abc_4b_3) and ballad meter, see Fussell, *Poetic Meter*, 138.

24. Cowper—to cite just one poet besides Wordsworth who maintained a clear distinction between the forms $a_4b_3a_4b_3$ and $a_4b_3c_4b_3$—writes nearly thirty of his Olney Hymns and much occasional verse in the stanza $a_4b_3a_4b_3$; when he turns to parody of the popular ballad in "John Gilpin," he also turns to the authentic ballad stanza, $a_4b_3c_4b_3$.

25. For a representative statement of this view, see Ostriker, *Vision and Verse*, esp. the historical overview in chaps. 1 and 2 ("The Conservative Background" and "The Liberal Background").

26. Here and throughout this discussion, quotations from the *Rime* are from the *LB* 1798 text as it appears in Butler and Green, *Lyrical Ballads, and Other Poems* (Appendix IV: "Non-Wordsworthian Poems in *Lyrical Ballads*").

27. On the general issue of stress timing and its effects, see Attridge, *Rhythms of English Poetry*, 70–74, 96–101.

28. Line 10 of the 1800 text has "here" for "hear"; a misprint (Butler and Green, *Lyrical Ballads, and Other Poems,* 109 app. crit).

29. Hallam Tennyson comments on the "contest," held in May 1835: "My father and Fitzgerald . . . had a contest as to who could invent the weakest Wordsworthian line imaginable. Although Fitzgerald claimed this line, my father declared that he had composed it." *Alfred, Lord Tennyson: A Memoir by His Son* (London: Macmillan, 1897), 1:153.

30. For another example of this kind of emblematic use of form in *LB*, see "Lines Written at a Small Distance." At the precise point at which the speaker asserts an opposition between a "Our living Calendar" and the "joyless forms" of abstract measurements of time from which he and the addressee of the poem shall escape, the verse form shifts (from aba_4b_3 to $a_4b_3a_4b_3$).

31. Additional evidence concerning Wordsworth's habitual practice of regarding line endings as "indicative of a conscious pause" is provided by Mark Reed, who notes that members of the Wordsworth family frequently omit appropriate punctuation at line endings in MSS of *The Prelude.* See *13-Bk Prelude* 1.102–3.

32. Harmon, "Rhyme in English Verse," 378–79.

33. See Lee M. Johnson, who calls "Lycidas" a "triumph of conceptual form" and compares its play of irregularity and regularity with Wordsworth's *Ode: Intimations of Immortality* (*Wordsworth's Metaphysical Verse,* 202–3). Johnson describes "Lycidas" as a sequence of variously irregular *canzoni* ending in a perfect *ottava rima* stanza "serving as a *commiato* of the whole."

34. See Marina Tarlinskaja, *Shakespeare's Verse,* 278; See also Bryan Crockett, "Word Boundary and Syntactic Line Segmenation in Shakespeare's Sonnets," *Style* 24 (1990): 600–610.

35. This copy, found in a set of *LB* (1800) at the State University of New York at Buffalo, is described and transcribed in the appendix of Brian G. Caraher's *Wordsworth's "Slumber" and the Problematics of Reading* (University Park: Pennsylvania State University Press, 1991), 263–70. It is "signed and apparently dated" ["20th July 1848"] by Wordsworth:

> She lived unknown, and few could
>   know
> When Lucy ceased to be;
>   But She is in her grave—and oh
>   The difference to Me.!

Caraher makes no comment on the possible prosodic function of the underlining.

36. See Caroline Strong, "History and Relations of the Tail-Rhyme Strophe in Latin, French, and English," *PMLA* 22 (1907): 371–417. Jerome Mitchell calls special attention to a medieval tradition of lyric use in "Wordsworth's Tail-Rhyme 'Lucy' Poem," *Studies in Medieval Culture* 4 (1974): 561–68.

37. See my *Numerous Verse,* 57–60.

38. Collier, *Seven Lectures,* li–lii.

39. Among other poems in Wordsworth's *Poetical Works* that use "trochaic" rhythm for the effect of enchantment are "Song for the Spinning Wheel" (composed 1812), and "Hymn for the Boatmen, as they Approach the Rapids under the Castle of Heidelberg" (1820).

40. For a discussion of parallels between "The Chase" and "Hart-Leap Well" (and of Wordsworth's departures from ballad narrative form), see Parrish, *Art of the Lyrical Ballads,* 131. Parrish is not concerned in this instance with the kinds of issues that occupy me here.

41. In the preface to *Annus Mirabilis,* Dryden calls the stanza "more noble, and of greater dignity, both for the sound and number, than any other verse in use amongst us." For a discussion of the history of the stanza in the late seventeenth and early eighteenth centuries,

see Susanne Woods, *Natural Emphasis: English Versification from Chaucer to Dryden* (San Marino, Calif.: Huntington Library, 1984). Woods calls the stanza "historically the predecessor of the [pentameter-couplet] explosion in narrative and discursive poetry" (275).

42. Commentators have often noted the discrepancy between the style and approach of the two parts, but usually have tended to see the division as a disunifying fault. Such is the implicit view of Parrish, for example, who sees Wordsworth's choice to narrate Part First directly as an "abandonment" of some of the more "daring and original" techniques through which the *LB* explore psychological depths of speakers. By not making the shepherd the dramatic speaker of the tale, Parrish says, Wordsworth focuses attention in Part First on "incidents, not psychology" (*Art of the Lyrical Ballads*, 132).

43. For Wordsworth's comments on the "glee" with which he composed the poem, see the Fenwick note (Butler and Green, *Lyrical Ballads, and Other Poems*, 354). Wordsworth tells John Wilson in a letter of 7 June 1802 that he "wrote the poem with exceeding delight and pleasure" (*EY*, 355).

44. Percy comments on the five-line variant in "Sir Cauline," and remarks upon its rarity: "There is something peculiar in the metre of this old ballad; it is not unusual to meet with redundant stanzas of six lines; but the occasional insertion of a double third or fourth line, is an irregularity I do not remember to have seen elsewhere" (1:90). Coleridge was of course familiar with the poem in Percy, from which he also may have borrowed the name of his heroine in *Christabel*. See also Wordsworth's comment on "the exquisite ballad of Sir Cauline" in the Essay, Supplemental to the Preface (1815). (*Prose* 3:75).

45. See Fraistat, *Poem and the Book*, 86; Parrish compares Wordsworth's and Coleridge's common but dissimilar use of Bürger's "Lenora" in "The Idiot Boy" (parodic and mock heroic) and the "Ancient Mariner" (in which the ballad is taken "more seriously"). See *Art of the Lyrical Ballads*, 88–89.

46. Mary Jacobus provides a useful discussion of Wordsworth's complex and creative engagement of ballad themes and narrative style for comic purposes, in "The Idiot Boy," in *Bicentenary Wordsworth Studies*, ed. Jonathan Wordsworth, 238–65 (Ithaca, N.Y.: Cornell University Press, 1970). The view presented here of Wordsworth's engagement of the metrical tradition of balladry is intended as a complement to her analysis.

47. Among the reasons why repetition is often desirable in poetry, Wordsworth mentions "a spirit of fondness, of exultation and gratitude, [from which] the mind luxuriates in the repetition of words which appear successfully to communicate its feelings" (*PW* 2:513).

48. These six poems are "The Reverie of Poor Susan," "A Character," "The Two Thieves," "The Childless Father" (all in the stanza aabb$_4$, anapests), "Written in Germany on one of the Coldest Days of the Century" (a$_4$b$_3$cc$_4$b$_3$, anapests), and "Rural Architecture" (aa$_4$b$_3$cc$_4$b$_3$, anapests).

49. See *STCL* 3:112, for a letter to Wordsworth in which Coleridge asserts that triple meters have a tendency to act upon the reader "a priori and with complete self-subsistence."

50. See Elizabeth Sewell, *The Orphic Voice: Poetry and Natural History* (New York: Harper and Row, 1971). Citing Wordsworth's "The Power of Music" and other poems in such "unpretentious street-ballad-like meter" (e.g., "Poor Susan"), Sewell comments that "like so many of Wordsworth's poems, its complete apparent simplicity and naivete make it the kind of thing we find utterly unacceptable when young, when we are looking for stronger stuff. ... But later on, the more one looks into this type of Wordsworthian poem, the more one comes to see in it, and I believe this would be true of almost any poem of this kind he wrote. They show a profound subtlety, infinitely removed from sophistication, a subtlety whose precondition is the simplicity of the approach and of the subject" (317). For other aspects of the anapestic line and stanza in the romantic period and in Wordsworth, see Hollander, "Wordsworth and the Music of Sound," 68 and *Vision and Resonance*, 200–202; and Margaret Garner, "The Anapestic Lyrical Ballads: New Sympathies," *Wordsworth Circle* 13 (1982): 183–88.

51. On the prevalence of "rising" tendencies in English speech and verse, see Attridge, *Rhythms of English Poetry,* esp. 67–70, 111–14.

52. For another example of this tendency, see Wordsworth's use of a half-meter stanza (abab$_3$), for the song carolled by the "Angels" in "The Egyptian Maid" (ll. 355–86). The stanza and the angelic chorus are both unique in Wordsworth's corpus.

53. This is very nearly the same meter that Roethke uses for another poem in which an adult speaker attempts to create rhythmically a sense of the measures of a childish feeling:

> We romped until the pans
> Slid from the kitchen shelf
> My mother's countenance
> Could not unfrown itself.
>
> ("My Papa's Waltz," ll. 5–8)

5. "INFINITELY THE MOST DIFFICULT METRE TO MANAGE": CHARACTERISTICS OF WORDSWORTH'S BLANK VERSE

1. Gill, *Salisbury Plain Poems,* 288. The text of "The road extended o'er a heath" appears in appendix 1 (289) as fragment 16 (a). See Sheats, *Making of Wordsworth's Poetry,* 119 and 273 n. 13 for a brief discussion of the poem as indicative of Wordsworth's emerging mature style.

2. This survey is limited to verse written between mid-1796 and early 1800. It therefore excludes very early work—such as the Miltonic blank verse that Wordsworth wrote at Cambridge—and translations. For descriptions of the early (mostly fragmentary) blank verse, see Reed, *CEY,* General Chronological List, nos. 20, 22, 23, 26, 28b, 31, 46; for the translations, see Bruce E. Graver's forthcoming edition in the Cornell Wordsworth series. For the rationale behind exclusion from consideration of juvenilia and unpublished early work, see above, chapter 3, note 29.

3. On the imprecision of Wordsworth's terminology—"long" and "short"—see above, chap. 1, note 12.

4. For Wordsworth's opinions on the appropriateness of "trochaic endings" in dramatic blank verse, see *LY* 3:381, an 1842 letter to Quillinan in which Wordsworth discusses Sir Henry Taylor's *Edwin the Fair.* Wordsworth complains that Taylor's verse, "owing to the want of trochaic endings in the lines," is "very often rather fit for didactic or epic poetry than the dramatic."

5. This total for Milton is somewhat inflated, as book 1 contains several passages that are, even for Milton, heavily enjambed. W. Jackson Bate's count for all of *Paradise Lost* is 59 percent, which is still considerably higher than any eighteenth- or nineteenth-century practitioner of the form. Bate calculates Blair's enjambments at only 25 percent. Thomson and Young also enjamb less frequently than does Milton. Bate estimates perhaps 50 percent or not much below as the norm for most eighteenth-century blank verse. (*Stylistic Development,* 81).

6. Some context may be supplied by Bate's remark that, except for Akenside, Cowper, and the Elizabethan blank verse of Robert Blair, it is "questionable whether the use of the unbroken line rose much even in eighteenth-century blank verse" above the 29 percent that he counts in *Paradise Lost.* For Bate, Keats's use of an unbroken line in 43.4 percent of the verses in *Hyperion* "is, as far as I know, unequaled except by Surrey in English" (*Stylistic Development of Keats,* 80–81).

7. On relations between four- and five-beat verse, see chapter 3.

8. Wordsworth invites comparison between his poem and odes in a note appended to "Tintern Abbey" in editions from 1800 through 1805: "I have not ventured to call this Poem an Ode; but it was written with a hope that in the transitions, and the impassioned music

of the versification would be found the principal requisites for that species of composition" (Butler and Green, *Lyrical Ballads, and Other Poems*, 357).

9. For a comparison of Southey's blank verse with Wordsworth's work on "The Ruined Cottage," see Jonathan Wordsworth, *The Music of Humanity* (New York: Harper and Row, 1969), 62–66. I quote Southey's "Hannah" from Jonathan Wordsworth's text, 63–64; rpt. from the *Monthly Magazine* 4 (October 1797). See also Sheats, *Making of Wordsworth's Poetry*, 145–48.

10. Figures for "Tintern Abbey" have been given above—55.6 percent of the lines are enjambed and the percentage of midline full stops relative to total full stops is 65.8 percent. Figures for other parts of the *LB* sample are as follows: "Lines Left upon a Seat in a Yew-Tree"—49 percent enjambed; 60.8 percent midline full stops; "The Brothers"—49 percent enjambed; 51.7 percent midline full stops; "A Narrow Girdle of Rough Stones and Crags"—55.8 percent enjambed; 30 percent midline full stops; "There Was A Boy"—58.8 percent enjambed; 45.4 percent midline full stops; "The Old Cumberland Beggar"—48 percent enjambed; 53.5 percent midline full stops; "Nutting"—60.7 percent enjambed; 52.6 percent midline full stops; "Written with a Slate Pencil upon a Stone . . . upon One of the Islands at Rydal"—60 percent enjambed; 55.5 percent midline full stop; "To Joanna"—43.5 percent enjambed; 28 percent midline full stops; "There is an Eminence—of these our hills"—52.9 percent enjambed; 28.6 percent midline full stops; "Michael"—44.9 percent enjambed; 29.8 percent midline full stops.

11. See Pound's definition of poetic rhythm: "Rhythm is a form cut into TIME, as a design is determined SPACE." In "Treatise on Metre," in Gross, *Structure of Verse*, 235.

12. In Wordsworth's careful structuring both of this introductory verse paragraph and of the poem as a whole—particularly his gradual accumulation of descriptive detail and his amassing of smaller formal structures into larger and more comprehensive structures—Lee M. Johnson has found evidence that Wordsworth constructed the poem according to strict geometrical proportions: "['Tintern Abbey' is] a modified Pindaric ode in the form of a double golden section, which is built upon the lesser details of repeated images and the ornamental patterns of simple binaries" (*Wordsworth's Metaphysical Verse*, 60).

13. Wordsworth's interest in sonnetlike patterns and effects in blank verse is illustrated by a comment to Henry Crabb Robinson in which the poet calls a passage of fourteen lines in *Paradise Lost* "a perfect sonnet without rhyme" (*Henry Crabb Robinson on Books and Their Writers* [London: J. M. Dent, 1938], 2:484). Johnson (*Metaphysical Verse*) argues for the presence of blank verse sonnets throughout Wordsworth's blank verse (see esp. 33–35, 72–74). Johnson does not mention "Animal Tranquillity and Decay" in his discussion of blank verse sonnets.

14. The obvious clash between the sketch and the ending, and its "disquieting" effects, have of course been noted frequently by commentators. For a recent summary of opinion, see Patrick Campbell, *Lyrical Ballads*, 112–14. None of the many commentators on the poem has addressed himself specifically to metrical style. The phrase "abrupt down-fall" is used by Coleridge with reference to "The Sailor's Mother" (*BL* 2:71; see above, chapter 2). Note that Wordsworth says in the 1800 Preface that "it has also been part of my general purpose to attempt to sketch characters under the influence of less impassioned feelings, as in the Old Man Travelling, The Two Thieves, etc. characters of which the elements are simple, belonging rather to nature than to manners, such as exist now and will probably always exist" (*Prose* 1:128).

15. A hint of Wordsworth's theoretical interest in aesthetic open-endedness may be seen in a comment made to Crabb Robinson concerning sonnet structure. A too pat summation, or as Wordsworth puts it a "sharp turning at the end [of a sonnet] with an epigrammatic point" is held to be "absolutely a vice." See *Henry Crabb Robinson on Books and Their Writers* 2:485.

16. Letter of 12 September 1857 to James Mottram, Jr., Esq. See *The Correspondence of Henry Crabb Robinson with the Wordsworth Circle, 1808–1866*, ed. Edith J. Morley (Oxford: Clarendon Press, 1927), 2:820. See also Robinson's statement that Wordsworth had in 1815

singled out "A Night-Piece" and "Yew-Trees" as "among the best for the imaginative power displayed in them" (*Henry Crabb Robinson on Books and Their Writers* 1:166).

17. Other evidence of the close linkage of these two poems in Wordsworth's mind is their close proximity in collective editions beginning in 1815 (where they are poems 3 and 4 in the Poems of the Imagination; in 1850, they are separated by "Airey-Force Valley," published 1842). In addition, work toward "Yew-Trees" appears in DC MS 80 just after a copy of "A Night-Piece." See Curtis, *Poems, In Two Volumes*, 669.

18. The texts of "A Night-Piece" and "Yew-Trees" used in this chapter are the first published versions, from *Poems* (1815). For early work on "A Night-Piece," see Beth Darlington, "Two Early Texts," in *Bicentenary Wordsworth Studies* (425–48), and Butler and Green, *Lyrical Ballads, and Other Poems* (276–77). For early work on "Yew-Trees," see Curtis, *Poems, In Two Volumes*, 606, 669–71 ("Ewtrees") and 605, 665 ("That vast eugh-tree, pride of Lorton Vale").

19. See Attridge, *Rhythms of English Poetry*, for a discussion of this very disruptive (and consequently very rare) kind of "inversion" (209). The effect is outlawed by classical prosodists, and is specifically ruled out on the basis of its rarity by some generative metrists. Tarlinskaja finds only seventeen examples in thirteen hundred lines of nondramatic blank verse (*English Verse*, 283, table 43). Tarlinskaja's tables list Wordsworth's preferences for inversion thus: inversions caused by monosyllables—first foot (72 percent), fourth (16 percent); third (8 percent), second (4 percent), fifth (0 percent); inversions caused by polysyllables—first (97 percent), fourth (2.9 percent).

Wordsworth is reported to have singled out an instance of the "diabolus" in Milton. Arguing that Milton "sometimes indulged himself" in "lines which, if not in time, you could hardly call verse," Wordsworth cites *Paradise Lost* 3.36:

    And Tiresias and Phineus, prophets old
    B̄ o B   B o B o B

He goes on to note "the sweet-flowing lines which followed, and with regard to which he had no doubt the unmusical line before had been inserted." "Personal Reminiscences (1836), by the Hon. Mr. Justice Coleridge," in *The Prose Works of William Wordsworth*, ed. Alexander B. Grosart (London: Moxon, 1876), 3:430.

20. Walker provides a convenient summary of critical discussion of the "impersonal" or "elided" subject in "Yew-Trees," in "Wordsworth's 'Haunted Tree' and 'Yew-Trees' Criticism." The chief articles in the argument summarized by Walker are Michael Riffaterre, "Interpretation and Descriptive Poetry: A Reading of Wordsworth's 'Yew-Trees,'" *New Literary History* 4 (1973): 229–56 and Geoffrey H. Hartman, "The Use and Abuse of Structural Analysis: Riffaterre's Interpretation of Wordsworth's 'Yew-Trees,'" *New Literary History* 7 (1975): 165–89.

21. Johnson, *Metaphysical Verse*, 52–57. Johnson argues that "Yew-Trees" is, like many important passages of Wordsworth's blank verse, geometrically regular, structured metrically as a pythagorean golden section. The opening sentence, about the Lorton Yew, comprises 12.4 lines. These 12.4 lines are approximately 0.62 of the remaining 20.6 lines (the second sentence, about the Borrowdale Yews). The ratio of part 1 to part 2, then, is identical to the ratio of part 2 (20.6 lines) to the whole (33 lines). The presence of this geometrical structure as the chief organizing pattern of the linguistic minutiae of the poem is, for Johnson, evidence that the poem is "essentially metaphysical." It requires for its full realization the reader's recognition that "the forms of nature are not only natural but also supernatural in relation to the abstract powers and the immaterial forms of geometrical thought" (57).

22. Kelley, *Wordsworth's Revisionary Aesthetics*, 166.

23. On syntactic stress hierarchies, see Attridge, *Rhythms of English Poetry*, 67–70.

24. On Wordsworth's probable way of proceeding with regard to the complex issue of

elision, see the Introduction to this book, and the discussion of the letter to Thelwall in chapter 1, above.

25. Robert Bridges includes this cluster of sounds under his "Rule of L": "unstressed vowels separated by an 'l' may be elided"; for example, "popular, populous, *articulate, credulous, groveling, perilous*" (*Milton's Prosody* [London: Oxford University Press, 1921], 30–33; emphasis added).

26. MS B, ll. 168–70, in Beth Darlington, ed. *Home at Grasmere* (Ithaca, N.Y.: Cornell University Press, 1977), 48.

27. Ricks, "Wordsworth: 'A Pure Organic Pleasure from the Lines,'" 4.

28. See Sheats, *Making of Wordsworth's Poetry*, 156.

29. Incidentally, Ricks does not discuss this characteristic of Wordsworth's blank verse endings.

30. *Henry Crabb Robinson on Books and their Writers* 2:479.

31. Walker, "Wordsworth's 'Haunted Tree' and 'Yew-Trees' Criticism," 72.

32. *The Letters and Prose Writings of William Cowper*, ed. James King and Charles Ryskamp, 2:308 (Oxford: Clarendon Press, 1979–84). See Ostriker's comment on Cowper's blank verse: Cowper, according to Ostriker the one "genuine original" of late-eighteenth-century blank verse, anticipates Wordsworth's manner, "but with less prosiness" (*Vision and Verse*, 26).

33. See *PW* 3:441–42. Wordsworth acknowledges his debt to Cowper, Burns, and Percy, who "powerfully counteracted the mischievous influence of Darwin's dazzling manner, the extravagance of the earlier dramas of Schiller, and that of other German writers upon my taste and natural tendencies."

34. See the chapter "Milton's Fame in the Eighteenth Century," in Raymond Dexter Havens, *The Influence of Milton on English Poetry* (Cambridge: Harvard University Press, 1922), esp. 6–13. On the issue of the pervasiveness of the Miltonic voice in Wordsworth's memory, see Thomas and Ober, *A Mind For Ever Voyaging*, 68–69.

35. Compare Coleridge's assessment: "The language and versification of the Paradise Lost are peculiar in being so much more necessarily correspondent to each than those in any other poem or poet. The connexion of the sentences and the position of the words are exquisitely artificial; but the position is rather according to the logic of passion or universal logic, than to the logic of grammar. Milton attempted to make the English language obey the logic of passion as perfectly as the Greek and Latin. Hence the occasional harshness in the construction" ("Unassigned Lecture Notes," appendix A of *Lectures 1808–1819* 2:427.)

36. Compare Wordsworth's comments in the "Essay Supplementary to the Preface" of 1815, on the unnaturalness of expression in MacPherson's "Ossian" compared with natural phenomena: everything in nature is "perfectly distinct" but never "defined into absolute independent singleness" (*Prose* 3:77).

37. See "It is a Beauteous Evening," l. 8; *13-Bk Prelude* 2.324; *14-Bk Prelude* 2.305.

38. Page, "Wordsworth and the Psychology of Meter."

39. James K. Chandler, "Romantic Allusiveness," *Critical Inquiry* 8 (1982): 476.

40. Within the limits of her own argument, it is perfectly appropriate that Page emphasize this element, as her chief interest is the specifically psychological implications of Wordsworth's metrical manner. For a brief but suggestive comment on Wordsworth's internalized Miltonic voice, see Ernest de Selincourt's edition of *The Prelude* (Oxford: Clarendon Press, 1959), xlii: The Miltonic, De Selincourt comments, would have been "a natural and indispensable element in [Wordsworth's] own speech."

41. This point represents the source of my chief disagreement with Page. To her claim that "it is as if Milton's style and voice had to be exorcised in the process of writing before Wordsworth could retrieve those earlier, pre-literary memories which yield such rich meaning" (294), I object that the stream of words and the preliterary powers of sound are too completely interwoven in the poetry itself to admit of any such complete separation or

sequencing. The choice, in other words, is not between Milton and the Derwent; it is between a voice more or less influenced by Milton. Both the Miltonic and the "natural" Wordsworth are "Wordsworth." Both are engaged in a process of channeling the Miltonic voice (so inextricably associated with nondramatic blank verse) in original ways.

42. O. B. Hardison, Jr., *Prosody and Purpose in the Renaissance* (Baltimore, Md.: Johns Hopkins University Press, 1989), 22.

43. The text cited here is the first published version of the "Prospectus," in *The Excursion* (1814). For early work on the "Prospectus," see Darlington, *Home at Grasmere*.

44. These lines develop from a passage (ll. 1002–14 of MS B of *Home at Grasmere*) generally acknowledged to have been written later (probably 1806; perhaps 1805) than the remainder of the Prospectus (probably spring 1800 to early spring 1802). Although of course it would be possible to regard the prosodic contrast (or clash) of the passage with what has gone before as evidence of a falling off from the original inspiration of the "Prospectus" (or as one more example of prosodic "inconstancy"), I assert here (as I have asserted throughout this book) that such contrast, even in an extreme degree, is a chief aesthetic aim of Wordsworth's metrical art. Darlington summarizes the evidence for dating the "Prospectus" in her introduction to *Home at Grasmere*, 19–22.

45. See Tarlinskaja, *English Verse*, table 44, 285–86. Compare these twenty-four occurrences of stress-final pairing with "linkage" (or juncture inversion caused by autonomous polysyllables) with the 1,939 occurrences of stress-final pairing without linkage (or juncture inversion caused by monosyllables) in Tarlinskaja's counts. On "linkage," see Attridge, *Rhythms of English Poetry*, 265.

CONCLUSION: ON THE POWER OF SOUND

1. "On the Power of Sound" was placed last in the *Yarrow Revisited* volume in which it first appeared (in 1835), and is the last of the "Poems of the Imagination" in *PW* (1836–37). In a letter to Alexander Dyce (23 December 1837), Wordsworth comments that such placement is an indication of his own high opinion of the poem: "I cannot call to mind a reason why you should not think some passages in 'The Power of Sound' equal to anything I have produced; when first printed in 'Yarrow Revisited,' I placed it at the end of the Volume, and in the last edition of my poems, at the close of the Poems of Imagination, indicating thereby my *own* opinion of it" (*LY* 3:502). This is the poem, too, the versification of which prompted Barron Field's prediction, cited in the Introduction to this book, that "one day" readers would come to appreciate how "deeply" Wordsworth "studied the sound as well as the sense of poetry" (*LY* 3:355 n. 4).

2. For a discussion of Wordsworth's poem in the context of the Orpheus myth, see Sewell, *Orphic Voice*. Sewell reads the poem as an Orphic quest, or a myth of "myth looking at itself." It is a poetic investigation of the roots of poetic power, stressing the activity of mythologizing as a means for breaking down dichotomies of mind and body, science and poetry, and pointing the way for creative cooperation between theology and natural science.

3. Alfred North Whitehead, *Science and the Modern World* (New York: Macmillan, 1925; New York: Free Press, 1967), 37.

4. For a fuller discussion of this passage in relation to Wordsworth's metrical art, see chapter 5.

5. In addition to the studies mentioned here, see also Stein, *Wordsworth's Art of Allusion*. The conclusion to Stein's study argues for the importance of "On the Power of Sound" for an understanding of Wordsworth's commitment to echo as the chief figure in his "spousal verse" (see esp. 218–20).

6. "Apostrophe and Lyric Voice in *The Prelude*." Reprinted from *Lyric Poetry: Beyond New Criticism* (Ithaca, N.Y.: Cornell University Press, 1985), 158.

7. "Wordsworth and the Music of Sound," in *New Perspectives on Coleridge and Wordsworth: Selected Papers from the English Institute,* ed. Geoffrey H. Hartman (New York: Columbia University Press, 1972), 45.

8. See above, chapter 4, note 16.

9. There are four stresses in l. 11 of stanza 1; five stresses in l. 12 of stanzas 1, 8, 9, 11; five stresses in ll. 9 and 10 of stanza 11; five stresses in l. 16 of stanza 14 (last line of the poem).

10. These are the lines as they appear in "On the Power of Sound." In draft toward "The Triad," they read thus:

> There is a world of spirit
> Whose motions by fit music are controlled,
> And glorious is their privilege who merit
> Initiation in that mystery old.
>
> (*PW* 2:294 app. crit.)

11. See the discussion of similar effects in Wordsworth's blank verse in chapter 5.

12. See Keats's sonnet "If by dull rhymes our English must be chained" in *Poems of John Keats,* ed. Jack Stillinger (Cambridge: Harvard University Press, 1978), 368.

13. Dyce was to publish fifteen of Wordsworth's sonnets in *Specimens of English Sonnets* (1833). Wordsworth's comments are offered as advice should Dyce see fit to include in his volume "a short preface upon the Construction of the Sonnet" (*LY* 2:604).

14. Johnson observes the exact metrical equivalence of the two halves of the stanza in *Wordsworth's Metaphysical Verse,* 235–6 n.71.

15. "To a Skylark" ("Ethereal minstrel!"), l. 12.

Bibliography

PRIMARY SOURCES CITED

Addison, Joseph. *The Spectator.* 5 vols. Edited by Donald F. Bond. Oxford: Clarendon Press, 1965.
Anderson, Robert. *Ballads, In the Cumberland Dialect.* Alnwick: W. Davison, n.d.
Anderson, Dr. Robert, ed. *Works of the British Poets.* 13 vols. London: John and Arthur Arch, 1795.
Averill, James, ed. *An Evening Walk.* Ithaca, N.Y.: Cornell University Press, 1984.
Birdsall, Eric, ed. *Descriptive Sketches.* Ithaca, N.Y.: Cornell University Press, 1984.
Blair, Hugh. *Lectures on Rhetoric and Belles Lettres.* 2d ed. 3 vols. London, 1785.
Blake, William. *The Poetry and Prose of William Blake.* Edited by David V. Erdman. Garden City, N.Y.: Doubleday, 1965.
Butler, James, ed. *The Ruined Cottage and The Pedlar.* Ithaca, N.Y.: Cornell University Press, 1979.
Butler, James, and Karen Green, eds. *Lyrical Ballads, and Other Poems, 1797–1800.* Ithaca, N.Y.: Cornell University Press, 1992.
Byron, George Gordon, Lord. *The Complete Poetical Works.* Edited by Jerome J. McGann. 5 vols. New York: Oxford University Press, 1981–86.
Bysshe, Edward. *The Art of English Poetry.* 1708. Reprint. Augustan Reprint Society, No. 40. Los Angeles: William Andrews Clark Memorial Library, 1953.
Cockin, William. *The Art of Delivering Written Language.* London, 1775.
Coleridge, Samuel Taylor. *Biographia Literaria; or, Biographical Sketches of My Literary Life and Opinions.* Edited by James Engell and W. Jackson Bate. 2 vols. Princeton, N.J.: Princeton University Press, 1983.
——. *Collected Letters of Samuel Taylor Coleridge.* Edited by Earl Leslie Griggs. 6 vols. Oxford: Clarendon Press, 1956–71.
——. *Lectures 1808–1809: On Literature.* Edited by R. A. Foakes. Princeton, N.J.: Princeton University Press, 1987.
——. *The Complete Poetical Works of Samuel Taylor Coleridge.* 2 vols. Edited by E. H. Coleridge. London: Oxford University Press, 1912.
Collier, J. Payne. "Introductory Preface" to *Seven Lectures on Shakespeare and Milton [by Samuel Taylor Coleridge].* London, 1856.
Cowper, William. *The Complete Poetical Works of William Cowper.* Edited by H. S. Milford. New York: Oxford University Press, 1902.
——. *The Letters and Prose Writings of William Cowper.* Edited by James King and Charles Ryskamp. Oxford: Clarendon Press, 1979–84.
Curtis, Jared, ed. *Poems, in Two Volumes, and Other Poems, 1800–1807.* Ithaca, N.Y.: Cornell University Press, 1983.
Darlington, Beth, ed. *Home at Grasmere.* Ithaca, N.Y.: Cornell University Press, 1977.

———, ed. "Two Early Texts: *A Night-Piece* and *The Discharged Soldier.*" In *Bicentenary Wordsworth Studies in Memory of John Alban Finch,* edited by Jonathan Wordsworth, 425–48. Ithaca, N.Y.: Cornell University Press, 1970.
De Selincourt, Ernest, ed. *The Letters of William and Dorothy Wordsworth, The Early Years, 1787–1805.* Revised, Chester L. Shaver. Oxford: Clarendon Press, 1967.
———, ed. *The Letters of William and Dorothy Wordsworth, The Later Years, Part I, 1821–1828.* 2d ed. Revised, Alan G. Hill. Oxford: Clarendon Press, 1978.
———, ed. *The Letters of William and Dorothy Wordsworth, The Later Years, Part II, 1829–1834.* 2d ed. Revised, Alan G. Hill. Oxford: Clarendon Press, 1979.
———, ed. *The Letters of William and Dorothy Wordsworth, The Later Years, Part III, 1835–1839.* 2d ed. Revised, Alan G. Hill. Oxford: Clarendon Press, 1982.
———, ed. *The Letters of William and Dorothy Wordsworth, The Later Years, Part IV, 1840–1853.* 2d ed. Revised, Alan G. Hill. Oxford: Clarendon Press, 1988.
———, ed. *The Letters of William and Dorothy Wordsworth, The Middle Years, Part I, 1806–1811.* Revised, Mary Moorman. Oxford: Clarendon Press, 1969.
———, ed. *The Letters of William and Dorothy Wordsworth, The Middle Years, Part II, 1812–1820.* Revised, Mary Moorman and Alan G. Hill. Oxford: Clarendon Press, 1970.
———, ed. *William Wordsworth: The Prelude.* 2d ed. Revised, Helen Darbishire. Oxford: Clarendon Press, 1959.
De Selincourt, Ernest, and Helen Darbishire, eds. *The Poetical Works of William Wordsworth.* 5 vols. 1940–49. Reprint. Oxford: Clarendon Press, 1952–59.
Dryden, John. "Essay of Dramatic Poesy." In *The Essays of John Dryden,* vol. 1. Edited by W. P. Ker. Oxford: Clarendon Press, 1926.
Dugas, Kristine, ed. *The White Doe of Rylstone; or, the Fate of the Nortons.* Ithaca, N.Y.: Cornell University Press, 1988.
Emerson, Ralph Waldo. "The Poet." In *The Collected Works of Ralph Waldo Emerson,* vol. 3. Cambridge: Harvard University Press, 1983.
Field, Barron. *Memoirs of Wordsworth.* Edited by Geoffrey Little. Sydney: Australian Academy of the Humanities, 1975.
Gill, Stephen, ed. *The Salisbury Plain Poems of William Wordsworth.* Ithaca, N.Y.: Cornell University Press, 1975.
Grosart, Alexander B., ed. *The Prose Works of William Wordsworth.* 3 vols. London: Moxon, 1876.
Hazlitt, William. *The Complete Works of William Hazlitt.* 21 vols. Edited by P. P. Howe. London: Dutton, 1930–34.
Johnson, Samuel. *Lives of the English Poets.* Edited by George Birkbeck Hill. Oxford: Clarendon Press, 1905.
———. *The Rambler.* Edited by W. Jackson Bate and Albrecht B. Strauss. 3 vols. New Haven, Conn.: Yale University Press, 1969.
Keats, John. *The Poems of John Keats.* Edited by Jack Stillinger. Cambridge: Harvard University Press, 1978.
Manwaring [Mainwaring], Edward. *Stichology.* London, 1737.
Moore, Thomas. *Tom Moore's Diary.* Edited by J. B. Priestley. Cambridge: Cambridge University Press, 1925.
Owen, W. J. B., ed. *The Fourteen-Book Prelude.* Ithaca, N.Y.: Cornell University Press, 1985.
———, ed. *Wordsworth and Coleridge: Lyrical Ballads, 1798.* 2d ed. Oxford: Oxford University Press, 1969.
Owen, W. J. B., and J. W. Smyser, eds. *The Prose Works of William Wordsworth.* 3 vols. Oxford: Clarendon Press, 1974.
Parrish, Stephen, ed. *The Prelude, 1798–1799.* Ithaca, N.Y.: Cornell University Press, 1977.

Peacock, Markham L. *The Critical Opinions of William Wordsworth.* Baltimore, Md.: Johns Hopkins University Press, 1950.
Percy, Thomas. *Percy's Reliques of Ancient Poetry.* Edited by Ernest Rhys. 2 vols. New York: E. P. Dutton, 1906.
Pope, Alexander. *The Correspondence of Alexander Pope.* Edited by George Sherburn. 5 vols. Oxford: Clarendon Press, 1956.
——. *The Poems of Alexander Pope.* General ed. John Butt. 11 vols. New Haven, Conn.: Yale University Press, 1943–69.
Reed, Mark L., ed. *The Thirteen-Book Prelude.* 2 vols. Ithaca, N.Y.: Cornell University Press, 1991.
Robinson, Henry Crabb. *The Correspondence of Henry Crabb Robinson with the Wordsworth Circle, 1808–1866.* Edited by Edith J. Morley. 2 vols. Oxford: Clarendon Press, 1927.
——. *Henry Crabb Robinson on Books and their Writers.* London: J. M. Dent, 1938.
Say, Samuel. *An Essay on the Harmony, Variety, and Power of Numbers (1745).* Augustan Reprint Society, No. 55. Los Angeles: William Andrews Clark Memorial Library, 1956.
Scott, Sir Walter. *The Chase, and William and Helen (1796).* Oxford: Woodstock Books, 1989.
——. *The Complete Poetical Works of Sir Walter Scott.* Edited by Horace E. Scudder. Boston: Houghton Mifflin, 1900.
Shenstone, William. *The Works in Verse and Prose of William Shenstone.* London, 1764–69.
Smart, Christopher. *The Poetical Works of Christopher Smart. Volume II: Religious Poetry, 1763–1771.* Edited by Marcus Walsh and Karina Williamson. Oxford: Clarendon, 1983.
Southey, Robert. *Selections from the Letters of Robert Southey.* Edited by J. W. Warter. London, 1856.
Steele, Joshua. *Prosodia Rationalis.* London, 1779.
Tennyson, Hallam. *Alfred, Lord Tennyson: A Memoir by His Son.* London: Macmillan, 1897.
Thelwall, John. *Selections for the Illustration of a Course of Instructions on the Rhythmus and Utterance of the English Language.* London, 1812.
Webb, Daniel. *Remarks on the Beauties of Poetry.* London, 1762.
Wordsworth, Christopher. *Memoirs of William Wordsworth.* London, 1851.
Wordsworth, Jonathan, M. H. Abrams, and Stephen Gill, eds. *The Prelude 1799, 1805, 1850.* New York: Norton, 1979.

SECONDARY SOURCES CITED

Abrams, M. H. *Doing Things with Texts.* Edited by Michael Fisher. New York: Norton, 1989.
——. *The Mirror and the Lamp: Romantic Theory and the Critical Tradition.* New York: Oxford University Press, 1953; New York: Norton, 1958.
——. *Natural Supernaturalism: Tradition and Revolution in Romantic Literature.* New York: Norton, 1971.
Alter, Robert. *The Pleasures of Reading in an Ideological Age.* New York: Simon and Schuster, 1989.
Arnold, Matthew. "Wordsworth." In *The Complete Prose Works of Matthew Arnold.* Vol. 9 of *English Literature and Irish Politics.* Edited by R. H. Super. Ann Arbor: University of Michigan Press, 1973.
Attridge, Derek. *The Rhythms of English Poetry.* London: Longman, 1982.
Aubin, Robert A. *Topographical Poetry in XVIII-Century England.* New York: Modern Language Association of America, 1936.
Barstow, M. L. (see Greenbie).
Bate, Walter Jackson. *The Stylistic Development of Keats.* New York: Modern Language Association, 1945.

Bauer, N. Stephen. "Wordsworth and the Early Anthologies." *Library*, 5th ser., 32 (1972): 37–45.
Bialostosky, Don. *Making Tales: The Poetics of Wordsworth's Narrative Experiments*. Chicago: University of Chicago Press, 1984.
———. *Wordsworth, Dialogics, and the Practice of Criticism*. Cambridge: Cambridge University Press, 1992.
———. "Wordsworth's Dialogic Art." *Wordsworth Circle* 20 (1989): 140–48.
Bloom, Harold. "Introduction." In *William Wordsworth's The Prelude: Modern Critical Interpretations*, edited by Harold Bloom. New York: Chelsea House, 1986.
Brewster, Paul G. "The Influence of the Popular Ballad on Wordsworth's Poetry." *Studies in Philology* 35 (1938): 588–612.
Bridges, Robert. *Milton's Prosody*. London: Oxford University Press, 1921.
Brogan, T. V. F. *English Versification, 1570–1980. A Reference Guide with a Global Appendix*. Baltimore, Md.: Johns Hopkins University Press, 1981.
Butler, James A. "The Muse at Hawkshead: Early Criticism of Wordsworth's Poetry." *Wordsworth Circle* 20 (1989): 140.
Campbell, Patrick. *The "Lyrical Ballads" of Wordsworth and Coleridge: Critical Perspectives*. London: Macmillan, 1991.
Caraher, Brian G. *Wordsworth's "Slumber" and the Problematics of Reading*. University Park: Pennsylvania State University Press, 1991.
Chandler, James K. "Romantic Allusiveness." *Critical Inquiry* 8 (1982): 461–87.
Cooper, Lane. *A Concordance to the Poems of William Wordsworth*. London: Smith and Elder, 1911; New York: Russell and Russell, 1965.
Crockett, Bryan. "Word Boundary and Syntactic Line Segmentation in Shakespeare's Sonnets." *Style* 24 (1990): 600–610.
Culler, A. Dwight. "Edward Bysshe and the Poet's Handbook." *PMLA* 63 (1948): 858–85.
Curran, Stuart. *Poetic Form and British Romanticism*. New York: Oxford University Press, 1986.
Darbishire, Helen. *The Poet Wordsworth*. Oxford: Clarendon Press, 1958.
Ferguson, Frances. *Wordsworth: Language as Counter-Spirit*. New Haven, Conn.: Yale University Press, 1977.
Fink, Z. S. *The Early Wordsworthian Milieu. A Notebook of Christopher Wordsworth with a Few Entries by William Wordsworth*. New York: Oxford University Press, 1958.
Fraistat, Neil. *The Poem and the Book*. Chapel Hill: University of North Carolina Press, 1985.
Fussell, Paul, Jr. *Poetic Meter and Poetic Form*. New York: Random House, 1979.
———. *Theory of Prosody in Eighteenth-Century England*. Connecticut College Monograph No. 5, 1954.
———. "Some Observations on Wordsworth's 'A Poet!—He hath put his heart to school.'" *Philological Quarterly* 37 (1958): 454–64.
Garner, Margaret. "The Anapestic Lyrical Ballads: New Sympathies." *Wordsworth Circle* 13 (1982): 183–88.
Gill, Stephen. *William Wordsworth: A Life*. Oxford: Clarendon Press, 1989.
———. *William Wordsworth: The Prelude*. Landmarks of World Literature. Cambridge: Cambridge University Press, 1991.
Graver, Bruce E. "Wordsworth and the Language of Epic: The Translation of the *Aeneid*." *Studies in Philology* 83 (1986): 261–85.
———. "Wordsworth's Georgic Beginnings." *Texas Studies in Language and Literature* 33 (1991): 137–59.
———. "Wordsworth's Translations from Latin Poetry." Ph.D. diss., University of North Carolina, Chapel Hill, 1984.
Greenbie, M. L. [Barstow]. *Wordsworth's Theory of Poetic Diction*. New Haven, Conn.: Yale University Press, 1917.

Gross, Harvey, ed. *The Structure of Verse: Modern Essays on Prosody.* Rev. ed. New York: Ecco Press, 1979.

Guest, Edwin. *A History of English Rhythms.* 1838. Reprint, edited by Rev. Walter W. Skeat, London, 1882.

Häublein, Ernst. *The Stanza.* London: Methuen, 1978.

Hardison, O. B., Jr. *Prosody and Purpose in the Renaissance.* Baltimore, Md.: Johns Hopkins University Press, 1989.

Harmon, William. "Rhyme in English Verse: History, Structures, Functions." *Studies in Philology* 84 (1987): 365–93.

Hartman, Geoffrey H. "The Use and Abuse of Structural Analysis: Riffaterre's Interpretation of Wordsworth's 'Yew-Trees.'" *New Literary History* 7 (1975): 165–89.

———. "Wordsworth's Descriptive Sketches and the Growth of a Poet's Mind." *PMLA* 76 (1961): 519–27.

———. *Wordsworth's Poetry 1787–1814.* New Haven, Conn.: Yale University Press, 1964.

Hartman, Herbert. "Wordsworth's 'Lucy' Poems: Notes and Marginalia." *PMLA* 49 (1934): 134–42.

Havens, Raymond Dexter. *The Influence of Milton on English Poetry.* Cambridge: Harvard University Press, 1922.

———. *The Mind of a Poet.* Baltimore, Md.: Johns Hopkins University Press, 1941.

Hollander, John. *Images of Voice: Music and Sound in Romantic Poetry.* Churchill College Overseas Fellowship Lectures, No. 5. Cambridge: W. Heffer and Sons, 1970.

———. *Melodious Guile.* New Haven, Conn.: Yale University Press, 1989.

———. *Rhyme's Reason: A Guide to English Verse.* Enlarged ed. New Haven, Conn.: Yale University Press, 1989.

———. "Romantic Verse Form and the Metrical Contract." In *Romanticism and Consciousness,* edited by Harold Bloom, 181–200. New York: Norton, 1970.

———. *Vision and Resonance: Two Senses of Poetic Form.* New York: Oxford University Press, 1975.

———. "Wordsworth and the Music of Sound." In *New Perspectives on Coleridge and Wordsworth: Selected Papers from the English Institute,* edited by Geoffrey H. Hartman, 41–84. New York: Columbia University Press, 1972.

Jacobus, Mary. "Apostrophe and Lyric Voice in *The Prelude.*" Reprinted from *Lyric Poetry: Beyond New Criticism.* Ithaca, N.Y.: Cornell University Press, 1985. In *William Wordsworth's The Prelude: Modern Critical Interpretations,* edited by Harold Bloom, 145–59. New York: Chelsea House, 1986.

———. "The Idiot Boy." In *Bicentenary Wordsworth Studies in Memory of John Alban Finch,* edited by Jonathan Wordsworth, 238–65. Ithaca, N.Y.: Cornell University Press, 1970.

———. *Tradition and Experiment in Wordsworth's "Lyrical Ballads."* Oxford: Clarendon Press, 1976.

Johnson, Lee M. *Wordsworth and the Sonnet.* Anglistica, vol. 19. Copenhagen: Rosenkilde and Bagger, 1973.

———. *Wordsworth's Metaphysical Verse: Geometry, Nature, and Form.* Toronto: University of Toronto Press, 1982.

Jones, John. *The Egotistical Sublime: A History of Wordsworth's Imagination.* London: Chatto and Windus, 1954.

Jordan, John E. *Why the "Lyrical Ballads"?* Berkeley and Los Angeles: University of California Press, 1976.

Kelley, Theresa. *Wordsworth's Revisionary Aesthetics.* Cambridge: Cambridge University Press, 1988.

Land, Stephen K. "The Silent Poet: An Aspect of Wordsworth's Semantic Theory." *University of Toronto Quarterly* 42 (1973): 157–69.

Legouis, Emile. *The Early Life of William Wordsworth.* Translated by J. W. Matthews. New York: Dutton, 1932.
Malof, Joseph. *A Manual of English Meters.* Bloomington: Indiana University Press, 1970.
Mayo, Robert. "The Contemporaneity of the *Lyrical Ballads.*" *PMLA* 69 (1954): 486–522.
McKusick, James C. *Coleridge's Philosophy of Language.* Yale Studies in English, 195. New Haven, Conn.: Yale University Press, 1986.
Minahan, John A. *Word Like a Bell: John Keats, Music and the Romantic Poet.* Kent, Ohio: Kent State University Press, 1992.
Mitchell, Jerome. "Wordsworth's Tail-Rhyme 'Lucy' Poem." *Studies in Medieval Culture* 4 (1974): 561–68.
Moorman, Mary. *William Wordsworth, A Biography: The Early Years, 1770–1803.* Oxford: Clarendon Press, 1957.
———. *William Wordsworth, A Biography: The Later Years, 1803–1850.* Oxford: Clarendon Press, 1965.
Morris, Bryan. "Mr. Wordsworth's Ear." *Wordsworth Circle* 10 (1979): 113–21.
O'Donnell, Brennan. *Numerous Verse: A Guide to the Stanzas and Metrical Structures of Wordsworth's Poetry.* Studies in Philology, Texts and Studies Series 86, no. 4. Chapel Hill: University of North Carolina Press, 1989.
Omond, Thomas Stewart. *English Metrists: Being a Sketch of English Prosodical Criticism from Elizabethan Times to the Present Day.* Oxford: Clarendon Press, 1921.
Ostriker, Alicia. *Vision and Verse in William Blake.* Madison: University of Wisconsin Press, 1965.
Owen, W. J. B. *Wordsworth as Critic.* Toronto: University of Toronto Press, 1969.
Page, Judith W. "Wordsworth and the Psychology of Meter." *Papers on Language and Literature* 21 (1985): 275–94.
Parrish, Stephen. *The Art of the "Lyrical Ballads."* Cambridge: Harvard University Press, 1973.
Payne, Richard. "'The Style and Spirit of the Elder Poets': The *Ancient Mariner* and English Literary Tradition." *Modern Philology* 75 (1978): 368–84.
Perkins, David. "How the Romantics Recited Poetry." *Studies in English Literature, 1500–1900* 31 (1991): 655–71.
Piper, William Bowman. *The Heroic Couplet.* Cleveland: Case Western Reserve University Press, 1969.
Pottle, F. A. *The Idiom of Poetry.* Ithaca, N.Y.: Cornell University Press, 1946.
Potts, Abbie Findlay. *Wordsworth's Prelude: A Study of Its Literary Form.* Ithaca, N.Y.: Cornell University Press, 1953; Octagon Books, 1972.
Pound, Ezra. "Treatise on Metre." In *The Structure of Verse,* edited by Harvey Gross, 234–40. New York: Ecco Press, 1979.
Preminger, Alex, ed. *The Princeton Encyclopedia of Poetry and Poetics.* Enlarged ed. Princeton, N.J.: Princeton University Press, 1974.
———. *The Princeton Handbook of Poetic Terms.* Princeton, N.J.: Princeton University Press, 1986.
Preminger, Alex, and T. V. F. Brogan, eds. *The New Princeton Encyclopedia of Poetry and Poetics.* Princeton, N.J.: Princeton University Press, 1993.
Reed, Mark L. "The Speaker of *The Prelude.*" In *Bicentenary Wordsworth Studies in Memory of John Alban Finch,* edited by Jonathan Wordsworth, 276–93. Ithaca, N.Y.: Cornell University Press, 1970.
———. "Wordsworth, Coleridge, and the 'Plan' of the Lyrical Ballads." *University of Toronto Quarterly* 34 (1965): 238–53.
———. *Wordsworth: The Chronology of the Early Years, 1770–1799.* Cambridge: Harvard University Press, 1967.

———. *Wordsworth: The Chronology of the Middle Years, 1800–1815.* Cambridge: Harvard University Press, 1975.
Ricks, Christopher. "Wordsworth: 'A Pure Organic Pleasure from the Lines.'" *Essays in Criticism* 21 (1971): 1–32.
Riffaterre, Michael. "Interpretation and Descriptive Poetry: A Reading of Wordsworth's 'Yew-Trees.'" *New Literary History* 4 (1973): 229–56.
Ruoff, Gene W. "Wordsworth on Language: Toward a Radical Poetics for English Romanticism." *Wordsworth Circle* 3 (1972): 204–11.
Saintsbury, George. *A History of English Prosody.* 3 vols. London: Macmillan, 1906–10.
Schneider, Ben Ross, Jr. *Wordsworth's Cambridge Education.* Cambridge: Cambridge University Press, 1957.
Sewell, Elizabeth. *The Orphic Voice: Poetry and Natural History.* New York: Harper and Row, 1971.
Shaver, Chester L., and Alice C. Shaver. *Wordsworth's Library: A Catalogue Including a List of Books Housed by Wordsworth for Coleridge from c. 1810 to c. 1830.* New York: Garland, 1979.
Sheats, Paul D. *The Making of Wordsworth's Poetry, 1785–1798.* Cambridge: Harvard University Press, 1973.
———. "'Tis Three Feet Long and Two Feet Wide': Wordsworth's "Thorn" and the Politics of Bathos." *Wordsworth Circle* 22 (1991): 92–100.
Smith, Barbara Herrnstein. *On the Margins of Discourse.* Chicago: University of Chicago Press, 1978.
———. *Poetic Closure.* Chicago: University of Chicago Press, 1968.
Steele, Timothy. *Missing Measures: Modern Poetry and the Revolt against Meter.* Fayetteville: University of Arkansas Press, 1990.
Stein, Edwin, Jr. *Wordsworth's Art of Allusion.* University Park: Pennsylvania State University Press, 1988.
Strong, Caroline. "History and Relations of the Tail-Rhyme Strophe in Latin, French, and English." *PMLA* 22 (1907): 371–417.
Tarlinskaja, Marina. *English Verse: Theory and History.* The Hague: Mouton, 1976.
———. *Shakespeare's Verse: Iambic Pentameter and the Poet's Idiosyncrasies.* New York, 1987.
Taylor, Dennis. "Hardy and Wordsworth." *Victorian Poetry* 24 (1986): 441–54.
———. *Hardy's Metres and Victorian Prosody.* Oxford: Clarendon Press, 1988.
Thomas, W. K., and Warren U. Ober. *A Mind For Ever Voyaging: Wordsworth at Work Portraying Newton and Science.* Edmonton: University of Alberta Press, 1989.
Walker, Eric C. "*Biographia Literaria* and Wordsworth's Revisions." *Studies in English Literature, 1500–1900* 28 (1988): 569–88.
———. "Wordsworth's 'Haunted Tree' and 'Yew-Trees' Criticism." *Philological Quarterly* 67 (1988): 63–82.
Wasserman, Earl R. *Elizabethan Poetry in the Eighteenth Century.* Illinois Studies in Language and Literature, 32. Urbana, 1947.
Wesling, Donald. *The New Poetries.* Lewisburg, Pa.: Bucknell University Press, 1985.
Whitehead, Alfred North. *Science and the Modern World.* New York: Macmillan, 1925; New York: Free Press, 1967.
Williams, Ann. *Prophetic Strain.* Chicago: University of Chicago Press, 1984.
Wimsatt, W. K., Jr. *The Verbal Icon.* Lexington: University of Kentucky Press, 1954.
Wimsatt, W. K., Jr., and Monroe Beardsley. "The Concept of Meter: An Exercise in Abstraction." *PMLA* 74 (1959): 585–94. Reprinted in *The Structure of Verse*, edited by Harvey Gross, 150–67. New York: Ecco Press, 1979.
Woodring, Carl. *Politics in English Romantic Poetry.* Cambridge: Harvard University Press, 1970.

Woods, Susanne. *Natural Emphasis: English Versification from Chaucer to Dryden.* San Marino, Calif.: Huntington Library, 1984.
Wordsworth, Jonathan. "As with the Silence of the Thought." In *High Romantic Argument: Essays for M. H. Abrams,* edited by Lawrence Lipking. Ithaca, N.Y.: Cornell University Press, 1981.
———. *The Music of Humanity.* New York: Harper and Row, 1969.
Wright, George T. *Shakespeare's Metrical Art.* Berkeley and Los Angeles: University of California Press, 1988.
Wu, Duncan. *Wordsworth's Reading 1770–1799.* Cambridge: Cambridge University Press, 1993.

Index

Abrams, M. H., 265n.61
Addison, Joseph, 39
Akenside, Mark, 137, 155, 170, 266n.16
Alter, Robert, 250n.9, 253n.4
Anderson, Robert, 111
Arnold, Matthew, 251n.10
Attridge, Derek, 11–16, 32–37, 131, 209, 234, 252n.23, 259n.20, 272nn.19, 23
Aubin, Robert A., 73
Averill, James, 260n.12

Bakhtin, M. M., 251–52n.17
Ballad prosody, 10, 63–67, 266–67n.20, 267n.21. *See also* Ballad stanza
Ballad stanza, 63–66, 116–17, 131–55, 165–69, 267nn.22, 23, 24
Barstow, M. L. *See* Greenbie, M. L.
Bate, Walter Jackson, 26n.21, 270nn.5, 6
Bauer, N. Stephen, 266n.10
Baumgarten, Alexander, 265n.61
Beardsley, Monroe, 67
Beattie, James, 4, 72, 114, 253n.2, 266n.16
Bialostosky, Don, 251–52n.17, 258n.10, 265n.5
Birdsall, Eric, 264n.50
Blair, Hugh, 262–63n.32, 263–64n.44
Blair, Robert, 270nn.5, 6
Blake, William, 5, 73, 115, 251n.16, 260n.9
Blank verse: of Cowper, 185–90, 226, 227; of Milton, 10, 39, 185–90, 225–37, 270n.5, 273n.35; Milton's influence on Wordsworth's, 225–37; sonnet structure in, 202–3, 271n.13; of Southey, 195–96, 271n.9; of Wordsworth, 117, 120–22, 182–225; Wordsworth's theory of, 156, 179–82, 226–27, 270n.4
Brewster, Paul G., 267n.23
Bridges, Robert, 216, 234, 273n.25
Brogan, T. V. F., 254n.13, 267n.23

Browning, Robert, 5
Bürger, Gottfried August, 159, 269n.45
Burns, Robert, 4, 10, 59, 273n.33
Byron, George Gordon, Lord, 164
Bysshe, Edward, 9, 93, 252n.18

Campbell, Patrick, 266n.14, 271n.14
Caraher, Brian G., 268n.35
Cento, 131, 243, 266n.16
Chandler, James K., 228
Chatterton, Thomas, 137
Chaucer, Geoffrey, 5, 10, 36, 81, 115, 155
Cockin, William, 39
Coleridge, Samuel Taylor, 4, 10, 40, 91, 266n.10; on *Descriptive Sketches*, 100–101; on meter and diction, 49–56, 58–60, 66, 257nn.1, 2; on metrical art, 8; on Milton's blank verse, 273n.35; on the poet, 49, 198, 259n.3; on Shakespeare's verse, 259n.3; on Wordsworth's "inconstancy of style," 4, 8, 50–52, 178, 250–51n.10
Coleridge, Samuel Taylor, works of
—*Christabel*, 5, 251n.16, 255n.16, 269n.44
—"Day Dream, A," 54
—"Dejection: An Ode," 54
—"Foster Mother's Tale, The," 119, 201, 265n.6
—"Lines: On An Autumnal Evening," 101–2
—"Lines to a Beautiful Spring in a Village," 262n.27
—"Love," 120
—"Nightingale, The," 118
—"Nil Pejus est Caelibe Vita," 54
—"Ode to the Departing Year," 54
—"Rime of the Ancient Mariner, The," 5, 116–17, 136, 137–40, 145, 146, 165–69, 265n.3

—"Three Graves, The," 267n.22
Collier, J. Payne, 156
Collins, William, 64, 137, 155
Concordia Discors, 73, 108
Corbet, Richard, 163–64
Cowper, William, 4, 39–40, 54, 81, 264n.58, 267n.24, 273n.33; blank verse of, 185–90, 226, 227
Crockett, Bryan, 268n.34
Culler, A. Dwight, 252n.18
Curran, Stuart, 1, 2, 262n.25

Daniel, Samuel, 4
Darbishire, Helen, 110
Darwin, Erasmus, 72, 273n.33
Davenant, William, 160
Deconstruction, 3, 250n.9
Della-Cruscans, The, 86
Denham, John, 107
DeQuincey, Thomas, 259n.2
DeSelincourt, Ernest, 80
Diabolus in prosodia. See Second-foot inversion
Dryden, John, 9–10, 79, 107, 260n.9, 264n.58; influence on Wordsworth, 4, 110, 160, 268–69n.41; on rhyme and meter, 39, 40–42
Dugas, Kristine, 267n.21
D'Urfey, Thomas, 163
Dyce, Alexander, 246, 274n.1, 275n.13
Dyer, John, 110

Ecclesiastes, 72
Elegiac stanza. *See* Heroic stanza
Elision: in eighteenth-century verse, 9, 261–62n.24; in Milton's blank verse, 39; in nineteenth-century theory, 10, 30–31, 254–55n.15, 255n.16; in Wordsworth's blank verse, 83–84, 182, 207–8, 216–19, 231–33; in Wordsworth's early verse, 80–83, 92–93, 95; in Wordsworth's stanzaic verse, 152, 268n.35
Emerson, Ralph Waldo, 40
Enjambment: in Cowper's blank verse, 188–90; in Milton's blank verse, 188–90; in Wordsworth's blank verse, 180, 181–82, 188–97, 203, 209–10, 218–20, 228–32; in Wordsworth's cross-rhymed stanzas, 146–47; Wordsworth's opinions on, 27, 150, 268n.31

Ferguson, Frances, 265n.5
Field, Barron, 1–2, 6, 274n.1
Finch, Anne, 4
Fitzgerald, Edward, 144, 268n.29
Fleming, John, 259n.2
Fraistat, Neil, 265n.7, 269n.45
Fussell, Paul, 38–39, 163–64, 251n.15, 256nn.31, 33, 265n.4

Garner, Margaret, 269n.50
Gascoigne, George, 65
Gill, Stephen, 1, 179–80, 253n.7, 265–66n.8
Gillies, Robert Pierce, 180–81, 261n.20, 266–67n.20
Godwin, Catharine Grace, 179
Godwin, William, 256n.29
Goldsmith, Oliver, 72–73, 101–4, 259n.2, 264n.47
Gomm, William Maynard, 256n.36
Graver, Bruce E., 262n.29
Gray, Thomas, 54, 62–63, 155, 160, 259nn.2, 17
Greenbie, M. L. [Barstow], 261n.22, 262n.29
Greenwood, William, 72
Guest, Edwin, 254–55n.15

Hamilton, William, of Bangour, 262n.28
Hamilton, William Rowan, 42, 179, 260n.13
Hardison, O. B., Jr., 230
Hardy, Thomas, 115, 254n.11
Harmon, William, 16–17, 58, 151
Hartman, Geoffrey, 262–63n.32, 272n.20
Hartman, Herbert, 267n.23
Häublein, Ernst, 253n.6
Havens, R. D., 226, 259n.2
Hazlitt, William, 5, 11, 36–37, 111, 261n.23
Heroic couplet, 9, 73, 75–83, 90–114
Heroic stanza, 159–63, 268–69n.41
Herrick, Robert, 137
Hiatus, 80, 93
Hogg, James, 266–67n.20
Hollander, John, 1, 36, 242–43, 250n.6, 251n.12, 269n.50
Hopkins, Gerard Manley, 251n.12
Horace, 155–56
Hughes, Ted, 255n.21
Hutcheson, Francis, 253n.2
Hutchinson, Mary, 120

Jacobus, Mary, 242, 269n.46
Jewsbury, Maria Jane, 260n.13

Johnson, Lee M., 213, 255n.20, 268n.33, 271nn.12, 13, 272n.21, 275n.14
Johnson, Samuel, 10, 73, 226, 254n.9, 261n.20
Jones, John, 51, 257–58n.5
Jonson, Ben, 4

Keats, John, 270n.6
Kelley, Theresa M., 213, 264n.50
Knight, Richard Payne, 254n.9

Lamb, Charles, 226
Land, Stephen K., 249n.4
Langhorne, William, 262n.28
Legouis, Emile, 91, 259–60n.4, 262–63n.32

McKusick, James, 256–57n.40
MacPherson, James, 6, 259n.2, 273n.36
Mad Song stanza, 163–65
Malof, Joseph, 131, 261n.18
Manwaring [Mainwaring], Edward, 39
Mathews, William, 111–12, 265n.59
Mayo, Robert, 115
Milton, John, 4, 36, 42, 109, 179, 260n.9; blank verse of, 10, 39, 185–90, 225–37, 270n.5, 273n.35; "L'Allegro" and "Il Penseroso," 87; "Lycidas," 151–52; stress-contour rhyme in, 212, 220–21
Mitchell, Jerome, 268n.36
Moore, Edward, 126
Moore, Thomas, 41, 256n.35

Native measure. *See* Ballad stanza
Newton, John, 226

Omond, Thomas Stewart, 253nn.5, 8
Orpheus, 170–71, 230, 239, 274n.2
Ossian. *See* MacPherson, James
Ostriker, Alicia, 25n.16, 260n.9, 267n.25, 273n.32

Page, Judith W., 228–29, 273n.40, 273–74n.41
Parrish, Stephen, 265n.5, 269n.42
Parry, Charles Henry, 252n.20
Patmore, Coventry, 254n.11
Pause, placement of: in Cowper's blank verse, 185–90; in Milton's blank verse, 185–90; in Pope's verse, 9–10, 76–79, 101–2; in Wordsworth's blank verse, 185–201; in Wordsworth's early verse, 76–79, 101–4, 108
Payne, Richard, 265n.3
Percy's *Reliques*: ballad stanza and meter in, 117, 132, 136–37, 144–45, 269n.44; influence on Wordsworth of, 10, 129, 267n.21, 273n.33; Mad Song stanza in, 163–65
Perkins, David, 3, 250n.6, 252n.22, 253n.7
Pope, Alexander, 4, 9–10, 73, 76–83, 260n.9, 264n.58; *Windsor Forest,* 101–2, 106–10
Pottle, Frederick, 101, 262–63n.32
Potts, Abbie Findlay, 260–61n.15, 264n.47
Poulter's measure, 163–64
Pound, Ezra, 200, 271n.11
Priestley, Joseph, 253n.2
Prior, Matthew, 54, 258n.7
Prosodic terms defined: beats and offbeats, 12; dislocation, 31–36; double offbeat, 15–16; duple rhythm, 16; implied offbeat condition, 15–16; initial inverse condition, 15–16; meter, 12, 48; meter *v.* rhythm, 31; metrical set, 15, 33, 36–37; promotion and demotion, 13–15; rhythm, 12; stress and unstress, 12–15, 252n.24, 254n.12; stress-final pairing, 15; stress-initial pairing, 15; syllable, 252n.24; verse, 32–33
Prosodic theory: of Derek Attridge, 11–16, 32–37, 131, 209, 234, 252n.23, 259n20, 272nn.19, 23; of Edward Bysshe, 9–10, 93; of Samuel Taylor Coleridge, 8, 49–61, 66, 255n.16, 257nn.1, 2; eighteenth-century, 9–10, 31, 38–40, 73–84, 91–93; of George Saintsbury, 5–6, 11, 115, 138; of Robert Southey, 82, 255n.16; of John Thelwall, 26–31, 37, 38–39, 65, 82, 253n.5, 255n.16; twentieth-century, 2–3, 31
Pythagorean tradition, 240–43

Quillinan, Edward, 270n.4

Reed, Mark L., 257n.4, 265n.7, 268n.31
Reynolds, Joshua, 253n.2
Rhyme, terms defined: assonance, 17; augmented, 17; consonance, 17; homoeoteleuton, 17; promotion and demotion, 16–17, 58
Richardson, Samuel, 126

Ricks, Christopher, 218–19, 253n.7
Riffaterre, Michael, 272n.20
Robinson, Henry Crabb, 257n.41, 271nn.13, 15, 271–72n.16
Roethke, Theodore, 270n.53
Ruoff, Gene W., 258n.10

Saintsbury, George, 5–6, 11, 115, 138
Schneider, Ben Ross, 110–11
Scott, John, 90
Scott, Walter, 10, 159, 261n.18
Second-foot inversion, 11, 81, 117, 209, 272n.19
Sewell, Elizabeth, 269n.50, 274n.2
Shaftesbury, Anthony Ashley Cooper, 3rd Earl of, 254n.14
Shakespeare, William, 4, 10, 36, 72, 126, 152, 250n.8, 259n.3
Sheats, Paul, 219, 262n.29, 262–63n.32, 263n.43, 264n.50, 265n.60, 266n.19, 270n.1
Shelley, Percy Bysshe, 5, 115
Shenstone, William, 83
Sidney, Philip, 167
Smart, Christopher, 155, 156
Smith, Adam, 253n.2
Smith, Barbara Herrnstein, 256n.34
Smith, Charlotte, 4, 86
Sonnet, 42, 86, 246–47, 271n.15. *See also* Blank verse: sonnet structure in
Sotheby, William, 257n.2
Southey, Robert, 59, 82, 122–23, 156, 266n.9, 271n.9. *See also* Blank verse
Spenser, Edmund, 4, 36, 48, 54, 137, 156, 221
Spenserian stanza, 118
Steele, Joshua, 26, 254n.13
Steele, Timothy, 250n.6
Stein, Edwin, 251n.11, 274n.5
Stress-contour rhyme, 212, 220–21
Strong, Caroline, 268n.36
Swinburne, Algernon Charles, 5–6, 115

Tail-rhyme stanza, 62, 133, 155–59, 258n.16, 268n.36
Tarlinskaja, Marina, 184, 233, 268n.34, 272n.19, 274n.45
Taylor, Anne, 72, 74, 113
Taylor, Dennis, 254n.11
Taylor, Henry, 270n.4
Tennyson, Alfred, Lord, 115, 144, 268n.29

Tennyson, Hallam, 268n.29
Thelwall, John, 26–31, 38–39, 65, 82, 96, 253n.5, 255n.16
Thomson, James, 4, 64, 94, 114, 262n.28, 266n.16, 270n.5

Verse: accentual, 138–40, 255n.16; accentual-syllabic, 5, 9–10, 15–16, 36–37, 119, 138–40; compared to dance, 39, 40; defined, 32–33; equated with geometric form, 39, 40, 255n.20; measured by "cadences," 29–31
Virgil, 72, 107

Walker, Eric, 224, 257n.3, 272n.20
Waller, Edmund, 9, 79
Walsh, William, 79
Wasserman, Earl R., 258n.7
Webb, Daniel, 77
Weismiller, Edward R., 255n.16, 261–62n.24
Wesling, Donald, 106
Whitehead, Alfred North, 240–41
Whitman, Walt, 115, 251n.12
Williams, Ann, 256–57n.40
Wilson, John, 269n.43
Wimsatt, William K., 67, 105
Woodring, Carl, 251n.14
Woods, Suzanne, 268–69n.41
Wordsworth, Christopher, 97
Wordsworth, Dora, 247
Wordsworth, Dorothy, 120, 267n.21
Wordsworth, Jonathan, 233–34, 249n.4, 271n.9
Wordsworth, William: critical reputation of, 1–6, 8, 50–52, 178, 249–50n.5, 250–51n.10; on distinction between poetry and prose, 3, 21, 28, 254n.9; and fitting of language to meter, 7–9, 22–26, 37–43, 48–67, 150, 155, 201, 234–37; on intertexture in verse, 28–29, 48–49, 54, 126; on metrical dislocation, 29–37, 180, 181; and passion of meter, 26–37, 177–78; on the poet, 1–2, 3, 22, 42–43, 51–52, 61, 249n.4, 258n.15; and principle of similitude in dissimilitude, 6–9, 21–37, 48–50, 60–61, 66–67, 113–14, 119–20, 177–78; range of stanzas and verse forms of, 4, 117–23, 248; on the real language of men, 23, 24, 38–40, 44, 256n.34; on the sonnet, 246–47, 271n.15; on symbolic function of meter, 44–47; and use of Cumberland dialect, 110–12

INDEX • 289

Wordsworth, William, works of
— "A Poet!—He hath put his heart to school," 41, 42
— "A slumber did my spirit seal," 121, 137, 152–54, 176
— "A whirlblast from behind the hill," 121
— "Alice Fell," 50
— "Andrew Jones," 121
— "Anecdote for Fathers," 50, 117, 119, 143, 154, 173, 265n.6
— "Animal Tranquillity and Decay," 179, 201 6, 265n.6
— "Ballad, A," 137
— *Borderers, The*, 119, 180, 183
— "Brothers, The," 120, 182–83, 201
— "Cento," 266n.16
— "Character, A," 122, 269n.48
— "Childless Father, The," 122, 269n.48
— "Complaint of a Forsaken Indian Woman, The," 118, 119, 124–28, 136, 176
— "Convict, The," 118, 119, 120
— "Description of a Beggar," 180
— *Descriptive Sketches*, 9, 71–75, 90–94, 95–114, 186, 259–60n.4, 260n.12, 262n.30
— "Egyptian Maid, The," 270n.52
— "Ellen Irwin," 122, 137, 155
— "Emigrant Mother, The," 125
— *Evening Walk, An*, 9, 71–75, 90–106, 110–14, 185–86, 259n.4, 262n.30
— *Excursion, The*, 183, 201
— "Expostulation and Reply," 117, 118, 136–49, 154–55, 265n.6
— "Female Vagrant, The," 118, 119, 265n.6
— "Force of Prayer, The," 137, 267n.21
— "Fountain, The," 121, 136, 154
— "Fragment, A" ("The Danish Boy"), 121, 134, 136
— "Goody Blake and Harry Gill," 63–67, 118, 119, 136, 167
— "Green Linnet, The," 170
— *Guilt and Sorrow*. See William Wordsworth, works of: "Salisbury Plain"
— "Hart-Leap Well," 122, 123, 155, 159–63, 269n.42
— *Home at Grasmere*, 218
— "Humanity," 51
— "Hymn for the Boatmen," 170, 268n.39
— "I Heard a Thousand Blended Notes," 110
— "I Wandered Lonely as a Cloud," 143
— "Idiot Boy, The," 51, 118, 119, 121, 155, 163–69, 265n.6
— "Idle-Shepherd Boys, The," 121, 134–35
— "If Nature, for a favorite child," 122
— "Kitten and the Falling Leaves, The," 89, 170
— "Last of the Flock, The," 51, 118, 119, 124–26, 265n.6
— "Lines Composed a few miles above Tintern Abbey," 118, 176, 179, 185, 191–94, 195–201; geometric pattern in, 271n.12; as ode, 270–71n.8; in relation to Wordsworth's stylistic range, 8, 51, 90, 117, 178; view of youthful poet in, 75
— "Lines left upon a Seat in a Yew Tree," 179, 183
— "Lines Written as a School Exercise at Hawkshead," 75–82, 101
— "Lines Written at a Small Distance from my House," 117, 143, 268n.30
— "Lines Written in Early Spring," 117, 154
— "Lines Written near Richmond, upon the Thames at Evening," 63–66, 118, 119, 120, 121, 259n.18
— "Lines Written with a Slate pencil . . . Rydal," 185
— "Louisa," 155
— "Lucy Gray," 121
— *Lyrical Ballads*, 9, 63, 115–24, 161, 177–78, 179–206, 265n.3, 266n.10
— "Mad Mother, The," 51, 118, 119, 124–26, 128–30, 136, 265n.6
— "Michael, " 120, 184, 189–91, 194–95, 201, 265–66n.8
— "My Heart Leaps Up," 35–36, 143
— "Night-Piece, A," 180, 206–25
— "Oak and the Broom, The," 122
— "Ode: Intimations of Immortality," 54, 90
— "Ode: The Morning of the Day Appointed for a General Thanksgiving," 156
— "Ode to Duty," 54
— "Old Cumberland Beggar, The," 32, 33–35, 96, 201
— "Old Man Travelling." See William Wordsworth, works of: "Animal Tranquillity and Decay"
— "On Seeing Miss Helen Maria Williams Weep at a Tale of Distress," 85–86, 87, 90, 95
— "On the Power of Sound," 9, 238–48, 266n.16, 274n.1

—"Pet-Lamb, The," 122, 123, 173–75, 177
—*Peter Bell*, 118, 163
—"Poems founded on the Affections," 51, 125
—*Poems, in Two Volumes*, 123, 170
—"Poems of the Fancy," 51
—"Poems of the Imagination," 51
—"Poems on the Naming of Places," 201
—"Poems Referring to the Period of Old Age," 51
—"Poems Written in Youth," 75
—"Poet's Epitaph, A," 122
—"Power of Music," 170–71
—Preface to *Lyrical Ballads*, 3–4, 7–9, 21–25, 28, 37–38, 42–47, 119, 169
—Preface to *Poems* (1815), 1–2, 40, 46–47, 242
—Preface to *The Excursion*, 123
—*Prelude, The*, 7, 51, 120, 180, 248; elision in, 84; enjambment in, 218–19, 228–29; view of youthful poet in, 71–72, 112, 114
—"Prospectus" to *The Excursion*, 112, 180, 231–37
—*Recluse, The*, 113, 247–48
—"Reverie of Poor Susan, The," 122, 171, 176, 269n.48
—*River Duddon, The*, 200, 246
—"Rob Roy's Grave," 136
—*Ruined Cottage, The*, 119, 120, 180
—"Rural Architecture," 122, 269n.48
—"Ruth," 122, 155–59
—"Sailor's Mother, The," 8, 50, 52–61, 66, 202
—*Salisbury Plain*, 118, 119
—"September 1819," 155
—"Septimi Gades," 155
—"Seven Sisters, The," 266n.13
—"She dwelt among th'untrodden ways," 121, 150–52, 176, 268n.35
—"Simon Lee," 118, 119
—"So Fair, so sweet, withal so sensitive," 170
—"Song for the Spinning Wheel," 268n.39
—"Song for the Wandering Jew," 122, 158, 172–73, 178
—"Sonnet written by Mr. ____ Immediately after the Death of his Wife," 83
—"Stepping Westward," 25–26
—"Strange Fits of Passion," 121
—"Tables Turned, The," 117, 118, 137–40, 145–49, 154
—"There is an Eminence—of these our hills," 185, 201
—"Thorn, The," 62–64, 66, 118, 119, 121, 130–36, 155, 168
—"Three years she grew in sun and shower," 122, 155
—"Tintern Abbey." *See* William Wordsworth, works of: "Lines Composed a few miles above Tintern Abbey"
—"'Tis said that some have died for love," 122, 123, 175–77
—"To a Sexton," 122
—"To a Skylark" ("Ethereal minstrel!"), 248
—"To a Skylark" ("Up with me!"), 170
—"To Joanna," 183, 184
—"To M. H.," 201
—"To My Sister." *See* William Wordsworth, works of: "Lines Written at a Small Distance from my House"
—"To the Cuckoo," 170
—"To the Daisy," 170
—"Two April Mornings, The," 121, 143
—"Two Thieves, The," 122, 269n.48
—"Triad, The," 244, 275n.10
—"Vale of Esthwaite, The," 86–90, 95, 97, 111
—"Waterfall and the Eglantine, The," 122, 155
—"We Are Seven," 117, 119, 173, 265n.6
—*White Doe of Rylstone, The*, 267n.21
—"Wishing Gate, The," 155
—"Wren's Nest, A," 170
—"Written in Germany on one of the Coldest Days of the Century," 122, 269n.48
—"Written in March at the Foot of Brother's Water," 51, 89, 170
—"Yes, it was a mountain echo," 170
—"Yew Trees," 206, 212–25, 245
Wright, George T., 250n.8, 255n.8
Wu, Duncan, 254n.9

Young, Edward, 270n.5

The Passion of Meter
was composed in 9½-point Didot leaded 3 points
on an IBM PC-based system with Linotronic L300 output
by Inari Information Services, Inc.;
printed by sheet-fed offset on
50-pound Glatfelter Supple Opaque natural stock
(an acid-free, recycled sheet),
notch bound over binder's boards in Holliston Kingston cloth,
and wrapped with dustjackets printed in two colors
on 100-pound enamel stock finished with matte film lamination
by Thomson-Shore, Inc.;
designed by Will Underwood;
and published by
The Kent State University Press
KENT, OHIO 44242

OHIO UNIVERSITY LIBRARY

Please return this book as soon as you have finished with it. In order to avoid a fine it must be returned by the latest date stamped below. All books are subject to recall after two weeks or immediately if needed for reserve.